LEO STRAUSS

and ANGLO-AMERICAN

DEMOCRACY

LEO STRAUSS
and ANGLO-AMERICAN
DEMOCRACY

A Conservative Critique

GRANT N. HAVERS

NIU Press
DeKalb, IL

© 2013 by Northern Illinois University Press
Published by the Northern Illinois University Press, DeKalb,
Illinois 60115

Library of Congress Cataloging-in-Publication Data
Havers, Grant N., 1965–
Leo Strauss and Anglo-American democracy : a conservative
critique / Grant N. Havers.
    pages cm
Summary: "Interprets Leo Strauss's political philosophy from
a conservative standpoint and argues that Strauss was a Cold
War liberal. Suggests inattention to Christianity is crucial to
the Straussian portrayal of Anglo-American democracy as a
universal regime whose eternal ideals of liberty and constitutional
government accord with the teachings of Plato and Aristotle, rather
than the Gospels"—Provided by publisher.
ISBN 978-1-5017-7438-6 (paperback)   — ISBN 978-1-60909-094-4
(e-book)
    1. Strauss, Leo. 2. Political science—Philosophy. 3.
Conservatism—Philosophy. 4. Political science—United
States—History. 5. Political science—Great Britain—History. I.
Title.
JC251.S8H38 2013
320.52092—dc23
2013012135

To My Love,

Therese

Fides quaerens intellectum

Contents

Preface

It has been over twenty-five years since I read my first book by Leo Strauss. At the time, I was enrolled in a graduate seminar course in the Social and Political Thought Program at York University in 1987, which focused on the complex relation between the Bible and philosophy. One of the course texts was Spinoza's *Theologico-Political Treatise*. Brayton Polka, the professor in the course who later supervised my doctoral dissertation on Spinoza, was deeply critical of Strauss. Yet he included Strauss's *Spinoza's Critique of Religion* in the course's bibliography of secondary sources. Although this work, which first appeared in German in 1930, was my first introduction to Strauss, it was not an introduction to the phenomenon of "Straussianism." The only inkling I had of Strauss's wider influence up to that point was gleaned from my undergraduate reading of the essays of George Grant, a Canadian conservative philosopher who generally had nothing but praise for Strauss. For most of my graduate study, I read Strauss as a profound interpreter of Spinoza as well as one of the few twentieth-century philosophers who actually took seriously the relation between reason and faith. I was intrigued that a philosopher of Strauss's high caliber even wrote on the Bible. As a born and bred Protestant who has never been persuaded that the Thomistic synthesis of Aristotelian philosophy and biblical revelation withstands scrutiny, I was impressed that a man of Strauss's intellect repudiated any attempt to suppress the tensions and differences that existed between "Athens" and "Jerusalem." Yet I was unaware at this time that Strauss had inspired a movement in political philosophy that had an impact far beyond the halls of academe. Although a Straussian scholar served on my dissertation committee, I had no idea there was a wider political debate, a veritable *Strausskampf,* over the true meaning of this philosopher's ideas and objectives.

My original apolitical understanding of Strauss that was nurtured in graduate school eventually gave way to a more intense interest in his influence on post–World War II conservatism, an influence that was already deeply reflected in the ideology of "neoconservatism." While seeking a full-time teaching position in the 1990s, I was persuaded that Strauss's recovery of Greek political philosophy as the only way to address modern relativism and nihilism was reliably conservative. Since my parents raised me to revere the defenders of traditional English constitutionalism as well as the statesmanship of Lincoln and Churchill, the Straussian praise of these figures resonated with me. It did not occur to me at the time that Strauss's line of thinking fits best into Cold War liberalism, a relatively new political tradition that was anti-conservative in many respects. This new version of liberalism, after all, stressed the importance of spreading liberal democratic ideals around the world, especially in the struggle against a totalitarian regime that had its own far more brutal version of universal credos.

As my own political views shifted sharply to the Right, it gradually dawned on me that "Straussianism" was a supremely important phenomenon precisely because Strauss and many of his most politically active students had almost succeeded in transforming conservatism, particularly its Anglo-American incarnation, into a doctrine that called for the democratization of the world. What all this had to do with distinguished conservatives such as Edmund Burke—who were deeply skeptical of political abstractions that justified grand projects of social engineering—was (and still is) beyond my comprehension. By the time that the second Iraq War had begun in 2003, a renewed debate over the meaning of Straussianism and neoconservatism crossed over from academe into the blogosphere, where instant experts on Strauss sprouted like mushrooms. At this time, I was gradually coming round to the view that Straussianism was a formidable adversary of everything that remotely stood for conservatism in the modern age. As a conservative Christian, I was also particularly troubled that Strauss gave short shrift to the influence of Christianity on Western political philosophy. What was doubly frustrating to me and other conservatives around this time was that the mainstream debate over Strauss was largely confined to an argument between leftist opponents of Strauss who saw him as a far rightist and his supporters who defended him as a liberal with some conservative tendencies. Very few critiques from the right-wing side of the spectrum have garnered popular attention. Although I wrote extensively on the Straussian reinvention of the American political tradition in my first book, a study of Abraham Lincoln's political theology, it recently occurred to me that Strauss and his students deserved their own book from a perspective that often receives little attention in today's debates. The purpose of this book, then, is to show how Strauss and his students offer a defense of Anglo-American democracy that is conservative in name only.

During this long journey from my study of Strauss to my critique of Straussianism, I have benefited immensely from the knowledge of others who have been longtime participants in the *Strausskampf*. I am eternally grateful to Paul Gottfried, who urged me to write this manuscript just as he was completing his own book on Strauss, for painstakingly reading and commenting on several drafts of this study. Without the benefit of Paul's unsurpassed knowledge of conservatism, I would not have been able to write this book. When Paul and his co-editor Claes Ryn published an essay of mine on Leo Strauss and Willmoore Kendall in the journal *Humanitas* in 2005, to which they both wrote critical replies, their kind attention to my work provided an additional catalyst for this book-length study of Strauss. I thank both Paul and Claes for encouraging further intellectual percolations. Peter Minowitz, who knows more than anyone about the intricate details of the controversies surrounding Strauss's legacy, also took the time to read the manuscript in rough as well as to offer invaluable suggestions that saved me from making more than a few unsubstantiated claims about Strauss and his students. Calvin Townsend also deserves my profound thanks for engaging in a decade-long dialogue with me about the subtle differences and disputes that have arisen in the Straussian movement since Strauss's death in 1973. Conversations with Phillip Wiebe, Christopher Morrissey, and Raymond Tatalovich on topics ranging from medieval scholasticism to American republicanism have encouraged me to reconsider many snap judgments about the relation between philosophy and politics. It was also a great blessing to have two first-rate anonymous peer reviewers who carefully and insightfully offered necessary suggestions for revising the text. Finally, I am very grateful to both Amy Farranto, acquisition editor of Northern Illinois University Press, for overseeing the early stages of the manuscript review, and Susan Bean, managing editor of NIU Press, for diligently helping me hammer out a readable manuscript that is suitable for readers who are not as obsessed with Strauss as I am.

And to my wife, Therese, I owe all my love for exuding patience, moderation, and wisdom as she supported my seemingly endless quest to figure out the mystery that is Leo Strauss. This book is justly dedicated to her.

LEO STRAUSS
and ANGLO-AMERICAN
DEMOCRACY

Introduction

It has been forty years since the death of Leo Strauss, yet there is little evidence that the debate over his legacy shows any sign of abatement. A prolific scholar who managed to inspire a whole new approach to political philosophy when he taught in the United States from the late 1930s until his death in 1973, he is in retrospect perhaps an unlikely choice for inspiring any political program. This quiet, gentlemanly figure, who delighted in detecting secret meanings in great philosophical texts, never ran for office, advised a politician, or joined a political party. Yet Strauss has provoked a wave of controversy that continues to wash over academe to this day and occasionally even spills over into the popular media.

For over a quarter of a century, most critics of Leo Strauss have portrayed this political philosopher as an enemy of liberal democracy who built a vast intellectual movement in the United States in order to foster an extreme right-wing agenda devoted to perpetual war and class hierarchy.[1] These critiques echoed in loud, shrill tones throughout the mass media when the second Gulf War commenced in 2003. At this time, various leftists spied a sinister conspiracy of Straussians, working in the Bush administration, who cajoled the American people into supporting the invasion of Iraq with a mix of subterfuge and exaggeration. Apparently Strauss, who died in 1973, was still haunting the minds of foreign policy experts in the United States. Worst of all, the influence of his thought was breeding a right-wing neo-fascist conspiracy that would undermine liberal democracy.[2]

This leftist critique of Strauss has generally been countered by his numerous followers (often called "Straussians") who insist that their teacher was a sincere defender of the democratic regime and the liberal ideals of freedom and equality. These acolytes have documented how Strauss saw in both Britain and the United States the last best hope to counter the dangers of tyranny in our time. In the words of Heinrich Meier, a prominent European admirer, Strauss actively encouraged his students to defend the very "foundations" of the modern American regime.[3] William Kristol, a famous Straussian journalist who is the editor of the *Weekly Standard*, rather brazenly draws this connection between Strauss's philosophy and the defense of Anglo-American democracy when he celebrates the West's unique identity for building on liberalism as well as "the older traditions of Athens and Jerusalem," praises Britain and the United States for preserving liberal civilization from secular totalitarianism during World War II, and calls on all free democratic nations today "that hold aloft and carry the torch" of the West to stand with Israel in the war against radical Islamic terrorists. Quoting from Strauss's description of Israel as an "outpost of the West that exists in the East," Kristol looks to America to continue its mission as the chief defender of Western civilization.[4] This heartfelt support for the Anglo-American tradition, Straussians insist, is consistent with Strauss's deep sympathy for liberal democracy as a whole. Since this debate over Strauss's philosophy has been mostly conducted by leftist critics and liberal supporters of this thinker, few voices from the conservative side of the political spectrum have succeeded in shifting the discussion beyond its traditional contours.[5]

It is the purpose of this study to critique Leo Strauss's political philosophy and movement from the Right.[6] In my judgment, Strauss's leftist critics have not successfully made their case that the target of their scorn is a man of the Far Right. Indeed, I am inclined to believe that he shares some important assumptions with the Left. For this reason, I accept the positive portrayal of Strauss, mainly advanced by his followers, as a sincere defender of liberal democracy. As a conservative critic of Strauss, however, I intend to expose the defective reasoning that he and his students have marshaled in favor of this cause. Specifically, I evaluate the problematic nature of Strauss's support of the most successful experiment in the democratic tradition—the Anglo-American tradition. Strauss's portrayal of this tradition arguably does more harm than good, despite his best intentions, for two principal reasons. First, he interprets the principles or foundations of Anglo-American democracy as philosophically eternal credos that have been known to humanity since the time of Plato and Aristotle. Second, he represents these principles as politically universal ideals that must be cultivated by all peoples, regardless of time and place. In neither case does Strauss provide a *conservative* defense of this tradition, despite what many of his supporters insist.

At this point it is necessary to clarify what I understand as the meaning of "Straussian" and "conservative," since these terms are often conflated. At a rudimentary level, "Straussian" refers to anyone who has studied the major texts of Leo Strauss and generally accepts his interpretation of the philosophical tradition. (Throughout this study, I will not employ this term as a pejorative word that necessarily always implies cultic attachment to Strauss.) More specifically, this interpretation rests on the assumption that certain political philosophers from the time of Plato to early modernity have written "esoterically" or have concealed their most subversive thoughts in a cryptic code that can be understood only by a few careful readers. Since these philosophers have feared political persecution, they have been required to engage in this concealment.[7]

This Straussian hermeneutic of suspicion has some passing importance to the argument that I present in this study, especially within the context of explaining why exactly Strauss and his students go to such lengths in downplaying or ignoring the role of Christianity in shaping the Anglo-American tradition. (Strauss and his followers do not believe that any political philosophers are sincerely religious, even though the latter may appear to be pious when it is politically expedient or when it is necessary to cultivate this image in order to avoid persecution.) Far more important to my discussion, however, is the Straussians' rejection of *historicism*—or what they take to be an overemphasis on historically specific traditions (which they sometimes call the "ancestral") at the expense of truly universal ideals.[8] Closely related to this anti-historicism is Strauss's celebration of the philosophy of "natural right," or the principle that there is a universal human nature above and beyond differences between historical traditions. In Strauss's view Plato, Aristotle, and their medieval heirs provided the most sophisticated account of natural right. The modern age, however, has embraced historicism and eschewed any suggestion of natural right, which has led to the near triumph of ideologies that threaten liberal democracy in our time. Strauss's call for a recovery of Greek political philosophy, then, also amounts to a call to defend the one regime that upholds the natural right belief in a universal human nature (and universal ideas of liberty and equality), liberal democracy. These tenets of Straussianism, which tend to reinvent the Greeks as more liberal and democratic than they truly were, are absolutely central to my discussion because they constitute a rejection of the philosophical (historicist) defenses that have shored up the Anglo-American tradition. It seems that Strauss and his students seek to defend this tradition on universalist grounds, not historicist ones. Put another way, they somehow want to preserve this tradition without the conservatism that emphasizes the historical relativity of its ideas and institutions.

What I mean by "conservative" here refers to a dedication to the rule of law, constitutional government, separation of church and state, and Christianity as a leavening influence on politics and society: these are important principles that characterize the history of the Anglo-American tradition. Its most important defenders (including Edmund Burke, Alexander Hamilton, and Sir Winston Churchill) are obviously central to my discussion, as are the political philosophers who established the groundwork for this tradition (Spinoza, Locke, Montesquieu, Smith, and so on). None of these thinkers looked to Plato and Aristotle in order to defend liberal democracy as a universal regime; in fact, they were severely critical of both Greek thought and statecraft. Although I do not doubt that Strauss and his students sincerely believe in the highest principles of what they take to be liberal democracy, they usually reinvent this tradition as a modern version of ancient Greek civilization in order to press their message that Anglo-American civilization is a universal tradition that has existed at least in principle since Plato and Aristotle. As a result, they misrepresent the very historical and philosophical underpinnings of this tradition.

Readers who are familiar with the long-standing battle between "neoconservatives" and "paleoconservatives" over the meaning of conservatism will instantly recognize the ideological context that my study reflects. One long-standing critique of Strauss from the paleoconservative camp is that he and his neoconservative followers fail to ground their defense of the tradition, ancient and modern, in any historical foundation. Paleoconservatives like Paul Gottfried who associate true conservatism with an unabashed appreciation for the historical differences that separate peoples from each other have been highly critical of the Straussian (and neoconservative) belief that "universal" ideals of justice and politics are known to all human beings regardless of the historical traditions that distinguish one people from another.[9] This paleoconservative critique, with which I am broadly sympathetic, is no mere nostalgic longing for throne and altar. Rather, it is rooted in a deeply felt desire to preserve what is best in the conservative tradition from ideological adulteration.

Straussian revisionism particularly undermines what is traditionally most precious to Anglo-American conservatives, or what amounts to the historical distinctiveness of the Anglo-American tradition. The most dangerous implication of this ideology is that it seeks the spread of democratic values on a global basis, in defiance of the historically relative nature of these values. The rule of law, constitutional government, and the separation of church and state are not easily transplanted beyond the historic confines of Anglo-American civilization, as recent wars of democracy in the Middle East and Central Asia have sadly demonstrated. Although it is not obvious that Strauss would have supported a "neoconservative" foreign policy of global democracy-building, as many of his critics claim, his critique of the traditional conservative (e.g., Burkean) preference for historically grounded ideals over universal credos that celebrate human equality provided a compelling intellectual rationale for this policy.

Yet this book is not just another analysis of the relation between Strauss and the neoconservative movement, whose members do not all count as Straussians anyway. In this study, I intend to subject the key principles of Strauss's thought to a philosophical and historical critique. Throughout this study, I contend that it is hard to justify how the ideals of Anglo-American civilization match those of the ancient Greeks, despite Straussian efforts to conflate these in the hope of presenting a defense of liberal democracy as the "universal" regime that is best for all human beings. Although not all students of Strauss identify every aspect of Greek political philosophy with Anglo-American statecraft, they ultimately follow Strauss in drawing important connections. While Strauss and his followers emphasize the great differences between the ancients and the moderns, they are also inclined to single out the Anglo-American regime and its greatest statesmen (Lincoln, Churchill) as the defenders of classical ideals that date back to the age of Plato and Aristotle. This project creates a huge set of methodological difficulties, since Strauss and his students have to explain away ancient Greek practices like slavery or infanticide that the Anglo-American political philosophers found horrifying. The Straussians face a conundrum of their own making. If they identify ancient Greeks with modern Anglo-Americans too closely, they have to explain massive differences between the two civilizations of the West. If they admit that there are huge distinctions to be drawn between the two, then they must acknowledge that the "eternal" principles of Anglo-American democracy may not be so eternal, since they are not rooted in the Greeks.

Equally disturbing to the conservative mind is Strauss's inattention to the pivotal role of Christianity in shaping the Anglo-American tradition. This lacuna in Strauss's hermeneutic has always perplexed me. Like many Canadians, I first discovered Strauss's thought in my undergraduate years through the writings of George Grant, a Canadian Tory Anglican philosopher who considered Strauss to be the greatest political thinker of his age. As Grant himself noted at times, however, it is never clear why Strauss either pays so little attention to Christianity or dualistically opposes philosophy (reason) to revelation (faith). As a graduate student working on my doctoral dissertation, which compared the ideas of Spinoza and Freud, I came to appreciate the power of Strauss's mind and his compelling interpretation of Spinoza, even though I could not fully grasp why Strauss is almost silent on the contribution that Christianity has made to the Western tradition of political philosophy.[10] Students of Strauss often disagree on the exact role of Christianity in this tradition. Some contend that Christianity had no role whatsoever in shaping the American Founding (e.g., Michael Zuckert) while others claim that this faith provided a moral impetus to important modern movements like the abolition of slavery during the Lincoln presidency (e.g., Harry Jaffa). Generally, however, there is near consensus in the Straussian camp, even among Catholic students (e.g., Ernest Fortin), that the *political* influence of Christianity on philosophy is almost nil, whatever its impact on moral teachings.

Ultimately, I understood later in life that this omission of Christianity as an influence on political philosophy, particularly in the modern period, is more politically driven than philosophically and historically justified.[11] As I have argued in my study of Abraham Lincoln's political philosophy, Strauss's students misrepresent the sixteenth president as a defender of "eternal" democratic values that owe more to Plato and Aristotle than to the biblical tradition.[12] In this study, I demonstrate the lengths to which Strauss and his followers have gone in misrepresenting both English and American ideas as the continuation of Hellenic political ideas. This lack of attention to Christianity, though historically unjustified, is crucial to Strauss and his students since they portray Anglo-American civilization as so *universal* that it owes nothing to a single religious faith.

The legacy of Strauss lies, then, in his movement's success in undermining conservative defenses of the Anglo-American tradition. In practical terms, Strauss and his followers have managed to reinvent Anglo-American conservatism as a tradition devoted to the spread of universal democratic ideals around the world. The costly nature of this historical revisionism has only served to undermine an accurate understanding of both the Anglo-American regime and its foundations. The ultimate irony is that Strauss and his students, who genuinely seek to preserve Anglo-American democracy, present a misleading portrait that may even endanger the survival of this tradition.

In chapter one, I discuss why Strauss and his students have favored Anglo-American democracy, and why they believe it needs to be saved from doctrines that deny the universality of its credos. Straussians generally fear that both the English and the American peoples have not been well served by their intellectual class, which has often uncritically imbibed dangerous modern ideas like positivism, relativism, and historicism, all of which question the objective superiority of liberal democracy. Far from being a guru of the fascist Right, as his leftist critics contend, Strauss is determined to shore up liberal democracy. His philosophy of "natural right" is deliberately preoccupied with the search for universal, ahistorical principles that are known to all human beings by nature. If Strauss has any misgivings about modernity, it is the tendency to ignore the fundamental goodness of the one regime that comes closest to recognizing this human equality—liberal democracy. As a result, his mission has been to save Anglo-Americans from their openness to ideologies that legitimize, in his view, undemocratic ideas like Nazism or Communism. Yet the Straussian rejection of historicism is a fateful one, since it leads to a devaluation of what is historically distinctive about Anglo-American civilization. In repudiating historicism, Strauss and his students must reinvent Anglo-American civilization as a model that is universally valid for all human beings. This project imposes a burden of "democratic universalism" that is beyond the historic range of this civilization.[13]

In chapter two, I explain why Strauss and his followers insist that "Athens" (Greek political philosophy) is the most decisive influence on what is best in the Anglo-American tradition, and why there is practically no evidence for this central assumption. A close reading of *The Federalist* as well as other writings that influenced the Founders and Framers reveals that both Greek political philosophy and history were rejected—not emulated—in the early American tradition of political philosophy. In the process, I explain why Strauss and his students go out of their way to ignore the Christian (Protestant) heritage that undergirds Anglo-American civilization while they gloss over some of the most unattractive features of Greek political life (e.g., slavery, infanticide). It is far too "historicist," in their eyes, to claim that the Protestant character of the American Founding was an essential influence on the political ideas and debates that convulsed America during the Revolutionary Era. The consequence of this revisionist history is that the Straussians judge America according to its adherence to a rather mythologized version of "Athens," which is far more liberal and democratic than the real version of this ancient polis. Yet this romantic praise of the Greeks is far less apparent in the writings of Jefferson, Hamilton, Tocqueville, or Lincoln than their celebration of Christian morality as a leavening influence on the republic's early politics.

In chapter three, I show how Strauss and his students, despite the appearance of conservative tendencies, are far more comfortable with leftist liberal ideals that call for the universalization of liberty and equality. Their leftist critics ignore Strauss's egalitarian view that all human beings, regardless of tradition or culture, can grasp the principles of "natural right." Any idea that conflicts with natural right is historicist. Following the logic of this argument, it would then have to follow that historically relative ideas like conservatism and Christianity are obstacles to a proper understanding of natural right, if the former are portrayed as essential influences on the West. As a result, Strauss does not fully object to the leftist dismissal of conservatism and Christianity as spent forces in modernity. Moreover, he accepts the leftist view that religion is dogma, an irrational force that must give way to more rational (e.g., Platonic-Aristotelian) arguments in favor of democratic virtues. What Strauss and his students ignore, however, are the best attempts of the Anglo-American tradition to defend religion—Christianity—as a quasi-rational influence that insists on the practice of charity (agape) in the political sphere. Strauss's dualistic separation of "irrational" religion from "rational" philosophy leaves him unwilling to appreciate one of the most important contributions that Anglo-American political philosophy makes to the human condition: the defense of a faith that insists on the practice of charity in political life. Although this hermeneutic is present in the writings of Hobbes, Locke, Burke, Lincoln, Churchill, and others in the Anglo-American pantheon, Strauss dismisses as Machiavellian subterfuge the idea of religion as a leavening influence on politics. Readers are then left with a truly bewildering contradiction emanating from Straussian writings. It is not obvious that the portrayal of the Anglo-American tradition is well served by defenders who portray it as resting on a cynical, deceitful foundation.

The implications of this misrepresentation of the Anglo-American tradition as Machiavellian to the core receive further discussion in chapter four, where I discuss and critique the false Straussian representation of Churchill. The Straussian version of this great statesman, who is admired (besides Lincoln) above all others in their pantheon of heroes, reinvents him as a devotee of ancient Greek political ideas, even though there is little evidence that Churchill showed any interest in the Greeks. On the few occasions where he exhibited such an interest, Churchill was usually appalled at the Greek tolerance of slavery and violence. Churchill also celebrated Christianity as an essential benevolent influence in the West that made modern constitutional government possible. Yet none of this fits into the "Great Man" theory of history that students of Strauss apply to Churchill, as an individual who defied the currents of historical change (e.g., the rise of Hitler) while he promoted democracy as the best regime for all human beings. This highly romanticized portrait of Churchill ignores the statesman's historicist doubts about the ability of all peoples (at least those uninfluenced by the English) even to understand democracy, just as it ignores his rather pessimistic views about the survival of democracy in an age of massification. Curiously, Strauss and his students do not share these worries, since they are confident that an education in the "Great Works" of political philosophy, as they read them, is the best hope to save the West from undemocratic ideas.

In chapter five, I explain why some Anglo-American conservatives have been mistakenly attracted to Straussian ideas, and what this attraction reveals about the state of Anglo-American conservatism today. To this end I discuss two distinguished political philosophers from the Anglo-American tradition, the Canadian George Grant and the American Willmoore Kendall, as instructive examples of Christian conservatives who were not students of Strauss yet embraced his thought. They even helped to disseminate Strauss's ideas in their respective nations, without fully understanding his profound anticonservatism. Grant, as a High Tory Anglican conservative, interpreted Strauss's "return" to the Greeks as a rallying cry for the restoration of long lost traditional virtues. Kendall, a defender of majority-rule democracy, similarly appreciated Strauss's defense of the "timeless" and "eternal" as an essential philosophical bulwark to the relativistic liberalism of their time. Grant's and Kendall's worries about postwar liberalism, particularly its aggressively secular character and hostility to Christianity, led them to Strauss. Yet neither man fully understands the high price that Strauss requires his conservative admirers to pay as they repudiate their own ancestral traditions. Grant and Kendall never grasped the fact that Strauss was a liberal, not a conservative, who was just as opposed as any postwar liberal to any attempt to ground the Western tradition of political philosophy in a Christian foundation. Strauss's liberalism is not open to conservative (ancestral) ideas that interfere with true devotion to the universal ideals of liberal democracy. The examples of Grant and Kendall serve as a warning to other like-minded conservatives that Strauss does not support Anglo-American conservatism in traditional ways.

Is there anything positive that Anglo-American conservatives and liberals can learn from Leo Strauss? In the last chapter, I answer this question in the affirmative. Strauss's teaching on the tension between "Athens" and "Jerusalem" may, despite his intent, provoke a new historical awareness of what separates Anglo-American civilization from the rest of the world. Although Strauss is hardly the first thinker in history to spy major differences between Greek paganism and biblical revelation, his studies of these distinctions may indirectly help conservatives understand what is truly unique about the West. In teaching that the conflict between Athens and Jerusalem is at the heart of the "secret vitality" of Western civilization, Strauss despite his best intentions, which usually impel him to emphasize the "universal," offers an argument in favor of the historically distinctive character of the West. Anglo-American conservatives (like me) can appreciate his insight that no other civilization has struggled so deeply with these tensions. More importantly, Strauss's teachings on the strict nature of biblical morality, whose concept of charity has no equivalent in Greek thought, serves as a warning to anticonservative thinkers like Jürgen Habermas and Charles Taylor in the modern Anglo-American West who seek to water down biblical ideas for the purpose of advancing a version of democracy that is even more egalitarian than Strauss's version. Strauss, to his credit, believed that this dilution of biblical morality for the sake of advancing the cause of equality and democracy in the world ignores what is historically unique about the biblical tradition. Although Strauss looked to the Greeks rather than the Bible in order to present a rational argument in favor of democracy, even he cannot escape from his own insight that the biblical tradition shapes the West in ways that have dramatic political implications. Ultimately, the Anglo-American tradition's indebtedness to biblical morality also raises tough questions for neoconservatives, particularly with regard to the viability of spreading Western ideals to parts of the world that have not been exposed to a biblical heritage. This lesson of Strauss may be his most enduring one, as both the established Left and the Right in the Western world today try to universalize their values in a desperate attempt to reinvent a world that is often hostile to Anglo-American ideals.

1

Saving Anglo-Americans from Themselves

"In defending modern civilisation against German nihilism, the English are defending the eternal principles of civilisation."[1] Leo Strauss delivered these stirring words in a lecture at the New School for Social Research in February 1941, when it was far from obvious that Britain, standing alone against Hitler, would win (or even survive) this deadly struggle. Yet the historic significance of Strauss's words goes far beyond the context of World War II, since his clear support for the cause of England ultimately redefined what conservatives in the Anglo-American tradition would stand for well into the Cold War and post–Cold War periods: the defense of *eternal* principles that stand above the current of history.

Strauss, who had fled from a Germany veering toward Nazi takeover in 1932, had good reason to resent the numerous appeasers of Hitler who claimed the Führer was a great leader who represented the next wave of unstoppable historical change. Perhaps for this reason, Strauss scorned those who were tempted to portray Hitler as anything more than a "tool of

'History'" who did not even understand the "new epoch" he was ushering into existence. Instead, the rise and success of Hitler demonstrated, at least to Strauss, the absurdity of reading into "History" any ultimate meaning that could provide a foundation for prudent political judgment. Appeals to "History" were so ambiguous that they could justify the bad as well as the good. Without a "standard which is stable and not changeable," a standard that is above History, any judgment based on the currents of historical change would have to lead to *nihilism*, the ultimate denial of the "rulership of reason" in favor of defending the most monstrous regime in history.[2]

This attack on the authority of History is not simply a rejection of the nineteenth-century idea of Progress, which had already been forcefully challenged by the carnage of World War I. Nor is Strauss, who was an avid reader of history, rejecting the study of historical fact. The study of history is not the same as appealing to the authority of History. In his American exile, Strauss is calling for nothing less than the abandonment of any standard of politics or morality that is merely relative to its historic period. For this reason, he privileges the "eternal principles" over the merely historical ones. Without these timeless standards, the West will sink into nihilism and, ultimately, death.

The obvious question that arises here is "What are these eternal principles?" The purpose of my study is twofold: to understand what Strauss meant by these trans-historical principles that he attributed to the best traits of Anglo-American civilization, and to evaluate the implications of his teaching on the Anglo-American tradition of democracy that he cherished. It was his fondest hope that his American students would continue to take up the defense of these ideals in the perilous days of the Cold War. Strauss's attempt to identify the cause of the Anglo-American West with credos that stand above and against History is not only his most lasting contribution to postwar political philosophy. It is his most enduring contribution to the cause of Anglo-American democracy in our time.

It is a major premise of this study that Strauss's support for Anglo-American democracy is sincere. Unlike his numerous leftist critics who accuse him of secretly hiding a right-wing contempt for liberal democracy, I believe that Strauss should be taken at his word. In fact, I agree with his equally numerous defenders that his most important teaching is to find "new resources" for the liberal tradition he attributes to English and American civilization.[3] However, I shall contend that Strauss's reasons for defending Anglo-American democracy may actually do the cause more harm than good. Strauss's radical rejection of History in favor of Nature is ultimately a rejection of the conservative tradition that is at the heart of the civilization he is determined to protect.

Before I embark on a full critique of Strauss's concept of History, it is essential to explain why he and his students have been so successful in redefining what the West should uphold as principle. Much has been made of the connection between Strauss and "neoconservatism," an ideology that first emerged in the early 1970s and has now become associated with the utopian project of democratizing the Moslem world through the use of American firepower. The purpose of this study is not to be another book on the relation between Straussianism and neoconservatism. Although the rise of neoconservatism is hard to imagine without the influence of Strauss, it is misleading to argue—as many critics do—that he and his movement bear *sole* responsibility for providing the intellectual rationale behind this foreign policy. Strauss would never have enjoyed the success he did in the Anglo-American world had there not already been a fertile ideological soil in which to plant his teachings. Although Strauss himself had more doubts than his American students about the wisdom of equating love of God with love of country and may well have opposed the post–Cold War policy of exporting American ideals by force, there is no question that he believed in the superiority of Anglo-American ideals.[4] Even if it is simplistic to blame the Iraq War on the application of Straussian ideas, his belief in "eternal" principles uncannily coheres with an Anglo-American ideal that long predates neoconservatism: the will to see the peoples of the world and the Anglo-American West in fundamental agreement over what is universally right.[5] Long before the beginning of Strauss's American exile, the Anglo-American tradition of political philosophy was already turning away from historical standards of judgment to trans-historical ideals that paved the way for the triumph of neoconservatism. For this reason, this book is as much a study of Strauss as it is a study of the principles that underlie Anglo-American democracy.

Why Did Strauss Succeed in the Anglo-American Sphere?

In his *Lectures on the History of Philosophy*, Hegel praises modern eighteenth-century England for creating a "rational politics" that encourages her countrymen to reflect upon "their inward political and economic relationships."

In particular, Hegel admires English political institutions for encouraging the freedom of conscience that makes possible this philosophical reflection. Despite his keen eye for historic and cultural diversity, Hegel is also confident that this "philosophy of reasoning thought" has become "universal." He even holds out the implicit hope that all peoples can adopt ideals that are historically specific to the English.[6]

Although Hegel represents the philosophy of "History" that Strauss pejoratively associates with historicism and nihilism, there is substantial agreement between the two thinkers on the virtues of the English. The fact that England offers to the world *universal* principles, which can be understood by all rational human beings, clearly appealed to both of these distinguished German thinkers. In "German Nihilism," Strauss praises the English for upholding "the old and eternal ideal of decency, of rule of law, and of that liberty which is not license."[7] Unlike the German nihilists, who prejudicially separate human beings based on race and culture, the English defend eternal principles of the good precisely because these are universal principles. In this context, Strauss and his students typically praise liberal democracy as the best regime for all human beings. Although Strauss never quite offers a rigorous definition of what he means by "liberal democracy," it is not hard to glean from his writings its historic origins. In his 1962 "Preface" to his early work on Spinoza, Strauss explains that liberal democracy was first conceived in opposition to the medieval "kingdom of darkness" that denied human freedom. In this new democratic regime, however, "universal human morality" and religious freedom are the cardinal political foundations.[8] (For this reason, Strauss goes on to say, it is the first regime that extended full political rights to Jews.) Although Strauss portrays the Dutch Jew Spinoza as the first defender of liberal democracy, it is Anglo-American civilization that actualizes this regime. Strauss's praise of liberal democracy is akin to Churchill's famous defense of "Civilisation" in a 1938 speech that employed this term as its title. "There is freedom, there is law; there is love of country; there is a great measure of goodwill between classes; there is a widening prosperity. There are unmeasured opportunities of correcting abuses and making further progress." It is not surprising that prominent Straussian scholars have looked to this speech as a classic defense of the best regime. This speech, as Thomas Pangle observes, inspires Western liberal democracies to "revivify" their understanding of "their highest purposes" and form an alliance as a bulwark against their enemies from the Left and the Right.[9]

In this defense of liberal democracy, there are a number of assumptions that cry out for scrutiny. For one thing, it is not obvious that liberalism and democracy fit as well as Strauss and his students seem to suggest. Spinoza, that great philosopher of liberal democracy, certainly treasured intellectual freedom, but he did not believe that women or slaves deserved the rights of democratic citizenship. Moreover, he lamented the democratic violence that the Puritans unleashed on the Stuart monarchy during the English Civil War, only to replace this institution with the dictatorship of Cromwell.[10] As Paul Gottfried has persuasively argued, the earliest liberals were generally hostile to the very idea of a mass democracy that would give the vote to all human beings, lest this extension of the franchise lead to the destruction of liberty.[11] Even Churchill, that hero of the Straussian pantheon, was generally opposed to the rise of democracy if this meant the end of Victorian virtues and liberties. Although Strauss cannot be accused of being a naïve defender of modern democracy, in light of his awareness that liberal freedom has led to discrimination against his own people,[12] he never gives the impression that liberalism and democracy are a fatal mix that may undermine one in favor of the other.

If Strauss and his students have any consistent worries, they involve the recurrent possibility that even the most democratic of peoples may lose faith in this regime and, worst of all, be unwilling to fight for its survival. We shall see Strauss emphasize that only a few Englishmen, and not necessarily the nation's greatest philosophers, uphold these ideals. As he observed in a letter to Karl Löwith one year after the end of World War II, one is more likely to find within "Anglosaxony" (sic) the presence of philosophical minds at work in the "historical faculties" than in "pure philosophy."[13] Strauss apparently never abandoned the hope that there are always a handful of Anglo-American minds who understand the big picture. For this reason, he credits the famed English liberal Lord Acton for teaching that an overemphasis on the historical origins of ideas may subvert otherwise decent regimes.[14]

The Historicist Threat to Liberal Democracy

What Strauss fears most, especially in the Cold War period of his American exile, is that the old German nihilism which caused World War II is enjoying victory in the nation struggling to maintain the "eternal principles" he once associated with the England that defied Hitler. In *Natural Right and History*, which Strauss published at the University of Chicago twelve years after his lecture on German nihilism, he warns Americans that the nation their country defeated in war may impose on them "the yoke of its own thought."[15] That yoke is Historicism, the ideology of appealing to History as the source of all political judgment. Only the United States represents the last, best hope to protect what is eternally true from the threat posed by those ideologues who believe in the historically relative. Lest any critic thinks that Strauss is an historicist for siding with the Anglo-American tradition while he blames the Germans for all that is wrong with modernity, his student Harry Jaffa cautions that this reading is dead wrong. Although no one "appreciated better than he—nor was anyone more grateful than he—for the strength no less than the decency of Anglo-American democracy," the nihilism and historicism that plagued the age was radically modern, not unique to the German mind.[16] It took a civilization dedicated to eternal principles to defeat this plague.

What, then, is eternal about the United States, a nation known for its brazen love of technological progress? It is well known to readers of Strauss that America's tradition of "natural right," particularly its adherence to the "self-evident" truths of universal liberty and equality, is, in his judgment, the most effective modern bulwark against historicism. Despite his misgivings toward the philosophy of Locke, Strauss admires America for retaining an awareness of what is naturally good for humanity. Since Locke and the American Founders clearly have an appreciation for an unchanging human nature that seeks what is universally good for all human beings, the republic still represents the most powerful obstacle against Historicism in its most lethal (that is, German) form.[17]

What exactly is wrong with Historicism? Why does Strauss emphatically assert that this ideology is destructive to all that is true and (eternally) good in the world? Historicism is not to be confused with the historical study of ideas, that is, an awareness of the historical context in which great thinkers and statesmen have labored. Strauss never opposes "history" per se, particularly when he refers to himself at times as an historian.[18] Historicism is more radical than this. The most serious criticism that he consistently offers throughout his oeuvre is that Historicism is self-contradictory: if it is true, then it is false (or at least trivial). Historicism suffers from the paradox of the liar. Since it teaches "that all human thoughts or beliefs are historical," historicism itself "can be of only temporary validity."

Because historicism denies the existence of transcendent or universal standards, there is no way of judging what is absolutely good or bad for human beings.[19] The political upshot of this teaching is a dire one since, from an historicist perspective, there is no way of judging the goodness or badness of a regime: democracy is reduced to the same level as tyranny. Taken to an extreme, Strauss believes that even the greatest modern historicists cannot distinguish between civilization and cannibalism if they apply historicism with consistency: the goodness or badness of both modes of being is relative to their historic periods.[20] To be sure, this last claim smacks of a polemical, straw man argument on Strauss's part: there is no evidence of an historicist who ever conflated civilization with cannibalism. It is also far from obvious that a reader can understand a great thinker's original intent (a cardinal tenet of Straussian hermeneutics) without understanding the kind of world this thinker inhabited.[21]

Nevertheless, Strauss is legitimately targeting a serious defect in some historicist thought (e.g., Marxism): its inability to account for its own quasi-absolute moral judgment, which then sacrifices people to some tyrannical end in the name of "History."[22] Strauss's keen sense of self-referentiality is motivated by his genuine determination to defend the most decent regime that humanity has ever known, Anglo-American liberal democracy. Still, as I argue throughout this book, Strauss's anti-historicist inattention to *historical* influences (like Christianity) on the Anglo-American tradition obscures the true foundations of the regime that he cherishes most.

Readers who are impressed with the common leftist complaint that Strauss is a right-wing xenophobe with hidden sympathies for fascist politics will likely find my portrayal of Strauss as a sincere liberal democrat here rather bewildering.[23] This conventional critique of Strauss rests on the assumption that he opposes liberal democracy and its universalist credos of freedom and equality in favor of the older European (especially German) prejudice that a small reactionary elite must rule the ignorant rabble with an iron fist. Strauss's famous "secret writing" thesis, or his long-standing argument that philosophers throughout history have concealed their most subversive thoughts in coded language in order to avoid persecution, has further encouraged the suspicion of critics that he is not truly being sincere when he supports liberal democracy.[24] According to leftist critics, up means down and black means white when Strauss gives lip service to the liberal cause, since he is actually concealing his distaste for freedom and equality with subtle hints that only a few astute readers can grasp.

For this reason, various leftists have associated Strauss with Old Right thinkers such as Joseph de Maistre and Carl Schmitt.[25] The main rationale behind this argument is that at times Strauss gives the impression he admires the "rule of the wise" that Plato and Aristotle famously articulated, and that he seeks to transplant this ancient lesson in democratic soil. Strauss presumably follows the Old Right's teaching that wise philosophical elites as far back as the age of Plato and Aristotle must employ religion, which they know to be false, for the "education of the many."[26]

Much has also been made of Strauss's respect for Martin Heidegger, whose Nazi sympathies have encouraged a cottage industry of scholarship that draws unsavory connections between his philosophy and the Third Reich. In the one essay that Strauss devotes to this major twentieth-century thinker, Strauss praises Heidegger as "the only great thinker in our time."[27] More ominously, at least to his leftist critics, Strauss also claims in the same piece that all "rational liberal philosophic positions have lost their significance" in his time.[28] Strauss then apparently demonstrates his visceral hatred for democratic rule when he agrees with Heidegger that the "official high priests" of "industrial mass democracy" have not prepared twentieth-century human beings for dealing with the "danger of universal philistinism and creeping conformism." As a result, Strauss urges his readers to "listen to the critics of democracy" as long as they are serious thinkers and not "blustering fools."[29] Critics such as Heidegger apparently convince Strauss to reject American democracy on the grounds that it is "metaphysically the same" as its enemy, Soviet communism. Both superpowers seek to create a "world society" that imposes the conditions of massification on human beings, whether they take the form of Soviet "iron compulsion" or American "soapy advertisement of the output of mass production."[30] Strauss's detestation for massification, or the creation of "lonely crowds" through the use of mass technology, has persuaded Shadia Drury that he is a sworn enemy of egalitarianism and democracy.[31] William Altman, a leftist critic of Strauss who echoes many of Drury's misgivings, adds that Strauss based his alleged opposition to liberal democracy on his study of Heidegger.[32]

What these readers ignore is that Strauss, in the same essay, reveals his determination to preserve what is left of Western liberal democracy from its enemies like Nietzsche and Heidegger. At the beginning of the article, Strauss worries that the philosophical revolution that Heidegger inaugurated is "beginning to affect even Anglo-Saxony."[33] This comment echoes his long-standing concern that German ideas, as we have seen, are unduly tainting the intellectual bloodstream of Anglo-American democracy. In the same passage in which he praises Heidegger as "the only great thinker in our time," Strauss also urges his philosophically minded readers to "find a solid basis for rational liberalism."[34] To be sure, he is convinced that Heidegger has made that goal even more difficult to achieve, in light of his powerful critique of mass technologized society. If there is anything about Heidegger's thought that genuinely worries Strauss, it is the former's argument that ethics is no longer a possibility. This attitude, in Strauss's mind, contributes to the relativistic and nihilistic portrayal of democracy as undeserving of any support on absolute moral grounds, since these grounds no longer exist. Heidegger's separation of ethics from philosophy, then, undermines the cause of liberal democracy in favor of a radical historicism that refuses all moral foundations.[35] There is every reason to believe, as I argue throughout this work, that Strauss attempted "to find a solid basis for rational liberalism" in order to counter the influence of Heidegger, even if the reasoning he employs is based on a rather romanticized view of Greek political philosophy (see chapter two). The fact that Strauss takes seriously Heidegger's critique of democracy may even suggest that he is worried that "postdemocratic nightmares" can follow these attacks.[36]

The larger problem with the leftist portrayal of Strauss as an opponent of liberalism is the unsubstantiated assumption that elitist misgivings about mass democracy are somehow automatically identical to the ideology of the Far Right. Yet Heidegger was hardly the only twentieth-century figure to worry about the implications of mass rule. On the opposite side of the political spectrum, the leftist Frankfurt School expressed near identical sentiments about the "creeping conformism" that mass democracy imposes through technology. When Strauss also laments the decline of a "democratic orthodoxy" that once appreciated the difficulty of finding rational justifications for freedom of speech and universal suffrage, he is lamenting the decline of intellectual support for the democratic regime as a whole. In targeting the new value-free political science, which does not even seek any such rational justifications, he is urging his readers to seek new arguments in support of democracy, not to join rightists in denouncing the democratic extension of the franchise.[37] In short, Strauss is hardly endorsing the Far Right when he complains that twentieth-century positivistic political scientists are failing to defend democracy, a development that the enemies of democracy might well have welcomed.

What leftist critics like Altman and Drury also ignore is that some of the most prominent twentieth-century defenders of liberal democracy have embraced the position that elites are as necessary for the proper functioning of this regime as are rhetorical fictions that encourage democratic patriotism within the masses. I argue in chapter four that Churchill, Strauss's favorite statesman, was similarly worried about the effects of mass democracy on politics and tradition. Other prominent twentieth-century liberals conveyed deep misgivings about mass democracy. Walter Lippmann, who admired Strauss's ideas, stressed the need for a specialized class of educated individuals to "manufacture consent" among the malleable citizenry of democracy. Reinhold Niebuhr, the famous left-liberal Protestant political theologian who was widely read by postwar presidents, similarly emphasized the essential use of "necessary illusions" that will keep the "average man" from drifting into "inertia," since rationality belongs only "to the cool observers" that make up the educated elite.[38] As Steven Smith has argued, Strauss is fairly typical among Cold War liberals for regarding the "educated mind as the best antidote to the pathologies of modern mass politics."[39] Smith could have added that Strauss stands with other Cold War liberals in believing that a special leadership class is needed to protect the citizenry of a liberal democracy from antidemocratic ideas.

The leftist portrayal of Strauss as an antiliberal would also enjoy more validity if its representatives could demonstrate that he supports, as the Far Right does, the natural superiority of some peoples over others. Does Strauss truly believe, like the European Far Right, that "culture and history are the 'identity card' of each people," and that there is no "essence" (nature) that unites humanity in common moral purpose?[40] Does Strauss ever claim, like Maistre, that he has never met "Man," and that talk of universal principles is absurd? If Shadia Drury is right, Strauss and his students are as racist as the Old Right.[41]

In fairness to these leftist critics, there are moments when Strauss admits that cultural diversity may get in the way of understanding principles that are beneficial for all of humanity. In *Natural Right and History*, Strauss acknowledges that the greatest teachers of natural right, both ancient and modern, recognize the basic anthropological truth that there are always "savage" human beings who do not perfectly fit into a civilized order.[42] Elsewhere, Strauss defers to the historic fact that some nations may have a "greater natural fitness for political excellence" than others.[43] These passing comments, however, do not constitute his most central teaching. As he observes in both of these passages, the fact that there are exceptional human beings or cultures that sometimes defy principles of natural right does not logically lead to the historicist conclusion that these principles are historically relative or, worst of all, cease to exist. Students like Allan Bloom are faithful to their teacher when they praise African American authors like W. E. B. DuBois for discovering in the "Great Works" of the Western canon a "common transcultural humanity" that recapitulates "the ever-renewed experience of books by intelligent poor and oppressed people seeking for a way out."[44]

Although a few critics of Strauss are willing to acknowledge that he is no racist, they still attribute to him a "fascism-lite" politics, since he and his students celebrate the Founding documents of America in a brazenly nationalistic manner.[45] Most specifically, they support a centralized form of leadership in the hands of a few. At best, this argument is a half-truth, since Strauss certainly gives the impression that only a wise few should rule. The fact that Strauss believes in the "rule of the wise" does not mean that he endorses tyranny, since the "rule of law" is to take the place of their rule. This Straussian teaching manifests, in principle at least, respect for the law that treats all human beings equally, the very foundation of liberal democracy.[46]

Can Anglo-American Democracy Survive?

Nevertheless, as we shall see, Strauss and his followers face a serious contradiction: if it is true that "the existence of civil liberties all over the world depends on Anglo-Saxon preponderance," can they survive without a foundation in the historically specific Anglo-American tradition?[47] Ultimately, Strauss understood himself to be a defender of universal principles, which just happen to be best defended in the Anglo-American tradition. It is hard to imagine anyone from the European Far Right, which detested English democracy, claiming that one should be a friend to (though not a flatterer of) liberal democracy.[48] Although Strauss refuses to flatter this regime in light of its defects (namely, its unwillingness to defend its own ideals, as we shall see), he is a friend precisely because this is the only regime that believes in a human nature that transcends history, culture, and tribe. As Bloom puts it, cultures, not liberal democracies, go to war against each other because they deny that all peoples enjoy the same nature and rights.[49] Unlike Maistre, Strauss believes in a universal human nature. "All natural right doctrines claim that the fundamentals of justice are, in principle, accessible to man as man. They presuppose, therefore, that a most important truth can, in principle be accessible to man as man."[50] Although Strauss sometimes comes across as a defender of "Western" civilization, in light of the West's contribution toward the teaching of natural right, he takes pains to emphasize that it is not only Westerners who can grasp universal (eternal) principles of justice. In an essay that defends the cause of liberal (and thus universal) education, Strauss issues the caution that the "greatest minds" do not necessarily come from the West and that only ignorance of the necessary languages prevents him from "listening to the greatest minds of India and China."[51] Strauss's defense of universalism or natural right fits very well into a Cold War liberal tradition in which prominent members of the American intelligentsia asserted that the republic represents ideals that are understandable to all human beings. As we shall see, Strauss also presents himself as a liberal who decries the eighteenth-century conservative abandonment of eternal ideals as a parochial and destructive reaction to Enlightenment universalism.[52] For this reason, Strauss persuaded quintessential Cold War liberals like Walter Lippmann that historicism in its most radical form is dangerous because it denies the permanence of a human nature as well as the eternal validity of principles that edify all of humanity.[53]

It may be tempting to think at this point that Strauss is offering a rather idealized version of Anglo-American civilization. It certainly is not a fashionable one in academe today, even in historically WASP-ish nations. Some historians and political scientists have continually sounded the alarm over the dangers that a "bigoted" Anglo-Saxon elite poses to the pluralistic, liberal tradition of the United States.[54] How can Strauss honestly believe that this civilization is so committed to universal principles in light of the prejudice and intolerance it has historically exhibited toward peoples who do not share an Anglo-Saxon background? Two years after he delivered his lecture on "German Nihilism," Strauss provided an answer to this question. In his lecture "The Re-education of Axis Countries concerning the Jews" (1943), in which he is preoccupied with the difficulty of creating liberal democracy in Germany once it is defeated by the Allies, he admits that the Germans have been very adept at pointing out the hypocrisy of the Anglo-Saxons who preach liberal democracy while they practice prejudice at home (e.g., Jim Crow) and imperialism abroad (e.g., India). Nevertheless, it is false, Strauss argues, to reduce Anglo-Saxon ideals to the mere practice of hypocrisy. What Germans fail to understand is the "spirit of compromise"—or the necessity of recognizing, as the English and Americans do, that a just law that exists in legal statutes but is not observed in practice still "acts as a humanizing influence."[55] Because of the tension between principle and practice that Strauss spies in Anglo-American civilization, he and his students are generally willing to overlook or qualify the most tribalist prejudices of their heroes (e.g., Churchill). The racialist rhetoric of Teddy Roosevelt, for example, can be largely forgiven because this president consistently held out the universalist view that republican self-government, with enough effort and firepower, can be spread all over the world. The racialist rhetoric of Woodrow Wilson, however, cannot be excused because this president was not sufficiently committed in practice to his overall belief that all peoples are capable of democratic rule.[56] The fact that Winston Churchill held racialist views about people's capacity for self-government does not, however, deter Straussians from portraying him as a democratic universalist (see chapter four).

What Strauss and his followers fear is not the outbreak of prejudice within Anglo-American civilization, the most tolerant civilization known to humanity in modern history. (For this reason, even non-Straussian neo-conservatives have attacked leftist promoters of multiculturalism for failing to appreciate the openness of the Anglo-American tradition while embracing a relativism that romantically celebrates the literature of the Third World, often based on the illiberal grounds of race and biology.)[57] What they fear most of all is a slackening of the commitment to support and even spread universal (democratic, eternal) ideals. It is not that Strauss supports *all* forms of universalism. His debate with the Marxist Hegel scholar Alexandre Kojève in the late 1940s clearly reveals that he opposes a communist version of universalism, culminating in the triumph of the "universal homogeneous state," that Cold War liberals always resisted. Yet he and his students genuinely worry about the decline of belief in American democratic universalism.

This fear is manifested throughout Allan Bloom's best-selling *The Closing of the American Mind*, which squarely blames this "closing" on the thoughtless tolerance Americans show toward undemocratic ideologies (which are mainly German in origin). Even if it is too polemical to accuse Bloom, as one leftist critic does, of offering "a Jewish youth's lament that the Wasps have abandoned the Greeks to let in the Blacks,"[58] Strauss and his students are anxious that Anglo-Saxon thinkers and politicians have become too tolerant of ideas that are contrary to the democratic mission of the Anglo-Saxon West.[59] Even in the atmosphere of victory after World War II, Strauss notes that the modern West has lost its "universal purpose" of making the world safe through the promotion of democratic ideals for all men and women around the globe.[60] The reason for this spiritual "crisis" of will is all too clear: the triumph of Historicism and its ideological cousins Positivism and Relativism. As Jaffa astutely observes, his teacher defended "Anglo-American constitutionalism *at its best*" and was well aware that it often had few defenders (aside from Lincoln and Churchill).[61] What troubles Strauss most of all in the Cold War period is that self-styled defenders of the English way of life have undermined their own cause when they appeal to historicist or relativist arguments. (Perhaps for this reason he praised readers who had a "natural preference" for the ennobling novels of Jane Austen over the existentialist fiction of Dostoyevsky.)[62] Strauss takes English liberals like R. G. Collingwood and Isaiah Berlin to task for ignorantly believing that they can defend their civilization *while* they deny, along historicist or relativist lines, that this civilization is eternally valid or has an absolute basis. Strauss laments the fact that, since the nineteenth century, English philosophy has not been properly committed to the defense of liberal democracy. The triumph of English positivism, which Strauss sometimes associates with Historicism, is a sure sign that even a decent civilization can go to the bad if it can no longer "objectively" condemn the enemies of democracy who simply express different "value judgments" about politics. Collingwood's rather casual remark that liberalism and despotism are simply "different"—not opposites—is precisely the sort of belief that Strauss condemns as a dangerously weak defense of democracy.[63] The positivistic reliance on science as the "backbone" of civilization is hardly an adequate response to anti-democratic nihilists who value war over brute facticity.[64] Americans are no better, according to Strauss, when the republic's liberals reject the "limits to diversity" imposed by natural right in favor of "the uninhibited cultivation of individuality."[65] In the pithy words of Bloom, Americans have thoughtlessly embraced "openness to closedness."[66] (Consistent with this line of thinking, James Ceaser faults the American pragmatist philosopher Richard Rorty for failing to defend liberal democracy on a rational foundation.)[67]

The weakening of Anglo-American will is, then, the greatest threat to the preservation of decent, democratic rule. As a political philosopher who constantly emphasizes the dangers of subversively questioning, as Socrates did, the ideals of a democratic regime, Strauss impressed upon his mainly

American students that the embrace of historicism and relativism at the highest leadership levels in Western democracy leads to disaster. Only rarely in history, including Anglo-American history, do we find statesmen of such high caliber as Abraham Lincoln who are determined to save constitutional government from its enemies, even if the price of survival is suppressing the civil liberties of those who misuse their freedom for the purpose of destroying freedom altogether.[68] Historicists of the Left as well as the Right are to blame, from a Straussian perspective, for treating Anglo-American liberal democracy as just another regime whose ideals are historically relative. Even historians with no attachment to the Straussian school have noted the relative decline of Anglo-Saxon (or WASP-ish) prejudice in the twentieth century that led to relativism or the devaluation of this civilization, not to a triumphant belief in "eternal principles."[69]

This intellectual rot from within Anglo-American civilization haunts students of Strauss to no end. Progressivist liberals like Carl Becker and John Rawls come under fire because of their failure to defend liberal ideals from a trans-historical standpoint. Despite the fact that Anglo-American progressivists believed, at least in the early twentieth century, that progress can benefit all peoples, this ideology dangerously relativizes the role and meaning of democracy in history. Progressivism leads, then, to opposition to democracy from the Left and the Right.[70] Harry Jaffa excoriates Becker for dismissing the Declaration of Independence as an outdated document that holds no absolute meaning for human beings all over the world who were desperately struggling against fascist and communist tyranny in the 1920s and 1930s.[71] Allan Bloom lambastes Rawls for abandoning the timeless principle of natural right in favor of a selfhood that seeks ends which are merely egoistic, and neither good nor bad in an absolute sense. Bloom's greatest fear (like Jaffa's) is that this false concept of justice, which fails to defend the "superiority of liberal democracy," will appeal to "the typical liberal in Anglo-Saxon countries" who is blissfully unaware that this argument is based on the ideas of liberal democracy's enemies, namely, historicists and relativists.[72]

Strauss's Search for the Universal

My focus on Strauss's thinking in his World War II and Cold War phases may invite the suspicion that I have not emphasized enough the political ideas of the early Strauss, which have received considerable attention from his leftist critics. According to Nicholas Xenos and William Altman, this early Strauss of the 1920s and 1930s, before his American exile, is most worthy of readers' attention since it is in this stage of life that Strauss exhibits sympathies for representatives of the Far Right like Schmitt, Heidegger, and Spengler. The fact that Strauss faults these men for having "paved the way for Hitler" presumably means nothing, since he made these remarks in 1941 in that anti-Nazi haven, the United States of America.[73]

Although I admit that my focus will almost exclusively be on Strauss in the period following his flight from Germany in 1932, I am unpersuaded that in his early years there is zero evidence of any preoccupation with universalism, which he later substantively developed in his American exile. Despite Bloom's claim that the Strauss of this early period was a "pre-Straussean Strauss," still under the spell of the historicist prejudice that reduced the ideas of the great thinkers to mere epiphenomena,[74] I am inclined to believe that Strauss even at this time was in search of a universal good that was intelligible to all human beings. As early as 1931, the young Strauss was lamenting the fact that the modern age was a "cave" of ignorance far worse than anything of which Plato warned in *The Republic*. The moderns in fact are so ignorant of the good that, unlike the Greeks, they need "history" in order to *ascend* to this cave.[75] As a Jewish student in Weimar Germany, Strauss's interest in debates over the meaning of Protestant theology encouraged him at least to raise some questions about the exclusivity of the religious life. From a philosophical perspective, was it truly valid to argue, as Schleiermacher and his followers had against the Kantian reliance on pure doctrine, that the understanding of absolutes like God's authority were intelligible only to those who "experienced" God? If that is the case, where does this leave those who are not Protestants, or even believers? It is not that Strauss was presenting the arch-rationalist argument, which he attributed to Spinoza, that only reason can make sense of religion. Strauss was even willing to admit that it was wrong to dismiss religious experience altogether in favor of reason. Indeed, Strauss was rejecting two opposing versions of exclusivist hermeneutics: one that restricted the understanding of faith only to those who have reason, and the other that restricted the understanding of faith only to those who have experienced God.[76] For this reason, Strauss disagreed with distinguished historians of ideas such as Eric Havelock and Eric Voegelin, during the Cold War, for insisting that *only* religious experience or fidelity to a particular religious tradition (e.g., Christianity) can illuminate human understanding about faith and politics.[77] To

be sure, Christian critics of Strauss, like the Thomistic philosopher Robert
Sokolowski, have fired back that Christian philosophy promotes universal
truths that are known to anyone who is willing to exercise his or her capacity for reason. The political truths that are known to all human beings do
not require Christian faith or experience of revelation.[78] If this is correct,
however, then Strauss could easily reply that there is still a universal good
beyond religion. In fact, both Aquinas's and Kant's dependence on Christianity effectively mitigates the possibility of a universal morality that is
rationally defensible to all (not just Christians).[79]

Once again, readers who are used to the leftist portrait of Strauss as a
philosopher of neo-fascism will find this reading of his ideas to be uncon-
ventional. Although my intent in this work is to critique the defective reasoning behind Strauss's support for liberal democracy as he understands it,
and not to review the vast literature on Strauss's alleged right-wing politics
as a young man, it is worth noting here that even in this early period the
evidence for his rightist sympathies is at best mixed. (For one thing, the
young Strauss may have voted for the center Left in the Weimar period.)[80]
In this so-called right-wing period when he was a student of philosophy
in Weimar Germany, there is even evidence that Strauss was in search of
a universal standard of the good that had little to do with the Far Right
politics that many leftist critics attribute to him. To be sure, much has been
made of supportive remarks he made in favor of right-wing causes both
before and after the rise of Nazism in Germany. Strauss's contempt for
the "rights of man," his support for Roman-style authoritarianism, and his
sympathy for a movement of the Right that might stop Hitler, all of which
he expressed in one lone letter to his friend Karl Löwith shortly after the
accession of Hitler (May 19, 1933), have been interpreted as proof positive
that he never had any true affection for liberal democracy. In the eyes of his
leftist readers, it is ominous that Strauss, who in 1932 had fled from Germany, appeals here to "fascist, authoritarian, and imperial principles" to decry the "shabby abomination" that is Hitler's Third Reich.[81] Additionally,
his friendship with Carl Schmitt, the philosopher of jurisprudence who
later defended the Nazi regime, has further inspired various suspicions that
Strauss was a lifelong ally of Far Right political movements.[82] As Paul Gottfried has argued, Strauss's hopes for a right-wing movement that might have
stopped Hitler in 1933 has more to do with pragmatic support of a leader like
Mussolini who "was widely regarded as the major adversary to Hitler on the
continent" than with any latent sympathy for the Far Right. (Gottfried adds

here that Strauss's rooting for Roman authoritarianism was quickly replaced by his praise for Churchill, the arch-opponent of Hitler, once Strauss arrived in England.)[83] Strauss's comments at this time must be put in a wider context that included other prominent Europeans who similarly hoped that Hitler would be overthrown by right-wing movements that were far less dedicated to revolutionary violence. Gottfried has also argued that Schmitt's realpolitik philosophy (based on Hobbes) has little to do with Strauss's celebration of "timeless" virtues.[84]

On a related philosophical note, it is evident that Strauss disagreed with Schmitt on what counts as universally true of humanity. In his famous essay on Schmitt's *The Concept of the Political* that he penned in the late 1920s, Strauss seeks a "horizon beyond liberalism."[85] Although his leftist critics have interpreted this comment as evidence of Strauss's lifelong antiliberal views, they fail to understand that Strauss, even in this early stage, is trying to shore up liberalism with a universal standard of nature that Schmitt's realpolitik philosophy presumably lacked.[86] In his critical analysis of Schmitt's political philosophy, Strauss takes aim at Schmitt's focus on "the philosophy of culture," which obscures any awareness of what is beyond culture. As Strauss puts it, "we may say in summary that liberalism, sheltered by and engrossed in a world of culture, forgets the foundation of culture, the state of nature, that is, human nature in its dangerousness and endangeredness."[87] Despite the obviously Hobbesian undertone in his remarks on the "state of nature," Strauss is already articulating his lifelong interest in defining what is universal.[88] What Strauss later calls the "ancestral" is similar to what he calls "culture" here, a concept of politics that is parochially concerned with particular human beings rather than human nature as a whole.[89] This preoccupation with particular traditions, which he spies in Schmitt's thought, obscures knowledge of what is universally known about all human beings. It is this knowledge that liberalism must recover. Once again, cultures go to war but liberal democracies do not. Whatever the merits of the distinction between culture and nature, it is clear that Strauss even in his Weimar period has little sympathy for the Far Right's preoccupation with what sets human beings apart from each other on cultural grounds.

This early interest in what is universally intelligible to all human beings perhaps goes a long way toward explaining why Strauss can be credited with being the most important intellectual influence in postwar conservatism and later neoconservatism, both of which were preoccupied with a search for "eternal" values.[90] This assertion is predictably controversial, since other intellects vie for the title of being the master guru of the movement. Reinhold Niebuhr, for example, arguably competes with Strauss for influence within both neoconservative and liberal ranks during the Cold War, since he was at least as universalistic in thought as Strauss. Niebuhr faults the foreign policy realist George Kennan for pouring too much doubt on the commendable American belief that the republic knows what is good for the world—namely, democracy.[91] Certainly it is undeniable that Niebuhr is much loved by prominent neoconservatives (e.g., Michael Novak) as well as presidents and politicians in both political parties.[92] I am inclined to believe, however, that Strauss's version of universalism is more in sync with Cold War liberalism than Niebuhr's version, precisely because Strauss does not restrict a proper understanding of democracy to any particular religious tradition. Strauss could never write, as Niebuhr does, that a prerequisite to true self-government is the assumption that *only* adherents to the Christian faith can understand both God and the ethic of charity that must underlie democracy.[93] As the Catholic philosopher James Schall astutely observes, Strauss was addressing readers who would be "scandalized" if they suspected that revelation, not reason, is essential for the virtuous life.[94]

Strauss took little interest in Niebuhr's thought except for a brief appreciative nod toward Niebuhr's efforts to reconcile Jews and Christians after the Holocaust.[95] Yet it is not hard to imagine where he would stand on the theologian's insistence that democracy must be understood along Christian lines. In Strauss's view, the intent to associate political philosophy or statecraft with any particular faith, culture, or civilization smacks of historicism.[96] On a more personal level, Strauss once recalled the treatment of German Jews at the hands of the Protestants in the Third Reich. Although he recognized that some Lutheran clergy helped the Jews in the early years of Nazi persecution, Strauss bitterly noted that not a single Protestant clergyman stood up for the political rights of Jews.[97] It is not surprising then that he refuses to accept Christianity as a universal faith that ought to inspire all human beings. To insist that one must be Christian (or religious) to embrace and practice democracy is a denial of natural right. It also raises the inevitable question, especially in the minds of leftist critics who may use it as an opportunity to question America as an "inclusivist" nation, What are non-Christians supposed to take from this teaching?[98]

Ultimately, it is impossible to separate a civilization's claims to be the guardian of universal ideals from the historic particularity of that same civilization. The "ether of universalism" threatens to burst "the boundaries of ethnicity," once the ideals of liberty and equality are applied to all human beings.[99] At the same time, however, the influence of religion on these ideals may be more important than Strauss acknowledges. If it is true that only Anglo-American civilization has made possible decent constitutional regimes that are dedicated to universal ideals, can they withstand the decline of the historical (and religious) foundations that made all this possible?[100] It is the purpose of this study to answer that question.

2

Athens in Anglo-America

It is well known that Leo Strauss portrayed himself as a political philosopher who sought the "recovery" of classical political philosophy. This recovery was essential in order to shore up the legitimacy of liberal democracy, which, although triumphant over fascism in World War II, was still threatened by communism in the Cold War. The urgency of this recovery, as Strauss explains in *Natural Right and History*, rests on his assumption that the philosophical ideas of the defeated enemy, Germany, have entered the intellectual bloodstream of the victor, the United States. "It would not be the first time that a nation, defeated on the battlefield and, as it were, annihilated as a political being, has deprived its victors of the most sublime fruit of victory by imposing on them the yoke of its own thought."[1] These ideas include value relativism and historicism, which undermine the traditional American faith in natural right (and therefore liberal democracy). Only a return to the political philosophy of Plato, Aristotle, and their medieval heirs can help beleaguered liberal democrats in the Anglo-American world win the intellectual war against these ideas; the classics alone can remind moderns of the "timeless ideals" that inoculate decent regimes against the dangers of ideologies that emphasize only the historically relative and contingent.

Passages like this give the impression that Strauss is a critic of modernity and would like nothing better than to challenge the most important foundations of modern political philosophy. Moreover, his supporters read him as an anti-modern for the most part. Stanley Rosen, an admiring reader and student of Strauss, identifies his philosophy with "paganism," which is radically distinct from both the biblical tradition and modernity.[2] Strauss's sharp distinctions between the ancients and the moderns have led sympathetic readers to portray him as a philosopher who repudiates the modern age.[3] Strauss has even been compared to modern-day Thomists who "vehemently deny" any association between ancient and modern versions of natural right.[4] Given the massive influence of Strauss's thought in the study of the American regime, it is no surprise that his supporters see themselves as scholars seeking "to improve American constitutionalism by returning to Aristotelian political science."[5] Even critics of Strauss often accept this conventional image. From the Right, Michael Novak accuses the Straussians of trying to introduce "pagan" ideas into the American Founding, at the expense of the Christian influence.[6] From the Left, Jean-François Drolet accuses Strauss of idealizing the "classical idea of the state" and threatening to manufacture an "elitist" democracy according to Platonic ideals.[7]

These readers may be exaggerating just how anti-modern Strauss's thought truly is. There is considerable reason to doubt that he repudiated *every* important modern idea, as we shall see. Unlike many Thomists, Strauss fully accepts the triumph of modern science over the "antiquated" cosmology of the Greeks.[8] It is also not obvious to every reader that Strauss is an unequivocal defender of the classics and opponent of the moderns, despite his predominant reputation as a defender of "Athens," or classical political philosophy. What Strauss and his students usually represent as "classical" or "timeless" ideals often sound more like post–World War II American liberal credos about democratic virtues. According to Paul Gottfried, the Straussians sometimes see classical ideals as the forerunner to the American regime.[9] Jennifer Roberts, in an extensive discussion of the various modernist attempts to reinvent Athens as a model of true democracy, has accused Strauss and his student Allan Bloom of holding up "for imitation an image of ancient Greece radically different from the world of Athenian democracy."[10] Nancy Levene has similarly argued that Strauss defends a "mythical" version of Athens that is far more dependent on modern ideas

than he is willing to admit.[11] Even Gregory Smith, a sympathetic reader
of Strauss, acknowledges that Strauss's version of Athens is a "hybrid" of
ancient and modern ideas.[12]

This controversy over the Straussian teaching on America may not be
surprising, since Strauss and his movement are often accused of practicing
"secret writing" in order to conceal the true intent of their thought. As I
have already noted, Strauss famously argued in *Persecution and the Art of
Writing* that philosophers from Plato to early modernity were compelled to
conceal their most subversive thoughts in order to avoid political persecution. Mindful of the fate of Socrates (who was executed by a democracy),
philosophers through the ages have attempted to avoid persecution and
even death by paying lip service to authority, at the surface level of the text,
while hiding their most critical ideas at the subterranean level of the text:
only a few wise readers can detect the latter through careful interpretation.[13] Whether this strategy makes sense in explaining the often conflicted
messages of the Straussian approach to the American regime is another
matter. After all, why would Strauss and his students hide their subversive
message in a relatively open regime that does not persecute dissenters?
Even Willmoore Kendall, one of the first prominent American admirers of
Strauss in the postwar period, predicted that one day "some future Strauss
will be needed . . . to ferret out the 'essential Strauss,' who no more than
Machiavelli is a man to blurt things out."[14]

While I do not claim to be this "future Strauss," my agreement with
those critics who are dubious about Strauss's self-portrait as a defender of
classical ideals will become obvious. Although most of these readers are
not primarily interested in the Straussian influence over political debates in
Anglo-American democracy, I agree with their general view that Strauss's
portrait of the classical tradition is suspect. Still, there is one major difference that deserves restatement. Whereas most of these critics (with the
exception of Gottfried) portray Strauss as an arch-conservative opponent
of liberalism, I take at face value, once again, Strauss's support for liberal
democracy: I do not believe he is a closet elitist of the Far Right.

My purpose in this chapter is to show that Straussian ideas, under close
scrutiny, turn out to make mythical and even false assumptions about the
classical tradition, which end up obscuring a proper understanding of the
American democratic regime Strauss and his followers sincerely wish to
preserve. Additionally, the Straussian approach to the American tradition
holds up a romanticized version of Athens while neglecting to give sufficient

weight to the Christian influence in that tradition. Even when Straussians acknowledge the influence of Christianity, it is usually subordinated to the greater influence of Hellas. If there is any secret agenda that Strauss and his movement had, it is to marginalize the importance of Christianity as the defining foundation of American political thought.[15]

Strauss's Qualified Anti-modernism

In his pivotal essay "Progress or Return? The Contemporary Crisis in Western Civilization," Strauss argues for a return to the wisdom of classical political philosophy as forcefully as he opposes the modern belief in progress. The main evidence he marshals against the idea of progress is that the "enormous increase of man's power" through the advancement of scientific and technological progress has not led "to a corresponding increase in wisdom and goodness." "Modern man is a blind giant" because he has lost the ability to distinguish between good and evil. Instead, he embraces either the fact-value dichotomy so dear to positivism or arbitrary and changeable terms like "progressive" and "reactionary" that have no meaning apart from their historic context. It is no wonder, then, according to Strauss, that progressivism has led to a "barbarization" that undermines the very heritage of Western civilization. Far from creating a civilization superior to all others, progressivism has robbed humanity of its ability to understand what a standard of superiority would even mean anymore. Strauss is not surprised, in his post–World War II context, that belief in progress has been replaced by belief in mere "change," now that progressivism has been discredited.[16]

Strauss's main criticism of progressivism, that it has failed to deliver its most ambitious promise of moral enlightenment, is not altogether surprising or original. As he himself admits in the same essay, prominent thinkers like Georges Sorel were dismissing the "wholly unwarranted hopes" of progressivism even before the cataclysm of World War I.[17] Moreover, what Strauss writes in this postwar essay largely parallels the ideas of his contemporaries in the Frankfurt School. In *Dialectic of Enlightenment*, Theodor Adorno and Max Horkheimer also denounce the idea of progress as a dead illusion that has replaced traditional bourgeois civilization with a scientifically contrived nightmare. Like Strauss, these Marxist critics have no sympathy whatsoever for the progressivist hope that technological advancement leads to human advancement.[18] In the aftermath of World

War II and the Holocaust, it is unremarkable that Strauss would share his contemporaries' disdain for the idea of progress.

What is remarkable, however, is that Strauss is vehemently attacking an idea that is at the core of the very civilization he cherishes. Unlike Adorno and Horkheimer, who denounced Western civilization as "fascist," Strauss admired the West for creating the liberal democratic regime. Strauss also admitted that it is hard to imagine this regime without relating its origins to the belief in progress. In *The City and Man* (1964), he sincerely laments the fact that the West, now in a potential death struggle with communism, has lost a sense of its purpose, since it no longer believes in the progressivist credo that the whole world must be made democratic. Thanks to the influence of positivism, which dismisses all ideas as ideology, the West can no longer rationally defend its own superiority against communism, which also promises a democratic world.[19] Despite its massive scientific and technical superiority over all other rivals, Western democracy has not been well served by its belief in progress, which positivistic social science has easily undermined.

Because of his opposition to the idea of progress and his support for liberal democracy, Strauss felt compelled to legitimize the one decent regime known to human beings on a foundation that was not, in his view, indebted to the progressivist faith. That foundation was classical political philosophy, as Plato and Aristotle articulated it. Strauss had to shore up the West, as he understood it, by recovering its ancient heritage. Although he is not the first or only twentieth-century thinker to portray the Hellenic tradition as being superior to the modern, Strauss stands out as a political philosopher who teaches that the concerns of Plato and Aristotle are not always opposed to those of their modern counterparts. The fact that the ancients and moderns proposed different solutions to the problem of politics should not obscure the truth, as Strauss understands it, that there is an eternal human nature. This teaching of the natural right tradition, as we have seen in chapter one, is the core teaching of Straussian hermeneutics. For this reason, Strauss did not see himself as a mere defender of the "West," since it is historicist to believe that only one civilization possesses high principles that are unknown to all other human beings. Political philosophers must repudiate the shared positivistic and historicist opinion that there are "no principles of understanding and principles of preference which belong to man as man, who can never go beyond a historically qualified humanity such as Western civilization."[20] What Strauss in principle seeks most of all is a recovery of the eternally valid credos of political philosophy, not an historicist return to Greek civilization. At times he even warns that attempts to "return" to antiquity (as in the case of Rousseau's political philosophy) typically advance radical versions of modernity.[21] Strauss hardly denies historic differences between antiquity and modernity. Yet he emphasizes that the moderns have simply forgotten the timeless truths regarding the theologico-political problem.[22] If it is true, as his student Stanley Rosen observes, that all political problems are the same throughout human history, then "the Greeks as Greeks become irrelevant."[23]

It is far from obvious that the regime of liberal democracy can survive or even be made intelligible without some reference to the progressivist faith that brought it into being. As Strauss himself admits, the authority of Socrates, Plato, and Aristotle "did not carry much weight" with the first great defender of liberal democracy, Spinoza.[24] It is also far from obvious, as we shall see, that Strauss and his followers can successfully abandon modern ideas, progressivist or otherwise, while they recover the classics. What most readers of Strauss, both critical and supportive, often ignore or misunderstand about Strauss is that his rejection of progress stems from a *modernist* foundation. It is true that Strauss sounds like an anti-modern conservative when he refuses to embrace the idea of progress since, in his view, this secular faith teaches that there are no eternal truths in politics. Once progressivism is wedded to the scientific method, it is impossible to escape the positivistic conclusion that democracy is itself a "value" that cannot be empirically measured.[25] Yet Strauss's rejection of progress also stems from a rather modern reading of what the Greeks meant by the "eternal," namely, the belief that humanity in general can understand the principles of natural right. These are accessible "to man as man." (Strauss even occasionally refers to "ancient egalitarian natural right.")[26] As I shall argue in this chapter, this egalitarian view of humanity not only ignores the xenophobic and tragically violent nature of Greek political life and theory. It also reinforces the traditionally modern, leftist goal of spreading democracy around the world.[27] Strauss ultimately rejects progress because it denies the fundamental equality of all human beings, their ability to understand right and wrong regardless of when they lived.

In fairness to the Straussian analysis, it is true that progressivism at times justified an exclusivist anthropology of human nature when its defenders (particularly Gobineau) made racialist distinctions between progressive and backward peoples.[28] Although we saw in the last chapter that there is evidence that Strauss also made distinctions between "savages" and enlightened human beings, these distinctions are secondary to his egalitarian view of human nature. While it would be a falsehood to claim that Strauss himself was a wholehearted progressivist, he shares at least the traditionally leftist belief in human equality. For this reason, Straussians like Ronald Pestritto have critiqued Woodrow Wilson because of his racist (and progressivist) belief that not all peoples are capable of democratic rule due to differing historical preconditions for self-government. The fact that Wilson, like Strauss, admires the English respect for the rule of law does not get him off the hook for "ethnocentrism," since he insists that only peoples with this background can make democracy work.[29] Although Wilson's defense of democratic ideals is commended from a Straussian perspective,[30] his historicist view of human nature cannot be tolerated. Wilson would be more acceptable if he had equated the English principle of respect for the law with a "timeless" respect for the same.

Strauss's project of providing a foundation for liberal democracy that avoids progressivism and even the most vulgar examples of modern political thought is, ultimately, rife with problems. As even Rosen has argued against his teacher, it is difficult to demonstrate the accessibility of eternal principles which have been "covered over" by historical changes that have occurred between the age of Plato and the age of modernity. It is even more difficult to demonstrate that the concerns of Plato are fundamentally identical to those of modern philosophers.[31] Nevertheless, Strauss must insist they are not so different, given his assumption that there is an eternal human nature. Although he certainly acknowledges that the moderns faced problems that were unknown to the ancients (e.g., technological change), Strauss emphasizes that there are timeless truths that are neither "ancient" nor "modern."

Strauss, we have seen, believes that the modern mind has not progressed beyond the wisdom of the past. As a result, the only hope for liberal democracy is to recover the timeless wisdom that vulgar modern movements like historicism, positivism, and progressivism have obscured. The big problem he faces, aside from the need to demonstrate that there is an eternal human nature of the sort he describes, is that he must account for the liberal democratic regime in eternal terms without relying on modern ideas in the process. That is to say, he and his numerous followers must demonstrate that the Anglo-American version of liberal democracy, as they understand it, is indeed primarily indebted to Greek political philosophy. If they are to avoid the scourge of progressivism, then they must legitimize this regime according to standards that are, historically, not modern. If America is to avoid the fate of being a permanent "blind giant" of modernity, then its foundations must not be exclusively based on flawed modern grounds. Strauss must avoid any serious dependence on modern ideas, especially progressivist ones, in order to recover classical political philosophy. Yet it is far from obvious that Strauss steers clear of the modern age altogether, particularly when he often significantly rejects pagan ideas that interfere with his defense of liberal democracy. For the remainder of this chapter, I evaluate the coherence of the Straussians' attempt to understand their favored regime, American democracy, according to the "timeless" standards of Plato and Aristotle.

Strauss, the Straussians, and American Democracy

In their study *The Truth about Leo Strauss: Political Philosophy and American Democracy*, Catherine and Michael Zuckert contend that "the Straussians do not form a unitary 'sect' with a party line."[32] In their view, the evidence clearly reveals a diversity of perspectives among the followers of Strauss who study the American Founding. The "East Coast" Straussians most famously represented by Allan Bloom apparently view America in tragic or pessimistic tones, as they fault the republic for embracing a naïve "openness" to dangerous historicist ideas from the Founding onward.[33] From this perspective, America has always been a flawed nation that never truly embraced the classical ideals which would have saved its collective soul from historicism and relativism. John Locke is no match for Rousseau, Nietzsche, and Heidegger. In contrast, the "West Coast" Straussians, led by Harry Jaffa, insist that the highest principles of the Founding echo and advance the political philosophy of Greek political philosophy. America in principle has always been an Aristotelian regime, and its greatest president Abraham Lincoln saved the nation from the evil of slavery by invoking timeless standards of "natural equality" that both Aristotle and the Founders defended as self-evident to all human beings. (Harvey Mansfield Jr., in his study of executive power, similarly argues that the American Constitution created an "Aristotelian regime formalized in writing.")[34] It was Lincoln's particular genius to restore the original meaning and role of the Declaration of Independence to its rightful place as the first political testament in modern history to create a regime that incarnated the highest principles of classical political philosophy.[35] A third offshoot of Straussian influence, which the Zuckerts label the "Midwest Straussians," is ideologically as well as geographically in between their brethren inhabiting America's coastlines. Martin Diamond, the main representative of this movement, agrees with his East Coast comrades that America never truly embraced classical principles, yet he agrees with his West Coast brethren that the republic has always possessed virtues that, however "bourgeois," make it worthy of preservation.[36]

The often elaborate distinctions that the Zuckerts painstakingly make between the students and followers of Strauss ultimately do not succeed in making their case against a unifying "party line" within the movement. Perhaps despite their best intentions, the Zuckerts show that there is broad agreement among the various Straussian camps on one crucial truth: *that the American regime must be judged according to classical standards of politics and ethics (as they understand them).* Whatever the merits of distinguishing between Bloom, Jaffa, and Diamond and their various epigones, there is absolutely no disagreement between them and their master on the necessity of understanding the American political tradition in terms that are ancient Greek in origin. A cursory glance at the works of Bloom and Jaffa reveals the core assumption that Greek political philosophy (in particular, Plato for Bloom, Aristotle for Jaffa) provides the means for addressing the crisis of modernity that afflicts America more adequately than do any modern authors. Even Diamond, whom the Zuckerts portray as the Straussian most critical of Strauss's famous distinction between the ancients and the moderns, conceded that the modern virtues are "lower" than the ancient ones.[37]

It is not hard to trace this line of thinking back to Strauss, who insisted that one must understand "the low in the light of the high."[38] The "low" was always the modern depths inhabited by Hobbes and Locke, whereas the "high" was always the heights occupied by Plato and Aristotle. Although Strauss never claimed, as his student Jaffa did, that America's regime is the incarnation of classical ideals,[39] he taught all of his students that even a relatively decent regime must be understood as well as defended on classical grounds. Even as the American tradition of natural right suffered from the defects of Lockean contractarianism, Strauss believed that this modern tradition, which so forcefully advocates the universality of liberty and equality for all, deserves a robust defense against modern totalitarianism from the Left and the Right. Indeed, Strauss went so far as to associate modern constitutional or liberal democracy with the teachings of the classics. In

On Tyranny, he claims that this regime "comes closer to what the classics demanded than any alternative that is viable in our age," although he cautions that the classical (Platonic) premise that "the wise do not desire to rule" still applies.[40] Like all of his students, Strauss shares a "hope" and a "faith" in America, even if he doubts that this faith is absolutely identical to the classical and biblical teachings.[41]

The students of Strauss are certainly not unique in contending that moderns must recover the classical virtues in order to address the spiritual and existential crises stemming from the vices of bourgeois civilization. In the introduction to a recent anthology that mainly includes essays on friendship by the followers of Eric Voegelin, the editors celebrate the superiority of Platonic and Aristotelian ideas of friendship over the Hobbesian ethic of pure self-interested calculation. Like the students of Strauss, these followers of Voegelin hold out the hope that "liberal democracy" (particularly its American manifestation) will be saved by a return to the ideals of the Greek polis, whose citizens saw each other as virtuous friends. Both modern liberalism and Christianity are threats to true friendship, since the first teaches that human beings are acquisitive rivals while the second teaches that human beings are sinful subordinates to God's authority alone. Somehow the damage inflicted by both Christianity and modern liberalism, which undermine the loyalty of citizens to their political regimes, will be undone through a recovery of the Great Works of antiquity.[42] In this vein, the Straussians and the Voegelinians are indistinguishable. Although Strauss was far more cautious than Voegelin in attributing the crisis of modernity to Christianity, both philosophers tend to celebrate the Greeks at the expense of the Christian tradition.[43]

The fact that Strauss's and Voegelin's students have also disagreed with each other at times should not blind readers to the far more central agreement between them on the superiority of classical virtue over modern vice. Even prominent critics of Strauss from the Catholic tradition fundamentally agree with him that the American regime must be defended on a classical foundation. Peter Augustine Lawler, who has criticized Strauss and his students for ignoring the contribution that a "Christian anthropology" has made to the tradition of political philosophy, nevertheless agrees with Strauss that true republican thought begins with the Greeks. For this reason, Lawler describes himself as a theologically inspired Straussian.[44] Although Lawler, as a Thomist, viscerally disagrees with Strauss on the wisdom of synthesizing Greek political philosophy (Athens) and biblical revelation (Jerusalem), they both agree that the lack of an Aristotelian tradition in the American regime necessitates a recovery of the classical virtues. Both men lament the influence of the Lockean tradition, which privileges cold calculation over the classical virtues of moderation and duty.[45]

The Straussian interpretation of the American Founding, whose powerful influence resonates with the ideas of both Voegelinian scholars and Catholic Thomists, deserves a vigorous examination, particularly its call for a return to Greek political philosophy. Should modern America be judged according to what these scholars understand as the ancient standards of the Greeks? This question is important because Strauss and his students pride themselves on understanding America's traditions as the Founders actually understood them. A cardinal tenet of Straussian hermeneutics is that every great political philosopher deserves nothing less than a reader who understands his original intent. For this reason, Strauss faults Spinoza for reading the Bible as one would read any human text. At the same time, Strauss promises he will read Spinoza on Spinoza's terms, even if his subject did not extend the same courtesy to Scripture.[46] As we have already seen, Strauss despises historicists for reducing a great thinker to his particular historical context, oblivious to the original philosophical rationale that drove the thinker to critique that context in the first place.

The Straussian Rewriting of American History

While it is a noble goal to avoid the reductionist tendency to identify a thinker solely with the intellectual currents of his time, this project does not necessarily justify the Straussian attempt to judge the American Founders and Framers according to the standards of the Greek political texts. To lift American political philosophy out of its own historic context and evaluate its merits and defects according to an "eternal" standard of statecraft is particularly problematic when one recognizes that *the American Founders themselves did not think in Greek terms*, as I argue in this chapter. If it is true that Greek political ideas are alien to the American political experience at its foundation, then the Straussians may stand guilty of violating their most cherished credo: to understand a tradition according to its own intent and original meaning.

Perhaps the most important philosophical document of the Founding is *The Federalist*, which has been much studied, if not always well understood in the Straussian movement, and is an appropriate place to start an examination of the Straussian attempt to "Hellenize" the American Founding. What a careful reading of this great work reveals is the determination of its authors (Alexander Hamilton, James Madison, and John Jay) to distinguish the incipient American republic from ancient Hellas. As early as in *The Federalist* No. 6 Hamilton warns that the ancient commercial republics of Athens, Sparta, Rome, and Carthage are not role models for a new America, since each of these was "as often engaged in wars, offensive and defensive." Even the Athens governed by the "celebrated Pericles" engaged in brutal wars of conquest against weaker peoples. *The Federalist* never strays from the position that ancient republicanism failed precisely because of its inability to staunch violence at home and abroad. In *The Federalist* No. 9, Hamilton finds it impossible to read the history of Greco-Roman republicanism "without feeling sensations of horror and disgust at the distractions with which they were continually agitated," including the succession of revolutions that threw up the grim choice between "tyranny and anarchy."

Why was ancient Greece plagued by violence? In *The Federalist* No. 18, Hamilton and Madison provide an answer to this question when they observe that the rule of the strong over the weak—the law of "might is right"—was tragically demonstrated by the strongest Greek cities that "awed and corrupted those of the weaker," leading to the inevitable triumph of the stronger party. In their view, the Greeks were more courageous than wise, since their adherence to violence makes them succumb to the "chains of Macedon" as well as "the vast projects of Rome." Athens, "the last hope of ancient liberty," ends up sharing the fate of the weaker peoples that it once subjugated in its glory days. It is also far from evident that *The Federalist* laments the death of Athens since, as "Publius" observes in No. 63, this polis never succeeded in creating a "safeguard" against the tyranny of its citizens' passions, which then tragically leads to the legal anarchy of "decreeing to the same citizens the hemlock on one day and statues on the next." The "narrow limits" in which the Greek democracies functioned are, if anything, a warning that American republicans must heed, not emulate.[47] (As the Straussian scholar Walter Berns correctly notes, Athens, like all ancient regimes, lacked a "written constitution," which is an innovation that belongs to the modern age. This defect in ancient statecraft undoubtedly contributed to political instability.)[48]

These key articles of *The Federalist* hit upon the fatal reversal that characterizes ancient Greek life. Hamilton understands well that Greek regimes failed precisely because they reverse into their opposites, based on the cyclical movement of time from fortune to misfortune. A strong city-state like Athens, as Thucydides dramatically narrates in his history of the Peloponnesian War, eventually ends up being a weak and defeated one. In the Melian Dialogue (which Thucydides recounts in book five), the hapless Melians, who are facing the tragic choice of death or enslavement at the hands of the Athenians, predict that one day Athens will be at the mercy of a stronger party (5.90).[49] (This prophecy is vindicated after Athens' army is wiped out in the Sicilian expedition and then later defeated by Sparta.) Hamilton well knows that the history of Greece is a history of violence in which fortune and misfortune are inherently changeable, as they fall indiscriminately on the stronger and weaker peoples. This reversal of fortune is equally philosophical and historical. In *The Statesman* (*Politikos*), Plato has the Eleatic Visitor describe in mythological terms how the cosmos itself experiences this fatal reversal (269c–274e). In the Age of Kronus, the god moves the rotation of the universe. In this age, the god takes such good care of the mortals that there is nothing but peace: conflict, work, and politics are nowhere to be seen. Yet the god ultimately abandons the cosmos and mortals to misfortune, when reversal occurs. "And the cosmos in twisting around and sustaining a shock, starts out with an impulse contrary to the beginning and end" (273a). The Age of Zeus then succeeds the Age of Kronus, bringing with it discord, war, and politics. Eventually the god takes control of the helm and restores the universe to its original condition. What is striking about this mythological account of the tragic nature of mortal life is that human beings can do absolutely nothing to stop the transitions from fortune to misfortune and back. Mortals are condemned to experience the cyclical movement of existence, from peace to war. The law of "might is right," which Hamilton identifies as the dominant law in Greek political life, is inescapable as mortals are at the mercy of the universe. It is no surprise, then, that Greek city-states never survived, as they inevitably moved from being conqueror to conquered.[50]

The tragic and violent nature of Greek city-states, including that of classical Athens, presents a monumental challenge to an intellectual movement that celebrates classical virtues at the expense of modern ones. Why should the early American republic be judged according to an historical period that *The Federalist* categorically rejects as one full of violence and devoid of virtue? One characteristic response from the Straussian school is to make a distinction between Greek political philosophy and Greek history, based on the rationale that the violence of the city-states was not mirrored or legitimized in the great philosophical texts. In a letter to Karl Löwith dated August 20, 1946, Strauss makes an early attempt at such a distinction when he warns his correspondent against the temptation of confusing the "Greek man-in-the-street" and even Greek poets with philosophers like Plato and Aristotle, who never believed in the simple-minded conventions of their time (e.g., religious worship of nature).[51] In a more scholarly context, Strauss, in *The City and Man*, notes Aristotle's agreement "with the liberalism of the modern age" because the Stagirite teaches that "Man transcends the city only pursuing true happiness, not by pursuing happiness however understood."[52] In short, Greek philosophy was distinct from the "city" (the political regimes of the day) in pursuing happiness over and above conventional opinions of the time. (This distinction is crucial to Strauss, since he can then portray liberalism as an eternal doctrine that goes all the way back to Plato and Aristotle and conservatism as a transient inclination that is concerned with the merely traditional and ancestral.)[53]

Yet this distinction between Greek political thought and the Greek city-states is not consistently upheld by Strauss. Nor can it be, precisely because it is one of his most central teachings that the wise philosopher who learns from the fate of Socrates must appreciate what is inherently good in a city like classical Athens. At the end of *The City and Man*, Strauss appreciates the French historian Fustel de Coulanges for revealing the "dark or remote side of the city." Yet he also faults him for paying insufficient attention to a truly "philosophical understanding of the city," which is different from the "prephilosophic" that is governed by religious dogma.[54] As is well known to all readers of Strauss, his most basic teaching is that philosophers need to show caution and restraint in attacking the irrational credos of their "city" or regime, if the latter secures to them a measure of philosophic liberty. (Strauss was fond of remarking that the fact that Socrates reached the age of seventy reveals just how tolerant Athens was toward its skeptical citizen's questioning.) In contrast to Coulanges, as he reads him, Strauss believes it is imperative for philosophers to avoid the fate of Socrates by celebrating a relatively decent (and democratic) polis even if that means dishonestly paying lip service to its dogmatic conventions.[55]

The distinction between Greek history and Greek political philosophy that Strauss proposes, however, is not nearly as clear-cut as he makes it out to be. For starters, it is not evident exactly where history ends and philosophy begins. (As we have seen, Plato and Thucydides do not differ on the inevitability of cyclical change.) Should Straussians side with the questioning Socrates or with the regime that executed him? Both options are problematic from a Straussian perspective. If they side with Socrates, they opt for relentless (and potentially nihilistic) questioning of a regime. If they side with Athens, they opt for a regime that is ruled by those whom Plato famously calls the ignorant "many." Willmoore Kendall, one of the first prominent American conservatives in the postwar era to embrace Straussian ideas, answered categorically on the side of Athens. In Kendall's view, democratic Athens had every right to try and execute Socrates, who dangerously questioned the very foundations of the city.[56] This reading of Plato's *Apology*, which recounts the trial of Socrates, is a risky one for students of Strauss to embrace wholeheartedly since this reading confirms the impression (shared by the authors of *The Federalist*) that Athens was tragically and interminably violent, and therefore unjust. Publius in *The Federalist* No. 63 even pointedly refers to the tragic fate of Socrates as an argument against holding up Athens as a model for America to emulate. "What bitter anguish would not the people of Athens have often escaped if their government had contained so provident a safeguard against the tyranny of their own passions? Popular liberty might then have escaped the indelible reproach of decreeing to the same citizens the hemlock on one day and statues on the next."

Strauss's genuine admiration for the modern principle of religious freedom would probably make him uncomfortable with Kendall's defense of Socrates's execution based on the charge of blasphemy against the gods of the state. Despite some misgivings over how liberal democracy makes it easier for anti-Semites to discriminate against Jews, Strauss never doubts that this regime affords the best political home for his people.[57] Nevertheless, Kendall's defense of ancient Athens is understandable, since it is never clear whether Strauss is defending Socratic freedom or the Athenian regime. On one hand, Strauss sometimes sounds like Kendall when he chastises the "youthful contempt" that the young Socrates had "for the political or moral things" that underlie Athens. This attitude presumably paved the way for Socrates' trial and death.[58] On the other hand, since Strauss is determined to spy a decent liberal tradition in classical Athens that permitted Socrates some measure of liberty, it is not obvious he would be absolutely comfortable with Kendall's understanding of Athenian democracy as violent and intolerant (even though Kendall meant it as a defense of

Athens). Unlike Kendall, Strauss even at times praises ancient Athens as a liberal defender of privacy. Strauss was hostile to Karl Popper's famous charge that the Greek city was a "totalitarian" society, with Plato as its chief defender.[59] Once again, however, it is unclear how the Greeks—Athens included—can be liberal in any sense, given the fate of Socrates. Even Jaffa admits that the very concept of individuality, which is central to the separation of church and state, did not kick in until the Christian Era.[60] Nevertheless, these admissions do not apparently deter Straussians from insisting on Athens as the true Founding tradition of political philosophy that must be emulated in America.

Despite Strauss's awareness of the violence of Greek history, based on his reading of Coulanges's work, he is loath to portray the dark side of Athens as enthusiastically as his follower Kendall did.[61] After all, Strauss insists that Greek philosophers enjoyed "a life in human freedom," as opposed to the obedience that biblical religion requires.[62] Nevertheless, philosophers once again must somehow reconcile themselves with the "prephilosophic" understanding of the city: they must learn to live in a decent democracy even if this means acceptance of unphilosophic dogmas that hold the regime together. If Strauss is correct, however, that Athens was a liberal city deserving of philosophers' devotion, does this teaching mean he and his students must gloss over the violence of Athens to which *The Federalist* itself points? Are Straussians asking Americans to emulate an ancient city that, frankly, was not even just?

In his essay on Thucydides, included in *The City and Man*, Strauss does not make clear why Greek statecraft should be a model for the moderns. Although he readily acknowledges that Thucydides' account of the Melian Dialogue—in which the Athenian admirals demand the unconditional surrender of the island of Melos for daring to be neutral in the Peloponnesian War—teaches the brutal political lesson that "might is right,"[63] Strauss still tries to extract from Thucydides' account a "universalism" that moderns presumably no longer grasp. While the political universalism imposed by Athens through imperialist means was doomed to failure due to incessant warfare, it is not obvious to Strauss that a more philosophical universalism also died with Athenian democracy. This universalism, which teaches a "manly gentleness," is as central to Thucydides as it is to Plato and Aristotle.[64] In erasing the distinction between Greek historiography and political philosophy, Strauss at least here attempts to portray Greek thought in general as less cruel than actual political practice. For this reason, Strauss chastises the historian Coulanges for allegedly ignoring the higher and nobler universalism of Athens over and above its political deeds.

Yet even Strauss cannot successfully gloss over the tragic nature of Greek life, whether in thought or in deed. By Strauss's own admission, Plato teaches that "chance rather than man or human wisdom" creates, and ultimately destroys, regimes.[65] This admission in Strauss's essay on Thucydides is not the only place in his oeuvre where he recognizes, however briefly, just how hopelessly violent the Greek cosmos was. In his essay "Jerusalem and Athens," which he completed three years after *The City and Man*, Strauss accurately describes Zeus, the king of the gods, as a deity that dooms human life to the endless misery of one race succeeding the other (just as Sparta conquered and displaced Athens): "there is no divine promise, supported by the fulfillment of earlier divine promises, that permits one to trust and to hope."[66] Strauss goes on to argue that the Greeks lack a concept of hope (since they do not believe in a revealing God that inspires hopes for universal peace),[67] as they struggled to exist in a universe in which humanity itself is devalued below nature. It is significant that Strauss does not restrict this belief in fatal suffering and tragedy to Greek literature. It is just as central to Greek philosophy and history.

It is even more significant that Strauss himself could not consistently stomach the full implications of the tragic view of history that the Greeks defended. Although he appreciates Oswald Spengler's *Der Untergang des Abendlandes* (1918) for its powerful indictment of modern progressivism, Strauss described as wrong and even "inhuman" Spengler's gloomy prediction that the West would inevitably decline.[68] Spengler's conflation of cultures with biological organisms fated to perish struck Strauss, along with many of Spengler's contemporaries, as a dangerous pessimism. In fact, Strauss usually associates such pessimism with the worst manifestations of historicism, which teaches that "all human thought" is dependent on the "fickle and dark fate" of historical change, "not on evident principles accessible to man as man."[69] As a defender of American liberal democracy, Strauss could hardly accept this extreme gloom. Yet he never reconciles his love of the Greeks, a tragically minded people, with his own rejection of fatalism and the cycles of fortune and misfortune. How can Strauss's rather modern rejection of Greek fatalism be compatible with his defense of liberal democracy, which, surely, rejects the inevitability of tragedy?

One of the most ambitious attempts to confront this question can be found in Paul Rahe's three-volume study *Republics: Ancient and Modern*

(1994). Rahe, who is a Straussian historian of both antiquity and modernity, boldly and comprehensively studies the massive differences between ancient and modern philosophies of republicanism. (Like Strauss, he is also well aware that Thucydides taught a fundamentally tragic view of life that has no modern counterpart.)[70] From volume one onward (which is dedicated to the study of classical Greek regimes), Rahe contends that "classical Greece has a special claim on our attention," since Greece provided "premodern republicanism in its pristine and purest form."[71] Is he, then, recommending Greece as a subject of study for moderns or, more ambitiously, as a role model to emulate? It turns out that Rahe provides two contradictory responses throughout his magnum opus, both of which can be traced back to Strauss. The first response lies in Rahe's argument that moderns must learn from the superior wisdom of the Greeks, with respect to their history and political philosophy. The Greeks presumably cared more about their polity than their modern counterparts, because their regime (fatherland) was so all-absorbing that the private realm was too restricted to interfere with political duties.[72] The bourgeois man's love of peace and commerce, for this reason, makes him a far less effective soldier than his ancient equivalent.[73] By the time that Rahe discusses the American regime, in his third volume, he declares in true Straussian tones that America was not a republic of virtue, since its greatest modern antecedents (Locke's and Montesquieu's political philosophies) had taught them to "look down not up" and judge themselves according to the standards of "the animal kingdom." In the process, the modern revolution (which must include America) "sows the seeds of its own destruction."[74] As a result, Rahe concludes a long discussion of the weak status of virtues in the modern age with the confident assumption that no modern has ever improved on the Greek teaching that man is a political animal whose deliberations "must lead him on to a concern with the just and even the good."[75]

It is not very clear to this reader how Rahe arrives at these conclusions when, elsewhere in his massive work, he presents his second answer to the question of Greece as a role model for America by documenting just how violent and unvirtuous the Greeks were. As early as his first volume, Rahe admits that every Greek city-state (Athens included) lacked a "civil society," a realm in which citizens could maintain certain private rights against the incursions of the regime (which he otherwise puzzlingly calls a "moral community").[76] Like Hamilton, Rahe recognizes that violence was the high price the Greeks paid for "the excitement of political life," which was manifested in various wars, xenophobia toward strangers, and tolerance of obnoxious practices like pederasty and slavery.[77] Perhaps most tragically of all, there was no true political "opposition" to the status quo, except during violent revolutions: the idea of peacefully tolerating opposition parties within a democracy is a modern idea.[78] It is no wonder, then, as Rahe notes, that the authors of *The Federalist* categorically rejected the Greek city-states as models for American republicans to imitate as they forged a new "science of politics."[79]

Once again, a possible way to reconcile the contradictory beliefs in the superior virtues of the Greeks with their insatiable violence goes back to Strauss himself. Like Strauss, Rahe at times draws a distinction between Greek political philosophy and the Greek cities. Aristotle, for example, urged careful town and family planning for the disordered city-states. Both he and Plato were critical of Sparta's violent ways.[80] Yet Rahe no more than Strauss fully escapes the conclusion that the greatest Greek thinkers ultimately accepted and celebrated the Greek way of life. Despite his famous criticisms of democracy after the death of his teacher, Plato, according to Rahe, still praised this regime as the one most open to philosophical liberty.[81] Plato as much as the Greek tragedian Aeschylus understands justice in the classically xenophobic manner of helping your friends and harming your enemies.[82] Moreover, Rahe cannot cite a single example of a Greek philosopher who critiqued the practice of slavery in antiquity. If it is not always clear where Strauss and his students stand on which Greece is to be emulated—the historic Greece or the philosophic Greece?—then their attempt to judge America by the standards of the Greeks also becomes less coherent. The message of *The Federalist* is far clearer on the Greeks than this Straussian distinction between history and philosophy allows.

I am not, of course, denying that the Founders and Framers read and even learned from the Greeks. *The Federalist* itself reveals that Hamilton possessed an impressive knowledge of ancient history. What I am contending is that this study of the Greeks ultimately led to a repudiation of Greek ideals, or at least, to a refusal to endorse these as the foundational credos for the new republic. As Clinton Rossiter has shown, while colonial interest in the histories of Herodotus, Thucydides, and Polybius was high, interest in Greek political philosophy was almost nil. "Aristotle enjoyed only a slight vogue, and Plato was virtually ignored."[83] Rossiter's comment on the lack of attention to Plato and Aristotle is supported, albeit briefly, in the pages of *The Federalist* itself. In *The Federalist* No. 49, Publius sternly opposes any reliance on the superior reason of a wise few to govern the new republic. Since reason "is timid and cautious when left alone, and acquires firmness and confidence in proportion to the number with which it is associated," there is no good reason to desire a "nation of philosophers" who would disregard this consideration. What Publius has in mind here is the danger of a leadership class governing according to its reason without the check of the people (or the community) against their authority. A "reverence for the laws" will not spring from this elitist rationalism, which the author dismisses as an unrealistic project anyway: "a nation of philosophers is as little to be expected as the philosophical race of kings wished for by Plato." What is desirable is that "the most rational government will not find it a superfluous advantage to have the prejudices of the community on its side."

It is imperative to recognize that *The Federalist* No. 49 is not making a surgical distinction between the wise few and the ignorant many, in the spirit of Plato, when Publius distinguishes between "rational government" and "the prejudices" of the community. For he later impresses upon the reader that it is the reason, not the passions, of the people "that ought to control and regulate the government." *The Federalist* No. 49 is perfectly consistent with the assumption expressed elsewhere in the work that the people are to be trusted as the final authority over the republic, since they possess a "deliberate sense" that checks and restrains political authority. In truly unPlatonic fashion, *The Federalist* places reason in the hands of the people and pours scorn on the classical dream of rule at the hands of the few. *The Federalist* No. 55 returns to this theme when Publius further repudiates the Greek dualism between the few and the many. Just as the new republic must not trust the wisdom of the few, so it should not trust the wisdom of the many. A tyranny of the majority is just as undesirable as a tyranny of the minority. "Had every Athenian citizen been a Socrates, every Athenian assembly would still have been a mob." These stirring words effectively accomplish what was, according to *The Federalist*, unknown to the Greek and Roman republicans: the reconciliation of the few and the many—or the end of all tragic, inevitable conflict between the two. Despite his own often uncritical endorsement of the Straussian-Platonist hermeneutic, Willmoore Kendall ultimately emphasized just how unique the American experiment was. For the first time in history, a conservatism had emerged that "adjourned *sine die* its quarrel with *democracy*."[84] Democracy was no longer doomed to the endless struggle between the tyrannical passions of the few and the anarchistic passions of the many.

It is a supreme irony that perhaps the most admirable feature of the American political tradition is the one that is least understood or appreciated by Straussian scholars who judge modern republicanism according to the flawed standards of the Greeks. What Peter Drucker called the "American solution" to the age-old problem of "extreme factionalism" is unique precisely because it rejects the need for an "unquestioned ruling class" that imposes its will on the people. The genius of American republicanism lies instead in tolerating factions, giving them their say, and allowing the people (who, as Kendall emphasized, are entrusted with political authority) to decide on their merits. In contrast to the republicanism of antiquity, factionalism no longer leads either to civil war or to anarchy, since the American principle of the "concurrent majority" prevents the people from electing a tyranny.[85]

The reader will rarely recognize, in the vast Straussian literature on the American Founding, acknowledgment of the fact that Greek virtues are not only opposed to the ideals of the new republic: they are in fact inferior to those of the moderns (including Americans). Although I have argued that Strauss and his students sincerely support a regime based on a universal commitment to liberty and equality (despite the leftist portrait of the movement as ideologically far to the Right), their reasoning in support of this position deeply conflicts with this commitment. Despite the overall teaching of *The Federalist* on the failures of Greek statecraft, Strauss was determined to read into the American experiment an aristocratic notion of politics that rests on Hellenic political philosophy. Strauss, for example, attributes to Jefferson the Greek belief in the "rule of the best" over those who are, presumably, inferior by nature.[86] Although we have seen *The Federalist* categorically reject this sentiment of Jefferson (who did not participate in the deliberations on the Constitution), this fact has not deterred scholars sympathetic to Strauss from projecting onto the American political tradition an indebtedness to Greek republicanism. In *The Greek Tradition in Republican Thought* (2004), Eric Nelson ambitiously contends that the Greek ideal of aristocratic rule is the true foundation of American politics. Nelson, whose study is influenced by the scholarship of Paul Rahe, insists that a "natural aristocracy" has always been the primary influence in the best political thought of the republic.[87] Although he never discusses *The Federalist*, and he even admits that Jefferson and other Founders rejected Plato, Nelson insists that Hamilton thought in Greek terms, particularly with respect to the need to avoid a class-divided society that results from the extreme inequitable distribution of wealth. Similar to Strauss's portrayal of Jefferson, Nelson believes that Hamilton looked to a class of *aristoi* to counter this defect of capitalism.[88]

In fairness to this sweeping historical revisionism, it is true that some prominent Americans have always looked to the Greek political texts for guidance. As Nelson puts it, the Greek "arrangement of elements that accords with nature" was attractive to Americans in the late eighteenth and early nineteenth centuries who understood justice as "instantiated by the rule of reason in the persons of the most excellent men": all this led to the creation of a regime that teaches virtue to its citizens.[89] What Nelson ignores, however, is the vehement opposition to Greek political thought that can be found in the writings of some of the most prominent Founders. In his defense of the American Constitution, John Adams describes "the dogma of Aristotle" as "the most unphilosophical, the most inhuman and cruel that can be conceived." Adams also warns that until "this wicked position, which is worse than the slavery of the ancient republics, or modern West Indies, shall be held up to the derision and contempt, the execration and horror, of mankind, it will be to little purpose to talk or write about liberty." Despite the various attempts of both Straussian and Thomistic scholars to apply Aristotle's notion of a "mixed regime," with a strong middle-class element, to the American Founding, Adams contended that Aristotle's version of the middle class is inconsistent with the thought of a philosopher whose principles include the defense of a truly happy and virtuous life. Adams pointedly asks, "but can you reconcile them with his other arbitrary doctrine, and tyrannical exclusion of husbandmen, merchants, and tradesmen, from the rank and rights of citizens?"[90] The rule of a wise few is just as far from the mind of Adams as it was from the authors of *The Federalist*. It is not self-evident to Adams that the Americans of his time should take lessons from a philosopher who was far more willing to tolerate serious and intractable class divisions than the Founders ever were.

Who, then, were the Americans that found this "natural" ideal to be most appealing? One need look no farther than the antebellum South, whose leadership class greatly enjoyed reading the political philosophy of Aristotle. What they understood to be the "natural" order of things predictably justified a society that sanctioned slavery. The master-slave relation that is so central to Aristotelian philosophy was the perfect justification for slavery, particularly since it was understood to be an unchangeable (natural) relation. The southern readers of both Plato and Aristotle supported democratic liberty and equality only insofar as these ideals accommodated slavery as well. Whereas *The Federalist* repudiated the classics for failing to provide stable and just forms of republicanism, many southerners praised the ancients for a noble and virtuous commitment to order that did not compromise on the natural inequality between slave and slaveholder.[91]

To my knowledge, no Straussian has systematically grappled with the undeniable fact that the American South was far more receptive to Greek political thought than any other region of the early republic. (Although Rahe never defends or excuses the brutality of Greek slavery, he still holds up ancient Hellas as the standard by which all Americans ought to measure themselves.) Nowhere in Harry Jaffa's comprehensive studies of Lincoln's political philosophy will the reader find any recognition of the historic fact that the defenders of the Confederacy enthusiastically defended slavery on the basis of Aristotelian philosophy. Instead, Jaffa takes pains to portray Aristotle as a critic of slavery who carefully distinguished between slavery by nature (which is just) and slavery by convention (which is unjust). Jaffa's version of Aristotle is a remarkably liberal and democratic soul who generally restricted slavery by nature to the mentally incompetent and forbade the enslavement of all other rational human beings.[92] Although Jaffa is willing to admit that there is an utter absence of "natural rights" in the ancient world, he never reconciles this admission with his false portrayal of Aristotle as an opponent of slavery.[93] The opponents of Abraham Lincoln below the Mason-Dixon Line, however, were quite happy to embrace Aristotle on their own illiberal terms.

The reason for the absence of natural rights in the ancient world, which effectively justified the practice of slavery, was well understood by Hamilton who, we have seen, was all too aware of the epidemic of violence that plagued the classical city-states. The utter changeability and instability of Greek politics are also fatally mirrored in the philosophy of Aristotle, reflecting once again the harsh fact that there is no clear distinction between Greek philosophy and statecraft. While Aristotle clearly distinguishes slavery by nature from slavery by convention, this distinction is itself subject to the changeability of politics in his most important works.[94] When Aristotle declares that slaves by nature are born into their servility while slaves by convention are victims of war, this distinction is more unstable than meets the eye.[95] Since war is the true source of all slavery both just and unjust, according to Aristotle, his distinction rests on the justice or injustice of the war itself. Although he never denies the injustice of enslaving a person of "superior rank" in an unjust war, he also never doubts that a just war can enslave those of "inferior rank" who are naturally fit for domination. It is never clear, however, who or what exactly decides which war is just and which form of enslavement is unjust. In his *Nicomachean Ethics*, Aristotle ultimately admits that the distinction between nature and convention is not as exact as he once thought, since human opinions on justice are utterly changeable: "with us [mortals] there is something that is just even by nature, yet all of it is changeable."[96] As Aristotle well knows, it is only the changeable nature of war that decides who is fit by nature for slavery. If mortal opinions on slavery, however, are based on the merely changeable, then the distinction between slavery by nature and slavery by convention must break down. How can we know with any certainty what is a just form of slavery if we rely on war, the conquest of the weak by the strong, to decide on the fate of the slaves?

As Alexander Hamilton learned well from his own reading of Greco-Roman history, the classical susceptibility to political chaos is driven by a fundamental ignorance of the necessity to check and restrain authority. The principle of checks and balances was "either not known at all, or imperfectly known to the ancients" (*The Federalist* No. 9) precisely because the ancients saw no need to restrain the authority of a master class (which owns slaves by nature). Yet this lack of restraint haunted the Greek mind, since the reality of war forever demonstrates the instability of notions of "justice," which rest, finally, on who has the power to enslave the weak. As Aristotle himself admits, there is no clear way of knowing who is a slave by nature if our understanding of nature itself is driven by the instability of incessant warfare.[97]

The Implicit Progressivism of Straussian Thought

It is significant that students of Strauss must at times employ progressivist arguments in order to deal with the brute fact of ancient Greek slavery. If it is true, as Jaffa admits, that there was no concept of natural rights in the ancient world, then when exactly does this idea emerge? More importantly, why did it emerge when it did? In his various writings on the significance of the American Founding, Jaffa contends that Christianity is not the primary source of natural rights, since the absolutist belief in the divine right of kings had dominated most of the Christian Era: "political authority descended from the top down, from God to kings and rulers, and that the obligation of the ruled was simply to obey."[98] It is not Jaffa's intention to fault the Christian monarchs of the past for creating an absolutist regime. In an essay on the "eternal" tension between reason and revelation, Jaffa describes the establishment of Christianity as a state religion in the fifth century AD as "understandable in light of the fact that every ancient city had attributed its law to its God." Even though this momentous decision led to a "theological despotism" enshrined in Rome with universalist pretensions toward world domination, it was still following the pagan template of identifying the regime with divine authority.[99] The fact that Jaffa so closely associates classical pagan statecraft with medieval absolutism is significant, since he then has no choice but to portray the American Revolution as an unprecedented event in human history. If this revolution is the only time in history when the sovereignty of the people was identified with the rule of law, or the will of the majority comported "with the equal rights of the minority," then this event indeed marks progress in human history. In order to explain the radical transition from ancient and medieval absolutism to modern liberalism, Jaffa has no choice but to embrace ideas that are both historicist and progressivist. In *Crisis of the House Divided*, the first volume of his massive study of Lincoln's political philosophy, Jaffa attempts to explain the vast difference between Aristotle's tolerance of natural slavery and Lincoln's dramatic opposition to any such belief by pointing to the massive historic changes that separate the fifth century BC from nineteenth-century America. The "economic scarcity" of Aristotle's time made dependence on slave labor an unavoidable necessity, in contrast to the "rapidly increasing abundance" of Lincoln's America. On a more philosophical (and progressivist) note, Jaffa further observes that the authors of the Declaration of Independence were writing for a readership that would grasp the universal principles it embodied. No such audience existed in the ancient world, Jaffa admits. The Declaration is intended for a "mass audience," not a wise few who might have entertained universal principles in "the interstices of society" (like the ancient Stoics).[100] There is no question, in Jaffa's mind, that the Declaration liberates all of humanity from past dogmas that defend absolutist authority.

Jaffa is perhaps aware of just how progressivist this argument is when he concludes this discussion with the observation that he has no interest in deciding whether "Lincoln's world or Aristotle's world was the better world."[101] In a sense, Jaffa has no choice but to make this statement since he is in principle opposed to the idea of progress. Only a progressivist historian could confidently claim that the abolition of slavery in the modern world was an achievement that far surpassed the wisdom of classical antiquity. Since Jaffa agrees with Strauss that "modern man" is essentially a "blind giant," he cannot make any progressivist claim. For this reason, Jaffa is unwilling to portray his hero Lincoln as a defender of progress.[102] Yet the contradiction that stems from Jaffa's denunciation of progressivism and his employment of certain progressivist ideas is not surprising, since he must adhere to a timeless view of politics while he celebrates a modern regime that is the first in history to defend natural rights.

Jaffa is not the only follower of Strauss who faces this theoretical cul-de-sac. In *Natural Rights and the Right to Choose*, Hadley Arkes follows his teacher Jaffa in portraying Aristotle as an opponent of slavery. Aristotelian philosophy is critically important in the fight against both slavery and abortion, since it is only this philosophy that adequately teaches what exactly the essence of humanity is. Since Aristotle portrays humanity as a creature that is capable of reasoning about the difference between good and evil, his theory of virtue ethics is essential in the struggle to defend the natural rights of all human beings. In Arkes's view, the defenders of a right to abortion are just as malevolent as the slave owners of the American South for denying the fundamental equality of all human beings, whether they are slaves or the unborn. The fact that both slavery and abortion deny some human beings their right to develop their capacity for rational thought reveals, according to Arkes, the triumph of historicism, positivism, and progressivism.[103]

Like Jaffa, Arkes faces the problem of explaining how an utterly modern philosophy like natural rights can spring from the works of a Greek philosopher who does not even refer to natural rights. Yet Arkes cannot admit that the philosophy of natural rights is a sign of progress that happened only because the moderns turned away from an ancient wisdom that tolerated slavery. Arkes makes no effort, for example, to reconcile the Greek toleration of infanticide with his portrayal of Aristotle as a defender of liberal equality. Although he admits, in a discussion of James Wilson's defense of natural rights, that the ancient Greeks commonly exposed defective newborn infants, he is silent on Aristotle's own tolerance of this practice.[104] Most significantly, he fails to mention that it was only with the rise of the Christian Era that these practices were abolished. Like Jaffa, Arkes must reinvent Aristotle as a liberal democrat in order to prove that basic moral beliefs like the right to life are timeless and universal, not historically specific.

Any lapse into progressivism leads to the dangerous conclusion that the Declaration is a document that celebrates rights as "defined by reference to history and economic forces rather than nature."[105] Yet it is hard to see how Straussians can consistently avoid this historicism without falsely attributing modern ideas to the Greek heritage.

It would be unfair to argue that Jaffa and Arkes completely ignore the influence of the one tradition, Christianity, that contributed to the rise of a natural rights philosophy. Despite his portrayal of Christian statecraft as a defense of "theological despotism," Jaffa admits that a belief in the "God-given right of people to rule themselves" is a modern (Protestant) idea that owes nothing to antiquity.[106] Arkes in turn notes the importance of the Golden Rule as Lincoln's main argument against slavery.[107] Yet this appreciation of the Christian influence is usually accompanied by the qualification that Christianity exerted relatively little political influence on the American regime, at least compared to Greek political philosophy. Even Jaffa, who portrays Lincoln as a president who upheld the Golden Rule as the best argument against slavery, portrays Christianity as an apolitical faith, based on the thirteenth chapter of Romans in which Saint Paul teaches that Christians must obey any regime as if it were appointed by God to rule over them.[108] Other Straussians, like Michael Zuckert, have gone even farther in claiming that American Lockeans (like Samuel West) had to make Romans 13 more political in meaning than it was intended to be, so that St. Paul's teaching could not be used as an excuse to support tyrannical regimes (like the British monarchy). This reinvention suggests at least to Zuckert that Christianity and even American Protestantism stood in the way of the Founding.[109] Even Straussians like Ernest Fortin who are most sympathetic to Christianity have concluded that the ethic of charity "is at best a pretty fuzzy thing" when it is applied to politics (even though this is clearly the opposite of Lincoln's understanding of charity).[110] For this reason, Americans must look to Athens, not Jerusalem, for their political education.

What is missing in this discussion, however, is the clear admission that the Christian tradition, particularly its Protestant manifestation, deserves far more credit for the philosophy of natural rights in America than anything remotely Hellenic. Just as Paul Rahe ignores the Calvinist foundations of American political thought,[111] so Arkes ignores the fact that a largely Protestant majority has opposed abortion without the help of Aristotle. Although I am not the first scholar to point to the lack of attention that Strauss and his students display toward the influence of Protestant theology on American political thought, my intention throughout this study is to expose the implications of this omission to its absolute limits.[112]

One disturbing implication arising from Arkes's analysis of natural rights is the constant emphasis he places on the preeminent influence of Aristotelian philosophy on debates over natural rights. His praise of President Calvin Coolidge as a fierce opponent of progressivism reveals the extent to which Arkes engages in historical revisionism, particularly when he focuses on a speech given by the president in 1926, on the 150th anniversary of the Declaration of Independence. Although he correctly portrays Coolidge as a defender of the Declaration, he also represents the Republican conservative president as a believer in the timeless or universal nature of this document. As a result, Arkes's version of Coolidge is that of a statesman who believes in the transhistorical nature of the Declaration's self-evident truths.[113] Coolidge, as Arkes portrays him, is an antiprogressivist since he believed that there "was no advance" beyond the truth of the Declaration. Yet Coolidge gives the impression in his speech that the Declaration is the grand result of historical progress. In affirming that the truths of the Declaration are "final," Coolidge is not denying that the Declaration itself marked the progress of humanity beyond a time when there was disbelief in its inalienable rights. Instead, Coolidge declares that a return to the time "when there was no equality, no rights of the individual, no rule of the people" would be a step back into tyranny. In short, progress ended with the Declaration: it is final in this sense. However, Coolidge also makes clear that people did not always believe in the Declaration. There was a time in history when its truths were denied, so it must follow that this document surpasses the wisdom of the past. What Arkes portrays as Coolidge's devotion to eternal truths is in fact a subtle understanding of the Declaration's role in advancing truths that were unknown to the ancients.

Nowhere in Coolidge's speeches on American political thought is there any sign of dependence on Greek political philosophy. Moreover, there is good reason to believe that the president considered that the ancients had nothing to teach about natural rights. Coolidge's implied dismissal of the Greeks is fundamentally no different in spirit from the suspicions that Adams and Hamilton expressed toward both classical history and thought. Yet it is essential for Strauss and his students to gloss over this fact in order to defend American democracy as an eternally valid regime. At the same time, they must take pains to demonstrate the superiority of the classics over the moderns. On both counts, however, the Straussian project can be found wanting. It is not evident that anything close to American democracy was conceived by Plato and Aristotle. Arkes never explains how New Deal liberalism is compatible with his favored traditions, even though he presents his book as a defender of its version of jurisprudence.[114] It is also unlikely that Calvin Coolidge, a favorite president of Arkes's, would have spied within the New Deal any defense of natural rights as Arkes understands them, given the statism of the 1930s. It is even less likely that Plato and Aristotle, who count as Arkes's philosophical heroes, would have supported a natural right to life on the part of the unborn.[115] Perhaps most importantly, it is far from obvious that the ancients' tolerance of slavery, wars of conquest, and infanticide make them suitable models for modern emulation. Is it truly edifying, then, to portray the Greeks in this revisionist way?

The usual Straussian response to these historically based objections is that Strauss and his followers are not seeking a literal return to the Greek city-states that allowed these practices. Strauss's students strenuously deny that their teacher had any nostalgia for ancient Athens.[116] In fairness to these students, it is accurate to claim that neither Strauss nor any of his students ever endorsed slavery or infanticide. Nevertheless, there is one big persistent problem with their denials that they romanticize ancient Greek life. As we have seen, the Straussians' distinction between Greek philosophy and Greek statecraft is not as clear as they make it out to be. It is far from obvious that Plato and Aristotle rejected the most oppressive aspects of Greek political life. This historical fact is a problem for a movement that upholds the "timeless" standards of classical virtue over the "timely" values of modernity. Strauss insists on reading the "low" in the light of the "high" in order to avoid the plague of relativism that undermines faith in liberal democracy.[117]

In accusing their opponents of "relativism," students of Strauss often ignore just how relativistic their favorite authors happen to be. Strauss and his students need to confront head-on the inconvenient fact that even Plato and Aristotle did not object to the practice of infanticide. As Adam Smith, one of the great heroes of the Anglo-American philosophical tradition, pointedly remarks in his *Theory of Moral Sentiments*, the "humane Plato" whose "love of mankind" informs all of his dialogues was never moved to condemn this practice. Indeed, Smith goes so far as to claim that both Plato and Aristotle appeal to the customs of their time, not timeless truths, in order to support such a practice. Yet an appeal to custom can surely be used in any attempt to justify any kind of evil. "When custom can give sanction to so dreadful a violation of humanity, we may well imagine that there is scarce any particular practice so gross which it cannot authorize."[118] What Smith rejects here is any clear distinction between the greatest Greek philosophers and the mores of their time. Smith's horror at the ancient tolerance of infanticide raises deeper questions about what ancient virtue was even worth when this custom could sanction any evil practice. It is implausible to argue, as Rahe does in this context, that Smith's observation does not detract from the "heroic and magnanimous" expressions of virtue of which the ancients were more capable than the moderns.[119]

Smith's observation is particularly inconvenient to students of Strauss, like Jaffa and Arkes, who hold up the Greek philosophers as opponents of slavery. In order to press the argument that Plato and Aristotle adhere to "timeless" standards of decency that apply to all of humanity, they must reinvent these Greek thinkers as opponents of the "relativism" that would support slavery. For this reason, both Jaffa and Arkes represent Abraham Lincoln as a statesman following in the tradition of these Greek ideals.[120] Their version of Lincoln is that of a neo-Aristotelian who opposed, like Aristotle, the belief that all slavery is just. (As we have seen, Aristotle distinguishes between slavery by nature and by convention.) Lost in this reinvention of Lincoln, however, is any recognition of the fact that the president never made a distinction between those who were justly enslaved (by nature) and those who were unjustly enslaved (by convention). It is hard to imagine Lincoln's fiery speeches against slavery inspiring the righteous indignation of Americans, as they did, had the president made a distinction between those who deserved slavery and those who did not. It is also hard to imagine how his administration in practice could have applied that distinction and emancipated only those slaves who were unjustly enslaved.[121]

It is not that Jaffa and Arkes ignore the Christian foundations of Lincoln's attack on slavery: both men recognize that the president appealed to the Golden Rule as a moral ethic clearly violated by slavery. In order to make their case that certain practices like slavery are eternally wrong, however, they have to bring Greek political philosophy onto the side of their argument. At the same time, they have to portray anyone who argues for the historical relativity of these arguments as a sinister figure. For example, Jaffa is outraged by the right-wing Catholic political philosopher Joseph de Maistre's denial that there is such a thing as a universal human nature. Pointing to Maistre's famous remark that he has seen "Frenchmen, Italians, Russians," and other peoples but he has never met "man" in his life, Jaffa portrays Maistre as an enemy of any notion of human equality.

In Jaffa's view, this French aristocrat stands against the Declaration of Independence, Plato, and Aristotle in refusing to accept that all human beings are equal, and that no one can legitimately rule over others as if they were "beasts."[122]

What Jaffa fails to recognize is that Maistre was also an opponent of slavery. Despite his opposition to the revolutionary violence that the French Jacobins practiced in the "name of equality," this conservative aristocrat celebrated Christianity as the one religion that made successful strides toward the abolition of slavery. Although Maistre, like Edmund Burke, opposed political revolutions that replace slavery with democratic tyranny, he was impressed by the fact that Christianity "started to labor especially and tirelessly for the abolition of slavery, something that no other religion, no legislator, no philosopher had ever dared to undertake or even imagine." Maistre adds that "slavery is the rule" where any religion other than Christianity "holds sway."[123]

While Maistre's intended readership consisted of those who had fallen for Jacobin propaganda directed against the backwardness of the Catholic faith, his argument against slavery is justifiably directed against Straussian thought as well. It is undeniably true that Maistre is appealing to what Strauss would call an "historicist" or "relativistic" position when he claims that only one faith, Christianity, has managed to abolish slavery and that no philosopher before the rise of this religion could have contemplated its abolition. Maistre's keen historical sense, which Jaffa otherwise condemns, in fact empowers his argument: that opposition to slavery is not universal in history, and that Christianity is distinctive in opposing this long-standing practice. It is the unique nature of Christianity that Jaffa and Arkes refuse to acknowledge, as they attempt to synthesize Aristotelian philosophy with biblical revelation.

Because of this omission on their part, they are deafeningly silent on why their American heroes often make arguments similar to that of Maistre on the subject of slavery. Although students of Strauss typically portray Alexis de Tocqueville as a modern thinker who follows Plato and Aristotle on the importance of rewarding virtue and preserving freedom,[124] even a cursory reading of *Democracy in America* reveals the author's signal lack of interest in the Greeks. Like his fellow French aristocrat Maistre, Tocqueville squarely credits Christianity for destroying slavery "only by asserting the rights of the slave."[125] Although Tocqueville admired American republican institutions far more than Maistre ever did, both men concur that it is Christianity alone that threatens the survival of slavery. The distinctive contributions Christianity has made toward social progress are also not lost on Alexander Hamilton, who is a hero of the Straussian pantheon for defending executive power.[126] Yet Hamilton praises Christianity alone for stripping war of "half its terrors." In language that is reminiscent of Maistre, Hamilton condemns the French Jacobins for renouncing Christianity and, as a consequence, relapsing into the "Barbarism" of revolutionary violence that this historic faith would have mitigated.[127]

Implicit in the arguments of Smith, Hamilton, Maistre, and Tocqueville is that the Christian ethic of charity (love thy neighbor as thyself) has inspired peoples to lead the fight against slavery, infanticide, and war (even if the Church has often fallen short in the consistent practice of this ethic). Yet these arguments are impossibly difficult to reconcile with the antihistoricist views of the Straussian school. Although Jaffa, Arkes, Rahe, and other Straussians acknowledge the importance of this ethic, they refuse to admit its primary importance in comparison to any alleged Greek influence. Other students of Strauss go farther in arguing that charity was never important to the American Founding (despite the writings of Jefferson, Hamilton, and others) because it imposed too many "demands" on human nature.[128] Despite this revisionist history, the main problem is that Straussians generally cannot account for moderns (including some of their heroes) who attribute to Christianity alone the achievement of ending injustices. Try as they might to avoid any progressivist thinking, it is hard for Straussians to defend the American Founding without at least implying that this regime avoided (and thus progressed beyond) the violent contradictions of Greek statecraft and political philosophy. If these authors are claiming that Jerusalem, not Athens, has contributed to the rise of the American regime, then they are historicists in the Straussian mind-set. Without this awareness of historical relativity, however, the Straussians falsely construct a vision of the American regime that is far more "timely" than they wish to admit. Ultimately, Strauss and his students want to have their cake and eat it too. Although they are sometimes willing to acknowledge the inhumane principles and practices of ancient Hellas, they still hold it up as the timeless standard of virtue that must strengthen and inspire Anglo-American democracy. This methodological inconsistency contributes to a confusing portrait of what makes the Anglo-American regime truly great.

3

Leo Strauss,
from Left to Right

During a conference dedicated to the ideas of Leo Strauss and Hannah Arendt in 1991, Harvey Mansfield praised Arendt for persuading the Left to abandon its traditional animosity toward the American Revolution. Mansfield, a distinguished Straussian political scientist at Harvard University, remarked that "it is because of her that the Left in America no longer attacks the American Revolution." After Arendt, Mansfield went on to say, the old polemic advanced by Charles Beard that the Revolution was the instrument of bourgeois property interest would no longer hold sway on the Left.[1] What is initially striking about Mansfield's observation is that it appears to conflict with the usual Straussian dismissal of Arendt's work. Strauss and his followers have typically condemned Arendt as a radical historicist who wrongly attempted to rehabilitate the reputation of her mentor, Martin Heidegger.[2] Since they see Heidegger as the philosophical version of

Hitler who mightily resisted the eternal principles of English civilization, they have usually reserved a special animus for anyone who falls prey to his influence.[3] Although Arendt and Strauss often give the impression that both are seeking a recovery of the wisdom that lay in Greek political philosophy, Strauss's students have made great efforts to distinguish her ideas from those of their teacher.[4]

Still, Mansfield's passing praise for Arendt is significant for two related reasons. First, it illustrates the overall Straussian position that leftists who happen to defend American democratic values are politically acceptable. (I shall leave unaddressed the assumption that Arendt is a figure of the Left, whose relevance goes beyond the present discussion.) In contrast, those on the Left and the Right who oppose these ideals or their enthusiastic promotion will face withering scrutiny. Second, neither Mansfield nor any other Straussian reader of Arendt takes aim at one of her most controversial teachings that she advanced in her classic study *On Revolution* (1963): that the American Revolution owed nothing whatsoever to the Christian heritage of the West. Arendt even goes so far as to claim that Christianity is apolitical, a claim shared by many students of Strauss such as Mansfield (see also chapter two).[5] Perhaps it is forgivable, from a Straussian perspective, to deny the influence of Christianity on American political ideas while one praises the greatness of the Revolution all the same. To date, several scholars have pointed to the near absence of attention that Strauss and Mansfield have given to the influence of Christianity on Western political philosophy.[6]

My purpose in this chapter is to show that Strauss was very much a political figure, despite the assurance of some of his defenders that "he saw politics neither from the Right nor from the Left but from above."[7] In particular, I argue that Strauss and his students do not necessarily oppose every assumption from the Left, despite the popular portrayal of his movement as an instrument of the radical Right. In fact, Strauss sounds rather leftist in his treatment of both conservatism and modern Christianity. It is Strauss's leftist dismissal of Christian theology that may compromise his overall defense of Anglo-American democracy, whose ideas have been historically shaped by the Christian tradition.

Readers of Strauss from the Left and Right may wonder how this political philosopher, who mainly influenced the post–World War II American Right, could ever be associated with anything "leftist." Strauss's leftist critics invariably portray him as an elitist opponent of liberal democracy with strong philosophical ties to the Far Right (see chapter one). His more appreciative readers (mainly his students) represent him as a Cold War liberal who admired conservative statesmen like Winston Churchill. Neither camp reads anything particularly leftist into his thought.

There are two reasons for this omission. First, Strauss was a fierce anti-communist who, like many of his contemporaries, saw Marxian ideology as a threat to liberal democracy. In a letter to Eric Voegelin in the early 1950s, Strauss sounds like a reactionary opponent of Marxism when he dismisses as the "root of the [modern] evil" Marx's famous imperative (from his *Theses on Feuerbach*) to "change the world" instead of just interpreting it.[8] Strauss also fiercely attacked the relativistic implications of Marxism that justified revolutionary violence in the name of "History."[9] Yet anti-communism by itself is not necessarily the same as anti-leftism. During the Cold War, some of the most visceral opponents of Stalinism were ex-communists who opposed the Soviet system without necessarily abandoning all leftist views in the process. (Many of these ex-communists later became neoconservatives.)[10] Although Strauss was never a communist, he likely supported the center left in Weimar Germany and, as an American citizen, even voted Democrat throughout the 1950s.[11] In short, he was not as conservative as his readers make him out to be, although he is still to the Right of his leftist critics who feel that his defense of liberal democracy does not go far enough. This attitude, however, may have more to do with the increasing radicalization of the Left in our time than with any latent "right-wing" politics in Strauss's thought.[12]

Second, most leftists would not join Strauss in celebrating the ancient Greeks, particularly when both Greek thought and statecraft were committed to rigidly hierarchical systems of power that allowed little room for either liberty or equality in the modern sense. Leftist critics have been suspicious of Strauss's love of Plato for this very reason and accordingly have associated him with figures of the Right who have also called for a recovery of this hierarchy in order to battle the excesses of democracy. Strauss and his students, however, attempt to locate a liberal tradition in the Greeks in order to advance their view that classical political philosophy is the standard by which the American regime is to be judged (see chapter two). Moreover, a few prominent leftists in the past have expressed nostalgic sentiments for the "glory that was Greece." Even Karl Marx, like many of his fellow German thinkers, at times lamented the loss of "freedom" that occurred when Western Christianity displaced Greek influence.[13] Although this nostalgia for the Greeks is generally passé among leftists today, there are still some occasional attempts by leftist scholars to read into the Greeks both liberal and egalitarian sentiments.[14] Still, Strauss and his students may be the last prominent example of a mass leftist movement in academe that celebrates the Greeks as proto-moderns.

It would be absurd to deny altogether that there is any sign of conservative (and anti-leftist) thought in the works of Strauss. At times Strauss manifests a certain respect for conservative thought, despite his misgivings toward historicists like Burke for celebrating the "ancestral." In his conclusion to *Thoughts on Machiavelli* (1958), Strauss even compares the "classics" (Plato and Aristotle) with modern conservatives who oppose political change, even though only the classics understood the dangers of technological change as well.[15] In his preface to *Liberalism: Ancient and Modern* (1968), Strauss further elaborates on how conservatism compares favorably with liberalism. He notes that the conservative love of the historical particularity of nation-states is friendlier to a "diversity regarding language, folk songs, pottery, and the like" than the liberal love of "universalism," which has more in common with the communists. (In this vein he praises Charles de Gaulle as an "outstanding European conservative.") Liberals, who advance the "universal homogeneous state" through methods that are far less violent than those of the communists, "are not sufficiently concerned with the fact that the tradition is ever being more eroded by the very changes in the direction of the Old World which they demand or applaud."[16] Yet these comments do not imply any deep adherence to conservatism on the part of Strauss since he goes on to remark that conservatism "is no longer politically important," as it has ceased to stand for "throne and altar," the traditions of the ancien regime in Europe. Instead, conservatism (especially the American version) simply continues the older version of Lockean liberalism. Strauss concludes this discussion by identifying his own position—that of classical political philosophy—with a premodern liberalism that opposes the conservative love of the ancestral and the traditional in favor of seeking what is good by "nature."[17] The fact that he rejects modern liberalism as a defective doctrine does not mean that he rejects liberalism in toto. The very title of his collection of essays suggests that Strauss privileges an "ancient" liberalism based on natural right far above a "modern" liberalism based on relativism and historicism. By the same token, Strauss accepts the typically modern view that true conservatism has had its day, and he makes every attempt to dissociate his thought from conservatism.[18] As I argue below, Strauss even sounds "leftist" in his dismissal of both conservatism and Christianity as enduring forces in our liberal age.

I am not the first scholar to spy some relation between Straussian thought and leftist ideas. Despite Milton Himmelfarb's claim that there have been no "Left Straussians," a few Straussians have gone as far as to claim that his hermeneutic is useful for leftist causes.[19] Thomas Pangle has contended that a Straussian reading of Plato's regime-psychology is compatible with the political personality studies of the Frankfurt School.[20] Both sympathetic readers such as Stanley Rosen and critical readers like Nicholas Xenos have remarked on the considerable similarity between Strauss's and the Frankfurt School's critique of modern reason as pure instrumentalism.[21] (Later in this chapter I devote some discussion to this similarity as well.) Near the end of his spirited defense of Strauss against the polemical attacks of the Left and Right, Peter Minowitz invites both feminists and multiculturalists to take up Strauss's ideas in the battle against ideological hegemony.[22] Even a leftist admirer of the American pragmatist philosopher Richard Rorty has coined the term "left-Straussianism" to underscore the parallels between Straussian philosophy and Rorty's left-leaning philosophy.[23] Although not all of these claims are thoroughly substantiated, they reveal that the Straussian opposition to leftism is far from uniform, particularly if leftists refrain from attacking the supreme goodness of American democracy.

Strauss himself set the tone here, since he tends to oppose the Left only when belief in the superiority of democracy is being threatened. (For this reason, students of Strauss often sympathize with the neoconservative view that democratic "values" must be portrayed as timelessly true.)[24] On a rare occasion where Strauss briefly alludes to the teachings of the Frankfurt School, he warns against its promotion of antidemocratic sentiments disguised as "objective" research. In an essay on the true meaning of political philosophy, Strauss briefly refers to the central theme of Theodor Adorno's *The Authoritarian Personality* when he faults the false value-neutrality of social scientists who distinguish between "democratic" and "authoritarian" personalities in a manner that reflects their personal value-laden preferences rather than true scientific judgment.[25] From Strauss's perspective, leftist social scientists are to blame for failing to provide any timeless foundation for democracy, free of subjective value-talk. Allan Bloom follows suit when he accuses the Left of dismissing the American Founding as a mere exercise in the enlightened self-interest (that is, value-laden preferences) of bourgeois property owners.[26] Harry Jaffa attacks the historian Richard Hofstadter, who was greatly influenced by the Frankfurt School, for undermining belief in Lincoln's grand concept of egalitarian democracy; Jaffa does not take aim at Hofstadter for ridiculing the Protestant faith and character of the president.[27] In short, the greatest crime of the Left has been its unwillingness to support American democracy with sufficient enthusiasm.

Nevertheless, Strauss's unhappiness with the Left in the Cold War period is not tantamount to a categorical rejection of all leftist or modern thought per se. As I argue for the remainder of this chapter, Strauss and his students largely agree with the traditional leftist dismissal of Christianity as an irrational influence on the political philosophy of the West. This fundamental consensus between Strauss and the Left, which has been neglected in most of the literature on Strauss, gravely affects their understanding of Anglo-American political thought. For Strauss was compelled to read out of this tradition any sign of a serious indebtedness to Christianity. Unlike the anti-democratic Far Right, which often faults Christianity for its universalistic morality (e.g., charity) that made modern democracy possible,[28] Strauss is ultimately critical of Christianity as a foundation for Anglo-American democracy because it is *not sufficiently universalist* (that is, intelligible to all human beings): it is sheer historicism to hold up one faith as the principal foundation of the West. As a result of this hermeneutical rationale, the very tradition that Strauss and his students wish to preserve as a repository of rationally accessible "eternal principles" is reinvented as a secular liberal artifice whose main inspiration is Athens, not Jerusalem.

These introductory observations are, admittedly, unorthodox when they are compared to the usual portrayal of Strauss as a man who both respected biblical revelation and opposed the secular Left's assault on Western civilization. Even Shadia Drury, one of the harshest critics of Strauss from the Left, contends that he lamented the decay of Christianity in the West due to its political utility as a source of morality.[29] Yet Strauss's fairly typical stance as a Cold War defender of the West should not obscure certain major convergence points between his thought and that of the Left.

Strauss's Leftist Critique of Bourgeois Christianity

In his study of the religious foundations of the American Founding, the Catholic neoconservative writer Michael Novak critically remarks that some Straussians, whom he describes as "on the right," share the position of "main-line academics on the left" that the most important American Founders were irreligious.[30] Although Novak does not substantiate this claim, I show in the remainder of this chapter that it is a fundamentally correct judgment about the Straussian view of not only America but modernity as well. Strauss's determination to portray the use of religion among modern political philosophers as purely political and cynical—thus Machiavellian—leaves both him and his numerous students unable to defend in a coherent way the legitimacy of the Anglo-American tradition. Because Strauss sets up an austere dualism between reason and revelation, in which no synthesis of the two is rationally defensible, he has no choice but to conclude that any use of religious (that is, Christian) themes and credos in the works of modern political philosophers must be insincere, and thus Machiavellian in purpose. He is also compelled to arrive at this conclusion because he stresses that modern political philosophers like Thomas Hobbes and John Locke are too preoccupied with defending political regimes that are open to all human beings to believe that Christian ideas count for very much in their understanding of politics. Yet Strauss's rather leftist love of political universalism, which reflects Cold War liberalism, may be a less important legacy of his thought than his portrayal of modernity as a Machiavellian project, which plays into the hands of radical leftists who contend that modern political ideas are simply expressions of ideological mystification.

Strauss's views on the trivial role of Christian faith in the formation of Western political philosophy, we shall see, shape his ultimate dismissal of conservatism as a viable tradition as well. As Hegel well understood, both Christianity and bourgeois conservatism are historically inseparable. Yet Strauss has no more time for "Right-Hegelians" than their opponents on the Left. In the one essay he devotes to the near triumph of Heideggerian historicism, Strauss dismisses conservative Hegelianism as an epiphenomenon of the nineteenth century. The monarchic state that was favored by Right-Hegelians, which provided limited liberty and equality to its citizens within the context of a class-divided state, was doomed to be displaced by Left-Hegelianism. This old Hegelian Right could never hold back the appeal of the Marxist promise of a classless society.[31]

This discussion brings us to Alexandre Kojève, the famous Marxist interpreter of Hegel who carried on a long correspondence with Strauss both before and after World War II, including a debate over Xenophon's *Hiero*. Both friends and foes of Strauss have usually portrayed him as an inveterate right-wing critic of Kojève. On the Right, George Grant and Barry Cooper have presented Strauss as a defender of classical (and thus conservative) political philosophy against Kojève's historicism. On the Left, Shadia Drury portrays Strauss as a Nietzschean far rightist who is determined to take on the Stalinist defender of the universal homogenous state.[32] What these readers overlook, however, is Strauss's partial acceptance of Kojève's leftist ideology. Like Strauss, Kojève tends to accept the Left-Hegelian triumph over its opponents on the Right, who have clung to obsolete beliefs like faith in a Christian God.[33] What is particularly relevant here is the absence of any attempt on Strauss's part to refute Kojève's typically Marxist view that Christianity has had its day, since the faith has been exposed as a myth based on the illusory belief that Jesus is the resurrected God.[34] Although it is tempting to portray Strauss as the "conservative" opposition against Kojève's radicalism, matters are not so simple.

It is far too easy to present Strauss as a visceral opponent of equality against Kojève's Marxist egalitarianism. To be sure, he opposes Kojève's Hegelian (secularizing) misuse of the Bible as a document that celebrates human equality on the grounds that it then allows Kojève to support the "universal homogeneous state" based on a specific religious foundation that is no longer viable. It is too convenient for Kojève, in Strauss's view, to claim that modern philosophy is just "the secularized form of Christianity" that makes this egalitarian regime possible while downplaying the fact that classical philosophy first entertained the idea of a universal regime (albeit one that was not as crudely egalitarian or free of class hierarchy as the universal homogeneous regime).[35] What Strauss is resisting here is not Kojève's defense of equality per se but his historicist reliance on a particular religion as the *one* true foundation of equality. As a Hegelian, Kojève could never accept Strauss's embrace of the Platonic ideal of the "wise few" ruling over the "ignorant many," as he makes clear throughout his dialogue with Strauss. Yet Strauss's defense of this Platonic statecraft in turn does not amount to a rejection of all expressions of equality, despite the claims of Shadia Drury.[36] Strauss opposes Kojève's historicism precisely because it denies a natural equality that is based on philosophy, which is more universal than revelation. Unlike the old European Right, Strauss still believes in a universal human nature that exists above and beyond the merely historical or ancestral. For this reason, Strauss holds out the frail hope, near the conclusion of his essay on Kojève, that there will always be "men" (*andres*) who will revolt against the universal homogeneous state. Moreover, there will always be philosophers who try to escape from the tyranny of this state, even though the "Universal and Final Tyrant" holds greater sway over the world than any classical tyrant from antiquity.[37] It is noteworthy that Strauss never claims that only one culture, faith, or civilization will produce these great figures that will rise up to challenge this tyranny. Any civilization can produce these great individuals because a universal human nature exists.

The fact that Strauss presents no defense of revelation against one of Kojève's most serious teachings—his dismissal of Christianity as historically obsolete—should invite pause. Although it may be tempting to argue, as many have, that Strauss refuses to defend Christianity from a leftist assault because he is a secret Nietzschean opponent of the faith, I believe this reading exaggerates the right-wing nature of his thought.[38] While Strauss at times gives the impression he is far more respectful of revelation than Kojève ever was, the reasoning behind his respect sounds like an acceptance of fundamental Leftist-Hegelian premises about the obsolescence of religion in general. Strauss, we have seen, always claims that philosophy cannot refute revelation, but it is important to understand why he insists on this truth.[39] In his pivotal essay "Progress or Return?" he goes as far as to claim that not a single modern Enlightenment critic of religion "refuted the most fundamentalistic orthodoxy."[40] This statement reflects his enduring view that religion is dogma, and philosophy must treat it as such. The absolute divorce of reason from revelation is at the core of Strauss's leftist position here. Although Strauss spent his entire philosophic career lambasting Spinoza for allegedly treating religion as useful myths and falsehoods, this critique should not imply that Strauss himself provides any rational reason for belief.

In one of the few commentaries he provides on a Christian author, Strauss contrasts John Calvin's theology with the irreligious philosophy of Spinoza. This contrast is so sharp in Strauss's mind that he claims Calvin "dispenses with all theoretical basis" in teaching that human beings must obey and fear—but not seek to understand—God.[41] Calvin's theology rests on an "enunciation of faith," not reason. A true philosopher cannot, then, be a believer since faith is identical to blind obedience.[42] Although his study of Spinoza is often considered an early and even immature version of his thought,[43] there is no evidence whatsoever in Strauss's later writings that he abandoned this dualistic separation of reason from faith. In a much later essay, Strauss sharply distinguishes between political philosophy, which is based on reason, and political theology, which is based on divine revelation.[44] The importance of this dualistic hermeneutic in Strauss's thought is hard to overstate, since it makes any attempt to spy rationality in faith almost impossible. It also throws into question Strauss's respect for the tradition of Anglo-American democracy, whose main defenders, I shall argue, mightily attempted to distinguish "true religion" from superstitious dogma. If Strauss believes that no distinction is possible, does the religious basis for this civilization fall by the wayside? And, if this is the case, does the irreligious Left score the ultimate victory over the Right?

As we have seen, Strauss sees no philosophic (theoretical) basis in theology, political or otherwise. At times Strauss may have been justified in thinking he was trying to save revelation from the crass attempts of modern authors to project political meanings onto religious texts. His critique of the famous attempt of Max Weber to read into Calvin's theology a rationale for capitalism should be read with this intent in mind. In Strauss's view, Weber was not reading Calvin on his own terms or according to his original intent.[45] Yet there is good reason to question Strauss's overall interpretation of Calvin's theology. Although Strauss is not the only reader of Spinoza to contrast this early modern philosopher with Calvin on the grounds that this early Reformation theologian appeals to non-rational concepts like the "testimony of the Holy Spirit" or divine illumination,[46] even Calvin admits that this special revelation must be *interpreted*. In his commentary on Genesis, Calvin offers a "theoretical basis" for making sense of the most miraculous claims within this book. In anticipation of the objection that Genesis makes unscientific assertions about the planets and the stars that a competent astronomer could easily refute, Calvin replies that Moses, the presumed author of Genesis, did not intend to write a work on astronomy. Instead, Moses "wrote in a popular style" that ordinary people are able to understand. The intent of Moses was to teach these people to praise the wonders of creation, not to explain the workings of heaven.[47]

At first glance, the distinction that Calvin sets up between science and faith should not trouble Strauss, since Calvin surgically separates reason from revelation as well. The fact that Calvin is careful not to call Moses a "philosopher" seems to be compatible with Strauss's hermeneutic. Yet Calvin goes on to argue that he has no intent of creating an antagonism between astronomy and revelation, since this science "is not only pleasant, but also very useful to be known: it cannot be denied that this art unfolds the admirable wisdom of God."[48] This statement appears to reflect the "theoretical basis" that Strauss believed to be absent in Calvin's theology, since Calvin is contending here that both science and revelation testify to the glory of God. Indeed, science would not even exist without divine blessing. Moreover, Calvin is offering an interpretation of Genesis when he reads into the narrative an implicit distinction between the purpose of science and that of biblical truth. Although Genesis does not literally teach this distinction, Calvin is confident that the creation story is intended by Moses to celebrate the miracles of God's providence, not to be taken literally as a work of science.

Strauss's rigid distinction between political theology and political philosophy, which parallels his attempt to oppose Calvinism to Spinozism, ultimately collapses for the same reason. Although he praises Calvin's *Institutes of the Christian Religion* as a great theological work that is nevertheless grounded in blind faith, Strauss ignores Calvin's own attempts to interpret the Bible in a manner comparable to the hermeneutic of Spinoza. When Calvin warns that the "vices and defects of men" require a regime that allows citizens to censor authorities for immoral "excess," he is, on Straussian grounds, going far beyond the original intent of biblical orthodoxy.[49] Although Calvin is not advocating the creation of liberal democracy here, both he and Spinoza interpret Scripture as a text that condemns the tyrannical abuse of power.[50] Additionally, Calvin is calling for a regime that institutionalizes some checks or restraints on those in authority. At least by Straussian criteria, it is hard to understand how Calvin could offer such an interpretation, since orthodoxy effectively shuts down all rational scrutiny of the Bible. Yet Calvin is demanding that citizens question those who claim to speak in the name of orthodoxy, lest they use Scripture as an excuse for oppression.

I dwell on Calvin's thought here, which was influential in America during the colonial and revolutionary periods,[51] in order to reveal the inadequacy of Strauss's leftist position on revelation and how, ultimately, it undermines his overall project: to defend the legitimacy of Anglo-American democracy. In his study of Spinoza, Strauss was fiercely critical of the Enlightenment's attempt to interpret the Bible as a work that teaches us how to live, not how to explain the scientific workings of the universe.[52] Any modern who interprets the Bible in this manner, especially Spinoza, receives Strauss's scorn. Even in his sole attempt to interpret the Bible (specifically, the book of Genesis), Strauss concludes that the Bible never offers any philosophical argument for creation whatsoever. The opposition between religion and cosmology (science) is absolute.[53] Not only does Strauss fail to see that Calvin interprets the Bible in a rationalist vein. He also fails to appreciate the modern—and Anglo-American—attempt to interpret the Bible in a way that distinguishes a true reading from a false one. This project Strauss deems impossible, since in his view Scripture is to be read without any philosophical bias whatsoever. Yet Strauss is then often at a loss to make sense of the Bible. It is significant that in "Progress or Return?" he admits some kind of interpretation is needed, even though no human interpretation can be "authoritative." Since only one interpretation "can be the true one," this reading must allude somehow to "objectivity."[54] Strauss, however, offers no such interpretation of his own, since in his view the objectivity of reason must remain silent on biblical truth.

At least one critic of Strauss has argued that this omission is a "shocking" one, but it is not so surprising in light of Strauss's overall arch-rationalist views on the roles of philosophy and faith.[55] Yet Strauss's refusal to read the Bible rationally parallels his refusal to engage the challenge of Spinoza's biblical hermeneutic. As Spinoza shows against the medieval Bible commentator Alfakhar in chapter 15 of his *Theologico-Political Treatise*, even if readers follow Alfakhar's fundamentalist insistence that they take seriously the literal meaning of the text and the prophets' intention, they would still need reason to understand the truth that the Bible reveals. If reason is made "subservient" to the Bible, then Scripture itself becomes unintelligible.[56]

What is relevant to my discussion here is, once again, Strauss's acceptance of the leftist (and modern) position that religion is a collection of dogmas that has nothing to teach those who live out the political life. At first glance, Strauss's defense of orthodox faith sounds conservative. Yet this conclusion may be too hasty. For Strauss's reading of Calvin is strikingly similar to that of Herbert Marcuse, who also argued that both Luther and Calvin teach blind obedience to authority as the true life of faith.[57] Although Strauss, unlike Marcuse, at least credits the Bible with teaching the virtue of humility while it insists on obedience to God, they both agree that this obedience is not based on reason.[58] I do not mean to suggest that Strauss has the same axe to grind against Protestantism as the Frankfurt School did. Unlike Marcuse, Strauss occasionally praises the Reformation for reducing the historic level of Christian violence against the Jews.[59] Nevertheless, Strauss has the same difficulty as Marcuse has in reading into the Bible any rational content. As a result, Strauss refuses to make any distinction between religion and dogma.

The upshot of Strauss's focus on modern Machiavellianism is that he is compelled to discredit some key modern political ideas that actually contributed to the rise and establishment of Anglo-American democracy. It is curious that Strauss, who genuinely admires the American Founding, nevertheless pours scorn on liberal Protestantism as a pseudo-religious tradition, since it was a liberal interpretation of Christianity that eased anxieties over the separation of church and state in the new republic.[60] Thomas Jefferson's famous version of the Bible, after all, deliberately emphasized the moral teachings of the Gospels at the expense of miracles, because he feared the recurrence of religious conflicts over the meaning of supernatural revelation.[61] Yet Strauss, as a critic of Spinoza, does not embrace the project of "liberal religion," the attempt to distinguish between "the core of the religious tradition and its periphery."[62] The Bible, in his view, must be accepted as the authoritarian text that requires obedience, not selective interpretation. Since Strauss stands fast here, it is difficult to see the compatibility between his austere hermeneutic and the Anglo-American tradition he so admires.

It is well known to readers of Strauss that he always dismisses the sincerity of philosophers who profess to be Christians. In his reading of two of the most important political philosophers of the English tradition, Hobbes and Locke, Strauss doubts these gentlemen truly believe in an orthodox faith, since any rational person would find it impossible to do so. For this reason, Strauss faults Weber and other scholars for overestimating the Protestant-Puritan influence on Hobbes.[63] Hobbes's use of religion is absolutely cynical in its support of a "bourgeois" usage of faith.[64] Moreover, an overemphasis on Hobbes's professed Anglican faith violates the principle of Straussian anti-historicism: the necessity of separating the greatness of a philosopher from the influences of his religious and cultural context.[65] In the case of Locke, Strauss invites his readers to note this philosopher's equally cynical attempt to read into the Bible's teachings on patriarchy an egalitarian defense of the social contract, which places parents and children on an equal footing.[66]

The fact that both Hobbes and Locke strenuously distinguish between Christianity (or "true religion") and mere superstition is, in Strauss's view, a Machiavellian dodge that should be treated with caution, if not dismissed. The inspiration behind this distinction (at least in Locke's philosophy) is Spinoza, who was the first modern philosopher to defend liberal democracy and to uphold Christian charity as the true basis of this regime.[67] Strauss not only dismisses Spinoza's defense of charity as a cynical attempt to devalue Judaism, his ancestral faith; he also accuses Spinoza of being entirely arbitrary for choosing this moral credo as the ultimate principle by which to interpret Scripture.[68] Strauss is similarly unimpressed with the efforts of Hobbes and Locke to make use of charity, the Golden Rule, as the standard of good citizenship because they read into Scripture a political meaning that is simply not there. The Bible, as Strauss understands it, does not support Hobbes's bourgeois monarchy or Locke's liberal democracy, even if these were relatively decent regimes.[69] In short, the great error that these English philosophers commit is to *interpret* the Bible, a text that defies all rational or political understanding.

There is a twofold irony within Strauss's portrayal of both Hobbes and Locke as two Machiavellian cynics. First, Strauss's commitment to understanding the original intent of the author would be more sensible if he devoted closer attention to the *intended* reader of the author. A preoccupation with original intent would surely be enriched by an attendant study of the reader (e.g., bourgeois Christian) for whom it is intended. It would then be easier to understand why Hobbes and Locke interpreted the Bible in a humane and decent manner that emphasizes its moral teachings. Yet, in his mature work (following his early study of Hobbes, which at least emphasized the bourgeois nature of his philosophy), Strauss refuses to focus on the intended readership of these two English philosophers because the question of who the reader is supposed to be is a matter for historians studying the context in which the authors wrote, not a political philosopher who is preoccupied with eternal truths. Second, Strauss's portrayal of Hobbes and Locke as philosophers who make broad generalizations about the nature of humanity, a feature of political philosophy as he understands it from Plato to Rousseau,[70] may be too literal an interpretation. Despite Hobbes's and Locke's numerous observations on the "nature" of humanity, Strauss may be too focused on the exoteric surface of their texts without being mindful of their esoteric bias that identifies what is "universal" and "natural" with what is simply bourgeois. Strauss's famously close, even conspiratorial, readings of texts with "secret meanings" may end up ignoring what is the real theological bias that lurks beneath the rhetoric of universalism.

It is not that Strauss is completely oblivious to the question of the intended reader; at times he even admits that Spinoza, who deeply influenced Locke, wrote for a "mercantile patriciate."[71] Yet he ultimately stands firm in his contention that Hobbes and Locke are writing for *all* readers, not simply the bourgeois readers of their time. In his review of C. B. Macpherson's classic study on the "possessive individualism" of Hobbes and Locke, Strauss rejects Macpherson's reductionist portrayal of Hobbes as a mere defender of a burgeoning capitalist order. Macpherson, like most Marxists, too quickly identifies Hobbes's focus on the "natural competitiveness" of humanity as a mere "reflex of the emerging market society." Instead, Macpherson is ignorant of Hobbes's overall view that signs of the "natural antagonism" which Hobbes attributes to humanity can be found not only in the bourgeois age but also "in the court of kings, in the most backward villages, among scholars, in convents, in drawing rooms, and in slave pens, in modern as well as in ancient times."[72]

The chief difficulty with this line of argument is that Strauss is giving insufficient attention to the type of reader that is most attracted to this interpretation. In particular, his appeal to certain Christian virtues makes sense if, and only if, a certain type of reader (e.g., a bourgeois Christian) is presupposed and even desired as the ideal citizen in the long run. Hobbes was clearly not pitching his message to the scholastics of his time who were still wedded to the ancient Greek distinction between the "wise few" and the "ignorant many." Instead, he was assuming that his readers embraced a natural equality that blurs and even eliminates the divisive distinction between classes of people that plagued antiquity. Given Strauss's intense sensitivity to the "ancient-modern quarrel," the reader may be forgiven for wondering why he cannot fully appreciate Hobbes's primary focus on the bourgeois reader who already rejects the anti-egalitarian qualities of scholasticism that stem from Aristotelian philosophy.

I am not the first scholar to fault Strauss for ignoring the bourgeois Protestant foundations of Hobbes's philosophy. J. G. A. Pocock has famously targeted Strauss for doubting the "theistic sincerity" of Hobbes, particularly with regard to the latter's rejection of the "Greek heritage" that was dominant in the universities of his time. In Pocock's view, Hobbes's hostility to the influence of Greek philosophy is driven by his Protestant animus toward the elitist ecclesiastics who misused the classic texts of Plato and Aristotle in order to justify a subversive theocratic politics.[73] In fairness to Strauss, Pocock's analysis does not completely refute the possibility that Hobbes may be playing fast and loose with religious symbolism in order to justify, in Machiavellian fashion, his own version of politics. It is significant, after all, that both Strauss and Pocock ultimately agree that Hobbes was a consequentialist who valued religion insofar as it fostered the best results for a stable political order. Pocock almost sounds like Strauss when he urges the reader to examine "the effects which [Hobbes's] words seem designed to produce" instead of the sincerity of his intent.[74]

Nevertheless, even if Strauss is correct in emphasizing the consequentialist nature of Hobbesian political philosophy, this hermeneutic does not fundamentally alter the fact that Hobbes was writing for a particular type of reader who, he hoped, would be most responsive to this line of argument. In chapter 13 of *Leviathan*, for example, where Hobbes famously affirms the "natural" equality of all men, the careful reader will clearly notice that Hobbes has no tolerance for scholastics who still think in terms of the "wise few" and the "ignorant many." In drawing attention to the fact that most human beings reject such a notion of equality, due to the "vain conceit" that their wisdom is superior to that of the "vulgar," Hobbes is not writing for readers who are already too committed to the classical pagan distinction between the wise and the ignorant. Those who are consumed by this sense of pride are not suited to join his social contract.

Strauss, in all of his studies of Hobbes, is well aware that Hobbes targets the Aristotelian concept of pride (magnanimity) as a vice, not a virtue.[75] Yet he refuses to accept the possibility that Hobbes's Protestant faith militates against the classical Greek celebration of pride. Instead, Hobbes is Machiavellian in subordinating virtues like magnanimity to the overall "social virtue of peaceableness."[76] The traditional Protestant suspicion of pride, which is evidence of original sin, presumably has no place in Hobbes's thought. Nevertheless, Hobbes's rejection of human pride as a divisive vice is perfectly consistent with his position, as he elaborates, in chapter 14, that all members of the social contract must obey the Golden Rule, the "law of the Gospel" that underscores the second law of nature: "whatsoever you require that others do to you, that do ye to them."[77] This ethic is identical to the renunciation of the right to take revenge against others in the social contract. If we do unto others as we would have them do unto us, then we must renounce our prideful, vindictive inclinations to take justice into our own hands. Hobbes, once again, knows that the Aristotelian scholastics did not teach this lesson, given their celebration of magnanimity as a virtue. For this reason, it is unlikely that Hobbes wrote for them as he urged his bourgeois Christian readers to abandon Greek philosophy altogether. Like the authors of *The Federalist*, Hobbes even offers good reasons to reject the Greek celebration of pride, since this teaching ultimately threatened civil war between the few and the many. At the very least, Strauss and his students should consider the validity of his attempt to question whether the Greeks were more virtuous than the bourgeois citizens of his time.

Hobbes's warning against believing in the "vain conceit" that one's wisdom is superior to that of others also implies that the classical teaching on pride as a virtue invites a violent return to the state of nature. His famous understanding of the natural condition of humanity as "nasty, brutish, and short" seems to fit into the bourgeois Christian mind-set that, I have argued, Hobbes is addressing in his works. Yet Strauss would reject this focus on the intended readership of Hobbes as Christian precisely because he sees no biblical foundation for the state of nature. Whereas Christians teach that human nature is fallen and in need of grace, Hobbes and Locke teach that humanity is self-serving and in need of good government. As a result, Strauss concludes that both the Hobbesian and the Lockean versions of the state of nature are, despite their differences, "alien" to the Bible.[78]

What Strauss ignores here is the common view of Hobbes and Locke that biblical morality is crucial in keeping a stable political order from sliding back into the state of nature. Even if a stable social contract replaces the power of divine grace, as Strauss suggests here, it does not change the fact that Hobbes and Locke are, once again, writing for a bourgeois Christian readership. I emphasize this fact because they also count on the *survival* of this readership. Despite Strauss's various claims that these English thinkers are writing for all human beings, not just the readers of their time, Hobbes and Locke give the impression that they desire the continued existence of bourgeois Christianity so that their social contract will also endure. To be sure, Strauss has a point when he portrays Locke as a political hedonist who assumes that citizens, even pious ones, desire governments that maximize pleasure.[79] Yet Locke never contends that it would be desirable for this hedonism to replace or overtake the influence of Christianity. When Locke writes in *The Reasonableness of Christianity* that it is better for "the mass of mankind" to learn their morality from the Bible than from the "sometimes intricate deductions of reason," he never gives the indication that the citizens of the social contract will eventually find a more suitable source of ethical teachings: "all the duties of morality lie there clear and plain, and easy to be understood."[80] Locke is as certain that this morality is most suitable to the greater number of people as he is that reason by itself cannot teach morality. Even if Locke is being consequentialist in affirming the utility of morality, it is also clear that he prefers one morality above all, the morality of the Bible. It is Scripture, albeit in bourgeois Protestant form, whose moral authority must continue to hold sway over the hearts of the citizenry. For this reason, Locke remarks in his *Letter Concerning Toleration*, his most famous defense of the separation of church and state, that the "Bonds of Humane Society" such as promises, covenants, and oaths "can have no hold upon an Atheist."[81] In short, a social contract without the leavening force of Scripture is doomed to return to the state of nature.

From a Straussian perspective, any emphasis on Locke's indebtedness to religion is dangerous, since it suggests that his concept of liberal democracy may require a Christian heritage that many peoples lack: this emphasis, then, detracts from the universal message of Lockean natural rights.[82] Yet this problem is one that challenges Strauss, not Locke or Hobbes. Since these preeminent English thinkers constantly assume, if not emphasize, that bourgeois Christianity must survive in order to teach morality to the masses, the burden of argument lies upon Strauss and his students to show how a liberal democracy can survive and even flourish beyond the theological origins that are foundational to this regime.

Once again, this austerely dualistic hermeneutic poses troubling consequences for the Anglo-American democratic tradition whose survival Strauss sincerely cherishes. He does not stop with his studies of Hobbes and Locke in questioning the foundations of this tradition. As readers of Strauss well know, he is critical of the father of modern conservatism, Edmund Burke, for inadequately defending his ancestral tradition on the basis of mere custom, and therefore historicism. From Strauss's perspective, there is nothing universally good about the English regime as Burke defends it, apart from the fact that it is an English one.[83] Although Strauss never claims to be a conservative anyway, in light of what he takes to be Burke's crudely conservative defense of the merely "ancestral," it is legitimate to raise the questions: What exactly does Strauss, as a self-styled liberal, wish to conserve in the English tradition? What is eternal about English civilization and, therefore, worthy of preservation?

Unsurprisingly, Burke's own answer is Christianity. Given Burke's strong Christian faith, some readers of Strauss have faulted him for exaggerating Burke's reliance on custom while ignoring his embrace of an absolute religious morality. The fact that Burke does not believe in the universal nature of the English regime should not, according to this argument, detract from his moral universalism, that is, his Christian faith.[84] Yet it is not hard to see why Strauss would reject this argument, since

Burke's reliance on Christianity as the source of a timeless moral standard would be further evidence of Burke's historicism. It should be obvious by now that Strauss would reject any claim of modern political philosophers to read the Bible with truly pious intent. Besides scrutinizing Burke's adherence to ancestral custom, Strauss questions Burke's misuse of theological notions like "Providence" for what seem to be Machiavellian purposes. Burke is as modern as Hobbes in manipulating theology for his own purposes.[85] In Strauss's mind, Burke's conservatism is perfectly consistent with his manipulation of religion. The only reason that Burke would make any role for religion in politics is to engage in "secularization," or the cynical (Machiavellian) conflation of God's design with political change. In the case of the French Revolution, Strauss's Burke is allegedly resigned to the victory of the revolutionaries because their triumph is ordained by God. In identifying Providence with History, then, Burke not only fails to grasp the "nobility of last-ditch resistance": he also ends up suppressing the "distinction between good and bad" in politics. Ironically, the father of modern conservatism as well as his admirers like Russell Kirk might as well be relativists because Burke's resignation to historical change, a process that is inspired by God's providence and thus beyond the control of human agency, leads them to replace the "good" with the "progressive," or what is in "harmony" with the movement of history itself.[86] In short, since Burke lacks any substantial idea of what is universally good for all of humanity above and beyond history, he has no choice but to go along with the relativistic currents of historical change that may be good only at the moment.

Yet Strauss fails to understand that Burke's Christian faith militates against any temptation of passively accepting the historical triumph of tyranny. In fact, Burke looks to the Bible to inspire in the hearts of its readers the rejection of political captivity. What is most striking about Strauss's reading of Burke as a defender of defeatism and resignation is his utter silence on Burke's robust attempt to distinguish true religion from superstition for the purpose of liberating humanity from tyranny. Like Hobbes and Locke, Burke takes pains to separate Christianity from its political abuses (superstitions). In his *Reflections on the Revolution in France*, Burke targets the "uncouth, pernicious and degrading superstition" of the Jacobin revolutionaries that must not be allowed to displace Christianity.[87] Yet Burke is not seeking to replace one superstition with another, since he later makes a distinction between the true faith and the abuses of its credos in politics. The fact that Christianity is misused as a "pretext" for tyranny does not mean that the faith itself teaches tyranny.[88] In one of his letters on the discontent that was bubbling over in the American colonies, Burke targeted those who corrupt and pervert Christianity by contending that "Christians are redeemed into captivity, and the blood of the Saviour of mankind has been shed to make them the slaves of a few proud and insolent sinners."[89] In short, Burke demands that human beings interpret the Bible as a book of true freedom and charity, not a pretext for bloodshed and enslavement.

Strauss is unwilling even to acknowledge the possibility of such an interpretation in light of his hostility to any politicized reading of the Bible. Yet it is hard to imagine how Strauss and his students could value the statesman whom they understand to be the greatest Englishman of all time, Winston Churchill. Like Burke, Churchill also interpreted the Bible as a work of liberation. In an essay on the Exodus narrative, Churchill claims to take this story literally and even urges the most scientifically minded readers to embrace this narrative as "the most decisive leap forward ever discernible in the human story." This story, in Churchill's judgment, is not mere myth to be dismissed with cynical ease. For the story of Exodus reveals the truth of a God who brings justice and mercy to all. This God, who was incomprehensible to "all the genius of Greece and all the power of Rome," is the one true deity.[90] Although Strauss admired the heroic efforts of his ancient ancestors, his reasons are altogether different from those of Churchill. Unlike Strauss, Churchill is not surgically separating religious truth from philosophical truth but instead, like his hero Burke, interprets the Bible as a liberating inspiration that can and must be understood by all human beings, philosophers and scientists included. Moreover, Churchill believes that the Exodus story teaches precisely what the pagan Greeks and Romans did not: belief in a God of universal justice.

None of Churchill's interpretation of Exodus fits well with a Straussian hermeneutic. Harry Jaffa, who greatly admires Churchill, demonstrates the degree to which he is locked into Strauss's hermeneutical straightjacket when he remarks that Churchill's essay on Exodus is not a "pious" reading of the narrative.[91] Although Jaffa never explains why Churchill's reading is impious, I assume that he is adhering to his teacher's view that true piety is dogmatic faith, lacking in a theoretical basis.[92] It is impossible to understand, however, why adherence to dogma is the same as piety. Like his fellow Englishmen Hobbes, Locke, and Burke, Churchill certainly reads into the Bible lessons on morality that can be understood in rational and philosophical terms. Moreover, Churchill apparently concurred with his distinguished philosophical ancestors that religion is not the same as superstition as long as it teaches mercy and justice. Although Strauss does not disparage these biblical virtues, he would refuse to call them rational ones. Shockingly, Strauss even goes so far as to claim that his own ancestral faith is a "heroic delusion" whose mysteries are inaccessible to philosophical understanding.[93]

Once again, it is possible that Strauss thought he was saving revelation from the Machiavellian misuse of its truths and credos. Yet he asks his readers and students to pay a high price for this salvage operation, for three reasons. First, he fails to distinguish between a true and a false understanding of the Bible, since he believes that reason cannot provide such a distinction. Second, he indirectly undermines support for the very civilization that he values most. One of the greatest achievements of English political philosophers, I have argued, is their determination, at least in early modernity, to separate true religion from its false perversions.[94] Without this distinction, it is impossible to condemn those who use "fundamentalistic orthodoxy" as a pretext for terrorism. As one critic of Strauss has pointed out, Strauss's hostility toward any rational reading of the Bible may allow theologians and pontiffs to "run wild with what they take theology to mean, that is, with their own private interests and passions in its guise."[95] It is also hard to answer the German nihilists who, Strauss believed, successfully exposed the hypocrisy of their English enemies, if all religion is superstition. If there is anything eternally valuable within the Anglo-American tradition, it is the sustained attempt to place the truth of charity above the tyrannical abuses of faith. Contrary to Strauss, the real choice is not between reason and faith. It is between true religion and philosophy on one side and adulterations on the other. Third, Strauss and his students give an undeserved victory to the Left, who have always taught that religious orthodoxy is so irrational that it has no place in political discourse.

Strauss's Costly Critique of Modern "Machiavellianism"

In the course of my previous discussion, I do not want to imply that Strauss and his students are themselves deliberately Machiavellian while they portray modern political philosophers as the apt pupils of the Florentine. Despite the numerous claims of Shadia Drury and others, I once again take Strauss at his word that he sincerely supports liberal democracy in the

Anglo-American tradition and does not seek to harm its legitimacy. If anything, he opposes the Machiavellian usage of religion, as he understands it, in order to protect both political philosophy and biblical revelation from this cynicism. Strauss genuinely laments the triumph of the Machiavellian view that a focus on "ideology," or the self-interested agenda of a ruling class, displaces the classical emphasis on "political philosophy," or the timeless wisdom of the ancients.[96] Despite his best intentions, however, Strauss's portrayal of moderns as Machiavellians sounds remarkably similar to the leftist suspicion that political philosophers are simply ideologues in disguise. Although Strauss does not go quite so far to claim, as Alfred North Whitehead famously did with respect to Plato's influence, that all of modern political philosophy is a series of footnotes to Machiavelli, he gives every indication that these moderns followed the Florentine in fighting "one and the same power," that of medieval ecclesiastical authority (or what Hobbes called "the kingdom of darkness") in politics.[97]

This identification of modern political philosophy with realpolitik is evident in Strauss's earliest monographs. In his study of Hobbes, Strauss writes like a classical Marxist when he portrays this English philosopher as a defender of bourgeois class interest.[98] Although Bloom dismisses this study as the work of a "pre-Straussean Strauss" who did not fully focus on the secret meanings contained within philosophic texts, I am once again unpersuaded that the early Strauss differs from the later Strauss on the ideological nature of modern political thought. Even Peter Minowitz, who admires the Straussian hermeneutic, admits that Strauss's focus on the "ruling ideas" of a particular modern period of history is just the reversal of Machiavelli's (and Marx's) emphasis on the "ruling class."[99] One way or the other, even the mature Strauss offers a hermeneutic of suspicion that casts doubt on the legitimacy of the modern project.

All of these concerns come to a head when Strauss critiques the political philosophy and biblical hermeneutic of Spinoza.[100] Although Spinoza is historically outside of the Anglo-American tradition, the fact that Strauss credits him with being the first defender of liberal democracy merits some attention here.[101] Moreover, the significant influence of Spinoza on John Locke, the premier defender of Anglo-American democracy, necessitates further discussion of Strauss's rather ambivalent attitude toward the Anglo-American tradition. As we have seen, Strauss admires this tradition for representing the "eternal" principles of civilization. These principles are not based on the merely ancestral or traditional. Yet he and his students tend to dislike the intellectual foundation upon which these principles have been defended, since it is well known that Strauss is a critic of both Spinoza and Locke. (For this reason, Straussians like Steven Smith insist that liberal democracy has a premodern basis in "Platonic" liberalism.)[102] What is this defective modern foundation that undermines modern liberal democracy?

This foundation is the liberal theology of the early modern age, a distorted version of Christianity that, Strauss believes, was made possible by Machiavelli. The general Straussian view of both Spinoza and Locke is that these great thinkers trivialized and misused biblical revelation for a Machiavellian purpose: to project a liberal democratic politics onto Scripture. In the process, these early moderns drained the Bible of any meaning. Worst of all, Spinoza and Locke end up dismissing the most supernaturalistic elements of revelation as "superstition" while they focus on the ethics of Scripture as most suitable to liberal democracy. Spinoza stands out in particular as "the hard-headed, not to say hard-hearted, pupil of Machiavelli and philologic-historical critic of the Bible," who lifts Machiavellianism "to theological heights."[103] Yet Spinoza is only the apt pupil of the man who first taught that the Bible must be understood in human terms, which leads to the conclusion that its truth is indistinguishable from myth. The triumphant influence of Machiavelli goes far beyond Spinoza. Strauss laments the fact that even Christian theologians of his time have uncritically accepted Machiavelli's portrayal of Scripture as largely mythical in content.[104]

This selective reading of the Bible, while necessary to the formation of liberal democracy, leads to the unfortunate consequence that revelation itself becomes a mere appendage to politics in modernity. David Janssens distinguishes Spinoza's "minimalist" faith from that of St. Paul on the grounds that Spinoza sees only "practical" value in Scripture.[105] Martin Yaffe, a translator of Spinoza's *Theologico-Political Treatise*, dismisses Spinoza's focus on the ethics of Scripture (or what he calls the "seven dogmas" in chapter fourteen of this work) as "instruments of behavior modification in biblical guise."[106] Ernest Fortin blames Spinoza for producing a version of Christianity that is "diluted, transmogrified, and barely recognizable."[107] Since Locke follows Spinoza's biblical hermeneutic (despite the former's more positive appraisal of miracles), he apparently merits blame as well for the devaluation of religion. According to Thomas Pangle, the "influence of the Spinoza-Locke axis led to the eclipse" of the "humanly gripping questions" about God and humanity's place in the universe.[108] Michael Zuckert and Paul Rahe, who concur with Pangle that Locke shares the same view of the Bible as Spinoza, accuse Locke of offering a "stripped-down" version of Christianity that is suitable only to liberal Christians, that is, believers who are not truly pious from a Straussian perspective.[109] Even Edwin Curley, a distinguished Spinoza scholar who is not a student of Strauss, sides with him in portraying both Spinoza and Hobbes as defenders of a "minimal" version of salvation that rests on the practice of charity.[110] (Why the practice of charity—a very demanding ethic, to say the least—is "minimal" is never quite explained by these authors.)[111]

Straussian readers of Spinoza can sound downright Marxist in their interpretation of the moderns as followers of Machiavelli (who, after all, inspired Marx as well, according to Strauss).[112] In tones that are reminiscent of Strauss's portrait of Hobbes as a defender of the English bourgeoisie, Yaffe dismisses Spinoza's celebration of his native Amsterdam's love of business as no more than a "glossy chamber-of-commerce" blurb. He additionally faults Spinoza for failing to explain how his strict biblical morality (the seven dogmas of faith that he lists in chapter 14 of his *Theologico-Political Treatise*) is compatible with a more libertine bourgeois order.[113] Yet neither Yaffe nor any other Straussian known to me adequately explains how the classical tradition of political philosophy, with its attendant love of strict hierarchy and slavery, could somehow be put into practice more effectively in the American democratic regime today. It is never admitted that Plato is far more alien than Spinoza to the cause of liberal democracy, given the latter's role (as Strauss presents him) in defending this regime for the first time in history.[114]

It is also legitimate to ask why readers like Yaffe reduce Spinoza, in quasi-Marxian fashion, to a mere defender of commercial society. Is this reading consistent with the Straussian rule that an author must be read on his own terms, without undue emphasis on his historical context? Moreover, there is ample evidence of a methodological double standard at work here. Strauss and his students never reduce Plato, Aristotle, or medieval authors to the status of being mere defenders of their regimes, since they emphasize that these premodern thinkers were in fact subtle (and secretive) critics of their status quo. A Straussian would never claim, for example, that Plato's or Aristotle's defense of "nature" is merely an attempt to shore up the economic institution of ancient slavery. The Greeks are somehow above these concerns, because of their love of the "timeless" virtues of philosophy and their disdain for the "timely" vices of practical life. Yet the same courtesy is not always extended to "Machiavellian" moderns like

Hobbes, Spinoza, or Locke. Why does the application of Straussian hermeneutics vary from ancient to modern?

The Straussian dismissal of the modernist usage of biblical morality in early modern social contract theory as insincere rests on the assumption that modern political philosophy overall is a continuation of Machiavellian themes. Despite his praise for the United States as the first nation that consciously defied Machiavellian ideas, Strauss also teaches that Machiavelli's interpretation of Roman republicanism deeply influenced the authors of *The Federalist* as well as moderns like Montesquieu whose works were widely read by the American Founders.[115] The predictable conclusion that arises out of this teaching, then, is that moderns only employ biblical morality as a foundation of the social contract because they are cynically making use of religion for political purposes. The undeniable and overwhelming presence of biblical charity in the works of Hobbes, Spinoza, Locke, and Montesquieu cannot possibly be sincerely believed, since, in Straussian terms, no true political philosopher is a believer. As Clifford Orwin puts it, Machiavelli is only the first of many moderns to "secularize" Christian compassion.[116] It is inconceivable to Strauss and his students that the early modern contractarians might have invoked charity for reasons that have nothing to do with a Machiavellian heritage. These "lukewarm Christians" end up advancing Machiavelli's aims by preferring their "earthly fatherland" to the "heavenly fatherland."[117]

There are ultimately three problems with Strauss's "Machiavellian" hypothesis. First, Machiavelli himself famously rejected biblical charity as an impractical credo for the rough-and-tumble world of politics.[118] Second, even if the modern usage of charity is stripped away from the biblical worldview, as many students of Strauss argue, this does not change the fact that even a minimalist use of charity can impose stark moral demands on the political sphere, which Machiavelli would have considered unacceptable.[119]

Yet the main reason that justifies a repudiation of the Straussian hermeneutic lies in the rather obvious fact that the early moderns chose biblical charity as the foundation of the social contract because, unlike Machiavelli, they believed it was superior to all other concepts of ethics. To my knowledge, neither Strauss nor any of his students ever explains why the allegedly cold-blooded rationalists of early modernity invoke charity instead of relying exclusively on the far more calculating ethic of utilitarianism as the foundational morality of the social contract. Even Hobbes, who famously portrays human beings as egoistic individuals competing against each other, insists that citizens in the contract obey the Golden Rule as a law of nature. It is not that Strauss fails to appreciate the legacy of Hobbes. At times he praises this early contractarian for employing biblical charity in a manner that ultimately led to a humane civilization. Because Hobbes "never wavered in his adherence to the golden rule," his version of the contract, as already noted, is far more decent than anything that the violent politics of the twentieth-century ever produced.[120] Yet Strauss never retreats from his assumption that this usage of charity, even if it has historically produced good results, has little to do with reason.

As we have seen, Hobbes and Locke count on the fact that even self-serving bourgeois individuals must practice charity toward each other, if religious and political freedom is to survive in their social contracts. It is not enough to demand that citizens simply treat each other as competitive rivals. Even Jefferson, who is harshly critical of the most authoritarian features of Christian rule in history, is confident that Christian charity is superior to all other versions of morality. In his words, this ethic was the "most sublime and benevolent," and "more pure and perfect" than anything that pagan philosophy had ever provided.[121] Jefferson's comments do not sound like the cynical thoughts of a Machiavellian statesman, who would not dare to teach that Christian morality is superior to ancient republican ethics. Yet Jefferson gives every impression that he believes in the truth of biblical charity.[122] Nor is Jefferson the first modern political philosopher to make this claim. In *The Spirit of Laws*, Montesquieu asserts that Christianity, "which ordains that men should love each other," has blessed every nation "with the best civil, the best political laws." Moreover, Christian principles are "infinitely more powerful than the false honour of monarchies, than the humane virtues of republics, or the servile fear of despotic states."[123] Like Jefferson, Montesquieu no doubt finds biblical morality to be useful to humanity. Yet the utility of this ethic does not take away from its superior truth, particularly when we remember that early modern minds did not necessarily distinguish utility from truth.[124] Most importantly, neither Montesquieu nor Jefferson ever insists, like Machiavelli, that charity is incompatible with the political life.

I have dwelled on the place of charity in early modern contractarianism to press the point that some of its most prominent defenders rejected the dualistic opposition between reason and faith, or between truth and religion. Despite the Straussian argument that attributes to all political philosophers the assumption that religion cannot be grounded in reason, moderns like

Montesquieu and Jefferson clearly prefer charity over any other ethics because they, rationally, find other ethical doctrines wanting. Like the authors of *The Federalist*, they consciously chose to reject the ancient model of politics because they preferred some version of Christian ethics. The fact that they distinguish Christian ethics from all other versions of morality reveals one of the achievements of Anglo-American politics: its insistence that all citizens adhere to a particular religious tradition in order to restrain and mitigate the evils of a commercial civilization. Once again, it is bizarre that Strauss and his students, who seek to defend Anglo-American democracy, dismiss this usage of the Christian faith as cynical, insincere, and false. (Ironically, in Straussian terms, Strauss is perhaps too "bold" in exposing the seedy origins of modern political philosophy while he defends the modern constitutional regime.)

Strauss's critique of modernity as a vast Machiavellian project has given the impression to many readers that he and his students are stalwart conservatives, determined to protect the sanctity of the Bible. (What is often ignored here is that most leftist readers of Spinoza agree with Strauss that this early modern liberal democrat is indeed a Machiavellian enemy of religion.)[125] It also sends the message that Strauss is opposed to both Spinoza and Locke on the philosophical grounds that revelation defies rational scrutiny and should, therefore, be left alone. Contrary to the critique of Strauss as an Averroist who promotes the use of faith for political purposes, he and his students appear to be arguing just the opposite.[126] What is often lost in this discussion of Strauss's critique of both Spinoza and Locke is an appreciation of the costly implications of this critique. Does Strauss's hermeneutic unwittingly confirm the leftist view that religion in modernist hands is a merely cynical example of realpolitik?

Jews and Liberal (Machiavellian) Democracy

Strauss's determination to separate religious faith from both reason and politics, which is the basis of his critique of Machiavellianism, also ultimately leaves his own ancestral faith without any possibility of philosophic defense. Despite his polemics against appeals to the traditional or ancestral as a legitimate basis for political philosophy, he also opposes Spinoza for devaluing Strauss's ancestral faith, Judaism. The implication of this exception is massively significant for his overall defense of Anglo-American democracy, since this regime institutionalized the liberal theology that made this alleged devaluation of both Judaism and Christianity possible.

At first glance, it is not particularly shocking to point out that Strauss was opposed to Spinoza for these reasons, especially when Strauss associates this Enlightenment philosopher with the liberal adulterations of Judaism and Zionism that Strauss embraced as a youth and later rejected. It is well known that Strauss turned on liberalized Judaism because, in his view, it accepted Spinoza's interpretation, which effectively abandoned both revelation and the special historical roots of Judaism. Maimonides, by contrast, appealed to Strauss because of his philosophical reluctance to attack the divine authority of revelation.[127] To my knowledge, however, no one has linked his critique of Spinoza to his overall attitude toward Anglo-American democracy. It is legitimate to ask these questions: Is it wise to reject every rational interpretation of Scripture in order to avoid Machiavellianism? Additionally, does Judaism, as Strauss portrays it, simply become an "ancestral" faith without any rational content? If religion is simply irrational, then how do we know whether it is true or not?

This line of thinking assumes that Strauss's preoccupation with the survival of Judaism is mainly or primarily ancestral, a controversial claim in the best of times. For if it is ancestral, then Strauss himself can be accused of practicing the very ideology that he otherwise opposes, historicism. To be sure, Strauss's concern with the survival of Judaism in the context of liberal democracy is understandable. Writing twenty years after the end of World War II and the Holocaust, Strauss is unconvinced that even a liberal democracy can fully protect the Jews. As he writes in his "Preface to the English Translation" (1962) to *Spinoza's Critique of Religion*, Strauss declares the Jewish problem "insoluble," because the liberal state protects both Jews and their enemies. (As a young man in Weimar Germany, Strauss embraced political Zionism and its goal of creating a Jewish state, for this very reason.)[128] The private sphere of life, which is central to liberal democracy, paradoxically allows Jews to practice their faith and anti-Semites to practice their hatred in the same climate of freedom.[129] This reasonable worry is not a sign of "ineradicable hatred" for liberal democracy, despite what some critics contend.[130] Rather, it is a conservative concern with the survival of one's tradition. The question is: Is there any way of reconciling this concern with Strauss's anti-historicism?

Naturally, students and admirers of Strauss have been reluctant to deal with or even acknowledge this massive contradiction, although there have been a few attempts at reconciliation of these opposing views. Milton Himmelfarb offers the standard view: Strauss simply believed that philosophy and Judaism cannot refute each other. The fact that Strauss favored his ancestral faith over any other has nothing to do with his philosophical pursuits. The tension between reason and faith must be accepted as inevitable, not as a conflict that invites an impossible synthesis of the two.[131] At best, Himmelfarb's explanation begs the question, since it is far from obvious that philosophy cannot refute the basic claims of revelation. Most importantly for my purposes, Himmelfarb has nothing to say about the incompatibility of two positions: Strauss's defense of his ancestral faith precisely because it is his own *and* his opposition to any historicist attempt to do the same. On similar grounds, Ted McAllister defends Strauss's appeal to the ancestral as a manifestation of his typical defense of "orthodoxy" against the atheistic assault of the Enlightenment.[132] Yet this defense also begs the question since, as we have seen, Strauss never spells out what exactly true religion or "orthodoxy" happens to look like. (For this reason, some critics have argued that Strauss's concept of "orthodoxy" has very little content.)[133] Hadley Arkes, who is just as sympathetic to Strauss's ideas as Himmelfarb and McAllister, offers a more philosophical attempt to understand this contradiction. Arkes at least appreciates the troubling nature of Strauss's apparent defense of his ancestral faith precisely because it is his own. Yet he seeks to address this problem by claiming that Judaism is a "religion of reason."[134] If that is a correct reading of Strauss, then it follows that his appeal to his ancestral faith is an act of philosophy, not historicism.

The problem with Arkes's reading of Strauss, however, is that the term "religion of reason" has far more to do with Hermann Cohen than Strauss.[135] Cohen, a neo-Kantian critic of Spinoza who was an influential defender of liberalized Judaism in early twentieth-century Berlin, was just as determined as Strauss to protect his ancestral faith, even though the reasoning behind his effort was vastly different from that of Strauss. Nothing could be less Straussian than Cohen's claim that the "concept of reason has to engender the concept of religion."[136] In an essay on Cohen, which he wrote near the end of his life, Strauss emphasized that Cohen, despite his opposition to Spinoza, was equally liberal in his treatment of Judaism. As Strauss points out, Cohen, like Spinoza, treated God as a mere "idea" and dismissed orthodox Jewish belief in both miracles and eternal punishment through hellfire.[137] What is particularly relevant to our discussion, however, is Strauss's lack of sympathy for Cohen's view, directed against Spinoza, that Judaism is a faith that is every bit as universalistic as Christianity. This attitude on Strauss's part may be surprising to some of his readers. Emil Fackenheim, who admired both Cohen and Strauss, respected Cohen in particular for emphasizing the universalistic message of Judaism.[138] In fact, it is so universalistic that Jews can easily embrace the tenets of liberal democracy, the most universalistic of political regimes. What worries Strauss here is that the historical particularity of Judaism will be lost in the liberal assimilation that Spinoza desired. Worst of all, Strauss is concerned, as we have seen, that the most liberal regime will not protect Jews from their enemies. As a result, Strauss concludes his essay on Cohen on a rather sour note when he observes that Cohen ultimately cajoles Jews into embracing "fidelity" to the liberal state, not to their nationality or identity.[139] If my reading of Strauss's critique of Cohen is correct, it is clear that he faults Cohen for advancing a liberal theology that ends up harming his own people. Although, to my knowledge, Strauss never explicitly calls Cohen a "Machiavellian," he certainly associates this great neo-Kantian philosopher with the pseudo-theology that made liberal democracy possible at the expense of the Judaic faith.[140]

The issue here is not whether Strauss is actually more sympathetic to Spinoza than meets the eye, since even he, as a young student, defended Spinoza against Cohen on the grounds that the former had to "politicize" Scripture in order to defend liberalism in a hostile and persecutory context. Other readers have also observed Strauss's occasional sympathy for Spinoza.[141] The issue at hand is whether it makes any sense for Strauss to portray his favored regime as Machiavellian to the core, even though by his own admission this is the only regime that has ever protected Jews.

In order to convey a sense of what is at stake here, it is worth comparing Strauss's thoughts on the relation between liberalism and Judaism to those of his fellow émigré Theodor Adorno. Both men share the same deep concerns about the survival of Jews under liberal democracy, a regime that had not prevented Hitler from coming to power in Germany. They also agree that modern rationalism is purely instrumental in form, wedded to a scientific method that defends a false dichotomy between fact and value.[142] Although Adorno is certainly classified as a philosopher far to the left of Strauss, it is significant that both thinkers also understand liberalism to be a fundamentally Machiavellian project.[143] Like Strauss, Adorno read the early modern defenders of liberalism as Machiavellian in intent. In *Dialectic of Enlightenment*, Adorno and Max Horkheimer portray Spinoza as a "Machiavellian" who teaches that Christian virtues like humility and repentance are "very useful despite their irrationality."[144] Adorno and Horkheimer also contend, like Strauss, that the "somber writers of the bourgeois dawn" such as Machiavelli, Hobbes, and Mandeville all openly "decried the egotism of the self," even as they were laying the theoretical foundations for a civilization that was based on this egotism.[145] Although Strauss, as a Cold War liberal, was far more sympathetic than Adorno to the cause of American democracy,[146] it is striking that Adorno is no more impressed than Strauss is with the liberal (Machiavellian) theology that underscores liberal civilization as a whole.[147] In his studies of both Kierkegaard and Heidegger, Adorno scorns this theology for reducing religion to mere moral sentiment after it is fully stripped of its supernaturalistic mystery.[148] Despite the tolerant nature of this theology, it has not served Jews well. Strauss and Adorno dramatically converge in their assumption that Enlightenment liberalism offered a cruel paradox to European Jews, in extending tolerance of Jews and the anti-Semites who sought to destroy them. This Machiavellian liberalism revealed, ironically, its lack of realism when the emancipated Jews of Europe discovered that their existence was threatened by emancipated Jew-haters. Just as Strauss warns against the liberal state's tolerance of "private discrimination" against the Jews, so Adorno lambastes liberalism for allowing the "beer-cellar politics of the anti-Semites" to thrive.[149] The cruelest irony, in the eyes of both Adorno and Strauss, is that this anti-Semitism destroyed the very liberal tradition that made it possible to flourish in the first place.

I dwell on the family resemblances shared by Strauss and Adorno to press the point that this focus on the dangers of liberal theology as a Machiavellian contrivance can play into the hands of leftist critics who seek to undermine Western liberalism. Unlike Strauss, Adorno was a cultural Marxist, who attacked liberal theology precisely because he despised Anglo-American liberalism as an oppressive lie that brought down ruin on his people. It will not do to argue, as one defender of Strauss does, that the relation between reason and revelation must remain an open question, in the absence of a rational interpretation of the Bible.[150] Even Strauss worried that the "victory of orthodoxy" was not an "unmitigated blessing," and that "it would be unwise to say farewell to reason" altogether.[151] Yet Strauss arguably says "farewell" when he refuses to interpret the Bible on rational grounds in order to root out the Machiavellianism that lurks within modern political philosophy.

The irony is that Strauss's determination to conflate a liberalized Christianity with Machiavellianism delegitimizes the one tradition that offered freedom to his own people. If it is true that liberal theology is a major foundation of the Anglo-American democratic tradition, then it would surely make sense to preserve it. Strauss's Cold War liberal opposition to the "historicist" privileging of one faith above all others notwithstanding, it is hard to imagine the universalism of Western democracy without its Christian foundation. In the absence of this tradition, it may be hard to maintain the "mild and easy-going" Anglo-Saxon humanitarianism that Strauss otherwise admires in this tradition.[152] If this tolerance disappears, however, due to his particular version of anti-Machiavellianism, then Strauss's own brethren will have to rely on a liberal universalism that is no longer supported on any theological grounds. At times even he admits that the philosophy of natural right is as much an act of faith as religious belief, one that rests on an "unevident premise."[153] It is far from obvious that liberalism will survive the decline of liberal theology. As Strauss well knew, Nietzsche predicted that biblical morality would not survive the death of the biblical God. It is just as likely that belief in human rights, which is rooted in Christianity, survives only as long as the faith persists.[154] If this liberalism is not as naturally felt as Strauss sometimes implies, then human beings in liberal democracies may embrace versions of historicism (the ancestral) that threaten vulnerable minorities like the Jews. Strauss's rather leftist search for a philosophical universalism that transcends all faiths and historical differences while making liberal democracy possible eventually has to hit the wall of the religious particularity that made this regime possible in the first place.

The Straussian devaluation of the Anglo-American focus on charity as "minimalist" and "trivial" also, ironically, harms the position of minorities in a liberal democracy. It is not only conveniently forgotten that Abraham Lincoln, a model statesman in the eyes of Straussians, upheld charity as a central political credo of the republic. It is also often forgotten that it may be more important to maintain biblical credos (e.g., the belief in the sanctity of human life) to shore up the moral legitimacy of the United States than to defend the American republic as a regime that owes nothing essential to its religious origins.[155] The fact that a liberal regime based on charity actually demands a great deal of virtue from its citizens as it insists on the extension of fundamental liberties to all citizens within that regime also receives scant attention. If this foundation of charity is merely an insult to religious orthodoxy, as Strauss and his students claim, then there may be no credible religious defense left to check those citizens who reject this liberalized version of Christianity. It is far from obvious that other interpretations of the Bible (or the Koran, for that matter) will inspire the better angels of our nature. In fine, the Straussian defense of Anglo-American democracy ends up undermining the very foundation that made it liberal in the first place.

4

Churchill, the Anglo-
American Greek?

In his lecture "What Can We Learn from Political Theory?" which he delivered at the New School for Social Research in 1942, Strauss praised Winston Churchill for defending Western civilization in accord with the timeless teachings of political philosophy. These teachings were not, Strauss made clear, based on biblical morality; they were in fact the ideas of Greek political philosophers. Churchill had made use of a tradition "founded by Socrates, Plato, and Aristotle," which was transformed but not "broken under the influence of the biblical virtues of mercy and humility." This tradition still provided "the most needed guidance as regards the fundamentals." Most importantly, the "cause" for which Churchill fought "would not exist but for the influence of the tradition in question."[1]

This was not the first time that Strauss had praised the great statesman or had associated his statecraft with the ancients. One year before this lecture, in "German Nihilism," Strauss had remarked that the manly defiance Churchill exhibited after the disaster at Dunkirk would have impressed young Germans who had once chosen Nazism over contemptible alternatives like the decadent bourgeois West as well as the "communist world revolution," both of which represented the discredited modern idea of progress. Churchill's stirring speech about "Britain's finest hour" was a powerful defense of liberal democracy that was reminiscent of Roman courage. With Churchill in mind, Strauss writes: "For one of their greatest teachers had taught them to see in Cannae the greatest moment in the life of that glory which was ancient Rome."[2] In his American exile, Strauss constantly taught his students to appreciate and learn from the history that Churchill both made and wrote. In a letter to Karl Löwith one year after the end of World War II, Strauss praised Churchill as a man who demonstrated that "the possibility of *megalopsychia* [greatness of soul] exists today *exactly* as it did in the fifth century, B.C." In fact, Churchill helped Strauss understand Aristotle.[3] The day after Churchill's death in 1965, Strauss once again praised Churchill in tones suggesting that the British prime minister was a statesman in the classical sense, when he contrasted the "indomitable and magnanimous statesman" with the "insane tyrant" who threatened to vanquish Britain, standing alone in defiance, in the perilous year 1940.[4] In short, as Harry Jaffa observes, Strauss admired Churchill "more than any other man of his time."[5] It was Churchill's opposition to Hitler that paralleled the "classical understanding" of tyranny that also animated the American Revolution.[6] Generally, Churchill's courageous and victorious resistance to Hitler is the obvious reason that Strauss and his students praise the man as the personification of all that is great about Anglo-American democracy.[7]

None of these citations should suggest that only Strauss and his students have celebrated this statesman. Most politicians of the Right in postwar Western democracies who had come of age during World War II never hesitated to invoke his memory.[8] Russell Kirk spoke for most American postwar conservatives when he praised the "fortitude" that Churchill exuded in 1940: Straussians like Carnes Lord have similarly praised Churchill's refusal to embrace defeatism.[9] It is well known to readers of Strauss and his followers that they celebrated Churchill as a fearless opponent of tyranny, perhaps even worshipping the statesman in a cultic manner that is comparable only to their adulation of Abraham Lincoln. Walter Berns, who studied with Strauss, celebrates Churchill, in an implicit comparison with Lincoln, as "the embodiment of the greatest cause in our lives: the preservation of government of, by, and for the people at a time when it was most imperiled."[10] Steven Smith contends that Strauss's "Platonic liberalism bespeaks a

Churchillian defense of democracy as the worst except for all the alterna-tives."[11] Joseph Cropsey, a first-generation student of Strauss, celebrates Churchill as a tough-minded democratic statesman who understood that the noble cause of liberal democracy must be defended at times through the calculated use of dissimulation, a talent well-known to classical states-men.[12] Francis Fukuyama praises Churchill for demonstrating during his wartime leadership "a degree of mastery every bit as great as that of states-men of pre-democratic ages."[13] From the Reagan era onward, Straussians in Washington have reportedly met on his birthday to sip brandy and smoke cigars.[14] As Anne Norton has argued, Churchill and Lincoln are the secu-lar "saints" of the Straussian movement.[15] Yet this strikingly enthusiastic admiration that Strauss's students have reserved for Churchill is based on a premise that is unique to their understanding of the West: that Churchill defended the *eternal* principles of civilization. Unlike Kirk and other post-war rightists, Strauss understood Churchill to be the guardian of timeless ideals, not simply the noble cause of British conservatism. Moreover, if Jaffa is correct, his teacher Strauss is as much the philosophical nemesis of Hei-degger (and other nihilists) as Churchill was the political foe of Hitler.[16]

It is not surprising to see why defenders of Anglo-American conserva-tism would admire an historical giant who, more than any other leader, pushed for the unity of the English-speaking peoples. Moreover, Churchill defended this purpose in the most universalist manner conceivable. Two years after the end of World War II, he held out the hope that this alliance "may save freedom, civilization, and democracy—and perhaps even roll away the curse of war forever from mankind."[17] In general, neoconserva-tives on both sides of the Atlantic have celebrated Churchill's homeland as a bastion of universal ideals that benefit all of humanity. Tony Blair became an honorary neoconservative, despite his leftist politics, when he pro-claimed in Churchillian tones during the start of the second Iraq War that the "liberty which we seek is not for some but for all, for that is the only path to victory in this struggle."[18] Neoconservatives, who are opposed to the old conservative (isolationist) suspicion of democratic interventions, look back with satisfaction to English statesmen like Canning, Palmerston, and Churchill who defended an imperialism that spread English liberal ide-als around the world.[19] It is not necessarily a neoconservative or Straussian invention to argue that the English tradition possesses a universalism of this sort. It was the British Conservative Party, after all, that opened the doors to Third World immigration in the 1950s, even though, ironically, Churchill and the Labour Party opposed this liberalized policy.[20]

Still, what Sir Michael Howard once called "Churchillmania" is most evident in the United States, in part due to the efforts of Strauss and his followers.[21] The American Straussian adulation of Churchill arguably fits best into what historians have dubbed the *Great Man* version of history, in which bold and courageous men in war and politics have defied, against all odds, the currents of historical change by performing noble deeds (even imperialist ones) that serve to inspire future generations. A great man like Churchill, as Harry Jaffa explains, is not the same as a gentleman who fights with gallantry and patriotism. In quoting Churchill's remark that the American Civil War was the last war fought by gentlemen, Jaffa notes that the Confederacy produced gentlemen like Lee, Jackson, and Davis who were fighting for the wrong cause. The Great Man has to fight on the side of high principle as well, even if that means defying historical change.[22]

Churchill, the prudential statesman, built on the "low but solid things" (like changeable human passions) in a democracy, as Strauss once put it,[23] but he still defied with manly courage the currents of his age. In *On Tyranny*, Strauss holds out the hope that there will "always be men (*andres*) who will revolt against a state which is destructive of humanity or in which there is no longer a possibility of noble action and great deeds."[24] Churchill himself admitted he understood history as "the tale of exceptional human beings, whose thoughts, actions, qualities, virtues, triumphs, weaknesses, and crimes have dominated the fortunes of the race."[25] Churchill's brave leadership in 1940, in Strauss's mind, no doubt dramatically contrasted with the cowardly historicists (including some of Churchill's own countrymen) who considered going along with the currents of change by contemplating a peace treaty with Nazi Germany.[26] Churchill's courage and wisdom, in the service of a democracy that did not always appreciate him, makes him an invaluable "anachronism" whom future democratic generations must emulate.[27] The "true human greatness" of Churchill allows us to "see the limits" of the ordinary human beings that populate democracy.[28]

Despite the overwhelming importance that Strauss and his students have attributed to Churchill and his legacy, leftist critics of Strauss have been almost silent on this central aspect of Straussian thought. Most leftist opponents of Strauss have been so determined to portray him as a guru of the Far Right that they rarely even mention his profound respect for Nazism's most dangerous enemy.[29] What has also received almost no critical discussion is why Straussians portray Churchill as a leader who, in the words of Strauss's 1942 lecture on political theory, appealed to a classical tradition that, fortunately, had not been "broken" by Christian virtues like mercy and humility. What is important to understand is the Straussian rationale behind the representation of Churchill as a classical, not Christian, statesman. What are the reasons behind this revisionist approach to history? Does this approach even effectively help their primary objective, which is to shore up support for "liberal democracy"?

Was Churchill a Pagan?

Several challenges face any scholar who wishes to portray Churchill as a classical statesman. Despite Strauss's own comparison of Churchill's leadership with Roman leadership, Churchill himself often scorned the "virtues" of the Romans. In *The Birth of Britain* (volume 1 of his *History of the English-Speaking Peoples*), he pointedly contrasted the failures of the Roman system of justice to provide due process and fair trials for the accused with the protections of these rights under English common law. In *The New World*, the second volume, Churchill compared the violence of the Cromwell era to the worst excesses of the Roman imperium.[30] To make matters even more difficult for those who portray Churchill as a classical statesman, there is little evidence that the great man even studied the works of Plato and Aristotle.[31]

Straussians like Jaffa eagerly quote Churchill's praise of Athens and Jerusalem as the two cities that "have counted more with mankind" than any other. "Their messages in religion, philosophy, and art have been the guiding lights of modern faith and culture."[32] To read Churchill on his own terms, as Strauss insists that serious scholars must do for any important figure, seems to reveal the statesman's dislike for the violence of pagan civilization. It is hard to reconcile Churchill's occasional praise for pagan Athens with his condemnation of the slavery and exploitation that characterized Greco-Roman civilization as a whole. Unlike Strauss and his students, Churchill refuses to draw any distinction between the classical political philosophers and the societies in which they lived. In fact, in a postwar speech on the superiority of Christian morality, Churchill goes so far as to condemn the pagan thinkers for their ignorance of the fundamental injustice that characterized their civilization. "They [the Greek and Latin philosophers] spoke of freedom and political institutions, but they were quite unaware that their culture was built upon detestable foundations." Perhaps most inconvenient to Strauss and his movement, Churchill credits Christianity, not Athens, with providing a moral foundation in which democracy "can reconcile the rights of the individual with the demands of society in a manner which alone can bring happiness and peace to humanity."[33]

None of these readily available facts has, to my knowledge, deterred Strauss or his students from claiming Churchill as one of their own. The fact that Churchill failed to appreciate or even seriously study the classics has probably not had much of an impact since Jaffa, Churchill's biggest booster among the Straussians, does not attribute any philosophical status to the statesman anyway. Instead, Churchill represents the "prephilosophic experience of political life" at its best.[34] Still, Churchill's own refusal to think in terms that sound classical (given his dismissal of Greco-Roman civilization) makes it hard to portray him as a pagan in the positive sense of the word. It is worth noting that Strauss and his students are not the only readers of Churchill who have portrayed him as a preserver of pagan statecraft. Patrick Buchanan, a paleoconservative critic of Churchill, associates the prime minister's "ferocity" in war with that of a "pagan in the Roman tradition." With this pejorative meaning of paganism in mind, Buchanan doubts that Churchill harbored any sincere Christian convictions, given his support for the fire-bombing of German cities during World War II.[35] (Ironically, Churchill also equated Nazism with "barbarous paganism" that derived "strength and perverted pleasure from persecution.")[36]

It is fair to conclude that what Buchanan means by "pagan," however, has little to do with the *mature* Straussian understanding of the classics. I emphasize "mature" because the young Strauss, as a political Zionist in the 1920s in Germany, also adhered to a similar meaning of paganism. When Strauss protested against the hierarchical and dictatorial Zionism of Walter Moses, he condemned this ideology as "pagan-fascist."[37] Yet Strauss at this time in his life was not seeking out the "eternal" standards of liberal democracy that would be his preoccupation in his scholarly career in postwar America. Whereas Buchanan equates paganism with cruelty and lack of mercy, the émigré Strauss and his American students identify classical pagan political philosophy with manly courage and resolve, the qualities of the "Great Man."

If Strauss is correct in contrasting the Platonic-Aristotelian tradition with a biblical tradition based on humility and mercy, however, is he then suggesting that Christianity is a religion of weakness that has no valuable role to play in the tough world of politics? To my knowledge, Strauss never *openly* faults Christianity for these failings, nor does he boldly portray Churchill as anti-Christian. In fact, he would be the first to attribute this teaching on politics to Machiavelli, whose thought he takes pains to repudiate as amoral.[38] Nevertheless, a few of his students and admirers have been more forthright in pressing the view that Churchill could not have afforded to be a good Christian and still persevere as a great practitioner of the political arts. In an illuminating essay on Churchill's account of the war in the Sudan, Paul Rahe contrasts the classical morality of Churchill with the Christian mores of Major Charles Gordon, who perished in the infamous Khartoum massacre in 1885. Whereas Gordon was a fine "Christian gentleman" who naïvely believed in a morality of "good intentions," which ultimately led to his demise, Churchill adhered to a "more manly moral code" and a "pagan" sense of honor that led him to appreciate a "morality of consequences."[39] (Major Gordon was clearly not a "great man.") Churchill's paganism presumably was more realistic and tough-minded in understanding the limits of British power than the hapless Gordon who believed in fulfilling moral duties toward a region of the world terrorized by Moslem warriors.[40] Pressing this sharp contrast even further, Rahe concludes that Churchill truly preserved the timeless (eternal) standards of political excellence, even if he was not a "believing Christian." In words that invoke the rhetoric of the American Founding, Rahe celebrates Churchill for believing in "nature's provision" or in "Nature's God," which is "essential to the spiritedness that gives rise in man to the noble and healthy desire to prevail."[41] Since Churchill allegedly adhered to "Nature's God" rather than the God of revelation, he was able to appreciate the unchanging yet harsh truths of politics, truths that are beyond the comprehension of a Christian.[42]

It is not hard to see why Strauss and his students are determined to portray Churchill as a stalwart defender of both pagan virtues and England's ideals. Churchill stands out as the greatest English statesman, in the Straussian view, because of his adherence to classical virtues. He is that rare individual who reaches greatness and rises above the mediocrity of mass democracy.[43] Despite their genuine love for the "eternal ideals" that England manifests at her best, there is the constant worry among Strauss and his students that many of England's (and America's) greatest leaders and thinkers do not understand what is at stake in the war against the enemies of liberal democracy. As I argued in chapter one, Strauss generally dislikes the English tradition of political philosophy. As early as his lecture on "German Nihilism," Strauss agrees to some extent with his fellow Germans that modern English philosophers caused a "debasement of morality" with their incessant focus on rights and materialism. This English vice unwittingly gave credence to the German nihilist view that modern civilization itself was debased and deserved to be overthrown.[44] There were only two things that saved England from the corrosive effects of German nihilism: first, the English spirit of "muddling through," which spurned the radicalism of German thought, and second, the manly example of that rare Englishman, Churchill, who defied the Nazis after the fall of France in 1940.[45] As Susan Shell has astutely argued, the shining example of Churchill in 1940 persuaded Strauss himself, who had been somewhat prejudiced against liberal democracy up to this point, to shift from being a "harsh critic" of the regime to becoming its "unhesitating supporter."[46]

Churchill's stature is exceptional, then, not only because he stood up against the "insane tyrant" Hitler. It is also because he understood, as so many of his countrymen did not, the necessary tension between paganism and revelation (or what Strauss famously called the conflict between "Athens and Jerusalem"). To my knowledge, the only other Englishman whom Strauss and his students credit with this exceptional awareness is Shakespeare.[47] For this reason, Strauss and his students take pains to associate Churchill with the "eternal ideals" that England manifests, ideals that are based on a premodern or classical foundation.[48] Churchill is decidedly not an adherent of the debased social contract tradition of Hobbes and Locke, as Strauss's admirer George Grant believed.[49] Nor is he an historicist, as Churchill's admirer Isaiah Berlin believed.[50] In the Straussian perspective, Churchill was not a mere modern who ignorantly adhered to the defective traits of his nation's own tradition of political philosophy, traits that contributed to the modern crisis of nihilism as Strauss understands it. How, then, did Churchill escape from this modern existential crisis that was incubated in his own nation? As Harry Jaffa explains, Churchill firmly rejected the Hobbesian (and modern) teaching that fear of violent death is the most important political passion. Instead, he manifested the Socratic teaching that living according to what is "intrinsically noble and just" is infinitely superior to an animalistic and cowardly life based on mere survival.[51] Put in political terms, Churchill chose to defy Hitler in 1940 instead of seeking a peace treaty with this tyrant.

As Strauss understands the English philosophical tradition, the Hobbesian teaching on the primacy of self-preservation was not the worst teaching to emerge out of Churchill's homeland. Although Strauss, in his early study of Hobbes, is willing to praise his subject for identifying the bourgeois virtues with the "virtues of civilized men," the reader should not conclude from this argument that Strauss fundamentally sympathizes with Hobbes.[52] Strauss's Hobbes is, after all, a philosophical successor to Machiavelli's project, which is to provide "an immoral or amoral substitute for morality" without any reference to a natural standard of justice. Even though Strauss believes Locke enjoyed a "resounding success" in the Anglo-Saxon world that was denied to Hobbes, this does not mean that Hobbes's influence has dissipated altogether.[53] Far worse than his teaching on mere survival is Hobbes's view that power is the other most important political passion. Strauss's Hobbes, then, is the precursor to Nietzsche and Schopenhauer.[54] The English heirs to Hobbes's legacy continue to advance the modern march to historicism and nihilism. Strauss has even less respect for Locke's philosophical acumen than for that of Hobbes, since at least Hobbes took the Greeks seriously (if only to dismiss them). Even Edmund Burke, an author who was much admired by Churchill, comes under fire for failing to appreciate the classical (pagan) virtue of noble "last-ditch resistance" against a tyrannical enemy. Instead, Burke embraced the historicist view that moderns must be resigned to the "fate" of unstoppable historical change.[55]

Whatever the validity of Strauss's portrait of English political philosophy, it should be apparent that Strauss's Churchill stands head and shoulders above his own nation's tradition, because he sought out the lessons of statecraft from a premodern tradition. He did not, however, seek political wisdom from Christianity. Even if Straussians overstate this last point, it must be recognized that Churchill at times profoundly recognized the huge tension between political morality and biblical ethics. In *The Gathering Storm* (the first volume of his magisterial history of World War II), in his conclusion to a chapter devoted to the West's surrender of Czechoslovakia to Hitler at Munich, Churchill celebrates the Sermon on the Mount as "the last word in Christian ethics." However, he immediately cautions that "it is not on these [Christian] terms that Ministers assume their responsibilities of guiding States." A much better guide to the political realm is honor, even though it is "baffling to reflect that what men call honour does not correspond always to Christian ethics."[56] The "element of pride" that informs the ideal of honor is not necessarily bad, despite what the New Testament teaches. In an essay on Marsilius of Padua, Strauss makes practically the same point as Churchill when he points to the tension between biblical morality and politics that Marsilius brings to the surface: "The demands of the Sermon on the Mount cannot be reconciled with the status and duties of governors and their lay subjects."[57] Instead, if honor is based on duty— rather than on an "exaggerated code" that leads to the "performance of utterly vain and unreasonable deeds"—then it is imperative that statesmen practice the former.[58] From Churchill's perspective, the appeasement of Hitler at Munich was an act of monumental dishonor.

Although it is plausible, as Strauss suggests, to attribute to Churchill an awareness of the tension between pagan honor and biblical morality, does this make Churchill a pagan statesman? I raise this question not because I believe that the prime minister was necessarily a devout Christian. Even if Buchanan goes too far in accusing Churchill of an utterly insincere religiosity, it is well known that he was not a regular churchgoer and even "regarded himself as a reverent agnostic—if not a pillar of the church at least a flying buttress."[59] In another context, Churchill sounded almost like a liberal Protestant when he portrayed his adherence to the "Religion of Healthy-Mindedness," a creed that required no beliefs beyond faithfulness toward friends and kindness toward the weak and poor.[60] It is legitimate to question, however, whether Churchill is a statesman in the Platonic-Aristotelian sense. The fact that Churchill adeptly spied a necessary tension between Athens and Jerusalem—to which he pronounced his fealty—does not necessarily mean that he was a modern-day Pericles. This discussion is important because it casts considerable doubt on just how universal or eternal the standards of Churchill's statecraft happen to be. If they are not eternal but in fact historical (that is, specific to Churchill's time and place), then the Straussian hermeneutic is thrown into question.

As we have seen, Churchill distinguished a healthy notion of honor and pride from an "exaggerated code" that leads to the "performance of utterly vain and unreasonable deeds." This superior understanding of honor presumably contributed to Churchill's magnanimity, which Strauss celebrates in the eulogy he gave after the statesman's death in 1965. (As readers of Churchill well know, magnanimity toward one's enemy was a virtue that, in his view, was an essential attitude for a victor to take in the aftermath of war.)[61] It is not obvious, however, that Aristotle explains the related notions of honor, pride, or magnanimity with this subtle understanding in mind. In his *Posterior Analytics*, Aristotle associates magnanimity with the "intolerance of insult" (as most famously expressed by the irascible Achilles) as well as indifference to fortune (as expressed by Socrates).[62] Neither manifestation of magnanimity, however, fits Churchill, even as Strauss portrays him. Churchill's praise of Lincoln's magnanimity in the aftermath of the American Civil War refers to the quality of mercy and intolerance of hatred, rather than insult.[63] Churchill also possessed greater moderation and good humor than Achilles in the face of mortal peril. Most importantly, Churchill was hardly resigned to the cycle of fortune and misfortune that Aristotle spies in Socrates; in fact, his defiance of Hitler in 1940 earns plaudits from his admirers (including Strauss and his students) because of his anti-fatalistic posture. The fatalism that Strauss associates with historicism is more similar to Socrates' resignation to the changeability of fortune than to Churchillian defiance.

Even if Strauss is right that Churchill recovered a classical tradition that had not yet been completely transformed by biblical humility and mercy (as he observed in his 1942 lecture), it does not follow that Churchill understood the virtues in the same way as the Greeks did. In his *Nicomachean Ethics*, Aristotle praises the magnanimous (or great-souled) man for looking down on those who are unequal to him. (In this vein, Strauss admits that biblical humility "excludes" magnanimity.)[64] As a modern democratic politician, however, Churchill would not easily get away with the rather open contempt that Aristotle's magnanimous man expresses toward ordinary souls. As a Liberal member of Parliament in the years leading up to the outbreak of World War I, Churchill poured contempt on aristocrats in the House of Lords who believed in their own "natural" superiority simply because they had the lands and titles to prove it. Churchill instead celebrated democracy as the "association of all through the leadership of the best." From this vantage point, Churchill had no patience with a hereditary class that failed to see any necessary relation between talent and greatness.[65] It is very hard to imagine Aristotle's magnanimous man, who would regard even the role of holding high office in a democracy as unworthy of him, ridiculing an aristocracy for believing they are superior by nature to the democratic mass.[66]

I am not suggesting that Churchill was a naïve democratic populist who always trusted in the wisdom of the people. Although he trusted in the good sense of British voters for the most part, he insisted that the people are truly a worthy people only if they respect constitutional government and spurn all violent, terrorist temptations.[67] In fact, Churchill and Strauss had similar misgivings about the rise of "mass democracy" in the twentieth century and its impact on the wider culture (see next section). Both men believed, as did Charles de Gaulle, that the rise of a "mass" people under-

mined the old liberal tradition that stressed individual greatness and inequality of talent.[68] I am simply questioning the validity of the Straussian
view that Churchill adhered to premodern ideals as the Greeks understood
them. Even if Churchill were interested in Greek ideas, which is far from
obvious, he faced the moral pressure of a biblical tradition that would have
been unthinkable to Aristotle. It would have been inconceivable for the
magnanimous man to praise, as Churchill did, the "universal God" of justice, mercy, and ineffable love that both Jews and Christians believe in, a
God who was beyond the comprehension of "all the genius of Greece and
all the power of Rome."[69] Aristotle makes no mention of any such deity
who loves all of humanity or demands that the magnanimous love the lowly
and the oppressed. Indeed, the magnanimous man is too "self-sufficient"
to be concerned with the suffering of others.[70] Churchill is, therefore, making a distinction between paganism and revelation that Strauss and his students would otherwise not make, namely, the superiority of biblical mores
over pagan ones.

It is probable that Churchill took from his bourgeois Protestant heritage a respect for biblical morality that he believed was universal in both
meaning and application. As we have seen, Churchill faulted the "detestable foundations" that Greco-Roman civilization was based upon, namely,
the tolerance and practice of slavery, which he pointedly contrasted with
the leavening force of a Christian ethics.

There is plenty of evidence in his writing that points to his belief that
Christianity was a vital—perhaps the essential—force of human progress
in history. The "pristine impulse of Christianity lifted men's souls" out of
the violence that characterized the twilight years of Roman Britain. In
America, it was the achievement of Christian ethics that strengthened the
cause of democratic equality.[71] To say the least, this Christian universalism
is not the eternal standard that Strauss and his students wish to uphold.
Paradoxically, however, it is this universalism that has made possible the
liberal democratic regime that they so cherish.

Mass Democracy or Liberal Democracy?

Since this study is a critical analysis of the reasoning behind Strauss's support for Anglo-American democracy, Churchill's views on the intricate
relationship between pagan and Christian civilization may turn out to be
less important than where he stands on the subject of modern democracy

itself. Was Churchill a defender of liberal democracy, as Strauss and his students define the term? It is tempting to answer in the affirmative since a few Straussians look to Churchill's text "Civilisation" (1938) as a profound articulation of what separates democracy from tyranny (see chapter one). What is at issue here is not whether Churchill and Strauss both supported the rule of law but whether they invoke the same line of reasoning in support of democratic institutions.

What makes a comparative discussion of Churchill's and Strauss's thoughts on democracy a challenge is that Churchill did not understand himself as a political philosopher. Even if it is true, as his official biographer Martin Gilbert has argued, that the "centre" of his political philosophy can be summed up as "the survival of parliamentary democracy" in England, Churchill never devoted a full-length study to the substance of democracy.[72] Nevertheless, this lacuna has not deterred every reader of Churchill from understanding him as a philosopher in the loose sense of being "a man who has touched life at many points" and can dispense wisdom through "pregnant observations" on a variety of topics.[73] Although Churchill was a statesmen and Strauss was a philosopher, this distinction should not deter us from venturing into a larger comparison of their political ideas that relate to the meaning of tyranny and democracy.

At a superficial level, Churchill and Strauss concur on several points. Even if Churchill had more respect for the idea of progress (and Christianity's role in advancing progress) than Strauss, both men generally shared the same doubts, which are fairly typical among twentieth-century figures, about whether the modern age had truly improved human nature. Even before the horror of World War I, Churchill pointed to the historic relativity of the word "progress." "Progress and reaction are no doubt relative terms. What one man calls progress another will call reaction."[74] World War I chastened Churchill's Victorian progressivism even further. As he recounts in his autobiography *My Early Life* (1930), the Great War reduced conflict to a "disgusting matter of Men, Money, and Machinery."[75] By the end of World War II and the onset of the Cold War, neither Churchill nor Strauss entertained any illusions about the inevitable triumph of democracy over totalitarianism.

On the subject of tyranny, there are also some predictable convergence points between Churchill and Strauss. Both men well understood the petty motivations that characterize the mind of the tyrant. In his portrait of Leon Trotsky, Churchill was struck by the gaping contradiction that defined this brutal Communist's personality: his belief in historical determinism and collectivism on one side and his ruthlessly selfish ambition on the other. "All the collectivism in the world could not rid him of an egoism which amounted to a disease, and a fatal disease." The reductionism of dialectical materialism, which privileges historical forces over individual action, did not deter the egoistic and vain Trotsky from seeking control of every government that he did not happen to lead.[76] Churchill's portrait of Trotsky is uncannily similar to Strauss's representation of the "Universal and Final Tyrant" in his debate with Kojève. This figure—who, like Trotsky, sought the violent re-creation of a world ungoverned by sacred or moral restraints—at bottom is also motivated by the all too human "desire for recognition." This tyrant seeks the respect of his contemporaries, even if he also intends to annihilate them.[77]

Perhaps the one Churchill text that puts into perspective his thoughts on mass democracy is his essay "Mass Effects in Modern Life," which he composed in 1932. This essay perhaps resonates most with readers (including students of Strauss) who are troubled by the rise of the mass democratic state in the twentieth century. Churchill's essay is of particular interest for adherents of the "Great Man" approach to history, since he poses the question "Is the march of events ordered and guided by eminent men; or do our leaders merely fall into their places at the heads of the moving columns?"[78] Can a "Great Man" survive or even triumph over the irreversible massification of modernity?

This essay was not the first time that Churchill had expressed gloomy thoughts about the survival of excellence. Twenty-six years earlier, in his essay "Liberalism and Socialism," he described the "whole tendency of civilisation" as moving "towards the multiplication of the collective functions of society."[79] In "Mass Effects," Churchill elaborated upon this theme. He laments the fact that the new twentieth century, already traumatized by the bloodiest war in history up to that time, suffered from a "marked lack of individual leadership." Whereas the Victorian age had "shone" with great statesmen, novelists, philosophers, and historians, the new age was governed by "blameless mediocrities" who do not compare well to their ancestors. Although science had progressed farther afield in this new age, it too had become a force for mediocrity in fashioning the technique that reduced most human beings to cogs within an administrative machinery. The much maligned Victorian age was a model of intellectual creativity compared to the new mass society, in which public opinion "is formed and expressed by machinery. The newspapers do an immense amount of thinking for the average man and woman." These media supply their readers "with such a continuous stream of standardized opinion" that "there is neither the need nor the leisure for personal reflection." The result is "enormous numbers of standardized citizens, all equipped with regulation opinions, prejudices, and sentiments, according to their class or party." Not all of this was bad. The "great diffusion of knowledge" that resulted from the mass production of literature was a true achievement, even though it was destructive of the "personal stress and mental effort" that characterized previous ages of enlightenment.[80]

One of the most shocking features of mass Western democracy is just how much it shared in common with its mortal enemy, communism. The Russian Bolsheviks carried this compulsion of the masses only to its "utmost extreme." The "Beehive" society that the Soviets forged in Russia after 1917 was only a particularly brutal example of the mass standardization that was already sweeping Western democracies.[81] What, then, did the leadership classes of the Western and communist regimes have in common?

Churchill notes that the "great emancipated nations" have become independent of famous guides and guardians. Instead, like their Bolshevik counterparts, they have reduced politics to what Lenin called "the administration of things." World War I had already prepared the ground for this revolution, since governments forged citizens into mass populations dedicated to the service of the state in war. To be sure, the war leaders felt themselves to be "uplifted above the general mass." Yet they could not be called heroes, since they made their decisions in anonymity, "banished from the fighting scene." The politicians of today are about as heroic as the leaders of vast corporations, who govern thousands of people as if they are mere automatons. War, politics, and business have become "mere office work." We now have "mass suffering, mass sacrifice, mass victory." Yet all this has been accomplished democratically. It is the "democratic plateau," armed with the tools of science and technology, that has reduced heroes and citizens to mere bureaucrats.[82]

At first glance, none of Churchill's pessimism about mass society should particularly trouble the defenders of Strauss. Daniel Mahoney, who has at least been influenced by the Straussian school, takes comfort from Churchill's cautiously optimistic view that the Bolsheviks have failed to replace human society with a society of collectivized ants. Since "human nature is more intractable than ant-nature," as Churchill assures his reader, there is still hope for humanity.[83] Strauss, who ultimately believed that the modern tyrant is even more dangerous than his ancient counterpart in attempting to re-create human nature with the power of modern science, may well have welcomed Churchill's views as expressed here.[84] Mahoney also concludes from his own reading of "Mass Effects in Modern Life" that great deeds performed by great men like Churchill are still possible, and even necessary, in "arousing democratic individuals from their slumbers."[85] Churchill reminds us of the "heights that politics, even democratic politics, may in principle attain."[86] Although Jaffa spends more time than Mahoney on Churchill's troubling admission that it was Western democracy, not Bolshevism, that first forged mass society and mass humanity, he also believes that the greatness of statesmen like Churchill offers the best chance of outshining the mediocrity that infects democracy.[87]

What both Jaffa and Mahoney reveal in their brief analyses of "Mass Effects in Modern Life" is an erroneous assumption that is characteristic of Strauss's thinking about democracy in general: *that the solution to the problems posed by mass democracy can be addressed by the greatness of a few individuals, whether they be philosophers or statesmen.* Yet Strauss's primary focus on the exceptional greatness of a few human beings is not well suited to understanding either Churchill or the problems of mass democracy. Strauss's distinctive understanding of this greatness is, ironically, incompatible with his hero's own analysis of history and the way in which power works.

In a couple of essays on the state of "liberal education" in a mass democracy, Strauss reveals that the primary solution to the leveling effects of this regime lies with a recovery of the "Great Works," specifically the works of Plato and Aristotle. In "Liberal Education and Responsibility," Strauss identifies the excellence of the ancient liberal tradition with these classics. Although he is too cautious to assert that the reading of these works is a "cure" for mass democracy and he gives no indication that a Platonic regime of philosopher-rule is possible, Strauss believes that the study of the classics is the "palliative" that is the best way of restoring political moderation to citizens in a liberal democracy. Even if the reading of these works will "remain the privilege and obligation of a minority," they will counter the temptation to embrace those immoderate enemies of liberal democracy Marx and Nietzsche. Strauss at least holds out the hope that "it may become true again that all liberally educated men will be politically moderate men. It is in this way that the liberally educated may yet again receive a hearing even in the market place."[88]

The caution that Strauss expresses in this essay contrasts rather sharply with the ambitions he expresses in "What Is Liberal Education?" Here Strauss expects that a "liberal education" will be the "counterpoison to mass culture, to the corroding effects of mass culture." Moreover, it is the "ladder by which we ascend from mass democracy to democracy as originally meant." The fact that liberal education will never be taken up by all human beings should not deter defenders of democracy, since the reading of the Great Works will lead to a new "aristocracy" that will teach "human greatness" to the citizens of mass democracy. Somehow, the most stultifying effects of mass culture, which is appropriated by the "meanest capacities," will give way to inspiring lessons on the great statesmen as well as the great philosophers.[89]

At first glance, Strauss's prescription for an aristocratic leadership to counter the vices of mass democracy sounds like old-fashioned conservatism. The preservation of ancient wisdom, which Strauss calls for, resonates with many conservatives to this day and even led to the initial impression that Strauss was attempting to restore the older tradition of natural law philosophy.[90] Moreover, in both essays on liberal education, Strauss calls for the "rule of gentlemen," or aristocratically minded individuals (like Churchill) who understand that there is more to life than material self-preservation. These individuals do not seek to reverse democratic rule. With a nod to Aristotle's *Politics*, Strauss contends that these men would re-create a "mixed regime" of aristocracy and democracy that will reinvigorate modern republicanism while it counters the low tastes of mass democracy.[91]

It should be clear by now that I do not share the views of Strauss's many leftist critics that he is proposing rule of democracy by an anti-liberal elite cadre of the Far Right. Once again, I take Strauss at his word when he celebrates "unhesitating loyalty to a decent constitution and even to the cause of constitutionalism."[92] His self-identification as a friend and ally, but not a flatterer, of democracy, is sincere.[93] As I have argued in previous chapters, Strauss is more modern than meets the eye here. His appeal to the premodern thought of the Western tradition, which is supposed to counter the leftist and rightist enemies of liberal democracy, rests on a rather romanticized version of the Greeks. Strauss is not even unique among twentieth-century liberals in claiming that new elites must govern mass democracy: as noted in chapter one, similar themes can be found in the works of Walter Lippmann and Reinhold Niebuhr, among others.[94] What is most pertinent to my discussion here, however, is whether Strauss's rather vague prescriptions bear any resemblance to Churchill's own understanding of modern history and the place of democracy within it.

It is striking that Strauss relies solely on intellectual means in order to counter the worst effects of mass democracy. Somehow the force of education alone will be the "counterpoison" to mass mediocrity, which breeds the deadly antidemocratic vices of communism and fascism. Yet it is never made exactly clear how all this is to be accomplished. A critical question that has been posed to Walter Lippmann's similar program for "liberal democratic regeneration" in the 1950s may be justly applied to Strauss as well: "How exactly does one create a civilized citizen with liberal virtues who will make a responsible use of freedom?"[95] The main reason, it seems to me, that Strauss cannot adequately answer this question is that his version of political science is not primarily concerned with the way in which institutions work. As we have seen, Strauss blames Machiavelli and his modern successors for shifting the focus away from "the formation of character to the trust in institutions."[96] Yet reliance on the virtue of those who teach about "human greatness" is a rather abstract strategy if they are up against mass forces that are already hostile to liberalism.[97]

Although I am not arguing against the value of careful and studious reading of Great Works within our intellectually impoverished democratic age, I question why this strategy is the most effective way of replacing mass democracy with liberal democracy. It is also far from obvious that Churchill himself understood the political reality of his time in such an intellectualized manner. Although Strauss and his students would heartily agree with Churchill's Victorian lament for a "real political democracy led by a hierarchy of statesmen, and not a fluid mass distracted by newspapers,"[98] it is unclear whether the statesmen to whom Churchill refers match up in any significant way to the idealized statesmen in the Straussian universe. What Manfred Weidhorn aptly describes as Churchill's own immersion in history probably fits Churchill's own understanding of what makes a statesman great.[99] Yet this quality led Churchill to understand modern history in two ways that Strauss and his followers would be compelled to reject.

First, it is well known that Churchill did not believe that all peoples are equally predisposed toward democratic rule or self-government. On the domestic front, Churchill often worried that the extension of the franchise to women or the lower classes would lead to a more socialist politics. Looking at the United States, in which he had ancestral roots on his mother's side, Churchill similarly believed that giving the vote to black Americans would beget a "sinister reaction."[100] On a wartime visit to America, Churchill surprised Vice President Henry Wallace with his racialist belief in "Anglo-Saxon superiority" as the necessary precondition for the successful spread of freedom around the world.[101] Nor were these just casual comments expressed in the heat of the political moment. In his *History of the English-Speaking Peoples*, Churchill doubted that "servile races" could throw off tyrannies, at least not without the assistance of English ideas and firepower.[102] Beyond the confines of Western civilization, peoples that had not experienced English influence were usually not capable of self-government (except perhaps the Japanese).[103]

Even peoples that had enjoyed some exposure to English principles were not necessarily inclined toward successful democratic rule, in Churchill's view. As the situation in India deteriorated in the 1930s, Churchill scorned the hypocrisy of the Brahmin class, who "mouth and patter the principles of Western Liberalism" while denying fundamental rights to the untouchables. It is quite apparent that Churchill thought the Great Works of philosophy would have no impact on this ruling elite in India, who cynically enjoyed "chopping logic with John Stuart Mill, or pleading the rights of man with Jean-Jacques Rousseau."[104] Churchill sounds positively Burkean in his outrage over the hypocrisy of the Brahmins. Burke famously used a similar argument against the Jacobins, whom he accused of laying down "metaphysic propositions" to an unprepared people while resorting to "barbarous tyranny" at the same time.[105] The Straussian hostility to Burke as a passive recipient of historical change is the exact opposite of Churchill's Burke, whose "soul revolted against tyranny" whether it was falsely justified in the name of democracy or monarchy.[106] Burke and Churchill are in full agreement over the need of peoples to inherit rights and duties from an historical tradition of their own making. Otherwise, the misuse of these rights for the purpose of violence and tyranny is inevitable.[107] The "historical jurisprudence" that Strauss spies in Burke's thought is, in Churchill's view, far preferable to the "metaphysical jurisprudence" that Straussians prefer.[108]

It may be tempting to respond that Strauss also occasionally doubts whether all human beings at all times can also embrace liberal democracy (see chapter one). In *Natural Right and History*, Strauss admits that the greatest teachers of natural right, both ancient and modern, recognize the basic anthropological truth that there are always "savage" human beings who do not fit perfectly into a civilized order. Strauss also defers to the historic fact that some nations may have a "greater natural fitness for political excellence" than others. Still, these passing remarks do not mitigate Strauss's far more egalitarian teaching that all human beings can understand the credos of natural right and thus become liberal democrats. In contrast to Paul Rahe and other Straussians, it is hard for me, however, to imagine how Churchill could have accepted the fundamental equality of all human beings by nature while he also stressed in detail the historical and religious differences that set human beings apart from each other. It is very likely that Churchill's "hierarchy of statesmen" required this rather historicist understanding of human diversity, as opposed to an egalitarian concept of human nature.

Second, it is far from clear that Churchill subscribes as closely to the "Great Man" theory of politics as his Straussian admirers do. As Weidhorn has rightly noted, there is a "lifelong oscillation" in Churchill's writings between his fascination with world-historical individuals and his resignation to historical determinism.[109] In his *History of the English-Speaking Peoples,* Churchill shows no reluctance to referring to "ruling classes" as one of the driving forces behind historical change in his native country. These "great men" are not necessarily virtuous. As Churchill soberly observes, in the long history of England it is evident that "capable rulers by their very virtues sow the seeds of future evil and weak or degenerate princes open the pathway of progress."[110] The class struggle between the landed classes and propertied (bourgeois) classes is one of the most defining historical dynamics, in Churchill's view, in such pivotal events as the rise of the Plantagenets or the Black Death.[111] In almost quasi-Marxian terms, Churchill also refers to the French Revolution as a victory for the "bourgeois" who had no interest in sharing power with the masses.[112] Even in his political speeches, the theme of class conflict is never far from his mind. Six years before the onset of World War I, Churchill lambasted employers in Britain for treating underemployed labor as a "surplus in a boom," only to be "flung back into the pool whenever there is a slump."[113]

This brief survey of Churchill's thoughts on the power of elites is particularly relevant to his understanding of mass democracy. Despite Churchill's oft-quoted statement that "democracy is the worst of all systems, except for all the others," his views on what distinguishes twentieth-century democracy from nineteenth-century liberalism are most relevant here. As a Victorian conservative, he lamented the passing of that "hierarchy of statesmen" who kept back the vices of mass rule and mass culture. Yet there is no evidence he thought that the tendency toward even greater massification was reversible, once that old elite had passed into history. (He certainly did not believe that "liberal education" could reverse this process.) Churchill's pessimism on the ineluctable rise of massification is remarkably similar to the thought of James Burnham, whose famous book *The Managerial Revolution* (1941) also gloomily predicted that a new "managerial elite" would displace the old bourgeois-capitalist order that defined the Victorian era.[114] This managerial elite, which is wedded to public administration and scientific technique, is practically identical to what Churchill describes as the "unheroic" managers of corporations and bureaucracies who are hostile to true individuality. Churchill understood as well as Burnham that this new managerial state was the fulfillment of democracy, not its antithesis.[115]

What also unites Churchill and Burnham is their agreement that mass democracy and Bolshevism are not fundamentally different in every sense. It is one of the central theses of Burnham's *Managerial Revolution* that the United States, under the New Deal, "moves in the same direction as Stalinism and Nazism."[116] Although some Straussians may accuse Burnham of practicing "moral equivalence," or the relativistic identification of a decent democracy with a vicious totalitarian regime, Burnham never suggests that the democratic features of America are identical to Soviet tyranny.[117] Nevertheless, the sheer centralization of control and knowledge in the hands of a small number of scientifically trained public administrators would sound the death knell for the bourgeois individualism that once resisted statist incursions into civil society.[118] What particularly joins the analyses of Churchill and Burnham is their prophecy that classical liberalism, including the "Tory defence of liberty," will be buried under the weight of the New Deal.[119] Although Churchill was far more nostalgic for the lost Victorian era than Burnham apparently was, both men faced with grim resignation the fact that the old liberal democratic regime was disappearing before their eyes. If that diagnosis is accurate, then why did Strauss and his students insist that "liberal democracy" was still alive, despite certain challenges (e.g., German historicism)?

It would be unfair to argue that Strauss and his students are completely oblivious to the displacement of constitutional liberalism by mass democracy in the twentieth century. Harry Jaffa, who spends more time than Mahoney in discussing Churchill's comparison of Western standardization with Bolshevism, even gloomily notes that "the regulation of opinion by the more impersonal process of standardization" in Western democracies may be more "insidious" and "more deadly to the soul," presumably be-

cause it is carried out with greater subtlety than it was in the far more brutal Soviet bloc.[120] Yet neither Jaffa nor Mahoney dwells sufficiently on the
full implications of Churchill's thoughts: that the old liberal tradition they
cherish, as Burnham also predicted, is long gone.[121]

Overall, it is not hard to imagine where Straussians generally would
stand on Burnham's ideas. Although Strauss admired Burnham's *Suicide of
the West* (1964) as a powerful indictment of modern liberalism's capitulation to Soviet communism, that is as far as his sympathy went.[122] Burnham's work on Machiavelli contrasted sharply with that of Strauss, since
Burnham ultimately accepted the Machiavellian view that power is the
plaything of ruling classes.[123] Although Strauss took pains to oppose this
Machiavellian influence on modern political thought, it is far from obvious
that Churchill would have abandoned his interest in class power merely for
the sake of an idealized "Great Man." It is even less apparent that Churchill
might have believed that the liberalism of the nineteenth century, which
Strauss ostensibly values, had survived the onslaught of massification. The
disintegration of English liberalism on the eve of World War I, which the
historian George Dangerfield so famously described, had far more to do
with pressures from the Left (e.g., the suffragette movement) and the Right
(e.g., the House of Lords) than with any philosophical abandonment of
Greek wisdom.[124]

I dwell on Churchill's focus on classes and historical forces in order
to sharpen the contrast between his concept of history and the Straussian image of Churchill as the "Great Man" who resisted the siren call of
historicism in his day. Significantly, one of Churchill's favorite writers was
the American historian Charles Beard, who took a similar approach to the
power of elites.[125] Yet this is the same historian whom Allan Bloom excoriates for undermining the American belief in the virtuous nature of the
Founding by stressing petty class interest as a prime motivation.[126] Perhaps
one reason that the students of Strauss have been silent on the historicism
of Churchill, aside from its incompatibility with a focus on the Great Man
and Great Works, is that these students are mainly American nationalists who are inclined to believe that America successfully transcended the
conflicts of the Old World. (Bloom's distaste with Beard's historiography
is perhaps an expression of this nationalism.) If this is the case, however,
then why should Strauss and his students reinvent Churchill as a statesman
wedded more to abstract slogans about the verities of democracy than to an
interest in the power of elites? It is not that Strauss and his students refrain

completely from the study of elite influence on political ideas. Strauss in his study of Hobbes categorized this English philosopher as a defender of bourgeois class interests. As already noted, some of his students have made similar claims about Spinoza (e.g., Martin Yaffe). Yet Straussians apply this reductionism to modern authors they dislike, not to heroes they celebrate. It is surely inconvenient to Straussians that Churchill, whom they portray as a statesman who acted and thought far above the concerns of class interests, actually understood history in terms that are hard to distinguish from the Hobbesian approach.

On a more practical level, it is hard to imagine how American mass democracy could ever accept the creation of a leadership class that, by Churchill's own admission, rested on the shoulders of a landed aristocracy and "country gentlemen."[127] If I have read Churchill correctly, this "ruling class" depended far more on their awareness of their historical distinctiveness as a people than on their exposure to the Great Works of antiquity. (This was certainly true of Churchill, as we have seen.) Despite the best efforts of Russell Kirk to argue that America also once had a Burkean aristocracy of the sort that Churchill thought indispensable, the predominantly Lockean capitalist nature of the republic arguably doomed that class to early extinction.[128] The very talk of a Burkean aristocracy would probably provoke derision from students of Strauss who have been hostile to Burke's historicism, partly on the grounds that he is hostile to a metaphysics of human nature.[129] Yet this historicism is no different from that of Churchill, who admired Burke as one of the greatest English conservatives of his time, without whom the defense of English tradition would have been inconceivable.

Strauss and his mostly American students may be guilty of what Churchill used to call an obsession with a "lofty Idea." This tendency, which Churchill spied as a particularly American one, rests on a love of abstractions at the expense of historical knowledge. It is well known that Churchill was impatient with Roosevelt's disdain for British imperialism, since it was driven by the rather naïve "Idea" that all peoples desire democratic rule.[130] The Straussian celebration of "liberal education" as the "counterpoison" to mass democracy may well have elicited a similar reaction from this great statesman.

From a Churchillian perspective, a leadership class of "Great Men" who do not understand their own historical distinctiveness may embrace the dangerous "Idea" that they represent all of humanity. In one of the few places in which Strauss, at least in his American period, refers to the "class interest" of particular philosophers throughout history, he describes this interest as simply the "desire to be left alone" to investigate the timeless questions.[131] It is far from apparent that the students of Strauss, who have often been able to wield some political influence, have consistently expressed this "desire to be left alone."[132] Perhaps the greatest irony here, however, is that the Straussian love of "liberal education" has often discouraged the asking of at least one timeless question that was of great interest to their hero Churchill: how exactly does the "Great Man" preserve his own historical tradition in a mass democratic age without a good dose of historicism?

5

The Anglo-American
Struggle with Strauss

The impact of Leo Strauss's ideas has been mainly although not exclusively felt in the Anglo-American world. In order to understand the various reasons behind this phenomenon, it is instructive to examine political philosophers who were influenced by his ideas. The Canadian conservative George Grant (1918–1988) and the American conservative Willmoore Kendall (1909–1967) come to mind precisely because they were, for a time, far more receptive to Strauss's ideas than those of any other twentieth-century thinker, despite the fact that neither man was a student of Strauss. Additionally, Grant and Kendall, who even corresponded with Strauss, discovered him when they were already established defenders of the conservative traditions in their respective nations. Despite their diverse backgrounds, both men had a common enemy in liberalism. Grant, a Tory descendant of the Loyalists who had fled the newly established American republic,[1] was determined to defend the surviving remnants of a conservatism that American liberalism threatened to confine to the dustbin of

history. Kendall, an American from the Oklahoma heartland, was a populist defender of majoritarian democracy who was equally determined to
preserve conservatism from the liberal establishment that threatened to
adulterate its meaning. Grant and Kendall also shared a Protestant heritage
that, as I shall argue, in part explains their attraction to Straussian political philosophy. Although Kendall converted to Catholicism late in life and
Grant was often a harsh critic of his ancestral faith, both men saw in the
Straussian hermeneutic a promising way of preserving what was best in the
Anglo-American Protestant tradition. Yet their embrace of Straussian ideas
was fateful, since they chose to support a political philosophy that is profoundly anti-conservative in its implications. The dramatic conflict between
conservatism and Straussian thought that shows up in the writings of these
distinguished conservatives serves as a warning for anyone on the Right who
is tempted to confuse Straussianism with Anglo-American conservatism.

George Grant's Journey from Protestantism to Straussianism

In 1947, the Canadian historian Harold Innis lamented the state of Christianity in his country. In his view, the Protestant churches in particular had
embraced an anti-intellectualism that was extremely detrimental to the vitality of the faith. Having lost its "curiosity for ideas," the Church was in
danger of being intellectually uninteresting to Canadians. In particular, the
churches had ignored the timeless lessons of ancient Greece—according
to Innis, who was raised in the Baptist tradition. The Greek preoccupation with the "training of character" had been entirely lost on the modern
church in Canada, which was instead overly preoccupied with the fashionable social issues of the day. This indifference to this important founding tradition of Western civilization would only doom the church to irrelevance and mediocrity. Nothing less than the survival of the West was at
stake: "The problem of the Church is the problem of Western civilization."[2]
    One of Innis's most admiring readers heartily agreed with these senti-
ments and tenaciously sought an alternative to the stagnant Protestantism
of his time. George Parkin Grant, like Innis, was well aware that his fellow
Protestants had lost the spiritual vitality their ancestors once possessed.
Grant was determined to look beyond his ancestral faith to remedy the
defects of modern Christianity, which had led to the triumph of parochi-
alism over true wisdom. The future of the modern university, which was

becoming enslaved to the imperatives of modern science and big business, was also at stake. Grant commended Innis for reminding both churches and universities alike that "the pure desire to know" is the true animating force of inquiry both religious and secular.[3] For this reason, it was essential to rediscover the timeless wisdom of Hellas.

No study of the relation between Strauss and Anglo-American universalism is complete without a discussion of George Grant, for this distinguished Tory nationalist and Anglican Christian political philosopher introduced Canadians to the ideas of Strauss in the post–World War II era. The reader does not have to look far to find the most effusive praise for Strauss in Grant's writings. In 1960, when Grant made the painful decision to resign from his teaching position at York University (which had demanded he teach a textbook that ridiculed Christianity), he praised Strauss as "the philosopher I admire most" and a "better philosopher than any practicing Christian I know on this continent."[4] Six years later, in an appendix to the new edition of his work *Philosophy in the Mass Age*, Grant enthused: "I count it a high blessing to have been acquainted with this man's thought."[5] At the deepest philosophical level, Grant credited Strauss with inspiring a massive intellectual sea-change in his own thought. Before Strauss, Grant had considered himself a Hegelian defender of progress. After studying Strauss's critique of progress and his call for a recovery of classical political philosophy, Grant rejected his old view that moderns "had overcome the inadequacies of ancient thought." In fact, Strauss had taught Grant that the ancients understood truths about both nature and the good that had been obscured by modern political philosophers.[6]

It is tempting to ask why Christians like Grant have even bothered to study a political philosopher who wrote so little on Christianity. (Recall Strauss's view that philosophers who claim to be Christian are being insincere.) In the case of George Grant, reasons for valuing Strauss are not so mysterious since, like many postwar conservatives (including, at least for a time, his fellow Tory philosopher Russell Kirk),[7] Grant understood Strauss as a traditional defender of the old classical virtues that had been most brilliantly articulated in the works of Plato and Aristotle. Most important for my discussion, Grant's disenchantment with the Anglo-Canadian tradition in which he grew up led him to Strauss. The irony is that Grant, in search of a truly respectable conservatism, unwittingly embraced an ideology that was even more radical than the Hegelian progressivism that once enchanted him.

Strauss put little value in the liberal Protestantism that influenced the theology of the modern age (see chapter three). Although the "starting point of Grant's life and thought was the liberal pragmatic Protestantism of the Canadian middle and upper classes between the world wars,"[8] Grant had also turned against this tradition by the 1950s. The difference between Grant and Strauss, however, is that Grant actually grew up within a strongly liberal Protestant tradition firsthand. Grant's ancestors, who still retained the old Loyalist suspicion of the United States, were fervent defenders of the British Empire as the glorious instrument of both God and civilization (in fact, the two were often identified). Grant was the grandson of two of the most prominent Tory nationalists in Canadian history. Sir George Parkin, his maternal grandfather, was the onetime headmaster of Upper Canada College in Toronto, a school whose sole purpose was to groom young Canadian men to take their place in the establishment. Parkin described himself as a "wandering evangelist of Empire" who was confident that British imperialism would civilize the world. Grant's paternal grandfather and president of the establishmentarian Queen's University, George Monro Grant was an unabashed Anglo-Saxon progressivist who also believed that the spread of British ideas was the work of divine providence. When Grant described Maude Parkin, his mother, as a "secularized Protestant who didn't believe a word of Christianity" even as she maintained her family's belief in progress through Anglo-Saxon hegemony, he was accurately describing the typical sentiments of nineteenth-century English Canada as a whole.[9]

Despite the nativistic sentiments expressed by many of Grant's Tory ancestors, there was also a sincere liberal belief in the equality of all human beings. At times Grant seemed to struggle with the tension between the conservative love of particular traditions and the universalistic demands of Christianity.[10] Yet he saw in Canadian Protestantism the uneasy, though attractive, conflation of English tradition and Christianity. Even if Grant turned away from the naïve optimism of the Victorian era, he never abandoned the egalitarianism that went along with this tradition.[11] Grant attributed this belief in equality to Christianity, the only faith known to him that taught there was something "intrinsically valuable" in all people.[12] This egalitarianism went hand in hand with Victorian imperialism, which called for the spread of civilization to all the corners of the world precisely because it fulfilled the Christian belief that all human beings are children of God. Even though these Canadian imperialists made a distinction between "stronger" and "weaker" races, they did not doubt that all peoples deserved the blessings of Anglo-Christian civilization.[13] Nor did these imperialists always support the violent imposition of British ideals on non-British peoples. Many took pride in the fact that Anglo-Saxon imperialism encouraged "the emergence of local nationalisms" and the preservation of cultural "diversity" among subject peoples.[14] Long after Grant abandoned his belief in progress, he still believed that the original genius of Canada lay in respecting the rights of different peoples—especially the Quebecois.[15] This Canadian manifestation of tolerance was also appreciated by Winston Churchill who, on a visit to Canada in 1929, praised the British way of life for allowing French Canadians to dwell "happily and in perfect freedom" within the empire while preserving their distinct identity, language, and history.[16] By the post–World War II era, this celebration of diversity had evolved into hostility toward any claim to Anglo-Saxon superiority. What Peter Brimelow calls progressivism of a "familiar Anglo-American type" led to the liberal view that "nationalism is ultimately an uncouth, reactionary and probably racist atavism, valuable only as a demolition tool."[17] How did all this happen?

The carnage of World War I led Grant as well as many of his countrymen to turn away from the most brazenly optimistic beliefs of their ancestral English tradition. Grant blamed the "Great War" for killing so many of the best English-speaking Canadians who had the talent and imagination to build a truly autonomous Canadian nation. The fact that the war also gravely weakened Britain and put it on the road to becoming a junior partner of the United States had a tremendous impact on Canadians who had once loyally believed in the enduring principles and power of the empire. Many of these Canadians had fought and died in the war, believing that "they were thereby guaranteeing freedom and justice in the world." Grant, who had been born two days after the signing of the armistice that ended World War I, was convinced that this war had been an imperialist struggle that had sealed Canada's fate as a satellite of the nation that succeeded Britain as the new hegemonic power in the world.[18]

Yet Grant also believed that there were deeper *religious* reasons for the "disappearance" of the once cherished hope that his country could one day become a nation all its own, free of empires both monarchist and republican. The descendants of the liberal Protestants who had forged a nation out of a wilderness and supported the egalitarian imperialism of empire were abandoning the dream of an autonomous Canada in favor of integration with the United States. By the 1940s, Grant was alarmed that the rapid modernization of Ontario, once the cradle of Canadian Toryism, was turning a bastion of conservatism into an outpost of American progressivism. Yet all this was being accomplished without firing a shot. Grant believed that the Protestant tradition of his ancestors had played a fateful role in softening up Canada for takeover. What were his reasons for such a blistering accusation?

In *Philosophy in the Mass Age* (1959), Grant turned his attention toward the Calvinist tradition that had had so much influence in shaping the currents of modernity. Although he credited Calvinism with an egalitarianism that challenged the stifling effect of Catholic hierarchy, this spirit of equality contributed to the most homogenizing effects of postwar liberalism. The modern Calvinist teaching that all human beings are equally willful creatures (which is not necessarily an accurate reflection of classical Calvinist theology) was, as Max Weber famously argued, a necessary catalyst for capitalism. This version of Calvinism eventually morphed into American pragmatism, which sought the eradication of all traditional and hierarchical barriers to progress and the open society. William James and John Dewey, in Grant's view, were similar to his Protestant ancestors who no longer believed in God yet clearly believed in progress.[19] By the 1960s, Grant's disdain for this decayed Protestant tradition had crystallized into a critique of modernity itself. Although he credited the earliest Protestant capitalists for liberating human beings from poverty and hunger, Grant also blamed Calvinism for creating a capitalism that not only dissolved all tradition but also manufactured a nightmarish technological society in which large governments and corporations made a mockery of words like "liberty," "individualism," and "equality" as they sought control over the lives of millions. It was bad enough, Grant pointed out in tones reminiscent of Innis, that these Protestants had no interest in the wisdom of the Greeks. It was even worse that they had little interest in preserving their own faith tradition. The "rough" Protestantism of America, with its "driving will to righteousness" drained of any caution or humility, had created a modern society that no longer even needed to pay lip service to the old Christian tradition. A faith in "providential intervention" effectively replaced the old orthodox Catholic and Anglican belief in miracles, only to be displaced by a belief in human will.[20]

I have briefly discussed Grant's preoccupation with the defective Protestantism of his time in order to provide some context to help explain his attraction to Straussian ideas. It is no accident that he gravitated toward

Strauss even as he was leaving his liberal Protestant past forever. What Grant sought was a sense of permanence, of timeless standards that remained true and absolute, above and beyond the chaotic dynamism of the American Protestant civilization that was engulfing his beloved Canada. Although he and his wife, Sheila, joined the Anglican Church of Canada in the 1950s, he recognized that Protestantism as a whole was not sufficient for the task of inspiring this awareness of the eternal things. Protestantism, after all, had massively contributed to the most corrosive effects of modernity.

It may at first glance be odd to connect Strauss and Grant so closely, in light of their apparent major differences over Anglo-American civilization. To be sure, Grant agreed with Strauss that the famed moderation of the English had rendered them, for a time, immune to the radical currents of modern philosophy that emanated from France and Germany.[21] Grant, unlike Strauss, however, never identified English ideals with the eternal principles of humanity. Moreover, Grant was deeply hostile to Churchill who, Strauss believed, defended these ideals more resolutely than any other Englishman. Far from being the virtuous classical statesman that Strauss and his students take him to be, Grant blamed Churchill, as a member of the Liberal Cabinet in 1914, for goading the English into the "intemperance" of World War I.[22] Grant even believed that Churchill may have hastened the demise of Canada as he moved Britain more closely (often more out of necessity than choice) into the orbit of the United States.[23] None of this was evidence of higher principle in Churchill who, Grant believed, was a fairly typical Anglo-Saxon racialist.[24]

Grant was also far more critical of Protestantism than Strauss was, precisely because he assigned a more powerful role to this faith tradition in Western political thought. Although Strauss was very critical of liberal theology, he did not spy an orthodox Protestant root in its foundations. Strauss was skeptical of talk of "secularization," or the popular twentieth-century thesis that all modern ideas were secular versions of biblical credos. Moreover, he chastised Eric Voegelin for confusing liberalism (in the guise of Spinoza's philosophy) with the Protestant tradition.[25] Yet Grant constantly emphasized that the most important ideologies of his time enjoyed a Protestant root. It was not only Calvinism in its American guise that was instrumental in fostering the triumph of the technological will to power. Protestantism as a whole had "become a tame confederate of the mass secular society."[26] Although Grant did not crudely identify Protestantism with modern liberalism, due to the stark historic differences between the stern morality of the former and the libertine ethic of the latter, he clearly thought that one had shaped the other in history. The tragedy of this process was that liberals no longer needed the Christian morality that once provided a moral foundation for their ideology: they were now free to embrace technological progress at the expense of vulnerable human beings (such as the unborn).[27] From a Straussian perspective, Grant was unduly emphasizing the influence of faith on modern political ideas that, frankly, had a secular (e.g., Machiavellian) root. Unlike Grant, Strauss never would have accepted at face value the apparent religiosity of modern political philosophers. Hobbes's profession of an Anglican faith, for example, did not persuade Strauss he was being sincere.[28]

Differences over Churchill and Protestantism aside, there are deeper distinctions between Strauss and Grant, at least in the eyes of Grant's defenders. Wayne Whillier believes that Grant's belief in Christian equality contrasts sharply with Strauss's embrace of the Greek notion of "natural difference."[29] Arthur Davis contends that "Grant drew the line against the Straussians on the Vietnam War, on the need to defend liberal democracy with the sword, and on their account of religion as inferior to philosophy and as a means of deceiving the people to keep them in order."[30] Gad Horowitz, who famously attributed to both Grant and his conservative ancestors a "Red Toryism" that challenged American liberalism, portrays Grant as an enemy of "capitalist inequality" who never would have sympathized with the Straussian love for elites and class-divided social orders.[31] There is some truth to all of these claims. It is true that Grant opposed the Vietnam War as an inevitable, genocidal outcome of American empire and liberal ideology.[32] It is also correct that Grant was genuinely puzzled by Strauss's "remarkable reticence" and even "contempt" for "certain forms of Biblical religion." Perhaps for this reason, Grant in the final years of his life gravitated toward the philosophy of Eric Voegelin, due to his perception that Voegelin wrote more profoundly than Strauss on the relation between philosophy and faith.[33] Horowitz is, like Drury, typically leftist in exaggerating the anti-egalitarianism of Strauss and his students. The fact that Strauss believes in "wise elites" does not make him utterly opposed to every kind of equality. Still, it is correct that Strauss, unlike Grant, never would have attributed the belief in human equality to Christianity alone—an act of historicism.

These criticisms leveled by Grant's leftist defenders, however, represent a classic case of missing the forest for the trees.[34] The differences between

Strauss and Grant over Anglo-American foreign policy in the twentieth century are far less important than their shared love of *universalism*. Whatever misgivings Grant had toward his ancestral Protestant tradition, he never abandoned the old Christian view that the truth is accessible to all human beings. Given his distaste for a Protestantism that had advanced capitalism and technological nihilism, Grant was naturally attracted to Strauss's position that the political philosophy of Plato provided an understanding of eternity that was desperately needed in an age of crude Hegelian progressivism.

In the one essay that Grant devoted to a discussion of Strauss's ideas, he took sides with Strauss against Alexandre Kojève, the famous Marxist interpreter of Hegel. Strauss and Kojève, who engaged in a debate in the late 1940s over the proper meaning of Xenophon's *Hiero*, appeared to offer positions that were starkly opposed to each other, at least in Grant's view. Strauss was a defender of Plato, the defender of trans-historical standards of justice and virtue that eschewed any utopian attempt to conquer or reinvent human nature. Kojève was the defender of Left-Hegelianism, who in true historicist fashion denied that any eternal standards existed and affirmed that the march of history had made Platonic philosophy obsolete. Grant took Strauss to be a true defender of classical tradition when he read Strauss's attack on the "universal homogeneous state," a global entity that threatened to impose a Stalinist leveling of all human beings, great and mediocre, into one common mass of self-satisfied consumers.[35]

Grant was careful not to call Strauss an unequivocal conservative since, in his view, conservatism was complicit with the modern project to advance progress toward the tyranny of the universal homogeneous state.[36] Grant's reticence here may also be due to his suspicion, as expressed in his essay on Strauss and Kojève, that Strauss did not completely disagree with his radical interlocutor on the history of political philosophy. Grant even wonders why Strauss does not challenge Kojève's view that philosophy in its modern manifestation had succeeded in demonstrating that all ideas at least in modernity must be understood as historical epiphenomena. The most disturbing upshot of Strauss's implicit acceptance of this rather historicist position is that Christianity itself may be a mere "worldly" phenomenon that has no access to eternity.[37] Nevertheless, Grant still understands Strauss as a Platonist who was sufficiently conservative to oppose the leveling egalitarianism of modernity, particularly its slavish promise to make all human beings into philosophers. Strauss's elitist view that only the wise few can embrace the philosophical life satisfied Grant that he was a true opponent of modernity's most radical currents.[38] What he failed to detect in Strauss, however, is the presence of a universalism that is at least as anti-conservative as that of Kojève.

Even though Grant was preoccupied with the fragile survival of his own country in an age of progress, he seemed to agree with Strauss that it was parochial for conservatives to appeal to the merely ancestral. Perhaps for this reason, Grant concluded *Lament for a Nation* with the admission that his "lament" was based on mere tradition, which is not the same as a philosophically respectable position.[39] Such a position, Grant thought, could be found in Strauss, who contended that true (Platonic) philosophy appealed to Nature, not to the ancestral or traditional. Moreover, this understanding of natural right was the most viable opposition to the leveling effects of the universal homogeneous state.[40]

What Grant missed, however, in Strauss's critique of this global tyranny is Strauss's admission that he was a *liberal* "in the original sense of the term."[41] Sympathetic readers of Grant's essay have also failed to understand, like Grant, that Strauss's rejection of "modern liberalism" is not a rejection of liberalism, or even modernity, altogether.[42] The difference, however, between Grant's conservatism and Strauss's liberalism comes through dramatically in their distinct critiques of liberalism itself. At first glance, their attacks on liberalism seem identical. Liberalism presumably spawns too much "openness" or "tolerance" toward ideas that are relativistic and even nihilistic. Sympathetic readers of Grant understand his attack on modernity to be one that rejects the liberal assumption that modern philosophy accepts all ideas as equally good.[43] Yet Strauss makes a sharper distinction between old and new liberalism than Grant ever did. Whereas Grant believes that liberalism in toto leads to relativism, Strauss believes that the older liberalism based on natural right imposes limits on diversity and individuality or, in short, rejects relativism.[44] This respect for a liberalism based on natural right is a key Straussian teaching that Grant ignored, due to his willingness to see Strauss as a Platonist (and therefore anti-liberal). If I am correct in arguing that Grant never understood Strauss's devotion to liberalism, then it is not hard to understand why Grant never grasped the full implications of Strauss's anti-historicism. Ever since the early years of his American exile during World War II, Strauss opposed liberalism for being "open" to ideas that were cherished by conservatives such as Grant. When Strauss condemns the "open society," he is warning liberals not to be open to nihilistic ideas that undermine liberal democracy.[45] (In Straussian terms, this amounts to openness to the "cave" of historicism.) These ideas include devotion to ancestral and historicist ideas. Unbeknownst to Grant, these ideas also include traditional conservatism.

The irony is that Grant fled from a corrosive liberalism, based on a decayed Protestantism, toward an alternative that is even more radical. In *Time as History* (1969), Grant fully reveals his indebtedness to Straussian hermeneutics. In this series of lectures on the impact of Nietzsche's philosophy on modernity, Grant reveals his absolute acceptance of Strauss's vilification of "historicist" thinking. The "historical sense" that Nietzsche so profoundly defended disastrously displaced any appeals to a higher "nature," and thus any understanding of what is good for all of humanity.[46] The elevation of History to the place of absolute authority meant that all actions, good and bad, could be justified according to the currents of historical change.

Grant drew certain conclusions from this critique of historicism that are, admittedly, out of sync with the Straussian love for an interventionist American foreign policy. Grant scorned Lyndon Johnson's remark that "History will judge my Vietnam policies" as vehemently as he castigated American political scientists like David Easton for failing to spy any connection between historicism and American empire-building.[47] Nevertheless, the Vietnam War was not the worst effect of modern historicism. Grant drew a straight line between historicism and the triumph of Nazism. Recalling his impression of Leni Riefenstahl's infamous documentaries of the Nazi era, Grant implicated radical historicists like Nietzsche and Heidegger in paving the way for the most monstrous regime in the twentieth century. Like Strauss, Grant believed that historicism led to Nazism because it had taught that there is nothing good or bad according to human nature. If this is the case, then there is no reason to reject what Grant calls Nietzsche's "spirit of revenge." Historicism erases any distinction between the noble and the vulgar. If there is no higher natural standard of greatness to which all human beings ought to aspire, then humanity must descend to the level of beasts. Grant ominously warns: "if one wants to understand what Nietzsche means by history, one must look at what he means by revenge."[48]

This argument fits very well into a Straussian hermeneutic. In *The Closing of the American Mind*, Allan Bloom devotes an entire chapter to the pernicious effects of the old German Right on the American liberal tradition. Although Grant had more respect for the New Left than Bloom did, both men, who shared a friendship, seemed to agree that the nihilism of the 1960s was attributable to German thought.⁴⁹ Grant sounds particularly Straussian when he also condemns the tendency of modern liberals to embrace the pure subjectivity of values. From this vantage point, Grant believed that the only alternative to the relativism and historicism that predictably sprang from this subjectivism was a rediscovery of Platonic eternity.⁵⁰ As a result Grant, like many postwar conservatives who embraced Strauss, put far more importance in the power of ideas than in historical forces. Although Grant occasionally scorned the New Left for failing to grasp the awesome power of institutions to co-opt dissent in a capitalist society, and he even displayed some interest in the institutional studies of the Frankfurt School (especially Marcuse),⁵¹ he ultimately believed that a focus on the historical context of ideas was a surrender to historicism. I am not the first reader of Grant to point out that he showed insufficient interest in the way that institutions actually make use of ideas in historical contexts.⁵² Nevertheless, my own reading perhaps uniquely emphasizes that Grant's infatuation with Straussian ideas contributed in large part to this lack of interest. It is well known to readers of Strauss that he taught the hard lesson that the study of institutions and historical contexts plays into the hands of Machiavelli, who was the first modern to reject the "eternal" ideals and pave the way for the triumph of historicism.⁵³

Ultimately, Grant did not comprehend the full implications of abandoning or demonizing historicism. Once this traditional defense of conservatism disappears, to which standard can one appeal as a protector of one's traditions? As a Christian, Grant wondered why Strauss paid so little attention to the most important faith tradition of the West.⁵⁴ It was also puzzling to Grant that Strauss opposed any synthesis of the traditions of Athens and Jerusalem and gave the impression that he valued reason more than revelation. Strauss's insistence that the philosopher be freed from revelation might possibly have reminded Grant of Protestants like Niebuhr who insisted that belief be freed from reason. Grant opposed any claim of "an inevitable split between Christianity and reason."⁵⁵ Yet it is lamentable that he failed to understand the connection between Strauss's antihistoricism and his avoidance of Christianity. Unlike Protestant theologians like Niebuhr, Strauss did not oppose the synthesis of Platonic Athens and Christian Jerusalem simply because he believed that revelation has no need for rational justification (although he sometimes gives that impression). Rather, he opposes any attempt to suggest that a philosophy of Nature requires the foundation of an historically particular faith.

Strauss thus opposes any attempt by Christian thinkers to portray Western civilization's necessary indebtedness to the faith, although some of his students have been much bolder than he was in pressing this point. This fact may be the real reason behind Strauss's rejection of Thomistic philosophy. Although Clark Merrill, like Gad Horowitz, believes Strauss is an elitist who opposes Christianity, and Aquinas in particular, simply because the scholastic tradition is more egalitarian than the Platonic-Aristotelian tradition, this critique misses the more fundamental point: Strauss seeks a universal philosophy that is intelligible to all human beings.[56] As he makes clear in *Natural Right and History*, it is difficult enough to reconcile the tough nature of biblical morality with the ethical "latitude" that statesmen require in the rough-and-tumble world of politics. Worst of all, the Thomistic identification of the virtuous life with Christianity, which then conflates the best regime with the City of God, obscures the classical teaching that by nature all human beings can understand the good.[57] Since Christianity is not universal, in light of its denial of nature's authority it cannot be the basis for truly eternal ideals. For this reason, some of Strauss's students and followers have vigorously pursued anyone who dares to argue that a Christian identity may be needed for the survival of liberal self-government. Ernest Fortin, for example, faults his fellow Catholic philosopher Frederick Wilhelmsen for seeking, in historicist fashion, "to ground philosophy in the experience of a particular tradition."[58]

In the context of North American politics, anyone who dares to associate Canada or the United States with a Protestant identity that is necessary for the proper functioning of liberal democracy faces Straussian attack. This treatment has been posthumously meted out to Grant himself. In her study of the Lockean foundations of the Canadian Founding, Janet Ajzenstat, a former student of Allan Bloom, takes aim at Grant for emphasizing the Protestant origins of this great event. Instead of focusing on "whether these ideas and institutions were universally good," Grant erroneously zeroed in on the tendency of the English-speaking Fathers of Confederation to embrace "their own," the English Protestant majority of the time. In her view (which is not substantiated by any textual evidence), Grant embraces a rather harsh "millenarian" Protestantism that encourages rulers to build a rigid theocratic hierarchy and to fear hellfire rather than the will of the populace. Ajzenstat's version of Grant, which inaccurately portrays him as a theocrat, also reflects the Straussian position that Christianity has no essential place in the politics of a modern liberal democracy today (even if it is historically important).[59] In a similar vein, Francis Fukuyama faulted Peter Brimelow, in a debate over open immigration in the 1990s, for emphasizing the "ethnic" (e.g., Anglo-Saxon) roots of American culture. Brimelow's apparent error was to link far too closely the culture of America with the particular ethnicity of one group.[60]

The irony here is that Grant was more Straussian than his supporters and detractors admit. Since Grant uncritically embraced Strauss's anti-historicism, he missed an historic opportunity to defend what was fundamentally good about the Canadian polity. To be sure, it is possible to spy in his writings the makings of a response. Despite his misgivings over his ancestral Protestant tradition, he never abandoned the belief in human equality that he thought was inseparable from its Christian origin. It was far from obvious that people would "go on believing in this principle" without sharing in the Christian tradition.[61] Indeed, the rise of legalized abortion in the 1970s persuaded him that the decline in traditional Christian belief would open the door to the cruelest actions.[62] The rise of a multicultural and multireligious Canada has also sparked some fear that not all cultural communities can effectively assimilate what is left of the old conservative Canadian ethic that Grant admired, however ambivalently.[63] If Anglo-American civilization truly loses its historic adherence to Protestantism, what will happen to the universalism that Strauss and so many others admire? Can there be universalism without the faith that brought it into being? Although Grant asked these questions, it never occurred to him that Straussian ideas were part of the problem rather than the solution.

The fashionable liberal view today is that Christianity has now become secularized, that in fact liberalism has retained the best of Christian morality minus the superstitious belief in God. Indeed, that is the position of the prominent liberal political scientist Michael Ignatieff, Grant's nephew, who, in acknowledging the Christian origins of human rights, cheerfully assures his readers that a "concept of the sacred" is no longer needed to teach charity and respect for all human beings.[64] As readers of Grant well know, he poured immense scorn on a "secularized Christianity," freed of the sacred, that did nothing to prevent the killing of the unborn.[65] Although Fukuyama, Leon Kass, and other students of Strauss have made comments similar to those of Ignatieff, it is not obvious that even Strauss himself would be so optimistic. As we have seen,

Strauss was fond of quoting Nietzsche on the futility of believing in biblical morality if one no longer believes in the biblical God. If the God of revelation no longer commands belief or adherence, can a universal morality based on natural right alone survive?[66] Although this question haunted George Grant to the end of his life, he never saw fit to scrutinize Strauss's role in marginalizing the essential importance of the Christian influence on this morality.

Willmoore Kendall and the Uniqueness of America

Although American students of Leo Strauss sincerely praise both Winston Churchill and English civilization for their virtuous stance against the forces of nihilism (namely, early twentieth-century Germany), they have often taken pains to distinguish the political ideas of the republic from those of England. In *How to Think about the American Revolution* (1978), Harry Jaffa contends that the Declaration of Independence owed absolutely nothing to an English heritage.[67] The author of this document, Thomas Jefferson, was defending a wholly original regime, a republic that unambiguously rejected the British monarchy against which the revolutionaries waged war. Moreover, the Declaration promulgated the rights of all human beings, not merely Englishmen. The Americans of the eighteenth century were true revolutionaries, not conservatives defending an illegitimate and discredited regime.[68]

At first glance, it may sound contradictory for Jaffa to deny the English influence on the American Revolution while he and other students of Strauss heap praise upon English civilization as the repository of eternal democratic ideals. Yet it is only an apparent contradiction that is easily resolved from a Straussian perspective. Jaffa defends Churchill and English civilization precisely because, in their defiance of Hitler in 1940, they manifested the eternally good, not simply the ancestral (e.g., English tradition). As fierce critics of historicism, which, in its conservative guise, appeals to what is merely traditional or customary, Strauss and Jaffa would never admire the English simply because they were English. It would, then, be a typical historicist error to portray the American Revolution as an exercise in recycling English principles, since this misrepresentation would undermine the eternal significance of its principles. The Americans of 1776 and the English of 1940 were standing up for unchanging democratic ideals, not the parochial concerns of their cultures.[69] Jaffa's argument naturally appeals to Americans who celebrate not only the utter originality of the American Revolution but also the new kind of conservatism that this earth-shattering event brought into being. For this reason, Strauss's anti-historicism and his praise for the natural right tradition have particularly resonated with Americans who believe that, for the first time in history, a people brought "nature down from the realm of philosophy" and introduced it "into the political world as the foundation of a new nation."[70]

Willmoore Kendall stands out as a classic example of an American conservative who became captivated by the anti-historicist message of Strauss and his students on these grounds. An influential figure in the postwar Right, Kendall dedicated his life to understanding what was truly unique about the American Founding.[71] Kendall was as opposed as his friend Jaffa to any suggestion that American ideas could not have emerged without a foundation in English history. American conservatism was that novel paradox that, to the surprise of the old Right of Europe, forever put an end to the quarrel between the elites and the people. (Unlike his fellow contributors at *National Review* in the 1950s and 1960s, Kendall was the sole anti-elitist.)[72] The genius of American democracy was to trust the "deliberate sense" of "We, the People" precisely because the people were conservative.[73] For this reason, Kendall insisted that a distinctively American political tradition was well established by 1776, and it had nothing to do with Edmund Burke.[74]

Why is a focus on Kendall's thought justified in this study of Strauss and Anglo-American democracy? As I shall argue, Kendall is an instructive example of an Anglo-American conservative who misunderstood Strauss as a conservative when he confused the latter's anti-historicism with a respectably conservative position. As a result, his conservatism often gets bogged down in a struggle to reconcile Strauss's universalism with Anglo-Protestant conservatism. Although it has already been pointed out that Kendall fails to understand that Strauss saw himself as a liberal, not as a conservative (see chapter two), there has been insufficient discussion of two important factors in their relationship.[75] First, why was Kendall, a conservative, drawn to an unconservative thinker? Second, to what extent did Kendall's own version of Anglo-American conservatism ultimately clash with Strauss's repudiation of the ancestral?

Kendall's Journey toward Straussianism

The respect that Kendall had for Strauss seems to have been reciprocated. Strauss, who carried on an eighteen-year correspondence with Kendall, once described him as "the best native theorist of your generation," a high compliment that he rarely bestowed on anyone.[76] Despite Strauss's popularity with the postwar Right, Kendall was the only prominent conservative with whom Strauss had a friendship. It is no exaggeration that Kendall was "the most (if not the only) eminent convert" to Strauss's ideas among American political scientists at the time.[77] Other noteworthy conservatives of the time were far less predisposed to Strauss. William F. Buckley Jr., in an introduction to an anthology of postwar American conservative works that included essays by Strauss and his former students, praised Strauss as "one of the most influential teachers of our age" while slyly noting that it is questionable to assume that there is such a thing as a "former" student of Strauss.[78] In any case, Buckley showed little sustained interest in Strauss beyond these sentiments. Kendall's other colleagues at *National Review* were either indifferent or downright hostile to Strauss. Russell Kirk, who was initially impressed with what he took to be Strauss's defense of the natural law tradition, later turned against the Straussian preoccupation with Lockeanism as the principal philosophy of the American Founding.[79] Although we have already noted that Strauss admired James Burnham's *Suicide of the West* for its incisive critique of liberalism, Burnham did not reciprocate any interest in Strauss, despite the fact that both he and Strauss had written influential studies of Machiavelli in the postwar era. It is likely that Strauss's belief in timeless virtues left Burnham, an arch-historicist student of realpolitik, rather cold.[80] Frank Meyer, another longtime contributor to *National Review*, disliked the statist implications of Straussian philosophy, which upheld the ideal of the ancient polis at the expense of individual liberty.[81]

Kendall, however, had nothing but high praise for Strauss, whose works he called "not required reading but Scripture for everyone who likes to think of himself as a Conservative."[82] Kendall even went as far as to celebrate the "Strauss revolution" as the "decisive development in modern political philosophy since Machiavelli himself."[83] Strauss's interpretation of Locke as a Machiavellian who sought to undermine Christianity persuaded Kendall to give up his earlier understanding of Locke as a sincere defender of majoritarian democracy constituted by Christian citizens.[84] He was equally full of praise for Strauss's students who, he predicted, might "revive the habit of political thought in the United States" while challenging "the

Liberal orthodoxy that is the main burden of the bulk of our current political science literature."[85] This support may well have played a decisive role in spreading the influence of Strauss during the Cold War, when Kendall enjoyed far more fame, as Strauss himself noted in correspondence.[86]

Kendall's own importance in the postwar Right is hard to underestimate. Jeffrey Hart considers Kendall to be the greatest influence on *National Review*, the magazine to which he contributed for almost ten years. Hart is not the only historian of the conservative movement to recognize Kendall's contributions.[87] To date, Kendall's writings on the importance of *The Federalist* have been credited with inspiring the students of Strauss (as well as Tea Party conservatives) to treat the Founding documents as sacred texts that define American conservatism while they oppose the expansion of the federal government's authority.[88]

It may be worth pondering why Kendall was even drawn to Strauss in the first place, considering the fact that he ultimately held some views that are not in sync with Straussian political philosophy. (Even Kendall admitted at times that his own appreciation of natural law theory, as a Catholic, was not neatly compatible with Strauss's own views.)[89] Additionally, Kendall's majoritarian populism does not seem to square well with Strauss's aristocratic inclinations.[90] My thesis in brief is that Kendall's understanding of American conservatism paradoxically led him to Strauss, but not without significant philosophical tensions between their ideas. Disillusioned with what counted as conservative thought in his time, Kendall, like Grant, was attracted to the "eternal" principles that Strauss seemed to promulgate. No true conservative, Kendall warned, could engage in a "flirtation" with relativism, historicism, or positivism.[91] Since Kendall firmly believed, however, that the Christian "picture of man" is essential to the survival of the American political tradition, his brand of conservatism would logically have to part ways, eventually, with the teachings of Strauss.[92] For reasons that will, I hope, become clearer in the remainder of this chapter, the example of Kendall serves as a warning to any Anglo-American conservative who believes that his tradition is compatible with radical anti-historicism.

Kendall's staunch faith in Christianity never deterred him from embracing Strauss's ideas. Like Grant, Kendall grew up in a Protestant milieu. Despite his conversion to Catholicism in the 1950s, he never gave up his respect for his ancestral faith tradition. Unlike Grant, Kendall never faulted his Protestant ancestors or contemporaries for failing to defend the conservative cause. A few of his closest readers have insisted that Kendall's conversion sheds far more light on his relation to Strauss than any other influence. Like most postwar Catholic conservatives who gravitated toward Strauss, Kendall opposed the relativism that was engulfing American universities.[93] Despite the fact that Kendall became a Catholic late in life, it is too quick to conclude from this that Catholicism was more influential on his thought than the Protestant tradition in which he grew up in rural Oklahoma. Although he admired prominent Catholic philosophers like John Courtney Murray, his respect does not necessarily translate into a Catholic approach to politics.[94] Kendall's admiration of Murray was driven by the fact that this distinguished Jesuit philosopher not only accepted the intrinsic goodness of the American regime but, unlike the Catholic Old Right, also trusted the virtuous nature of the American people.[95] This trust is central to Kendall's populist conservatism. Early in life, Kendall described himself as a "hinterland Protestant," a self-portrayal that is perfectly compatible with both his defense of majority-rule democracy and his abiding trust in the good sense of the Americans of the heartland.[96] Moreover, his Vanderbilt Lectures of 1964, eventually published as *The Basic Symbols of the American Political Tradition,* were a celebration of the Protestant people who defined and shaped America from the Mayflower Compact onward.

Kendall's populist defense of democracy set him apart from other conservatives, both Catholic and Protestant. A favorite target of Kendall was Russell Kirk for his aristocratic leanings. At first glance it may seem bizarre that Kendall would take Kirk to task, given their shared Anglo-Protestant roots and opposition to relativism and positivism. Yet Kendall was critical of the manner in which Kirk understood the Christian faith as a religion that, in its conservative guise, must resist change as well as non-theistic conservatism.[97] Kirk's focus on the unchanging and even dogmatic nature of Christian conservatism would, Kendall feared, drive potential conservatives out of the movement. Additionally, it was un-American to portray conservatism in the republic as a petrified tradition opposed to all change, since the very origins of this tradition lay in revolution.[98] The transcendent nature of Kirk's conservatism also mistakenly downplayed what was historically specific in American conservatism, namely, its Anglo-Protestant heritage. For this reason, Kendall criticized Kirk for entitling his famous work *The Conservative Mind* when the correct title should have been *The Anglo-American Conservative Mind.*[99] It is ironic, however, that Kendall embraced a political philosophy that was even more ahistorical than Kirk's.

Kendall versus the Straussians

Not all of Strauss's students are persuaded that the affinity between their master and Kendall is so obviously justified. Jaffa is willing to admit that Kendall was a "disciple" of Strauss but worries that he was not quite the apt pupil he made himself out to be. Jaffa and Kendall famously quarreled over the legacy of Abraham Lincoln, whose presidency and political rhetoric are practically sacrosanct in the Straussian movement. Kendall, in Jaffa's view, ultimately rejected the principle of equality that lies at the heart of Straussian political thought. Instead, Jaffa's Kendall offered a "distinctive American fascism, or national socialism."[100] Ironically, the anti-Straussian Shadia Drury agrees with Jaffa that Kendall represents an anti-egalitarian populism that is at odds with American conservatism, although she associates Kendall more closely with Strauss.[101] Debates over the legacy of Kendall continue to turn over his understanding of equality as well as his faith in the virtue of the "people."[102]

If Jaffa and Drury are to be believed, then anyone who questions the liberal ideal of equality must be from the Far Right of the political spectrum. Straussians like Jaffa can often support leftist critiques of traditional conservatism (see chapter three). Yet it is far from obvious that Kendall rejects *every* manifestation of equality. The fact that Kendall vigorously challenged Jaffa's interpretation of equality as the founding principle of American politics does not mean he was an inveterate anti-egalitarian. Kendall himself gave no such impression, even when he was attacking the Democratic Party and the civil rights movement for trying to impose an egalitarian agenda through the strategy of plebiscitary democracy (although he was one of the few conservatives of his time to support the 1964 Civil Rights Act).[103] In fact, he praised the Declaration as a document that rightly enshrined an equal right to justice and an equal right to live under a constitutionally limited government.[104] In a letter to Strauss in 1956, Kendall warned that any conservative position that rejected the limited equality that is a "first cousin" to Aristotle's *Ethics* "will end up delivering itself into the enemies' hands."[105] In his Vanderbilt Lectures on the American Founding that he delivered in 1964, Kendall contended that the usage of freedom and equality in the American experience went as far back as the Mayflower Compact (1620), whose signers believed that all peoples have a free and equal capacity to decide on the type of government they desire.[106] Moreover, Kendall's most stalwart defenders portray the man as a supporter of a very basic equality. M. E. Bradford, who also tussled with Jaffa over the legacy of Lincoln, contends that Kendall had no objection to equality as long as this meant "the aboriginal sameness of all men in their right to a certain order of political experience."[107] Francis G. Wilson believes that Kendall rejected "messianic egalitarianism" in favor of the Fourteenth Amendment, which grants equal protection under the law.[108] John Murley has plausibly argued that Kendall's critique of the Lincoln legacy has far more to do with rejecting the postwar reinvention of the president as a defender of the absolute and unlimited equality that justified the New Deal and the Great Society than with any visceral opposition to equality per se.[109] As I shall argue, however, Kendall's corporate view of equality, which supports the equal right of all peoples to form their own government,[110] is not nearly radical enough for those Straussians who demand that America export the ideal of equality to the rest of the world.

No qualification would satisfy critics like Jaffa and Drury who are equally convinced that Kendall was a man of the extreme Right. Unlike Drury, however, Jaffa and other students of Strauss have another reason to lambaste Kendall, a reason that receives far less attention in the literature. In their view, Kendall is too committed to the ancestral traditions of his own people. That is to say, Kendall is more historicist than universalist for their liking. It is not simply because he worried about how far a purely Lockean-Lincolnian view of natural rights would go in establishing equality in America.[111] What is particularly galling to Jaffa and others is that Kendall understood the essential Christian character of the American Founding in a way that militates against the spread of equality around the world. The fact that Kendall calls attention to the undeniable Christian influence at work in the origins of the republican tradition does not offend all students of Strauss, although a few readers have argued that his focus on the Protestant origins of America is too historicist.[112] Nevertheless, this attitude is not consistently shared in the movement. Jaffa himself has argued that the Declaration of Independence flows out of biblical morality and that the "rule of Christian gentlemen" was made possible for the first time in history by the establishment of America.[113] Allan Bloom similarly admits that it is hard to imagine the early republic without noting the egalitarian Protestantism that celebrated "every man his own interpreter" of the Bible.[114] Robert Kagan, a prominent American neoconservative who admires Jaffa's study of Lincoln, portrays the American colonists as "typical Englishmen" of the time who fervently believed in "the superiority of the Protestant religion."[115] James Ceaser takes note of Jefferson's view that the "Saxon" origins of his fellow Anglo-Americans were indispensable for their understanding of constitutional government.[116] Given these multiple recognitions of America's Anglo-Protestant heritage among Straussians and fellow travelers, Kendall's insistence on the role of Christianity provokes disdain only because of his related view that these Christian ideals do not justify a global democracy-building foreign policy (see below).

Kendall, Strauss, and the "Open Society"

Kendall sometimes did his best to apply Straussian principles to his own understanding of the American regime. One of the most famous examples of this effort was his argument that America was meant to be a relatively "closed" society, hostile to subversive ideas as well as political groups. Both Kendall and Jaffa relentlessly took aim at the "liberal" position (made famous by John Stuart Mill and Karl Popper) that a truly democratic society must be "open" to all ideas, no matter how hostile they are to basic norms and consensus.[117] Various leftist critics of Strauss (and Kendall) have had a field day pointing out how this common opposition to the ideal of the open society smacks of fascism and totalitarianism.[118] This leftist critique, however, is far off the mark since it fails to understand what truly distinguishes Strauss's and Kendall's concerns about the open society.

As early as in his lecture "German Nihilism," Strauss sounds the alarm about the falseness of the "open society." It is false because it promises an impossible regime. No functioning society can be conceivably open to all ideas. To claim that humanity is "progressing" toward this ideal begs the question, since it is not obvious that such a regime in practice is even compatible with the rather intolerant facts of human nature. Worst of all, this type of regime is not even desirable, since it is open to ideas that may destroy it. In this context, Strauss refers to the notorious Oxford Union debate in 1933 that ended with the pacifist declaration that English youth would never again fight another war for their nation.[119] Just as English and German liberal democrats had failed to provide cogent reasons in defense of their own ideals, the Americans that Strauss met after the war were displaying a similar lack of resolve. In *Natural Right and History*, Strauss takes aim at liberals who have tired of the older liberal tradition's impositions on "diversity or individuality" while pushing for "the uninhibited cultivation of individuality." This new liberalism, which rejects natural right, is presumably open to intolerant as well as tolerant ideas.[120]

It is important to recognize what Kendall, like Grant, missed in his reading of Strauss: that Strauss here is defending liberalism, not conservatism. Unlike Kendall, Strauss makes a careful distinction between a liberalism that is "closed" to illiberal ideas and one that is destructively open to them. Kendall more bluntly identifies the entirety of the liberal tradition with support for an open society. The typical "liberal" line, as Kendall reads Mill and Popper, is to advocate a totally unlimited tolerance of free speech, even if that speech is directed against a democratic regime.[121] (For this reason, Kendall defended Senator McCarthy's crackdown on communist subversives in the 1950s.) This difference in the approaches of Strauss and Kendall is important, since it opens up an even more substantive distinction between their two political philosophies. Strauss defends an older version of liberalism, based on natural right, precisely because he never abandons his view that the principles of justice and decency are intelligible to all human beings. He targets conservatism for denying this truth as it elevates the merely ancestral above the eternal. To my knowledge, however, Kendall never accepts this version of universalism.

It is tempting to gloss over this distinction since, at times, both Strauss and Kendall seem to be far less liberal than the liberals of their time. Both men were genuinely fearful of ideas that subvert the American faith in democratic values, especially relativism. Like Strauss, Kendall also attributes the fall of the Weimar Republic to an excessive tolerance of free speech that attacked democratic rule.[122] Nevertheless, Strauss opposes the ideal of the open society for decidedly *anti-conservative* reasons. As he makes clear in his new preface (1962) to his earlier study of Spinoza (1930), a liberal democracy, with its admirable commitment to belief in a "universal human morality," is often no match for citizens who embrace a nasty version of the ancestral.[123] Worst of all, liberal democracy even permits these prejudiced citizens (anti-Semites) the freedom to discriminate against vulnerable minorities (the Jews).[124] The only solution that Strauss even tentatively offers is that citizens be exposed to a "liberal education" that teaches them to esteem democratic virtues as much as possible. Now that "religious education" is no longer in vogue in a liberal democracy, it is up to the leaders or "natural hierarchy" of that regime to inculcate lessons in citizenship that will produce "politically moderate" citizens.[125]

By implication, then, conservatism is a drag on the teaching of these virtues. Yet this is a position that Kendall could hardly accept. Even in his most arguably "Straussian" essay, Kendall arrives at conclusions that are diametrically opposed to his mentor. In "The People versus Socrates Revisited," Kendall clearly sides with the "people" or the "multitude" against Socrates. As a conservative populist, Kendall believes that the people of Athens had every right to execute Socrates for his subversive questioning. Moreover, the "liberal" portrait of Socrates as a defender of free speech will not do, since Socrates had every chance to persuade his accusers of the rightness of his cause, even before he was put on trial. Every regime, even a relatively decent one like classical Athens, had a threshold of tolerance and Socrates crossed it.[126] At first glance, this line of argument sounds vaguely Straussian. Strauss sometimes distinguishes between two versions of Socrates: an historic Socrates who brashly questions the state and a fictional (Platonic) Socrates who is more cautious and subtle in his questioning.[127] Kendall undoubtedly appreciated Strauss's view that there are limits to questioning, but which kind of society, exactly, is being questioned?

Although Strauss is determined to defend a liberal regime from its excesses, Kendall is equally determined to defend a regime from liberalism altogether. For this reason, he invokes, in his various essays on free speech, the force of what Strauss would call the "ancestral." In his essay on Socrates, Kendall never claims that Athens represents an older version of liberalism. In fact, neither Athens nor Socrates counts as liberal in any sense. (Socrates is more concerned with the pursuit of truth at any cost rather than freedom of speech, as Kendall correctly notes.)[128] Kendall tends to fear the opposite of what Strauss fears: the demotion of the ancestral in a democratic regime. When Kendall refers to "orthodoxy" in his essay on Socrates, he has in mind certain religious beliefs that underscore the foundation of Athens and other democracies.[129] Although this position is reminiscent of Strauss's view that philosophers should leave religious orthodoxy alone, there is a subtle difference. Unlike Strauss, Kendall is deeply concerned with the survival of his ancestral faith, Christianity.

Here Kendall slips into an historicist logic that may well reflect in part his indebtedness to R. G. Collingwood, under whose tutelage he studied at Oxford in the 1930s.[130] It is particularly historicist of Kendall to worry about the threat that the open society's liberalism poses to Christianity.

In an essay on the Supreme Court's incursions into the realm of school prayer, Kendall worries that a society dedicated to all ideas will clamp down on any attempt to restrict the free flow of ideas in the private realm, including churches and religious schools. Ironically, the new liberalism will be very intolerant of any restriction, no matter how justified, on unlimited discussion of ideas.[131] With an uncannily prophetic sense of what actually happened to the role of the Supreme Court and federal government in the 1970s and beyond, Kendall predicts that the liberalism of the "open" society will break down the barrier between private and public when it outlaws any discrimination that is applied to intellectual or religious freedom.

Kendall decries exactly the opposite of what Strauss targets in liberalism. Whereas Kendall condemns liberal democracy for threatening to outlaw discrimination, Strauss laments the fact that liberalism does not do enough to undermine discrimination. Strauss blames the collapse of Weimar liberalism in part on adhering too closely to the separation between state and society, which then allows discrimination against Jews.[132] As long as a liberal democracy allows citizens to preserve the ancestral with absolute freedom, there will always be discrimination. What is a weakness to Strauss is, however, a strength to Kendall. It is decidedly un-Straussian of Kendall to believe that Americans must preserve the "privileged" status that Christianity enjoys in the political realm, since he is clearly endorsing a benign version of discrimination against other faiths.[133]

On a more sociological note, Kendall was distinctly and obviously proud of his own Anglo-American origins. Reflecting on the massive Republican defeat in the election of 1964, Kendall faulted Barry Goldwater for adhering to the "conquest" conception of American politics. It was no wonder that Goldwater lost, Kendall believed, because of his assumption that the hearts and minds of a people mesmerized by the Left had to be conquered anew. The candidate should have realized, as good "WASP" conservatives like Kendall did, that most Americans were already conservative and that no conquest was necessary.[134] The pessimism that, Kendall believed, drove not only Goldwater but other prominent conservatives of his time (including the contributors to National Review, which he left in the early 1960s)[135] ignored the justifiable sentiment that the majority of the American people felt conservatism "in their hips." Kendall left no doubt that American conservatism had to privilege the Anglo-Protestant identity over all others.

What Kendall proposes, then, in Straussian terms, is an "openness to closedness."[136] A truly functional democracy has every right to preserve orthodoxies that have historically shaped its traditions. For this reason, Kendall supports the right of peoples to decide on their own form of government. Yet the orthodoxies that Kendall defends are far less liberal than those promoted by Strauss and his students. As an opponent of natural right liberalism, Kendall has no sympathy for a doctrine that is so universal it encourages radical interventions at home and abroad.

Kendall and America's Mission in the World

At issue in the debate between Jaffa and Kendall over the role of America in the world is not only the meaning of equality: it is the very meaning of Christianity as well. Unlike many students of Strauss, Jaffa emphasizes the Christian origins of the United States. In contrast to Michael Zuckert, for example, Jaffa is convinced that the Declaration of Independence flows out of Christian morality.[137] At first glance, Jaffa even stands out among students of Strauss as a scholar who sees no tensions whatsoever between the principles of Christianity and the secular American Founding. This hermeneutic goes far beyond the emphasis that Strauss places on the irreconcilable tensions between faith and political philosophy.[138] The apparent difference between Strauss and Jaffa, however, on the relation between revelation and politics is less central than the basic agreement between them on the overarching importance of America's natural right principles and the necessity of all Americans (including Christians) to support them. In short, Jaffa has no objection to the faith of Christians as long as they support the spread of American equality around the world.

On this last point, Willmoore Kendall was clearly unsatisfactory from a Straussian perspective. Although both he and Jaffa supported the "mission" of the United States, they understood this project quite differently. In one of the few places where Kendall even refers to such a purpose, he interprets this mission as one that proves "to the world that self-government . . . is possible."[139] Jaffa by contrast believes that the mission of America is to export her ideals to the rest of the world. If the republic is truly committed to natural rights, then her citizens must understand that these rights are shared by all human beings, and that it is the task of the nation to uphold these rights everywhere.[140] Kendall's admiration for Straussian hermeneutics (including Jaffa's own scholarship), however, did not compel him to support any notion of natural rights if it carried the implication of aggressive statism at home and abroad. As he pointedly remarked in his review of Jaffa's *Crisis of the House Divided*, "there are better ways of demonstrating the possibility of self-government than imposing one's own views concerning natural right upon others."[141] What particularly troubles Jaffa is Kendall's position, as outlined in the Vanderbilt Lectures, that one can be a good American Christian *and* still oppose the spread of American equality throughout the world. As Jaffa argues in *How to Think about the American Revolution*, there is no tension whatsoever between belief in "Nature's God" (in the words of the Declaration) and the God of the Bible. If one believes in the Golden Rule, one must also believe in natural rights for all.[142]

It is not that Jaffa is oblivious to the danger of misusing the Bible for the age-old purpose of creating a New Jerusalem on earth. In *Crisis of the House Divided*, Jaffa takes aim at the millennialism that has driven many of the most radical movements in American history, which have surrendered reason to popular passion. Jaffa credits Abraham Lincoln for repudiating this "secularized Puritanism" that fuelled the extremism of both the temperance and the abolitionist movements.[143] Yet it is false to conclude from this testimony to political moderation that Jaffa rejects all forms of religious passion. In *How to Think about the American Revolution*, Jaffa embraces a "*secularized* version of the old religious millenarianism" that is the "very essence" of the American Revolution.[144] In short, Jaffa has no objection to religious passions if these are dedicated to democratic causes. Kendall, in contrast, worries about the "derailment" of America that would result from a program of "chosenness" dedicated to the adulteration of biblical symbolism.[145] Jaffa ultimately appreciates the radicalism of American Christianity more than Kendall does. In *The Basic Symbols of the American Political Tradition*, Kendall and Carey take pains to emphasize the moderate nature of American Christians who dedicated themselves to calm, reasonable deliberation in their creation of the Mayflower Compact and other covenants. What is missing in Kendall's discussion is any sympathy for the relative egalitarianism of American Christianity that has been a breeding ground for radical movements in the republic's history. Although Kendall recognizes these periods of radicalism, he dismisses them as "derailments" (in the terminology of Eric Voegelin) that otherwise do not detract from the general sobriety of the virtuous American people, one that is devoted to "humanity, civility, and Christianity." Yet this "people" has always been wedded to a belief in a personal God that treats all human beings equally.[146]

Unlike the Christian traditions of the Old World, the leveling effects of the "American Religion" have created a uniquely egalitarian Christianity that Jaffa draws upon in order to press his argument that America is the chosen nation that must spread equality far and wide. Far from being the "universal nation," however, America is grounded in a faith tradition that is historically specific to a radical Protestant heritage, one that is not easily reproducible across the globe.

Yet Jaffa is not troubled by the historical relativity of the beliefs that American Christians hold about God and the universe, as long as they embrace American democratic ideals. In this respect, he believes this was Lincoln's understanding of Christianity. Lincoln was so disinterested in the differences dividing Christian churches that he never joined any denomination.[147] What is paramount is the belief in human equality, a credo that Jaffa believes is "independent of the validity of any particular religious beliefs."[148] For this reason, Jaffa exhorted the Moral Majority of the 1980s to join the Republican Party and embrace "natural law" teachings that are consistent with a more universal understanding of human equality.[149] The greatest political sin, then, is not the abandonment of traditional Christian mores. Rather, the most terrible crime is for American Christians to oppose the ideal of exporting equality around the world. Americans are not worthy of their "mission" if they, like their Israelite forefathers, abandon the credo of natural rights.[150] This belief must be sincerely and fervently felt, if the mission is to succeed. In this vein, Jaffa even finds a few of his fellow Straussians wanting. In his review of Allan Bloom's *The Closing of the American Mind*, Jaffa lambastes the author for promoting the cynical Machiavellian view that the belief in American equality is a pleasing illusion that has no basis in reality.[151]

My discussion of Jaffa's hermeneutic of the American regime may be vulnerable to the charge that I have focused on only one stream of Straussian thought, which does not even accurately reflect the teachings of the master. Robert Kraynak plausibly contends that Strauss would have opposed the synthesis of Greek political philosophy and biblical revelation that Jaffa defends; in a different vein, Shadia Drury faults Jaffa for ignoring Strauss's doubts about the viability of American democracy.[152] These readers have a point, since Strauss himself never specifically endorses a policy of democratic globalism. Unlike Jaffa, Strauss doubts that America's mission in the world is based on "divine premises." Moreover, Strauss would have had none of Jaffa's eagerness to secularize biblical themes for political purposes, since this attempt begs the question as to what is biblical and what is simply a Machiavellian attempt to misuse the Bible; it is also far from obvious that Strauss sees Christian charity as an ethic that is compatible with statecraft.[153] Nevertheless, it is not hard to see some substantive connection between Strauss's anti-historicism and Jaffa's primary emphasis on the universal nature of American ideals.

Jaffa's critique of Kendall and other conservatives who oppose the universalization of American equality is not only consistent with Strauss's defense of the natural right tradition; it also sheds light on why Strauss and his students worry about the survival of Anglo-American liberal democracy. Strauss had little faith in English liberals like Berlin and Collingwood who valued their country's decent political traditions while (in his view) they devalued them as historically relative. In a similar vein, Kendall did not provoke much confidence in Jaffa when he opposed the expansion of natural rights at home and abroad. Although Kendall sounds Straussian when he opposes any "flirtation with positivism, historicism, or relativism," he still rejects Jaffa's view that natural rights are fundamental to the Founding.[154] For this reason, Strauss and his students believe that appeals to the merely "ancestral" (that is, unnatural) inevitably lead to a weak and flawed defense of liberal democracy. The driving force of this assumption may in part explain why some neoconservatives (not all of whom are Straussians) have purged old-style conservatives and libertarians from their movement, if the latter ever display any doubts about the wisdom of spreading the "eternal ideals" of liberal democracy to lands far beyond America's shores.[155]

Kendall's confusion over the true meaning of Strauss's political philosophy serves as a sobering warning for any conservatives, Christian or otherwise, who are attracted to his teachings, for they are faced with a stark choice: either they subordinate their faith to a belief in natural right or they risk being accused of historicism (or worse). As Kendall himself often (perhaps unwittingly) showed, there is no logical way that a conservative Christian can suspend his fidelity to the ancestral or embrace the universalistic implications of natural rights. It is not that Kendall thought all conservatives ought to be observant Christians; in fact, he condemned conservatives like Kirk and Meyer for insisting on this point.[156] However, he insisted that American conservatives, Christian or not, need to preserve what is distinctive about their nation, including traditions that are not transferable to other countries. Like most conservatives of his time, Kendall supported a restricted immigration policy according to cultural identity. He even went as far as to praise America for preferring British immigrants over Albanian ones, based on the assumption that the British were more "desirable" in light of their connection to the historic roots of the republic.[157] Yet Kendall never recognized, to my knowledge, that this slightly nativistic attitude conflicted with the Straussian view that there is one good regime for all human beings, based on the natural capacity of reason that is shared by all. When Kendall parroted the Straussian view that good government is "discovered" by all human beings according to nature, rather than created by them based on historical circumstance, he never brought up the difficulty that this perspective must then open the doors of a regime to all human beings, regardless of their ancestral ties.[158] Most importantly, the resultant ideals stemming from this regime would have to be exported to the rest of the world, whose peoples would "naturally" understand and embrace them. Although Kendall, we have seen, never supported such a project, it is well known that millions of American evangelical Protestants have embraced (as Jaffa hoped) the identification of Christian morality with the universalization of the American regime's ideals around the world. This development may well confirm Kendall's worst fears about the susceptibility of Americans to grand, quasi-religious causes.[159]

What Kendall never grasped about the Straussian perspective on natural rights is the bedrock assumption that nature is more important than identity (or what Straussians dismiss as conventionalism or historicism). If this assumption is correct, then human beings are malleable enough to fit into any democratic regime, as long as they develop their natural capacities to reason. What "reason" presumably means here is to accept the validity of natural right teachings. Although this assumption may appear to coincide with the Judeo-Christian position that all human beings can grasp the Golden Rule (the truth is written on the hearts of all human beings [2 Corinthians 3:2–3]), it is far more inclusive than even Christianity. For Strauss and Jaffa claim that even human beings without any exposure to biblical revelation can respect liberal democracy. That is to say, human beings with conflicting views about morality or peoples that have no sympathy with biblical charity can still be good citizens of this regime. (If there are serious conflicts, then a statist program of "democratic patriotism" may be necessary in order to inculcate the appropriate values among citizens.)[160] In pressing this argument, Strauss and his students go far beyond the social contract tradition which, from Spinoza onward, has insisted that Christian charity be the moral foundation of a true democracy. It is safe to say that, in the eyes of both Grant and Kendall, this Straussian move would be an unwelcome one. Once again, Strauss and his followers leave us with a contradiction. They want to preserve an historically specific identity—the Anglo-American—while they also present it as a tradition that is universalizable. Yet the most universal feature of this tradition—Christianity—is not the favored one for most students of Strauss. In the final chapter, I shall argue that even Strauss cannot escape from the historical and religious particularities of the Anglo-American West.

6

Leo Strauss and the
Uniqueness of the West

In the introduction to *The City and Man*, Strauss explains why the recovery of political philosophy in the context of the Cold War is so important. The "crisis of the West," which is ultimately a battle of ideas, cannot be addressed by the authority of religion alone. "It is not sufficient for everyone to obey and to listen to the Divine Message of the City of Righteousness, the Faithful City." The dangers of relativism, historicism, and communism, all of which threaten the liberal democracies of the West, must be countered by solid, rational argument. "Man" must understand his relation to the City (the good regime of democracy) through "the proper exercise of his own powers." It is more urgent to reestablish political philosophy as the "rightful queen of the social sciences" than to obey faith and show "that political philosophy is the indispensable handmaid of theology." In an increasingly secular age, it seems antiquated to Strauss to return to religion as the solution to the challenges of modernity. As he puts it, "even the highest lawcourt in the land is more likely to defer to the contentions of social science than to the Ten Commandments as the words of the Living God."[1]

This oft-quoted passage gives the impression that Strauss takes little interest in the enduring influence of biblical revelation on Western civilization. Even a sympathetic reader like George Grant, late in life, concluded that Eric Voegelin wrote more profoundly than Strauss about the relation between reason and revelation, as we have seen. Nevertheless, it is too hasty to conclude that Strauss has nothing to teach about the biblical tradition and its relation to the West. We have already seen how Strauss's privileging of Athens over Jerusalem does not allow him or his students to escape successfully from the influence of biblical revelation. On a few occasions, however, Strauss offers some instructive lessons on what the Bible can teach to our secular age. Strauss's appreciation of the distinctive features of Scripture may even help the present age understand how the Bible inevitably shapes the politics of our time. In this concluding chapter I do not intend to revise my overall view in this study that Strauss and his students generally seek to downplay the influence of Christianity on Western political philosophy. However, I do intend to extract a lesson from Strauss's major essays on the Bible that will help us comprehend why the Anglo-American West, now more than ever, needs to understand its biblical (Christian) origins.

Admittedly, it has not always been obvious to many readers that Strauss offers important insights on the Bible. Ernest Fortin, one of his most prominent Catholic students, once openly wondered why so few Christian theologians have appreciated or even taken seriously the ideas of the master. Fortin lamented this situation, as he insisted that his teacher "may have performed as great a service for theology as he has for philosophy." Furthermore, he assured Christians that they have much to learn from Strauss, whose ideas could help them regain some of the "lost credibility" that Christian theologians have suffered in the modern age.[2] Although Fortin was mainly addressing his fellow Catholics, I believe his invitation to learn from Strauss should be taken up by anyone who takes biblical religion seriously. Despite the undeniable fact that Strauss wrote very little about the Christian influence on political philosophy, focused exclusively on the Old Testament on those rare occasions that he turned to the Bible, and usually accused medieval and modern authors of manifesting less than sincere respect for faith in their works, I believe that Strauss's understanding of what he famously calls the "theologico-political problem" teaches a hard lesson about the relation between religion, politics, and morality that is instructive for the present age.

Strauss's pivotal distinction between Athens and Jerusalem, which he brilliantly defends in a few essays, contains this lesson. In his most important essays on this subject, Strauss contends that Greek political philosophy and biblical revelation are fundamentally different from—and even opposed to—each other. The conflict between Athens and Jerusalem is an "antagonism" that breathes a special vitality into the civilization of the West.[3] One might also add that Strauss is describing a unique feature of the West that, despite its pretensions to universalism, has no equivalent in other civilizations. Although we have seen Strauss refuse to defend the West simply because, as historicists would argue, it has Western ideals (as opposed to universal ones),[4] even he is forced to admit the historic peculiarity of this tension. What, then, precisely makes the Athens-Jerusalem antagonism unique to the West? And what is the "secular conflict" that arises from this tension?[5]

While Strauss sometimes frames this distinction as simply the difference between a life of "autonomous understanding" on one side and a life dedicated to "obedient love" of God on the other, there is more to this distinction than meets the eye.[6] Strauss also teaches that the morality of "obedient love" is unique to biblical revelation precisely because it is absent in Greek thought as a whole. In particular, the command to "love thy neighbor" (charity) has no counterpart in the tradition of Athens. If Strauss is correct on this point, then the contemporary political scene in the Western world faces a serious challenge: how can an ethic of *universal* obligation— love of all humanity—be taught to all human beings if this ethic is based in a *particular* faith tradition?[7] More specifically, how can current defenders of the Anglo-American liberal tradition, who are intent on finding a universal morality that all human beings can understand, make use of this biblical ethic for their own purposes without fully acknowledging the particular foundation of this ethic? As I shall show, the most prominent defenders of liberal democracy in our time cannot have it both ways: they cannot appeal to the authority of biblical morality *and* sever it from the wider tradition of Jerusalem at the same time. Yet this separation is exactly what secular liberals must attempt to do, given their historic hostility to faith.

Jerusalem and Athens

At first glance, it may appear that I am exaggerating the extent of the difference that Strauss sets up between Athens and Jerusalem. After all, Strauss himself sometimes gives the impression that both traditions fundamentally concur on the most basic ethical issues. In his essay "Progress or Return?"

he observes that both Greek philosophy and the Bible agree on the immorality of murder, theft, and adultery. Additionally, both traditions condemn the worship of human beings by other human beings.[8] As we have seen in earlier chapters, Strauss was stressing, at least as early as his World War II period, the stark differences between a biblical morality based on mercy and humility and one that is based on the tough-minded world of statesmanship.[9] Additionally, there are some important differences to which Strauss refers even in the context of locating common ground between both traditions. Strauss never strays far from his fundamental view that these two traditions disagree on "what completes morality."[10] Shortly after observing that there is basic agreement on morality, Strauss pointedly observes that the Greek concept of magnanimity, or a feeling of pride in one's superiority, contrasts sharply with the biblical ideal of humility. Moreover, whereas the Bible equates poverty with piety, Greek philosophy is "heartless in this as well as in other respects."[11] The distinction to which Strauss is alluding here suggests that biblical morality demands a greater belief in human equality over and above anything that the Greeks were prepared to tolerate. Although Strauss hardly believes that the biblical prophets were radical egalitarians, given their support for the patriarchal family,[12] the God of revelation demands absolute obedience to a morality that humbles all human beings so that they spurn belief in the superiority of the "wise few" that are central to the philosophies of Plato and Aristotle.

In his essay "Jerusalem and Athens: Some Preliminary Reflections" which he wrote almost fifteen years after "Progress or Return?" Strauss returns to the subject of what precisely distinguishes one tradition from the other. Once again, Strauss takes note of the egalitarian content of Scripture. The new Covenant that God establishes with humanity after the Flood, for example, makes both "partners," although not equal partners.[13] Nevertheless, all of humanity is subject to a covenant created by a God that is inconceivable to Greek philosophy. The sheer devotion that this God manifests toward His creation is utterly absent in Aristotle's understanding of the unmoved mover, who "surely does not rule by giving orders and laws." Instead, Aristotle's god is pure thought, a deity that is completely indifferent to the concerns of mortals.[14] Unlike the Bible, as Strauss understands it, Greek philosophy depreciates the importance of humanity, which receives no moral strictures from a higher power. The God of revelation by contrast loves fallen humanity so much that He blesses His creation with a covenant of laws.[15] (One might add here that He demands that all human beings, not simply the "ignorant many," obey these laws.) Indeed, this God loves humanity so much that He will eventually bless humanity with a messianic age of universal peace. Strauss correctly notes in this context that no Greek political philosopher could ever believe in this promised "cessation of war."[16]

Strauss's distinctions between Athens and Jerusalem, which I have only sketched here, have often provoked considerable controversy across the political spectrum. A few of his students have downplayed the radical implications of this distinction. Thomas Pangle, for example, portrays the Athens-Jerusalem distinction as one that merely parallels the more ancient quarrel between philosophy and poetry. Both of these conflicts reflect the age-old "theological-political problem" that began with the emergence of Platonic political philosophy and not just with the rise of biblical monotheism. The quarrel between reason and revelation is more about the best way to teach moral lessons than about disagreement over what morality is supposed to teach. When Pangle says that what is "most essential in the quarrel between Plato and the Bible is already present in the quarrel between Plato and the poets," he is not only suggesting (without demonstration) that the Bible is simply poetry.[17] He is also strongly implying, without demonstration, that the Greek poets taught the same lessons about morality as the biblical prophets within a discourse that is literary, not rational. Whatever the differences between poet and prophet, then, they both relied on stories rather than reason in order to teach the core principles of morality.

What is troubling about this particular reading of Strauss is Pangle's view that the Greek poets simply fed to the ignorant masses pleasant "fictions" about the gods in order to "veil from man" knowledge of the universe (which, presumably, does not require religious belief).[18] It is far from obvious that Strauss himself would have been happy with Pangle's interpretation, for two reasons. First, in "Progress or Return?" Strauss denounced as "either stupid or blasphemous" anyone who sees revelation as a useful "myth" or fiction to employ in political struggles (e.g., against communism during the Cold War). To read the Bible as either myth or poetry betrays a cardinal tenet of Straussian thought: to read a text on its own terms. As Strauss went to great lengths to argue in his lecture on Genesis, it is unlikely that the author of the creation story wanted this narrative to be read as mythical. Anyone who reads it in this way does not seek to understand its original intent. As he argues in "Jerusalem and Athens," the Bible never creates a pantheon of mythical gods (which would violate the First Commandment). If there is any original intent to the Bible, Strauss believes, it is for readers to accept it as history, not myth.[19]

Second, it is not obvious that the Greek poets and the Bible understand divine authority in identical ways. To be sure, Strauss admits at times that the poets are closer to the Bible than they are to Greek philosophers in assuming an omnipotent deity. The Greek philosophers, unlike the poets or prophets, believe in an "impersonal necessity" (nature) that makes no claim to omnipotence. Yet the difference between Greek poetry and philosophy may be less than meets the eye, since Strauss admits at times that the belief in a "perfect" book or authority (namely, the God of revelation) is unknown to both the classical poets and philosophers.[20] Additionally, Strauss never attributes to any Greek poet the belief in a God that blesses humanity with the creation of a covenantal morality. (At times Strauss even distinguishes poetry from piety, while he acknowledges that poetry at the time was still the greatest threat to Greek philosophy.)[21]

Despite Pangle's attempt to downplay the difference between Athens and Jerusalem in the thought of Strauss, other readers have taken this distinction more seriously. Strauss's right-wing critics, who are often Thomists, reject even the slightest attempt to make this distinction. Frederick Wilhelmsen, the distinguished Catholic political philosopher, denounced this hermeneutic as an attempt to remove faith (especially Christianity) from the tradition of political philosophy. James Schall, another Thomistic critic, similarly insists that Strauss never succeeded in showing that "reason under the light of faith is somehow unreasonable."[22] George Grant was not a Thomist but was nevertheless uncomfortable with Strauss's rigid separation of reason from faith, since it may have reminded him of the traditional Protestant opposition to philosophy that had contributed to anti-intellectual obscurantism in that faith tradition.[23] Strauss's leftist critics, like Shadia Drury and William Altman, interpret the Straussian distinction between Athens and Jerusalem as his subtle attempt to embrace a far right (Nietzschean) rejection of Christian faith as a "slave morality" that threatens the Platonic rule of the wise few. Altman, who believes that Heidegger is the true source of the distinction between Athens and Jerusalem, even goes so far as to accuse Strauss of undermining his own ancestral faith, Judaism, when he insists that biblical revelation does not appeal, like Greek philosophy, to the authority of reason.[24] Critics without a particular political agenda, like Remi Brague, have simply dismissed Strauss's distinction as tantamount to a dualistic separation of faith and reason that fits the Islamic tradition of philosophy more appropriately than the Western, Christian tradition.[25] Even among students of Strauss there is some confusion over the meaning of the Athens-Jerusalem distinction. Harry Jaffa, who began his scholarly journey as a critic of the Thomistic synthesis of the Bible and Aristotelian philosophy, later in life has emphasized the fundamental agreement between the two traditions.[26]

What is often missing in this series of critiques is any attempt to appreciate the intellectual rationale behind Strauss's distinction. It is quite possible that Strauss's early interest in Protestant theology in the Weimar period provided the groundwork for this separation between Athens and Jerusalem, since Protestants at least since Luther have drawn a surgical distinction between Greek philosophy (especially Aristotle) and the Bible. Protestants in the early Reformation period looked as far back as the Roman theologian Tertullian who famously asked, "What hath Athens to do with Jerusalem?" for inspiration.[27] Given the long intellectual pedigree of this distinction, it would be inaccurate to claim that only Strauss has taught its significance. The English man of letters Owen Barfield, who was a major influence on the thought of C. S. Lewis, also argued that the ancient Hebrew denial of any importance to the power of nature rested on a visceral opposition to idolatry that falsely confuses God with natural phenomena. Unlike Strauss, however, Barfield contends that this biblical repudiation of idolatry has significantly affected the literature of the modern West.[28] Catholic liberation theologians have also made use of this distinction, although in a more brazenly political manner. The egalitarian implications of the Bible, which Strauss himself noted at times, has inspired some leftist Catholics to take aim at the Church's misuse of Aristotelian philosophy in order to shore up "unprogressive" systems like capitalism.[29]

At least within the post–World War II context of American political philosophy, however, Strauss is unique in teaching the distinction between Athens and Jerusalem. The fact that Strauss stands alone among twentieth-century political philosophers on the postwar Right in pressing the significance of this distinction is often ignored. Only his longtime correspondent Eric Voegelin comes closest, among right-wing political philosophers of the last century, to making similar distinctions between Athens and Jerusalem. Yet, as Strauss himself pointed out in correspondence, Voegelin was far more open to the possibility of synthesizing the two traditions. In Strauss's view, Voegelin paid insufficient attention to "the diametrically opposed solutions of the Bible on the one hand and of philosophy on the other."[30] The validity of this criticism is borne out at times in Voegelin's major studies of the Greeks. In his study of Plato, Voegelin sounds like Strauss when he claims that the hierarchical distinction between souls differs sharply from the "experience of creaturely equality before a transcendent God" as revealed in the Bible. Yet in the same study Voegelin also teaches, contra Strauss, that Plato and St. Paul fundamentally agreed that all human beings are "equal as brothers" and should love each other accordingly.[31] Unlike Voegelin, Strauss is far more consistent in drawing a sharp distinction between Athens and Jerusalem. I contend that Strauss's distinction should be treated seriously, especially by defenders of modern liberalism.

One of the most important lessons that Strauss draws from his distinction between Athens and Jerusalem involves their radically distinctive approaches to *nature*. In Strauss's view, Greek philosophy clearly teaches that there is such a thing as nature whereas the Bible does not. (There is not even a Hebrew word for nature, as Owen Barfield also observes.)[32] According to revelation, humanity is instructed to obey a covenant that is laid down by an omnipotent, loving God who is above nature, not identical to it.[33] This hermeneutic is consistent with Strauss's view that reason itself is natural, or shared by all human beings. Although Strauss does not deny that the Bible reveals a universal morality, it is not an ethic that natural reason discovers. Once again, Strauss concludes that the Bible essentially places the importance and role of humanity far and above nature (including heaven) itself, a belief that would be inconceivable to Greek philosophers like Aristotle (who believe that man is not the highest thing). As Strauss astutely observes in "Progress or Return?" the biblical God's preoccupation with humanity has no counterpart in Greek philosophy where such a concern is, "to put it mildly, a problem for every Greek philosopher."[34] It is revealing that neither Greek philosophy nor Greek poetry supports any belief in a divine covenant with humanity: Strauss notes that Zeus condemned mortals to endless hardship due to either his ill will or his lack of power to bestow eternal bliss. Despite the anthropomorphic features of Zeus, he is no more just to humanity than Aristotle's impersonal unmoved mover.[35]

Although this implicit distinction between divine law and natural law would not find favor among Thomists who otherwise often admire Strauss's thought, it teaches an important lesson to anyone who believes that the morality of the Bible can be taught without belief in a covenantal God. For if biblical morality is not natural (that is, known to all human beings by the sheer use of their reason), then it must be revealed to all humanity by God—who, once again, is above nature.

Christianity without God

In order to convey a sense of what is at stake here, it is instructive to contrast Strauss's approach to Athens and Jerusalem with that of the famous critical theorist Jürgen Habermas, whose cultural Marxist ideas have been very influential in the Anglo-American sphere. In recent years, Habermas has taken an interest in the relation between these two founding traditions of the West, particularly with regard to the ideas of the German theologian Johann Baptist Metz. Like Strauss, Habermas contends that Greek philosophy and biblical revelation are not easily made compatible. Following Metz's analysis, Habermas deplores the Platonization of Christian thought, although he admits that the synthesis of Greek philosophy and revelation made the Western philosophical tradition possible in the first place. However, modern philosophy works at its best if it attempts to rescue "the semantic potential of salvific thought," which Judeo-Christian theology always contained, even though Greek metaphysics obscured this potential.[36] What is most "salvific" about the Bible, according to Habermas, is the "polycentric" church that embraces multiculturalism and pluralism. In short, the Habermasian version of revelation is beneficial as long as it serves the goals of liberal democracy.[37]

Habermas's attempt at political theology (sketched only briefly here) has very little in common with Strauss's treatment of the relation between Athens and Jerusalem, aside from both philosophers' agreement that Greek metaphysics and the Bible are incompatible. Strauss would likely dismiss Habermas's thought as an exercise in "secularization," a dishonest attempt to dress up modern ideas in biblical symbolism without actually examining whether the Bible was meant to be used as an instrument for modern political agendas. Strauss would also likely detest Habermas's attempt to build a new, more universalistic society on the foundation of biblical morality. In *On Tyranny*, Strauss went so far as to accuse Kojève of "producing an amazingly lax morality out of two moralities [biblical and classical] both of which made very strict demands on self-restraint."[38] This "lax morality" seeks to create what neither classical nor biblical morality ever desired: a regime of "universal recognition" that rules over all of humanity. This universal recognition is similar to the "polycentric church" that seeks a more pluralistic society, based on the secularization of biblical morality.

Yet Habermas shows very little interest in Strauss's own contributions to the question of Athens and Jerusalem. Habermas, to my knowledge, is unaware of the parallels between his thought and that of Kojève and has typically dismissed Strauss, without any discussion or demonstration, as a guru of the Far Right and associated his thought with that of his onetime peer Carl Schmitt.[39] It may not be hard to see why Habermas is inattentive to the political philosophy of Strauss, since their own approaches to revelation are fundamentally at odds.

Like other prominent defenders of liberal democracy, Habermas believes that biblical (especially Christian) morality is essential in undergirding the foundations of a new, more tolerant social contract. Yet this "salvific" moral content can somehow be preserved even if it is separated from traditional Christian orthodox beliefs about God and salvation.[40] Indeed, this separation must happen so that peoples who are non-Christian can embrace liberal democracy. Habermas's version of Christianity requires that an enlightened Christian adopt a "reflexive position with respect to its own truth claim." If I understand Habermas correctly, he is insisting that Christians maintain their moral beliefs without insisting on their absolute truth. Any claim to absolutism would alienate peoples that do not herald from a Christian background or, worst of all, have even been oppressed by historically Christian civilizations. Ideally, the "majority [Christian] culture no longer exercises the power to define the common political culture, but rather it submits and opens itself to an exchange, free of coercion, with the minority cultures."[41]

It is instructive to compare Habermas's approach to Christianity with that of the Canadian philosopher Charles Taylor, whose ideas have also greatly influenced Anglo-American political philosophy. Habermas's analysis is very similar to Taylor's own treatment of the relation between historically Christian societies and non-Christian peoples. Like Habermas, Taylor acknowledges the historical importance of Christianity in shaping modern liberal morality. Taylor even goes so far as to claim that *only* the Christian tradition has been responsible for making possible important liberal freedoms like the separation of church and state. However, as a defender of liberal democracy, Taylor also believes, like Habermas, that the moral pressure to uphold these freedoms must come primarily from Christians, who need to recognize both the equal value and worth of all cultures, Christian or not.[42] It is no surprise that Habermas and Taylor have recently dialogued at length on the importance of preserving a biblical morality without the religious underpinnings that went along with it. In this exchange, Taylor agrees with Habermas that a truly neutral liberal state cannot favor Christianity, despite liberalism's debt to this faith. Although Taylor was more willing than Habermas to admit that religion may provide legitimate, publicly defensible "reasons" for moral belief, they both cheerfully concur that the religious content of the Christian faith is no longer essential for believing in a Christian morality that is essential to liberalism. As Habermas puts it, secularization no longer applies to the "universalization" of Christian belief.[43]

At first glance, Strauss may well sympathize with this attempt to universalize democratic credos without the use of religion.[44] As we have seen, he is generally supportive of liberal democracy because of its acceptance of all peoples, despite his misgivings over Kojève's usage of biblical morality to create a universal regime. Yet he would also be the first to point out that both Habermas and Taylor are radically departing from the original premises of the social contract tradition. Sympathetic readers of Strauss like Susan Shell and Daniel Tanguay have argued that, even in his pre–World War II stage, Strauss was bewildered by the fact that the liberals of his time were untroubled by the waning influence of the Christian tradition that once gave some moral foundation to liberalism. Liberalism, in short, had become a "diluted" Christianity.[45] Despite Strauss's misgivings over the secularization of Christianity, which in his mind begs the question about what is secular and what is biblical,[46] he was too careful a reader of Nietzsche not to spy the essential relation between belief in a revealing God and adherence to His moral commands.

It is significant that Spinoza, the philosopher whom Strauss dubs the first defender of liberal democracy, also relied on biblical morality to provide a foundation for this fledgling regime. In his early study, *Spinoza's Critique of Religion* (1930), Strauss notes that Spinoza derives his idea of natural right "not immediately from the human situation, from the necessities of man as man," but from God.[47] Although Strauss famously portrays Spinoza as a Machiavellian who does not sincerely believe in the truth of Scripture, he does not question the veracity of Spinoza's biblical hermeneutic in toto.[48] In fact, he agrees with Spinoza's famous view that religion, not reason, "teaches the multitude to love one's neighbor."[49] (Spinoza's views on the political utility of charity are no different from those of Locke, Montesquieu, Jefferson, or Hamilton.) This agreement is consistent with Strauss's view that biblical morality is revealed by God, not by nature. The problem here, as Strauss understands Spinoza, is that an irrational force like religion then becomes the basis for a regime that desperately needs rational defense. Strauss is uncomfortable with Spinoza's reliance on the "seven dogmas of faith" (including love of one's neighbor) as the foundations for liberal democratic citizenship, since these cannot survive the withering scrutiny of philosophy.[50] Additionally, these dogmas of belief will, as the Straussian scholar Martin Yaffe has argued, only encourage charitable behavior "among those for whom the biblical text is already authoritative."[51] If the Strauss-Yaffe reading of Spinoza is correct, then those human beings who have never accepted biblical revelation are unlikely to accept the ethical precepts that go along with it.

It is also very likely that Strauss would be unpersuaded by Habermas's view that the free exercise of reason will automatically lead to democratic outcomes. Strauss even leaves his readers with the stark conclusion that the irreligious authority of reason, severed from the leavening influence of biblical morality, does not necessarily lead to the conclusion that all class distinctions and hierarchies must disappear. In sharp contrast to Habermas's rather egalitarian assumptions about the public accessibility of reason, Strauss believes that certain expressions of reason can tolerate inequality. It is not that Strauss is necessarily promoting a Nietzschean view of political reality here. As a Cold War liberal who admired defenders of hierarchy (based on merit or talent) like Churchill, Strauss simply believes that a perfect equality is impossible.

For this reason, Strauss in "Jerusalem and Athens" takes to task Hermann Cohen for synthesizing reason and revelation in a manner similar to that of Kojève. Cohen makes the mistake of integrating the Platonic search for knowledge and truth with the prophetic hope for a more just (and egalitarian) society. Unlike Habermas and Taylor, Cohen does not acknowledge the Christian roots of this project. Worst of all, according to Strauss, he is fundamentally misunderstanding the vast difference between Plato and the Bible. Strauss admits that Plato, at least since the Middle Ages, is often considered the philosopher closest to the Bible.[52] Still, this historical fact does not mitigate the vast differences. Whereas Greek philosophy teaches that there is an unchangeable human nature, the Bible teaches that

God can perform miracles that change humanity.[53] While Plato is willing to tolerate a rigidly class-divided society ruled by a wise few, the biblical prophets believe in an omnipotent God who can transform human nature in such a way that these distinctions disappear altogether (in accord with the messianic promise of universal peace among men).[54] Although Cohen "does not say a single word about Christianity" in this context, Strauss implies that he is more dependent on this faith than he admits in seeking a more just society. Like Habermas, Cohen secularizes religious belief for his own political purpose (which is to build a socialist state). As Strauss puts it in an earlier essay on this neo-Kantian philosopher, Cohen was inconsistent in opposing the creation of a Zionist state while upholding socialism as the "sole end of the religion of Judaism."[55]

I dwell on Strauss's reading of Spinoza and Cohen here because it helps us understand the implications of Habermas's and Taylor's attempts to jettison the founding religious credos of the early social contract tradition. (As one student of the Straussian school has astutely argued, liberals like John Rawls, Richard Rorty, and Stanley Fish have also abandoned the early religious foundations of liberalism while they demand quasi-religious adherence to secular liberal credos.)[56] Because of his own hostility to religious belief, Habermas does not grasp how important religion may turn out to be in fostering a sense of guilt about past historic injustices. Although he may be on firm ground in assuming that Westernized, modern Christians can openly dialogue with other cultures about the history of religious oppression, he may be overreaching when he also insists that nonbelievers embrace a similarly pluralistic tolerance. As Paul Gottfried has persuasively shown, guilt over historic injustices is a Christian phenomenon that is usually taken seriously only by that faith's adherents.[57] Yet these challenges do not trouble Habermas, who is convinced that a biblical morality can and must be made rational, to the degree that it severs its historic relation to belief in an omnipotent, loving God. Perhaps the most utopian feature of Habermas's thought, which is radically distinct from that of Spinoza, is his insistence that reason *alone* can teach this morality. By contrast, Spinoza insisted on unquestioning obedience to charity, which reason cannot teach.[58]

As we have seen, Strauss's dissatisfaction with Spinoza's (and other moderns') reliance on biblical morality led him to Greek political philosophy, which in his view defended a version of liberalism that did not require the demanding ethic of the Bible. Reason can only weaken the "majesty of moral demands" to love and feel guilt, whereas the Bible strengthens these.[59] Although I have adamantly disagreed with Strauss's understanding of the Greeks in earlier chapters, one can learn from his appreciation of the distinctive features of biblical morality and its inescapable religious origins. Liberal democrats like Habermas and Taylor need the authority of revelation more than they recognize.

The Future of Anglo-American Democracy

Neoconservative defenders of liberal democracy would also do well to ponder the full implications of Strauss's distinction between Athens and Jerusalem. Although Strauss, as a self-described liberal, had at best a passing interest in conservatism (which he usually identified with no more than he identified with opposition to technological change),[60] conservatives may well learn from Strauss a telling lesson about Western identity. If the morality of Jerusalem is not, historically speaking, a universal morality that is known to all human beings, then ambitious attempts to spread biblical values (even in a liberalized form) to cultures that have no connection to the biblical tradition may be doomed to failure. In fairness to his critics from the Right, Strauss shares some of the blame for promoting a universalism that has served as an ideological rationale for expansionist foreign policy. Even though it is not obvious that Strauss himself would have supported global democracy-building,[61] and at times he even opposes versions of cosmopolitanism (the "universal homogeneous state") that deny historical particularity,[62] he bears some responsibility for inspiring the philosophical rationale for these global ventures. Because Strauss insisted, against opponents like Isaiah Berlin and others, that it makes no sense to defend a decent liberal regime unless that regime is absolutely valid for all human beings (and not "relatively valid" for the time being), his neoconservative admirers have had an easier job of holding up Western democracy as the best regime for all peoples.[63] When neoconservatives identify the "identity" of the West with this democratic universalism and object to their "relativistic" opponents who deny this universalism, they are clearly echoing a Straussian line. The Israeli neoconservative Natan Sharansky, for example, admires Strauss's student Allan Bloom precisely because Bloom opposed the "moral relativism" that undermines true democratic faith.[64] This line of reasoning, as I have argued throughout this book, dangerously ignores the historic and religious particularities that contributed to the rise of the liberal tradition in the West. If it is relativistic to argue that Anglo-American Christianity is essential to this tradition, then even some of Strauss's heroes (e.g., Churchill) must be called relativists.

It is arguable that Strauss and his students were successful in the postwar period because America's leaders at this time were under intense pressure to "universalize" the ideals of America. Caught in a mortal struggle with the Soviet Union, whose own brand of universalism was appealing to developing nations, it was convenient to downplay the historical relativity of American values. If they were merely specific to America's history, then they would not appeal to impoverished peoples who might be swayed by the siren song of Marxist-Leninism. In the terminology of the Canadian economic historian Harold Innis, America became a "space-oriented" nation preoccupied with spreading its ideas, not a "time-oriented" power concerned with preserving its traditions. This ideological effort became so successful that even major figures on the Right—most famously Strauss—were abandoning "history" for "nature" and "universalism" in the Cold War era.[65] What Strauss and his students spy as a lack of Anglo-American fervor for universalistic democratic ideals (see chapter one) is hard to reconcile with these postwar American attempts to abandon an historical sense of human differences across civilizations.

Still, Strauss's students who actually study the historic rise of liberal democracy have been no more notably successful in escaping "history" than their teacher. Francis Fukuyama, perhaps the foremost defender of this regime in our age, consistently argued in his best-selling post–Cold War book *The End of History and the Last Man* that liberal democracy no longer requires the Christian foundation that once made this regime possible. With a nod to Hegel, Fukuyama admitted that the "secularization" of Christianity was essential in order to build virtues like charity and compassion into the liberal mind-set.[66] However, Fukuyama confidently assures his readers, in a rather un-Hegelian manner, that all religions are capable of creating decent democratic regimes.[67] Since the heady days of the early post–Cold War era, even Fukuyama has had to admit that religions are stubborn things that teach different lessons about morality. In a detailed study of the social virtue of trust, he admits that Chinese Confucianism, unlike Christianity, does not teach "a universal obligation to all human beings" but in fact is preoccupied with serving blood relatives alone. More significantly, Confucianism does not even teach the importance of "private conscience" (in the Christian sense) as a check on political authority.[68] If

Fukuyama's comments are accurate, then it may be high time to have an honest conversation about whether all religions can encourage responsible self-government.

In one of the few places where he admits to the historic and religious uniqueness of the West, then, Strauss teaches a politically incorrect lesson about the politics of our age that both the Left and the Right should heed. Traditional conservatives, like the Catholic writer Leon Podles, have made use of Strauss's implicit view that biblical morality teaches a patriarchal form of love, which is not universal to all civilizations. Because the Bible teaches that God is "separate" from His creation, humankind is command-ed by this God to be a loving father of his children. By contrast, the pagan "fusion" of God with Nature encourages mortals, including fathers, to be cruel (like nature) to their progeny.[69] If Podles is correct that only the Bible teaches this practice of loving fatherhood, then it is all the more difficult to export biblically based ideals of morality to cultures around the world that do not celebrate either biblical charity or even the sanctity of life.

Debates over what is universal and relative within Western civilization will not go away anytime soon.[70] Even if a cosmic "clash of civilizations" be-tween the West and its historic rivals is not in the cards, the unique contri-bution that biblical morality has made to the West is bound to be a source of friction with peoples who do not embrace the seven dogmas of Spinoza. Despite the best efforts of Strauss to universalize Anglo-American political ideas, even he hit the wall of historic and religious particularity. If the Bible teaches a universal morality that all human beings must practice, it will never logically follow that this morality is *historically* universal. Although it is unlikely that the globalist Left and Right will take this message to heart, the survival of the Anglo-American West may well depend on its peoples heeding this lesson.

Notes

Introduction

1. Shadia B. Drury, *The Political Ideas of Leo Strauss*, with a new introduction by the author (1988; New York: Palgrave Macmillan, 2005) and *Leo Strauss and the American Right* (New York: St. Martin's Press, 1997); Stephen Holmes, *The Anatomy of Antiliberalism* (Cambridge: Harvard University Press, 1993), 61–87; Nicholas Xenos, *Cloaked in Virtue: Unveiling Leo Strauss and the Rhetoric of American Foreign Policy* (New York: Routledge, 2008); William H. F. Altman, *The German Stranger: Leo Strauss and National Socialism*, foreword by Michael Zank (Lanham, MD: Lexington Books, 2011).

2. Peter Minowitz, in *Straussophobia: Defending Leo Strauss and Straussians against Shadia Drury and Other Accusers* (Lanham, MD: Lexington Books, 2009), critically analyzes the ideological twists and turns of this emotionally charged debate. See my review of this study in *European Legacy* 16, no. 4 (2011): 553–554.

3. Heinrich Meier, *Leo Strauss and the Theologico-Political Problem*, translated by Marcus Brainard (Cambridge: Cambridge University Press, 2006), xviii. All of Strauss's students and defenders make the same argument as Meier. See also Thomas L. Pangle, *Leo Strauss: An Introduction to His Thought and Intellectual Legacy* (Baltimore: Johns Hopkins University Press, 2006), 75–82; Catherine Zuckert and Michael Zuckert, *The Truth about Leo Strauss: Political Philosophy and American Democracy* (Chicago: University of Chicago Press, 2006); Steven B. Smith, *Reading Leo Strauss: Politics, Philosophy, Judaism* (Chicago: University of Chicago Press, 2006); Minowitz, *Straussophobia*.

4. William Kristol, "The West Fights Back," *Weekly Standard* 18, no. 12, December 3, 2012.

5. A few book-length conservative critiques of Strauss stand out. See Paul E. Gottfried, *Leo Strauss and the Conservative Movement in America: A Critical Appraisal* (Cambridge: Cambridge University Press, 2012); Claes G. Ryn, *America the Virtuous: The Crisis of Democracy and the Quest for Empire* (New Brunswick, NJ: Transaction, 2003); Barry Alan Shain, *The Myth of American Individualism: The Protestant Origins of American Political Thought* (Princeton: Princeton University Press, 1994). Only Gottfried's book, to date, provides an extensive conservative critique of Straussian ideas. One of Gottfried's main complaints is the degree to which Straussians pay attention mainly to leftist critics, not critics from the Right. See my review of Gottfried's study in "Conservatism True and False in America: Evaluating Leo Strauss from the Right," at http://libertylawsite.org/2012/04/15/conservatism-true-and-false-in-america-evaluating-leo-strauss-from-the-right/.

6. Gottfried accurately refers to me as a conservative Christian critic of Strauss (see his *Leo Strauss*, 78–79), and especially of Strauss's interpretation of Spinoza.

7. See Leo Strauss, *Persecution and the Art of Writing* (Chicago: University of Chicago

Press, 1952). Willmoore Kendall, in his review of *Ancients and Moderns: Essays on the Tradition of Political Philosophy* (New York: Basic Books, 1964), an anthology of Straussian essays edited by Joseph Cropsey, notes that there are various ways of understanding the term "Straussian," ranging from anti-modernism to downright conspiracy theorizing. Kendall decides that the "mysterious something" that unites all Straussians is a focus on "secret writing." Kendall's review can be found in John A. Murley and John E. Alvis, eds., *Willmoore Kendall: Maverick of American Conservatives* (Lanham, MD: Lexington Books, 2002), 263–265. I discuss Kendall's own problematic reading of Strauss in chapter four.

8. Minowitz provides a useful definition of what counts as "Straussian," which parallels what I have written here. See *Straussophobia*, 22–23.

9. Gottfried, *Leo Strauss*. See also Paul Gottfried, *Conservatism in America: Making Sense of the American Right* (London: Palgrave, 2007).

10. Grant Havers, *Philosophy and Psychoanalysis: A Critical Study of Spinoza and Freud* (unpublished Ph.D. dissertation, Program in Social and Political Thought, York University, Toronto, 1992).

11. See Grant Havers, "Leo Strauss, Willmoore Kendall, and the Meaning of Conservatism," *Humanitas* 18, nos. 1–2 (2005): 5–25. At this time, I thought that Strauss was a *conservative* at least in the post–World War II American sense, an assumption that prompted critical replies by two distinguished conservative thinkers. See Paul Gottfried's "Strauss and the Straussians" and Claes Ryn's "Leo Strauss and History: The Philosopher as Conspirator" in the same volume of *Humanitas* (26–58). Since that time I have come to agree with their view that Strauss was an anti-religious Cold War *liberal*. Be that as it may, I have always agreed with these conservatives that Strauss's dismissal of Christianity is suspect.

12. Grant Havers, *Lincoln and the Politics of Christian Love* (Columbia, MO: University of Missouri Press, 2009), chapter 5.

13. Allan Bloom, one of Strauss's most famous students, refers to the term "democratic universalism" in the context of describing America's mission and its "liberalizing effects on many enslaved nations." See Allan Bloom, *The Closing of the American Mind: How Higher Education Has Failed Democracy and Impoverished the Souls of Today's Students* (New York: Simon and Schuster, 1987), 152.

1: Saving Anglo-Americans from Themselves

1. Leo Strauss, "German Nihilism," *Interpretation* 26, no. 3 (Spring 1999): 373.

2. Ibid., 363–364.

3. Clifford Orwin, "'Straussians' in the News: The World Trembles," *National Post*, June 17, 2003, A12. See also Pangle, *Leo Strauss*, 75–82; Zuckert and Zuckert, *The Truth*; Smith, *Reading Leo Strauss*; Minowitz, *Straussophobia*. All of these authors note Strauss's undying admiration of Churchill.

4. For Strauss's reluctance to equate "faith in America" with "hope for America based on explicit divine premises," see his "Progress or Return? The Contemporary Crisis in Western Civilization," in *An Introduction to Political Philosophy: Ten Essays by Leo Strauss*, edited with an introduction by Hilail Gildin (Detroit: Wayne State University Press, 1989), 257. See also Leora Batnitzky, *Leo Strauss and Emmanuel Levinas: Philosophy and the Politics of Revelation* (Cambridge: Cambridge University Press, 2006), 211; Minowitz, *Straussophobia*, 118, 158.

5. Clifford Longley, *Chosen People: The Big Idea that Shapes England and America* (London: Hodder and Stoughton, 2002), 14.

6. G. W. F. Hegel, *Lectures on the History of Philosophy*, vol. 3, *Medieval and Modern Philosophy*, translated by E. S. Haldane and Frances H. Simson (Lincoln and London: University of Nebraska Press, 1995), 313. See also G. W. F. Hegel, *The Philosophy of History*, translated by J. Sibree (Amherst, NY: Prometheus Books, 1991), 453–454.

7. Strauss, "German Nihilism," 372.

8. Leo Strauss, "Preface to the English Translation," in Leo Strauss, *Spinoza's Critique of Religion*, translated by E. M. Sinclair (New York: Schocken Books, 1982), 3. This preface was written in 1962. The original German edition of this work was published in 1930.

9. Winston S. Churchill, "Civilisation," in *Into Battle: Speeches by the Right Hon. Winston S. Churchill*, compiled by Randolph S. Churchill (London: Cassel, 1943), 35–36; Thomas L. Pangle, *The Ennobling of Democracy: The Challenge of the Postmodern Age* (Baltimore: Johns Hopkins University Press, 1992), 83–84. See also Daniel J. Mahoney, "Moral Principle and Realistic Judgment," in *Churchill's "Iron Curtain" Speech Fifty Years Later*, edited by James W. Muller (Columbia, MO: University of Missouri Press, 1999), 75–76. Mahoney adds, in Lincolnesque tones, that "for Churchill the English-speaking peoples are 'mankind's last best hope.'" (74)

10. On women and slaves, see Spinoza's last and incomplete work, *A Political Treatise*, chapter 11, sections 3–4. On the English Civil War, see Spinoza, *Theologico-Political Treatise*, chapter 18, section 4, paragraph 15. Throughout this work, I shall use Martin Yaffe's translation of *Spinoza's Theologico-Political Treatise* (Newburyport, MA: Focus Philosophical Library, 2004), and add the page numbers in parentheses after each citation. For a rigorous discussion of Spinoza's conservative—or illiberal—views on democracy, see Lewis Feuer, "Spinoza's Political Philosophy: The Lessons and Problems of a Conservative Democrat," in *The Philosophy of Baruch Spinoza*, edited by Richard Kennington (Washington, DC: Catholic University of America Press, 1980), 133–153. This essay marks a massive departure from Feuer's earlier portrait of Spinoza as a liberal. See his *Spinoza and the Rise of Liberalism* (Boston: Beacon Press, 1958). See also Grant Havers, "Was Spinoza a Liberal?" *Political Science Reviewer* 36 (2007): 143–174.

11. See Paul Edward Gottfried, *After Liberalism: Mass Democracy in the Managerial State* (Princeton: Princeton University Press, 1999), 38–40.

12. Strauss, "Preface to the English Translation," 6. For this reason, Strauss advises, "We are not permitted to be flatterers of democracy precisely because we are friends and allies of democracy." See "Liberal Education and Responsibility," in Leo Strauss, *Liberalism: Ancient and Modern*, foreword by Allan Bloom (Chicago: University of Chicago Press, 1989), 24.

13. Leo Strauss, "Correspondence concerning Modernity: Karl Löwith and Leo Strauss," *Independent Journal of Philosophy* 4 (1983): 107.

14. Leo Strauss, *Natural Right and History* (Chicago: University of Chicago Press, 1953), 7.

15. Ibid., 2.

16. Harry V. Jaffa, *The Conditions of Freedom: Essays in Political Philosophy* (Claremont, CA: Claremont Institute, 2000), 5. See also Zuckert and Zuckert, *The Truth*, 243.

17. At the beginning of *Natural Right and History*, Strauss quotes in an appreciative tone the famous reference to "self-evident" truths from the Declaration of Independence, while he expresses worry over whether the republic still cherishes "the faith in which it was

conceived and raised" (1). For an insightful discussion of Strauss's pro-American sympathies, see Gottfried, *Leo Strauss*, esp. 27–31.

18. In distinguishing the Bible from myth, Strauss describes himself as an "historian" not a theologian. See "Progress or Return?" 286. James W. Ceaser rejects the accusation that Straussianism teaches a contempt for the study of history. See James W. Ceaser, *Nature and History in American Political Development: A Debate* (Cambridge: Harvard University Press, 2006), 81. See also Catherine H. Zuckert, *Postmodern Platos: Nietzsche, Heidegger, Gadamer, Strauss, Derrida* (Chicago: University of Chicago Press, 1996), 125.

19. Strauss, *Natural Right and History*, 25. See also Strauss, *What Is Political Philosophy? And Other Studies* (Chicago: University of Chicago Press, 1988), 72–73.

20. Strauss, *Natural Right and History*, 3. See also his "What Is Political Philosophy?" in *Introduction to Political Philosophy*, 53.

21. For an illuminating discussion of these issues, see Kenneth B. McIntyre, "'What's Gone and What's Past Help…': Oakeshott and Strauss on Historical Explanation," *Journal of the Philosophy of History* 4, no. 1 (2010): 78–86.

22. See Strauss, "Relativism," in *The Rebirth of Classical Political Rationalism: An Introduction to the Thought of Leo Strauss*, Essays and lectures selected and introduced by Thomas L. Pangle (Chicago: University of Chicago Press, 1989), 19–21. Even Gottfried (*Leo Strauss*, 45) admits that Strauss's anti-historicism applies to Marxism. In the words of Peter Lawler, human beings become "History Fodder." See Lawler, "What Is Straussianism (according to Strauss)?" *Society* (2011): 52.

23. Drury, *Political Ideas*; Holmes, *Anatomy*, 61–87; Xenos, *Cloaked in Virtue*; Altman, *German Stranger*.

24. Strauss's argument for "esotericism" can be found in most of his works, but chiefly in *Persecution and the Art of Writing*. All of the leftist critics cited in the previous note agree that Strauss secretly undermines liberal democracy in his works.

25. Holmes, *Anatomy*, 62–63. See Drury, *Strauss and the American Right*, 91–96.

26. In "Progress or Return?" Strauss briefly refers to the Greek philosophical view that the "divine law" is mainly for the "education of the many," not the wise (286). Strauss similarly writes in *Natural Right and History*: "No premodern atheist doubted that social life required belief in, and worship of, God or gods" (169). See also Holmes, *Anatomy*, 63–65; Drury, *Strauss and the American Right*, 78–80.

27. Leo Strauss, "An Introduction to Heideggerian Existentialism," in *Rebirth of Classical Political Rationalism*, 29.

28. Ibid.

29. Ibid., 31–32.

30. Ibid., 41–42.

31. Drury, *Strauss and the American Right*, 71.

32. Altman, *German Stranger*, 223–224. I review Altman's book in detail in "The Final Volley in the Strauss Wars?" *European Legacy* 18, no. 1 (2013): 78–82.

33. Strauss, "Heideggerian Existentialism," 27.

34. Ibid., 29.

35. Ibid., 36. For the radical historicist rejection of morality, see Strauss, *What Is Political Philosophy?* 72–73. See also Gottfried, *Leo Strauss*, 50.

36. See Minowitz, *Straussophobia*, 153. The most serious "postdemocratic nightmares," from a Straussian perspective, come from the Right. Francis Fukuyama warns that "liberal democracy's tendency to grant equal recognition to unequal people" is most seri-

ously threatened by the Right. See Francis Fukuyama, *The End of History and the Last Man*, with a new afterword (1992; New York: Free Press, 2006), 299.

37. See Strauss, "An Epilogue," in *Introduction to Political Philosophy*, 155.

38. Walter Lippmann, *Liberty and the News*, with a preface by Robert W. McChesney (Mineola, NY: Dover, 2010), 1–2. This work was originally published in 1920. See also Reinhold Niebuhr, *Moral Man and Immoral Society: A Study in Ethics and Politics* (New York: Charles Scribner's Sons, 1932), 221. Both Lippmann and Niebuhr are discussed in Noam Chomsky, *Necessary Illusions: Thought Control in Democratic Societies* (Toronto: Anansi, 2003), 16–17. Chomsky accurately contends that Lippmann's and Niebuhr's views on the need for elites to educate the masses with appropriate political fictions fit well with the credos of Cold War liberalism.

39. Smith, *Reading Leo Strauss*, 15.

40. Tomislav Sunic, *Against Democracy and Equality: The European New Right*, preface by Paul Gottfried (Newport Beach, CA: Noontide Press, 2004), 141; Michael O'Meara, *New Culture, New Right: Anti-liberalism in Postmodern Europe* (Bloomington, IN: 1stBooks, 2004), 67. See also Thomas Molnar, *The Pagan Temptation* (Grand Rapids: Eerdmans, 1987).

41. Holmes, *Anatomy*, 14; Drury, *Strauss and the American Right*, 43. See also Drury, *Alexandre Kojève: The Roots of Postmodern Politics* (New York: St. Martin's Press, 1994), 254, 257. Yet Jaffa critiques Maistre's anti-egalitarian view of human nature. See Harry V. Jaffa, *A New Birth of Freedom: Abraham Lincoln and the Coming of the Civil War* (Lanham, MD: Rowman and Littlefield, 2000), 118–119. I discuss Jaffa's critique of Maistre in chapter two.

42. Strauss, *Natural Right and History*, 9.

43. Strauss, *What Is Political Philosophy?* 87.

44. Allan Bloom, *Giants and Dwarfs: Essays, 1960–1990* (New York: Simon and Schuster, 1990), 25–26. Bloom is contrasting DuBois's appreciation of the canon with the hostility that black activists (or Afrocentrists) show toward works written by dead white males.

45. C. Bradley Thompson with Yaron Brook, *Neoconservatism: An Obituary for an Idea* (Boulder: Paradigm Publishers, 2010), 250.

46. See Strauss, *Natural Right and History*, 114; Harry V. Jaffa, "Dear Professor Drury," *Political Theory* 15, no. 3 (August 1987): 317–318. Jaffa's essay largely addresses the objections made by Thompson and Brook, which are identical to Drury's criticisms.

47. Strauss, "What Can We Learn from Political Theory?" *Review of Politics* 69, no. 4 (Fall 2007): 518. Strauss gave this lecture in July 1942, at the New School.

48. Strauss, "Liberal Education and Responsibility," in Strauss, *Liberalism: Ancient and Modern*, 24: "We are not permitted to be flatterers of democracy precisely because we are friends and allies of democracy."

49. Bloom, *Closing*, 202. Walter Berns, who also studied under Strauss, attributes this opinion on the pacific nature of democracies to Thomas Paine. See his *Making Patriots* (Chicago: University of Chicago Press, 2001), 61–62.

50. Strauss, *Natural Right and History*, 28. Note that I am not literally identifying Far Right denials of a universal human nature with the historicist view that historical differences trump similarities among human beings. One can be an historicist without being a devotee of the Far Right. Carl Becker and Isaiah Berlin (discussed below) were liberals as well as historicists. Maistre, who was also an historicist, was by contrast absolutely opposed to liberalism, democracy, and the French Revolution.

51. Strauss, "What Is Liberal Education?" in *Liberalism: Ancient and Modern*, 7. In her attempt to associate Strauss with Carl Schmitt's politics, Drury accuses Strauss of supporting

an exclusivist, illiberal democracy that is hostile to immigrants and outsiders (*Strauss and the American Right*, 84–87). Yet she never takes account of the universalist sentiments that Strauss expresses here.

52. Milton Himmelfarb, "On Leo Strauss," *Commentary* 58, no. 2 (August 1974): 63.

53. Ceaser, *Nature and History*, 71–72.

54. See Allan J. Lichtman, *White Protestant Nation: The Rise of the American Conservative Movement* (New York: Atlantic Monthly Press, 2008), esp. 3. See my review of this book in *European Legacy* 15, no. 3 (2010): 375–376.

55. Leo Strauss, "The Re-education of Axis Countries concerning the Jews," *Review of Politics* 69, no. 4 (Fall 2007): 534. Strauss gave this talk at the New School in 1943. Strauss similarly worries that the Machiavellian teaching that all regimes begin with a violent crime may undermine American fealty to their own democracy, which often committed an "occasional deviation" from its own ideals of freedom and justice, particularly with regard to the treatment of Native Americans. See *Thoughts on Machiavelli* (Chicago: University of Chicago Press, 1958), 13–14.

56. James R. Holmes, *Theodore Roosevelt and World Order: Police Power in International Relations* (Washington, DC: Potomac Books, 2006), 69; Ronald J. Pestritto, *Woodrow Wilson and the Roots of Modern Liberalism* (Lanham, MD: Rowman and Littlefield, 2005), 253–266. See my review of Pestritto's book in *European Legacy* 13, no. 1 (2008): 112–113.

57. Gary Dorrien, *The Neoconservative Mind: Politics, Culture, and the War of Ideology* (Philadelphia: Temple University Press, 1993), 356. See also James Ceaser, "Multiculturalism and American Liberal Democracy," in Arthur Melzer, Jerry Weinberger, and M. Richard Zinman, eds., *Multiculturalism and American Democracy* (Lawrence: University Press of Kansas, 1998), 155. Unlike Dorrien, Ceaser is a Straussian.

58. John O'Neill, *Plato's Cave: Desire, Power, and the Specular Functions of the Media* (Norwood, NJ: Ablex Publishing, 1991), 5. Around this time, Henry Louis Gates Jr. described Bloom as a representative of the "cultural Right" and a defender of the remnants of "white, male culture" in the West. See Gates, "Whose Canon Is It Anyway?" *New York Times*, February 26, 1989.

59. Neoconservatives like Norman Podhoretz and Michael Novak have also worried about the "Wasp" establishment's capitulation to leftist protest movements. See Dorrien, *Neoconservative Mind*, 361–362.

60. Leo Strauss, *The City and Man* (Chicago: University of Chicago Press, 1964), 3–4.

61. Harry V. Jaffa, *How to Think about the American Revolution: A Bicentennial Celebration* (Durham, NC: Carolina Academic Press, 1978), 171 (my italics).

62. Strauss, *What Is Political Philosophy?* 104.

63. Leo Strauss, "On Collingwood's Philosophy of History," *Review of Metaphysics* 5, no. 4 (June 1952): 559–586. For Berlin, see Strauss, "Relativism," 17. Despite his disagreements with Strauss on the possibility of "eternal truths," Berlin still admired Strauss as a scholar. See Harry V. Jaffa, "Dear Sirs," in Harry V. Jaffa et al., *Crisis of the Strauss Divided: Essays on Leo Strauss and Straussianism, East and West* (Lanham, MD: Rowman and Littlefield, 2012), 163–165. For Strauss on the nineteenth century, see Strauss, *What Is Political Philosophy?* 65, and *Natural Right and History*, 192; also Leo Strauss, *On Tyranny: Including the Strauss-Kojève Correspondence*, edited by Victor Gourevitch and Michael S. Roth (Chicago: University of Chicago Press, 2000), 194. For R. G. Collingwood's view of democracy, see *The Idea of History* (New York: Oxford University Press, 1956), 119. For a useful discussion of Strauss on Collingwood, see McIntyre, "What's Gone," 76–79.

64. Strauss associates positivism with historicism in *Natural Right and History*, 16. He also associates relativism with historicism in *Natural Right and History*, 6. For Strauss's condemnation of faith in science as the bulwark against nihilism, see "German Nihilism," 363. For positivism's lack of opposition to undemocratic ideas, see Strauss, *Liberalism: Ancient and Modern*, 26.

65. On Americans, see Strauss, *Natural Right and History*, 5. Bloom similarly laments the fact that John Stuart Mill, who did not defend the philosophy of natural rights, was the last modern defender of liberal democracy. See *Giants and Dwarfs*, 382.

66. Bloom, *Closing*, 39.

67. Ceaser, *Nature and History*, 75, 85–86.

68. Harry V. Jaffa, "On the Nature of Civil and Religious Liberty," in *American Conservative Thought in the Twentieth Century*, edited by William F. Buckley Jr. (Indianapolis and New York: Bobbs-Merrill, 1970), 222.

69. Eric P. Kaufmann, *The Rise and Fall of Anglo-America* (Cambridge: Harvard University Press, 2004), 108–109.

70. Ceaser, *Nature and History*, 72–73.

71. Jaffa, *New Birth*, 84–86, 105–106.

72. Bloom, *Giants and Dwarfs*, 318. In a lecture on "Western Civ" that he gave at Harvard in 1988, Bloom also lamented the fact that postmodern leftists in the United States who decry any notion of universal standards of liberty and equality have no words of inspiration for the young Chinese movement for democracy that was later crushed by the communist regime (ibid., 31).

73. Xenos, *Cloaked in Virtue*; Altman, *German Stranger*; Strauss, "German Nihilism," 362.

74. Bloom, *Giants and Dwarfs*, 246.

75. Leo Strauss, *The Early Writings, 1921–1932*, translated and edited by Michael Zank (Albany: SUNY Press, 2002), 215. Strauss means here that moderns must learn by reading the classics as the alternative to the modern crisis.

76. See Strauss, *Early Writings*, 184–185. See also Samuel Moyn, "From Experience to Law: Leo Strauss and the Weimar Crisis of the Philosophy of Religion," *History of European Ideas* 33, no. 2 (June 2007): 189–90, 193. Ironically, Spinoza, whose philosophy Strauss generally critiques, also decries those authorities that boast of having "some Spirit besides this [reason] which renders them certain about the truth." See Spinoza, *Theologico-Political Treatise*, chapter 15, section 1, paragraph 64 (176).

77. For Havelock's "historicist" view that liberalism has its roots in the New Testament, not Platonic political philosophy, see Strauss, *Liberalism: Ancient and Modern*, 29–30. For the differences between Strauss and Voegelin, see Peter Emberley and Barry Cooper, eds., *Faith and Political Philosophy: The Correspondence between Leo Strauss and Eric Voegelin, 1934–1964* (University Park: Pennsylvania State University Press, 1993), 78. The letter to Voegelin is dated February 25, 1951. In his review of this book, Strauss's student Ernest L. Fortin notes Strauss's discomfort with Voegelin's "historicist" view that only human beings with a Christian background could access the "experiences" that make sense of the relation between reason and revelation. See Fortin, *Classical Christianity and the Political Order: Reflections on the Theologico-Political Problem*, edited by J. Brian Benestad (Lanham, MD: Rowman and Littlefield, 1996), 333.

78. Robert Sokolowski, *The God of Faith and Reason: Foundations of Christian Theology* (Washington, DC: Catholic University of America Press, 1982), 158.

79. See Batnitzky, *Strauss and Emmanuel Levinas*, 123. Batnitzky here targets "conservative Christian" readers who misunderstand Strauss's separation of Athens and Jerusalem and downplay his skeptical view that reason and revelation cannot be synthesized (129). Yet the only conservative Christians that she has in mind here are Thomistic readers of Strauss who are committed to this synthesis, not conservative Protestant readers (like myself) who accept Strauss's separation of these two traditions yet draw different conclusions from this hermeneutic. See chapter six.

80. Gottfried, *Leo Strauss*, 14.

81. Leo Strauss, "Letter to Karl Löwith," *Constellations* 16, no. 1 (2009): 82. For a leftist critique of this letter, see Altman, *German Stranger*, 227–228. See also Steven E. Aschheim, *Beyond the Border: The German-Jewish Legacy Abroad* (Princeton: Princeton University Press, 2007), 111.

82. Xenos, *Cloaked in Virtue*, 29–34; Drury, *Strauss and the American Right*, 81–96.

83. See Paul E. Gottfried, "Cryptic Fascist?" *American Conservative* (February 2011): 47. Gottfried's article is a long review of Altman's *German Stranger*.

84. On the vast differences between Schmitt and Strauss, see Paul Edward Gottfried, *Carl Schmitt: Politics and Theory* (New York: Greenwood Press, 1990), 116–117.

85. Leo Strauss, "Notes on Carl Schmitt, *The Concept of the Political*," in Carl Schmitt, *The Concept of the Political*, translated and with an introduction by George Schwab (Chicago: University of Chicago Press, 1996), 107.

86. Drury, *Strauss and the American Right*, 91–96; William Altman, "The Alpine Limits of Jewish Thought: Leo Strauss, National Socialism, and *Judentum ohne Gott*," *Journal of Jewish Thought and Philosophy* 17, no. 1 (Spring 2009): 28.

87. Strauss, "Notes on Carl Schmitt," 92. For a discussion of these issues, see Grant Havers, "Carl Schmitt, Leo Strauss, and the Necessity of Political Theology," in *Politics in Theology: Religion and Public Life*, vol. 38, edited by Gabriel R. Ricci (New Brunswick, NJ: Transaction, 2012), 15–31.

88. Xenos correctly notes Strauss's indebtedness to Hobbes in this essay, "Notes on Carl Schmitt" (*Cloaked in Virtue*, 54–58), even though Strauss by the 1940s had categorically abandoned Hobbes for Plato. In the context of his essay on Schmitt, Strauss also hoped that his own people, in true Hobbesian fashion, would create a new nation (Israel) that would secure their survival. See Gottfried, *Leo Strauss*, 22.

89. Strauss, "Progress or Return?" 284; Strauss, *Natural Right and History*, 12.

90. See Gottfried, *Conservatism in America*.

91. Reinhold Niebuhr, *The Irony of American History* (New York: Charles Scribners' Sons, 1962), 148.

92. Michael Novak, *The Spirit of Democratic Capitalism* (New York: Madison Books, 1991). See also Robert S. McNamara and James G. Blight, *Wilson's Ghost: Reducing the Risk of Conflict, Killing, and Catastrophe in the Twenty-First Century* (New York: PublicAffairs, 2001), 41.

93. Niebuhr, *Irony*, 150. See John P. Diggins, *Why Niebuhr Now?* (Chicago: University of Chicago Press, 2011), who notes that Niebuhr insisted, "until we consider certain Christian insights about human nature, we can never understand the nature of power in history" (117). Nevertheless, some sympathetic readers of Strauss, like the famous doyen of neoconservatism Irving Kristol, have appreciated Niebuhr's ideas. See Kristol, *Neoconservatism: The Autobiography of an Idea* (Chicago: Elephant Paperbacks, 1995), 484.

94. James V. Schall SJ, *Christianity and Politics* (Boston: St. Paul Editions, 1981),

236 (see also 252).

95. Leo Strauss, "Why We Remain Jews: Can Jewish Faith and History still Speak to Us?" in Leo Strauss, *Jewish Philosophy and the Crisis of Modernity: Essays and Lectures in Modern Jewish Thought by Leo Strauss*, edited with an introduction by Kenneth Hart Green (Albany: SUNY Press, 1997), 335. Strauss gave this lecture in 1962.

96. Strauss, *Natural Right and History*, 12, 138.

97. Strauss, "Re-education of Axis Countries," 537.

98. Noam Chomsky, "Reinhold Niebuhr," *Grand Street* 6, no. 2 (Winter 1987): 199–203. Chomsky faults Niebuhr for assuming that non-Christians would accept his "Christian" approach to democracy.

99. Kaufmann, *Rise and Fall*, 307.

100. See Paul Edward Gottfried, *The Search for Historical Meaning: Hegel and the Postwar American Right* (DeKalb: Northern Illinois University Press, 1986), 132–133.

2: Athens in Anglo-America

1. Strauss, *Natural Right and History*, 2.

2. Stanley Rosen, "Politics or Transcendence? Responding to Historicism," in Emberley and Cooper, *Faith and Political Philosophy*, 264. Elsewhere Rosen has admitted that Strauss has rather modern, even Kantian, notions about nature and the will. See Stanley Rosen, *Hermeneutics as Politics* (Oxford: Oxford University Press, 1987), 123–138.

3. Eugene F. Miller, "Leo Strauss: The Recovery of Political Philosophy," in *Contemporary Political Philosophers*, edited by Anthony de Crespigny and Kenneth Minogue (London: Methuen, 1976), 76–77. See also Ted McAllister, *Revolt against Modernity: Leo Strauss, Eric Voegelin, and the Search for a Postliberal Order* (Lawrence: University Press of Kansas, 1995).

4. Brian Tierney, *The Idea of Natural Rights: Studies on Natural Rights, Natural Law, and Church Law, 1150–1625* (Grand Rapids: William B. Eerdmans, 1997), 4.

5. Johnathan O'Neill, "Straussian Constitutional History and the Straussian Political Project," *Rethinking History* 13, no. 4 (December 2009): 473.

6. Michael Novak, *On Two Wings: Humble Faith and Common Sense at the American Founding* (San Francisco: Encounter Books, 2002), 58.

7. Jean-François Drolet, *American Neoconservatism: The Politics and Culture of a Reactionary Idealism* (London: Hurst, 2011), 85, 137.

8. See Strauss, *Natural Right and History*, 8; Strauss, *What Is Political Philosophy?* 47. In each passage, Strauss refers to the victory of modern science over Aristotelian teleology.

9. Gottfried, *Leo Strauss*, 10, 57, 102. Elsewhere, Gottfried questions how Platonic views on philosopher rule could be made compatible with modern mass democracy. See Gottfried, *Carl Schmitt*, 116–117.

10. Jennifer Tolbert Roberts, *Athens on Trial: The Antidemocratic Tradition in Western Thought* (Princeton: Princeton University Press, 1994), 13.

11. Nancy K. Levene, "Athens and Jerusalem: Myths and Mirrors in Strauss's Vision of the West," *Hebraic Political Studies* 3, no. 2 (Spring 2008): 116–117.

12. Gregory Bruce Smith, "Athens and Washington: Leo Strauss and the American Regime," in Kenneth L. Deutsch and John A. Murley, eds., *Leo Strauss, the Straussians, and the American Regime* (Lanham, MD: Rowman and Littlefield, 1999), 116.

13. Strauss, of course, also believes that moderns (e.g., Spinoza) were far too "bold"

in openly critiquing religion and, therefore, not as skilful as the ancients in the art of secret writing. See Strauss, *What Is Political Philosophy?* 171.

14. Willmoore Kendall, "Thoughts on Machiavelli," in *Willmoore Kendall Contra Mundum*, edited by Nellie D. Kendall (Lanham, MD: University Press of America, 1994), 456. This passage is from Kendall's review of Strauss's *Thoughts on Machiavelli*.

15. In a letter to Karl Löwith dated August 15, 1946, Strauss observes that the greatest exponents of the "ancient-modern quarrel" recognized "that the real theme of the quarrel is antiquity and Christianity." See Strauss, "Correspondence concerning Modernity," 106. This is a rare explicit example of Strauss's real opinion of Christianity. For a useful discussion of the various ways in which Strauss's students have often ignored or downplayed the influence of Christianity on political philosophy, see Gottfried, *Leo Strauss*, 72–81.

16. Strauss, "Progress or Return?" 258, 264, 268.

17. Ibid., 267.

18. For a brief comparison of Strauss and the Frankfurt School, see Rosen, *Hermeneutics as Politics*, 134–135. In chapter three, I draw some additional connections between Strauss and the Frankfurt School.

19. Strauss, *The City and Man*, 3–6. For a discussion of the modern replacement of political philosophy with ideology, see also Strauss's "Plato," in Strauss, *Introduction to Political Philosophy*, 208.

20. Leo Strauss, *On Plato's "Symposium,"* edited and with a foreword by Seth Benardete (Chicago: University of Chicago Press, 2003), 2–3.

21. Strauss, *Natural Right and History*, 252. In *The City and Man*, Strauss similarly cautions that the "classical principles" of ancient political philosophy are not "immediately applicable" to the problems of today even if they serve as "the indispensable starting-point" for understanding the crisis of modernity (11).

22. Strauss, *Persecution and the Art of Writing*, 27, 33.

23. Rosen, *Hermeneutics as Politics*, 128. Elsewhere Rosen dismisses the idea of a "return" to antiquity as both impossible and undesirable due to the beneficial influence of the Enlightenment on modern thought. See Stanley Rosen, *The Ancients and the Moderns: Rethinking Modernity* (New Haven: Yale University Press, 1989), 9–11. This position is not altogether distinct from Strauss's. Zuckert and Zuckert similarly doubt that Strauss would want to stack the Supreme Court with Platonic philosopher-kings (*The Truth*, 208). See also Zuckert, *Postmodern Platos*, 200.

24. Strauss, *Persecution and the Art of Writing*, 152. Spinoza admits his disinterest in the ancients in Letter 56 (to Hugo Boxel) of his correspondence. See Spinoza, *The Letters*, translated by Samuel Shirley (Indianapolis: Hackett, 1995), 279.

25. Strauss, "What Is Political Philosophy?" 16; Strauss, "Epilogue," 144.

26. Strauss, *Natural Right and History*, 28, 144. See also "What Is Liberal Education?" in *Liberalism: Ancient and Modern*, 7.

27. For a similar argument against Strauss, see Ryn, *America the Virtuous*.

28. Robert Nisbet, *History of the Idea of Progress* (New York: Basic Books, 1980), 288–291.

29. See Pestritto, *Woodrow Wilson*, 253–266. See my review of Pestritto's book in *European Legacy* 13, no. 1 (2008): 112–113.

30. See Francis Fukuyama, *America at the Crossroads: Democracy, Power, and the Neoconservative Legacy* (New Haven: Yale University Press, 2006). Although Fukuyama opposed the second Iraq War, he supports the "neo-Wilsonian" policy of spreading democratic values on a global scale.

31. See Rosen, *Hermeneutics as Politics*, 132, 138.

32. Zuckert and Zuckert, *The Truth*, 228. It may be objected here that the relation between Strauss and his students is not necessarily as close as I argue. For the record, I agree with Lawrence Lampert that Strauss "was responsible for Straussianism," even if he himself was not a Straussian. See Lawrence Lampert, *Leo Strauss and Nietzsche* (Chicago: University of Chicago Press, 1996), 132.

33. Zuckert and Zuckert, *The Truth*, 236.

34. Harvey C. Mansfield Jr., *Taming the Prince: The Ambivalence of Modern Executive Power* (New York: Free Press, 1989), 276.

35. Zuckert and Zuckert, *The Truth*, 244–245.

36. Ibid., 256–258.

37. Ibid., 258.

38. Strauss, "Preface to the English Translation," 2.

39. See Harry V. Jaffa, *The American Founding as the Best Regime: The Bonding of Civil and Religious Liberty* (Claremont, CA: Claremont Institute, 1990), 25–26.

40. Strauss, *On Tyranny*, 194. In "The Three Waves of Modernity," Strauss similarly asserts that liberal democracy "derives powerful support" from the premodern political philosophers (*Introduction to Political Philosophy*, 98). See also Strauss, *Natural Right and History*, 1–3, where he mainly warns against German historicism, which includes both the totalitarian Right (Nietzsche, Heidegger) and Left (Marx).

41. Strauss, "Progress or Return?" 257.

42. John von Heyking and Richard Avramenko, "Introduction: The Persistence of Friendship in Political Life," in *Friendship and Politics: Essays in Political Thought*, edited by John von Heyking and Richard Avramenko (Notre Dame, IN: University of Notre Dame Press, 2008), 7. The editors cite Strauss with approval on the conflict between Jerusalem and Athens. Allan Bloom similarly blames both Christianity and modern philosophy for teaching that man is "not naturally a political being" but is only concerned with his survival. See Bloom, "Introduction," in Jean-Jacques Rousseau, *Émile, or On Education*, introduction, translation, and notes by Allan Bloom (New York: Basic Books, 1979), 5.

43. See John J. Ranieri, *Disturbing Revelation: Leo Strauss, Eric Voegelin, and the Bible* (Columbia, MO: University of Missouri Press, 2009).

44. Peter Augustine Lawler, *Homeless and at Home in America* (South Bend, IN: St. Augustine's Press, 2007), 26. For Lawler's critique of Strauss, see his "Strauss, Straussians, and Faith-Based Students of Strauss," *Political Science Reviewer* 36 (2007): 3–12. See also James V. Schall, "A Latitude for Statesmanship? Strauss on St. Thomas," in Kenneth L. Deutsch and Walter Nicgorski, eds., *Leo Strauss: Political Philosopher and Jewish Thinker* (Lanham, MD: Rowman and Littlefield, 1994), 212–215.

45. See Lawler's introduction to Orestes A. Brownson, *The American Republic: Its Constitution, Tendencies, and Destiny* (Wilmington, DE: ISI Books, 2003), xliii–xlv, lxii, lxix.

46. Strauss, *Persecution and the Art of Writing*, 143, 146–147.

47. These critical observations of ancient Greek and Roman statecraft in the pages of *The Federalist* are uncannily similar to Spinoza's contention that the ancient Roman republicans failed to achieve political stability precisely because they continued to replace one tyrant with another, "or choose many tyrants in place of the one," without actually breaking the cycle of violence altogether. Eventually the republic yielded to the rule of the Caesars. See Spinoza, *Theologico-Political Treatise*, chapter 18, section 4, paragraph 18 (216–217). Despite the Straussian view that Spinoza was a Machiavellian, it has been plausibly argued that Spinoza in fact repudiates Machiavelli's uncritical praise of Roman republicanism here.

See Brayton Polka, *Politics and Ethics*, vol. 2 of *Between Philosophy and Religion: Spinoza, the Bible, and Modernity* (Lanham, MD: Lexington Books, 2007), 204–206. Despite Spinoza's and Hamilton's obvious rejection of Machiavelli's celebration of Greco-Roman republicanism, Strauss still insists that Spinoza and the authors of *The Federalist* were deeply influenced by the Florentine's reading of ancient history. See Strauss, *What Is Political Philosophy?* 47.

48. See Walter Berns, *Taking the Constitution Seriously* (New York: Simon and Schuster, 1987), 69–70. Although Berns, a prominent Straussian scholar, acknowledges this defect of ancient statecraft, it does not deter him from judging the American Founding according to the standards of Greek political philosophy. Some Straussians have even taken Berns to task for being too critical of America's lack of "virtue" in the Platonic sense. See Zuckert and Zuckert, *The Truth*, 202–209.

49. Clifford Orwin provides a useful discussion of the Melians' prophecy on the fate of Athens and its tragic dimensions in *The Humanity of Thucydides* (Princeton: Princeton University Press, 1994), 100–101.

50. Here I use the translation of Plato's *Statesman* by Seth Benardete (Chicago: University of Chicago Press, 1986), 22. For an excellent discussion of the pagan law of reversal, which permeates all Greek texts (philosophical, literary, and historical), see Brayton Polka, *The Dialectic of Biblical Critique: Interpretation and Existence* (New York: St. Martin's Press, 1986), 81–155. As Polka argues, Greek philosophy is not exempted from the effects of this reversal. Even Socrates, who spends his philosophic life exposing the ignorance of the "many," ends his life, as Plato recounts in *The Crito*, defending the virtue of obeying the "Laws" that the "many" instituted. See also Grant Havers, "Kierkegaard, Adorno, and the Socratic Individual," *European Legacy* (forthcoming). Kierkegaard is one of the few prominent modern thinkers who comprehend the fatal law of reversal and its importance in pagan Greek thought.

51. Strauss, "Correspondence concerning Modernity," 112.

52. Strauss, *The City and Man*, 49.

53. Strauss, *Liberalism: Ancient and Modern*, viii–ix.

54. Ibid., 240–241. See Numa Denis Fustel de Coulanges, *The Ancient City: A Study of the Religions, Laws, and Institutions of Greece and Rome* (Garden City, NY: Doubleday Anchor Books, 1956). This work was originally published in 1864.

55. Leo Strauss, "The Problem of Socrates: Five Lectures," in *Rebirth of Classical Political Rationalism*, 103–183.

56. Willmoore Kendall, "The People versus Socrates Revisited," in Willmoore Kendall, *Willmoore Kendall Contra Mundum*, edited by Nellie D. Kendall (New York: University Press, 1994), 149–167.

57. Strauss, "Preface to the English Translation," 3. It should be noted that Strauss is making a comment on the failure of Weimar Germany's bourgeois liberalism, not Anglo-American liberalism. Pierre Manent, a prominent French admirer of Strauss, mistakenly contends that Strauss is critiquing the entire liberal tradition of the West in this context. See his *La Raison des nations: Réflexions sur la démocratie en Europe* (Paris: Éditions Gallimard, 2006), 82–85.

58. Leo Strauss, *Socrates and Aristophanes* (Chicago: University of Chicago Press, 1966), 314.

59. Strauss, *What Is Political Philosophy?* 260. Here Strauss associates Kurt Riezler's "liberal" love of privacy with his feeling "at home" in the philosophy of ancient Greece. For Strauss's views on Popper, see *Persecution and the Art of Writing*, 21; Emberley and Cooper, *Faith and Political Philosophy*, 66–69.

60. See Jaffa, *American Founding*, 24. Even Strauss admits at times that medieval Christian philosophers enjoyed more freedom than their Jewish or Moslem counterparts. See his "How to Begin to Study Medieval Philosophy," in *Rebirth of Classical Political Rationalism*, 221–222. For a similar argument, see also Bernard-Henri Lévy, *The Testament of God*, translated by George Holoch (New York: Harper and Row, 1979), 77–87.

61. Ranieri argues that Strauss is indifferent to Greek political violence (*Disturbing Revelation*, 226, 243).

62. Leo Strauss, "On the Interpretation of Genesis," in Strauss, *Jewish Philosophy*, 373.

63. Strauss, *The City and Man*, 187, 191.

64. Ibid., 230, 236.

65. Ibid., 238.

66. Leo Strauss, "Jerusalem and Athens: Some Preliminary Reflections," in Strauss, *Jewish Philosophy*, 396.

67. Ibid., 403. Strauss also refers to the "cessation of evil" that is made possible by God's providence as revealed in the Bible (*Natural Right and History*, 144).

68. Strauss, "Heideggerian Existentialism," 41. For a discussion of Strauss's rejection of the tragic (pagan) view of life that Spengler embraces, see Grant N. Havers, "The Meaning of 'Neo-Paganism': Rethinking the Relation between Nature and Freedom," in *Humanity at the Turning Point: Rethinking Nature, Culture, and Freedom*, edited by Sonja Servomaa (Helsinki: Renvall Institute, 2006), 159–169.

69. Strauss, *Natural Right and History*, 19.

70. See Paul A. Rahe, "Thucydides' Critique of Realpolitik," *Security Studies* 5, no. 2 (Winter 1995–1996): 139–141.

71. Paul A. Rahe, *The Ancien Régime in Classical Greece*, vol. 1 of *Republics Ancient and Modern* (Chapel Hill: University of North Carolina Press, 1994), xxiii.

72. Ibid., 27.

73. Ibid., 107. Rahe even praises Sparta (ibid., 123, 125) for advancing the martial virtues more effectively than any other regime, ancient or modern.

74. Paul A. Rahe, *Inventions of Prudence: Constituting the American Regime*, vol. 3 of *Republics Ancient and Modern* (Chapel Hill: University of North Carolina Press, 1994), 59, 207.

75. Ibid., 230.

76. Rahe, *Ancien Régime*, 5, 16–17.

77. Ibid., 41–43, 59, 114, 141.

78. Ibid., 150–151.

79. Rahe, *Inventions of Prudence*, 39–44.

80. Rahe, *Ancien Régime*, 57, 124, 142.

81. Ibid., 176.

82. Ibid., 96.

83. Clinton Rossiter, *Seedtime of the Republic: The Origin of the American Tradition of Political Liberty* (New York: Harcourt, Brace, and World, 1953), 356.

84. Kendall, "The Part-Time Sage of Ithaca," in *Willmoore Kendall Contra Mundum*, 72 (his italics).

85. Peter F. Drucker, "A Key to American Politics: Calhoun's Pluralism," in *Liberalism versus Conservatism: The Continuing Debate in American Government*, edited by Willmoore Kendall and George W. Carey (New York: D. Van Nostrand, 1966), 445–446. Drucker's article was originally published in 1948.

86. Leo Strauss, "On Classical Political Philosophy," in *Introduction to Political Philosophy*, 68.

87. Eric Nelson, *The Greek Tradition in Republican Thought* (Cambridge: Cambridge University Press, 2004), 17, 213, 220, 226, 230. Nelson is not a typical Straussian, since he gives more credence than Strauss to the importance of the biblical (at least Old Testament) influence on modern political thought (through secularization). Nevertheless, he still follows Strauss on fundamental issues (like the Machiavellianism of Spinoza). See Eric Nelson, *The Hebrew Republic: Jewish Sources and the Transformation of European Political Thought* (Cambridge: Harvard University Press, 2010), 130.

88. Nelson, *Greek Tradition*, 200–201 on Jefferson and Plato, and 224–225 on Hamilton. Rahe (*Constituting the American Regime*, 23) also portrays Hamilton's thought as indebted to the Greeks, although, unlike Nelson, he spies in Hamilton an unacknowledged indebtedness to Machiavelli.

89. Nelson, *Greek Tradition*, 15.

90. John Adams, *The Works of John Adams, Second President of the United States: With a Life of the Author, Notes and Illustrations, by his Grandson Charles Francis Adams* (Boston: Little, Brown, 1856), vol. 5, chapter 9, *A Defence of the Constitutions of Government of the United States of America*.

91. Elizabeth Fox-Genovese and Eugene D. Genovese, *The Mind of the Master Class: History and Faith in the Southern Slaveholders' Worldview* (Cambridge: Cambridge University Press, 2005), 201, 274–275, 291, 293.

92. Jaffa, *New Birth*, 167; Jaffa, *The Conditions of Freedom*, 19–21.

93. Jaffa, *New Birth*, 375.

94. Some Straussians interpret this distinction as Aristotle's attempt to oppose slavery in his time and expose its morally ambiguous status (since it is not clear who is a slave by nature). See Mary P. Nichols, *Citizens and Statesmen: A Study of Aristotle's "Politics"* (Savage, MD: Rowman and Littlefield, 1992), 19–24. Yet she still admits that Aristotle unambiguously stands by his view that certain human beings deserve to be enslaved by nature.

95. Aristotle, *Politics*, book 1, chapter 6, 1255a 5–32. Here I use *The Basic Works of Aristotle*, edited by Richard McKeon (New York: Modern Library, 2001), 1132. It may be objected here that I am portraying Aristotle as a relativist who denied moral absolutes. Ironically enough, Strauss himself is occasionally accused of portraying Aristotle as a relativist on justice. See Schall, "A Latitude for Statesmanship?" 219–220.

96. *Nicomachean Ethics*, book 5, chapter 7, 1134b 25–29. Here I use *The Basic Works of Aristotle*, 1014.

97. Aristotle, *Politics*, book 7, chapter 2, 1324b 14–15.

98. Jaffa, *New Birth*, 135.

99. Harry V. Jaffa, "Leo Strauss, the Bible, and Political Philosophy," in Deutsch and Nicgorski, *Leo Strauss*, 208–209.

100. Harry V. Jaffa, *Crisis of the House Divided: An Interpretation of the Issues in the Lincoln-Douglas Debates* (Chicago: University of Chicago Press, 1982), 344–346.

101. Ibid., 346.

102. Ibid., 409. In a public forum at Rosary College in 1980, Jaffa coyly left it up to his audience to decide whether he was taking a "Hegelian" (that is, historicist) view when he credited Christianity, not paganism, for inspiring an awareness of guilt and redemption that is absent in Greek tragedy yet obviously present in Shakespeare's plays. Yet he stops short of claiming that Christianity "progressed" beyond paganism, even though this meaning is implied in his comments. See Harry V. Jaffa, *American Conservatism and the American Founding* (Claremont, CA: Claremont Institute, 1984), 68.

103. Hadley Arkes, *Natural Rights and the Right to Choose* (Cambridge: Cambridge University Press, 2002), 5, 68.

104. Ibid., 139.

105. Jason R. Jividen, *Claiming Lincoln: Progressivism, Equality, and the Battle for Lincoln's Legacy in Presidential Rhetoric* (DeKalb: Northern Illinois University Press, 2011), 31.

106. Jaffa, *New Birth*, 135. Elsewhere Jaffa makes a similar argument in stating that the Christian separation of religion from politics (based on Jesus' "unprecedented" distinction between Caesar and God) made modern constitutional government possible. See Harry V. Jaffa, "Too Good to Be True? A Reply to Robert Kraynak's 'Moral Order in the Western Tradition: Harry Jaffa's Grand Synthesis of Athens, Jerusalem, and Peoria,'" in Jaffa et al., *Crisis of the Strauss Divided*, 233, 238–239. See also his *American Founding*, 24–25. Yet Jaffa is still determined to draw Aristotelian themes from the American Founding, despite his own admission that Aristotle is silent on the separation of religious from political authority.

107. Arkes, *Natural Rights*, 3.

108. Jaffa, *New Birth*, 144–145.

109. Michael P. Zuckert, "Natural Rights and Protestant Politics," in *Protestantism and the American Founding*, edited by Thomas S. Engeman and Michael P. Zuckert (Notre Dame, IN: University of Notre Dame Press, 2004), 56–57. Throughout this essay, Zuckert downplays the influence of Protestantism on any political philosophy that came out of the Revolutionary era.

110. Fortin, *Classical Christianity*, 289. For Lincoln, see Havers, *Lincoln and the Politics of Christian Love*, 54–86 (esp. 57).

111. For Rahe's omission, see Paul Gottfried, "Concepts of Government," *Modern Age* 37, no. 3 (Spring 1995): 267. This article is a long review of Rahe's three-volume study.

112. Shain, *Myth of American Individualism*; Glenn Moots, *Politics Reformed: The Anglo-American Legacy of Covenant Theology* (Columbia, MO: University of Missouri Press, 2010), 5; Mark C. Henrie, "Thomas Pangle and the Problems of a Straussian Founding," *Modern Age* 36, no. 2 (1993): 128–138.

113. Arkes, *Natural Rights*, 24–25.

114. Ibid., 73–74, 77. The description inside the cover to Arkes's book previews the theme that the new right to abortion (since *Roe vs. Wade* in 1973) "overturned the liberal jurisprudence of the New Deal and placed liberal jurisprudence on a notably different foundation."

115. Once again, Jaffa admits that the philosophy of natural rights was "unknown to the ancient world" (*New Birth*, 375) but does not let this fact interfere with his view that Aristotle opposed slavery.

116. Nathan Tarcov and Thomas L. Pangle, "Epilogue: Leo Strauss and the History of Political Philosophy," in *History of Political Philosophy*, 3rd edition, edited by Leo Strauss and Joseph Cropsey (Chicago: University of Chicago Press, 1987), 928. See also Gottfried, *Leo Strauss*, 56–57, 60.

117. Strauss, "Relativism," 13–26.

118. Adam Smith, *The Theory of Moral Sentiments*, edited by D. D. Raphael and A. L. Macfie (Indianapolis: Liberty Classics, 1982), 210. Smith refers to Plato's *Republic* 460c and 461c, and Aristotle's *Politics* 1335b 20–21.

119. Paul A. Rahe, *New Modes and Orders in Early Modern Political Thought*, vol. 2 of *Republics Ancient and Modern* (Chapel Hill: University of North Carolina Press, 1994), 89–90.

120. Jaffa, *Crisis of the House Divided*; Jaffa, *New Birth*. See Arkes, *Natural Rights*, esp. 3.

121. Jaffa may well respond to this argument by contending that slavery by nature is just because it involves the enslavement of mental incompetents. See his *Conditions of Freedom*, 19–21. Yet Lincoln never made such a qualification when he called for the end of slavery. For a detailed discussion of Jaffa's misrepresentation of Lincoln, see Havers, *Lincoln and the Politics of Christian Love*, chapters 5–6.

122. Jaffa, *New Birth*, 117–121. For Maistre's famous remark on never meeting "man," see his "Considerations on France," in *The Works of Joseph de Maistre*, edited and translated by Jack Lively (New York: Macmillan, 1965), 80. Maistre is attacking the references to "man" in the 1795 French Constitution.

123. Maistre, "The Pope," in *The Works of Joseph de Maistre*, 144–145. Stephen Holmes has tried to associate Strauss with Maistre (*Anatomy*, 62–63) but never discusses the vast differences between the two thinkers on the role of Christianity in Western political thought.

124. See Harvey C. Mansfield Jr., "Providence and Democracy," *Claremont Review of Books* 11, nos. 1–2 (Winter 2010–Spring 2011): 78. Elsewhere Mansfield admits that Tocqueville shows no interest in defining the "best regime" as Plato and Aristotle understood this term. See Harvey C. Mansfield Jr. and Delba Winthrop, "Editors' Introduction," in Alexis de Tocqueville, *Democracy in America*, translated, edited, and with an introduction by Harvey C. Mansfield Jr. and Delba Winthrop (Chicago: University of Chicago Press, 2000), xxxiii–xxxiv, l–lii.

125. Tocqueville, *Democracy in America*, vol. 1, part 2, chapter 10 (334). I discuss Tocqueville's thoughts on Christian charity and its implicit opposition to slavery in my *Lincoln and the Politics of Christian Love*, 50–52.

126. Carnes Lord, *The Modern Prince: What Leaders Need to Know Now* (New Haven: Yale University Press, 2003), 77–81.

127. Alexander Hamilton, "The War in Europe," in *The Papers of Alexander Hamilton*, vol. 20, *January 1796–March 1797*, edited by Harold C. Syrett (New York: Columbia University Press, 1974), 339–340. For an incisive discussion of Hamilton's views on Christianity and the importance of the ethic of charity, see Karl Friedrich-Walling, "Was Alexander Hamilton a Machiavellian Statesman?" in *Machiavelli's Liberal Republican Legacy*, edited by Paul A. Rahe (Cambridge: Cambridge University Press, 2006), 275–276.

128. Bloom, *Closing*, 165. Bloom is basing this argument on Strauss's view that Machiavelli succeeded in "lowering" the lofty aims of politics, as they were understood by classical and medieval authors, by replacing the demanding ethic of Christian charity with the self-serving ethic of calculation. See Strauss, *What Is Political Philosophy?* 43–44.

3: Leo Strauss, from Left to Right

1. Harvey Mansfield Jr., "Roundtable Discussion: The Influence of German Philosophy," in *Hannah Arendt and Leo Strauss: German Emigrés and American Political Thought after World War II*, edited by Peter Graf Kielmansegg, Horst Mewes, and Elisabeth Glaser-Schmidt (Cambridge: Cambridge University Press, 1995), 170. This conference, which featured prominent German and American experts on political philosophy, was held at the University of Colorado, Boulder, in September 1991.

2. For a detailed critique of Arendt's thought from a Straussian perspective, see Thomas L. Pangle, *The Spirit of Modern Republicanism: The Moral Vision of the American Founders and*

the Philosophy of Locke (Chicago: University of Chicago Press, 1988), 48–61. See also Minowitz, *Straussophobia*, 36–38; Ceaser, *Nature and History*, 74; Bloom, *Closing*, 152.

3. Harry Jaffa once declared that Strauss was the philosophical answer to Heidegger, just as Churchill was the political answer to Hitler. See Jaffa, "Dear Professor Drury," 324–325. Bloom similarly notes the insidious influence of Heidegger on American campuses. See *Closing*, 309–311. Strauss himself refers to Heidegger as "intellectually the counterpart to what Hitler was politically." See Leo Strauss, "An Unspoken Prologue to a Public Lecture at St. John's College in Honor of Jacob Klein," in Strauss, *Jewish Philosophy*, 450.

4. Some of Arendt's writings often share with Strauss remarkably similar views about the need to protect the classical tradition of political philosophy against modern "nihilists" like Marx, Kierkegaard, and Nietzsche. See Hannah Arendt, *Between Past and Future: Six Exercises in Political Thought* (New York: Meridian Books, 1963), 17–40. For a discussion of the philosophical affinities between Strauss and Arendt, see Grant Havers, "Between Athens and Jerusalem: Western Otherness in the Works of Leo Strauss and Hannah Arendt," *European Legacy* 9, no.1 (2004): 19–29.

5. Hannah Arendt, *On Revolution* (London and New York: Penguin, 1990). This book was originally published in 1963. Like Pangle, Arendt contends that Christian thought had little impact on the American Revolution (70–71). It is also significant that Mansfield follows Arendt in ignoring the influence of the Bible on the intellectual tradition of the West. In his study of the Machiavellian origins of the American Founding, Mansfield follows Strauss in contending that the Christian ethic of charity was too otherworldly and burdensome for the rough-and-tumble world of politics. See Mansfield, *Taming the Prince*, chapters 5–6 (esp. 115, 125). Additionally, his study of the philosophical approaches to gender and sexuality discusses the Greeks in detail yet ignores the Bible altogether. See Harvey C. Mansfield Jr., *Manliness* (New Haven: Yale University Press, 2006), and my review of this book in *European Legacy* 12, no. 6 (2007): 764–765.

6. See Gottfried, *Leo Strauss*, 72–81.

7. Smith, *Reading Leo Strauss*, 179.

8. Letter to Voegelin dated August 25, 1950, in Emberley and Cooper, *Faith and Political Philosophy*, 71. In a similarly conservative vein, Strauss elaborates upon the Platonic lesson that politics is akin to wine-drinking. From this analogy he cautions against overly bold innovations, such as the attempt to replace old laws with new ones: "[Drinkers] must drink wine, not in deed, but in speech" (*What Is Political Philosophy?* 31).

9. See his comments on Lukacs in Strauss, "Relativism," 19–21.

10. See John P. Diggins, *Up from Communism: Conservative Odysseys in American Intellectual History* (New York: Harper and Row, 1975).

11. Gottfried, *Leo Strauss*, 14, 70. Gottfried also notes that Strauss thought President Eisenhower was a "bit too far to the right for his taste" (35).

12. Ibid., 71.

13. See Roberts, *Athens on Trial*, 271. Roberts's study is an excellent critical analysis of the various ways in which moderns, including Strauss, read contemporary agenda into the history and political thought of classical Athens.

14. The philosopher Martha Nussbaum, who is not a Straussian, also comes close to offering a leftist appreciation of Aristotle. In the preface to the revised edition of her study *The Fragility of Goodness: Luck and Ethics in Greek Tragedy and Philosophy* (Cambridge: Cambridge University Press, 2001), she admits that there is no concept of "universal human dignity" in Aristotle's thought (xx). Yet she also contends that his understanding of fortune,

both good and bad, can help combat "racist or nationalist" sentiments that express hatred of humanity (xxxi).

15. Strauss, *Thoughts on Machiavelli*, 298. Elsewhere, Strauss warns of the "emancipation of technology, of the arts, from moral and political control" in modernity (*What Is Political Philosophy?* 37).

16. Strauss, *Liberalism: Ancient and Modern*, viii–ix. In an essay on Kurt Riezler, Strauss decries liberal "cosmopolitanism" for ignoring the power of nationalism in the modern age (*What Is Political Philosophy?* 236–237). In the last year of his life, Strauss referred to himself as a "hopeless reactionary." See Minowitz, *Straussophobia*, 163.

17. Strauss, *Liberalism: Ancient and Modern*, x.

18. For a useful discussion of this preface, see Gottfried, *Leo Strauss*, 62–64. Gottfried notes that Strauss's passing respect for conservatism in no way challenges his far greater appreciation for liberal democracy.

19. Himmelfarb, "On Leo Strauss," 64. Tracy Strong wonders whether "there could be a Straussianism of the Left in America," given leftist admiration for his onetime friend Carl Schmitt. See her foreword to Carl Schmitt, *The Concept of the Political*, translated and with an introduction by George Schwab (Chicago: University of Chicago Press, 1996), xx.

20. Pangle, *Leo Strauss*, 101.

21. Rosen, *Hermeneutics as Politics*, 134–135; Xenos, *Cloaked in Virtue*, 68. For an extensive discussion of the similarities between Strauss's and Adorno's critiques of modern instrumental reason, see Christopher Brittain, "Leo Strauss and Resourceful Odysseus: Rhetorical Violence and the Holy Middle," *Canadian Review of American Studies* 38, no. 1 (2008): 147–163. See also Havers, "Kierkegaard, Adorno."

22. Minowitz, *Straussophobia*, 288–289.

23. Melvin L. Rogers, "Rorty's Straussianism, or, Irony against Democracy," *Contemporary Pragmatism* 1, no. 2 (December 2004): 104.

24. Gottfried, *Leo Strauss*.

25. Strauss, *What Is Political Philosophy?* 21. Strauss is referring to Adorno's two-volume study, *The Authoritarian Personality* (New York: Harper and Row, 1950). His critical remarks here seem to conflict with Pangle's view that Strauss's analysis of Plato's regime psychology fits into the Frankfurt School's studies on political psychology. See Pangle, *Leo Strauss*, 101.

26. Bloom, *Closing*, 29.

27. Jaffa, *Crisis*, 364–381; Jaffa, *How to Think*, 3–6. For Hofstadter's indebtedness to the Frankfurt School, see David S. Brown, *Richard Hofstadter: An Intellectual Biography* (Chicago: University of Chicago Press, 2006), 89–90. I discuss Hofstadter's polemics against Lincoln's Protestantism in my *Lincoln and the Politics of Christian Love*, 100–103.

28. See Sunic, *Against Democracy and Equality*, 119–123.

29. Drury, *Political Ideas*, 123. According to Drury, Strauss blames Machiavelli, who dismisses Christianity as too otherworldly for the political sphere, for contributing to the decline of the faith in the West.

30. Novak, *On Two Wings*, 147.

31. Strauss, "Heideggerian Existentialism," 39–40.

32. See Barry Cooper, "The Revival of Political Philosophy," in *By Loving Our Own: George Grant and the Legacy of "Lament for a Nation,"* edited by Peter C. Emberley (Ottawa: Carleton University Press, 1990), 113. See also Drury, *Alexandre Kojève*, 143–159. Grant at least understood that Strauss is less opposed to historicism than meets the eye, since

Strauss, like Hegel, divides the history of modern philosophy into stages (e.g., the "three waves of modernity"). See George Parkin Grant, *Technology and Empire: Perspectives on North America* (Toronto: House of Anansi, 1969), 92. See also Zdravko Planinc, "Paradox and Polyphony in Grant's Critique of Modernity," in *George Grant and the Future of Canada,* edited by Yusuf K. Umar, with a foreword by Barry Cooper (Calgary: University of Calgary Press, 1992), 32–33.

33. Alexandre Kojève, "Hegel, Marx, and Christianity," *Interpretation* 1 (1970): 41.

34. See Kojève's review of the Right-Hegelian Gaston Fessard's anti-communism in Gaston Fessard, "Two Interpreters of Hegel's Phenomenology," *Interpretation* 19, no. 2 (Winter 1991–1992): 193.

35. Strauss, *On Tyranny,* 207. Strauss is responding to Kojève's argument on pages 172–173.

36. Drury, *Alexandre Kojève,* 143–159.

37. Strauss, *On Tyranny,* 209–211.

38. See Drury, *Alexandre Kojève,* 143–159; Lampert, *Leo Strauss and Nietzsche.*

39. Strauss, *Natural Right and History,* 75.

40. Strauss, "Progress or Return?" 305.

41. Strauss, *Spinoza's Critique of Religion,* 194. Strauss held this view of religion even as far back as the 1930s, before he came to America. At this time, Strauss rejected any possibility of a reconciliation between religious orthodoxy and Enlightenment rationalism. See his *Philosophy and Law: Contributions to the Understanding of Maimonides and His Predecessors,* translated with an introduction by Eve Adler (Albany: SUNY Press, 1995), 37–38. This book was originally published in German in 1935.

42. Strauss, *Spinoza's Critique of Religion,* 198. See Thomas L. Pangle, *Political Philosophy and the God of Abraham* (Baltimore: Johns Hopkins University Press, 2003), 91–92, 183; David Janssens, *Between Athens and Jerusalem: Philosophy, Prophecy, and Politics in Leo Strauss's Early Thought* (Albany, SUNY Press, 2008), 62. Pangle and Janssens closely follow Strauss's interpretation of Calvin and revelation as a whole.

43. See Bloom, *Giants and Dwarfs,* 246.

44. Strauss, *What Is Political Philosophy?* 13. Strauss wrote these remarks in lectures he gave at the Hebrew University in Jerusalem in 1954 and 1955.

45. Strauss, *Natural Right and History,* 59. For a useful discussion of Strauss's critique of Weber's analysis of Calvinism, see Nasser Behnegar, *Leo Strauss, Max Weber, and the Scientific Study of Politics* (Chicago: University of Chicago Press, 2003), 107–113.

46. Strauss, *Spinoza's Critique of Religion,* 195. See also Steven Nadler, *A Book Forged in Hell: Spinoza's Scandalous Treatise and the Birth of the Secular Age* (Princeton: Princeton University Press, 2011), 133.

47. John Calvin, *Genesis,* translated and edited by John King (London: The Banner of Truth Trust, 1975), 86. Spinoza similarly argues that Moses spoke primarily about ethics in a manner that was suited to his simple audience. See Spinoza, *Theologico-Political Treatise,* chapter 2, section 9, paragraphs 17 and 23 (26–27). It was not the intent of Moses or any of the prophets to provide a scientific account of the universe.

48. Calvin, *Genesis,* 86.

49. John Calvin, *Institutes of the Christian Religion,* translated by Henry Beveridge (Grand Rapids, MI: Eeerdmans, 1989), 657.

50. Spinoza's condemnation of "superstitious" authorities who invoke Scripture to justify oppression is a constant theme of his *Theologico-Political Treatise.* Like Calvin, Spi-

noza also understands the principal strength of the Bible as the greatest teacher of ethics. For Spinoza's indebtedness to Dutch Calvinism, see Graeme Hunter, *Radical Protestantism in Spinoza's Thought* (Burlington, VT: Ashgate, 2005). At times even Strauss admits that Spinoza makes use of Calvinist ideas, like the doctrine of predestination as an argument against free will, as well as the Christian emphasis on God's love. However, Strauss insists that Spinoza is being insincere and Machiavellian in his use of these credos, since he intends to undermine religious authority. See *Spinoza's Critique of Religion*, 201, 208.

51. Shain, *Myth of American Individualism*; Moots, *Politics Reformed*. See also Henrie, "Thomas Pangle," 128-138.

52. See Strauss, *Persecution and the Art of Writing*, 142-201.

53. Strauss, "On the Interpretation of Genesis," 369. Here he claims that there "is not a trace of an argument in support of this [biblical] assertion" that the universe was created by God.

54. Strauss, "Progress or Return?" 299.

55. See Brayton Polka, *Hermeneutics and Ontology*, vol. 1 of *Between Philosophy and Religion*, 253. Jaffa echoes Strauss in noting that God is "outside the order of nature" and thus beyond the comprehension of reason. See his "Leo Strauss, the Bible, and Political Philosophy," 210.

56. Spinoza, *Theologico-Political Treatise*, chapter 15, section 1, paragraphs 13-35 (170-173). See also Levene, "Athens and Jerusalem," 136. Remarkably for a critic of Spinoza, Strauss occasionally agrees with him in opposing any attempt to subordinate philosophy to religion (Alfakhar's position) or religion to philosophy (Maimonides' position). Every synthesis is actually an "option for Athens or Jerusalem." See his letter to Eric Voegelin dated February 25, 1951, in Emberley and Cooper, *Faith and Political Philosophy*, 78. See also Strauss, "Progress or Return?" 290.

57. Herbert Marcuse, *A Study on Authority*, translated by Joris de Bres (London: Verso Press, 2008), 34. Marcuse's argument is identical to that of Erich Fromm's *Fear of Freedom* (London: Routledge, 1991), which portrays both Lutheranism and Calvinism as forerunners of Nazism. Fromm was a member of the Frankfurt School.

58. Strauss, "Progress or Return?" 275; Strauss, *Natural Right and History*, 74.

59. Strauss, "Why We Remain Jews," 323. He may have had in mind Cromwell's England and Calvinist Holland, both of which accepted Jews who were refugees from Catholic persecution in Spain and Portugal (including Spinoza's ancestors who left Portugal and eventually migrated to Holland).

60. In his correspondence with Eric Voegelin (August 25, 1950), Strauss dismisses liberal Protestantism as a "pseudo-Protestantism, whose real basis is not Protestantism, but rather a radical secularization." See Emberley and Cooper, *Faith and Political Philosophy*, 71.

61. For Jefferson's liberal approach to the Bible, see Pangle, *Spirit of Modern Republicanism*, 81-84. Pangle interprets Jefferson's liberal theology as a descendant of the biblical hermeneutic that Spinoza and Locke first articulated. For an insightful critique of Pangle's analysis, which particularly targets Pangle's efforts to downplay the Protestantism at the core of the American Founding, see Henrie, "Thomas Pangle," 128-138.

62. Leo Strauss, "Freud on Moses and Monotheism," in Strauss, *Jewish Philosophy*, 303-304. See also his 1948 lecture "Reason and Revelation," in Meier, *Strauss and the Theologico-Political Problem*, 156. In this lecture, Strauss remarks that modern theology "stands or falls by the distinction between the central or true and peripheral or mythical elements of the Bible," a distinction that he attributes to Spinoza's influence.

63. Strauss, *Natural Right and History*, 61n. Since my study is focused on Anglo-American liberal democracy, it may be objected that I give too much attention to Hobbes, a defender of absolute monarchy. Given Hobbes's influence on the far more democratic Locke as well as his defense of natural equality, however, it is not much of a stretch to argue that Hobbes is, as Strauss argues, the founder of liberalism. See *Natural Right and History*, 182. For a useful elaboration of Hobbes's liberalism and its influence on feminism, see Mansfield, *Manliness*, 172-173.

64. Leo Strauss, *The Political Philosophy of Hobbes: Its Basis and Its Genesis*, translated by Elsa M. Sinclair (Chicago: University of Chicago Press, 1963), 121-126. The Clarendon Press (Oxford) first published this work in English in 1936.

65. Strauss, *Natural Right and History*, 199n.

66. Ibid., 215-219.

67. Strauss contends that Locke's views on miracles "tacitly" follow those of Spinoza. See *Natural Right and History*, 210. Spinoza's critique of miracles (see chapter 6 of his *Theologico-Political Treatise*) is crucial to his distinction between real religion and superstition, since the latter includes belief in miracles.

68. Strauss, *Spinoza's Critique of Religion*, 245, 248; Strauss, *Persecution and the Art of Writing*, 163, 173-175, 196.

69. See Strauss, *What Is Political Philosophy?* 171. Here he admits that Hobbes "never wavered in his adherence to the golden rule" and, compared to twentieth-century ideologues of tyranny, Hobbes incarnates "old-fashioned decency." That said, Strauss observes elsewhere that Hobbes was "deservedly punished" by his countrymen for his reckless ideas (*Natural Right and History*, 166).

70. Strauss argues in *Natural Right and History* (319) that the real turn from a preoccupation with the "universal" or "natural" to a focus on the merely "historical" and "ancestral" begins with Burke, not Rousseau, since this great English political philosopher's focus on mere tradition is a "preparation" for Hegel's more radical historicism. I discuss Strauss's critique of Burke below.

71. Strauss, *What Is Political Philosophy?* 171. In fairness to Strauss here, Spinoza praises the commercial citizenry of late seventeenth-century Amsterdam as most suited to the bourgeois Christianity he defends. See his *Theologico-Political Treatise*, chapter 20, section 6, paragraph 4 (235).

72. Leo Strauss, *Studies in Platonic Political Philosophy*, with an introduction by Thomas L. Pangle (Chicago: University of Chicago Press, 1983), 230. The full title of C. B. Macpherson's book is *The Political Theory of Possessive Individualism: Hobbes to Locke* (Oxford: Oxford University Press, 1962).

73. J. G. A. Pocock, *Politics, Language, and Time: Essays on Political Thought and History* (London: Methuen, 1972), 162, 192-193, 199-200. For a more recent discussion of Hobbes's Protestant faith and his corresponding rejection of scholasticism, see Michael Allen Gillespie, *The Theological Origins of Modernity* (Chicago: University of Chicago Press, 2008), 207-254.

74. Pocock, *Politics, Language, and Time*, 162. Strauss similarly writes that the "intrinsic validity" of biblical religion has no place in Hobbes's utilitarian social contract (*Natural Right and History*, 187). At times, Pocock is somewhat receptive to Strauss's studies, even praising his *Thoughts on Machiavelli* as "marvelously perceptive in some ways, as well as marvelously wrong-headed in others." See J. G. A. Pocock, "Prophet and Inquisitor, or, A Church Built upon Bayonets Cannot Stand: A Comment on Mansfield's 'Strauss's Machiavelli,'" *Political Theory* 3, no. 4 (November 1975): 385-386.

75. Strauss, *Political Philosophy of Hobbes*, 44–58.

76. Strauss, *Natural Right and History*, 187. Hobbes's focus on the "badness" of humanity presumably has origins in Machiavelli, who was the first to use this teaching against the classical ideal of rule by the wise. See Strauss, *Thoughts on Machiavelli*, 254.

77. Besides chapter 14, Hobbes appeals to the Golden Rule as the foundation (the "laws of nature") of the peaceable social contract in chapters 15, 17, and 26 of *Leviathan*. Here I use the edition of *Leviathan* edited by Michael Oakeshott (New York: Macmillan, 1962).

78. Strauss, *Natural Right and History*, 184, 215.

79. Ibid., 216–251.

80. John Locke, *The Reasonableness of Christianity, with a Discourse of Miracles and Part of a Third Letter Concerning Toleration*, edited by I. T. Ramsey (Stanford: Stanford University Press, 1958), 61, 66–67. Locke concludes this essay with the observation, which he already has repeated more than once, that the people are better off learning morality from the Bible since they have "not leisure for learning and logic, and superfine distinctions of the schools" (76). Locke's entire argument is similar to Spinoza's view that the Bible, not nature or reason, teaches morality to most human beings. See Spinoza, *Theologico-Political Treatise*, chapter 16.

81. John Locke, *A Letter Concerning Toleration*, edited and introduced by James H. Tully (Indianapolis: Hackett, 1983), 51. Spinoza similarly adds that covenants (social contracts) do not count with "Heathens," who do not practice biblical morality. See Spinoza, *Theologico-Political Treatise*, chapter 16, section 8, paragraph 20 (189).

82. Ross J. Corbett, "Locke's Biblical Critique," *Review of Politics* 74 (2012): 28.

83. Strauss, *Natural Right and History*, 294–323. In fairness to Strauss, at times he credits Burke with defending a conservatism that is somewhat compatible with "pre-modern natural law." Yet even this trace of eternal truths in Burke's writings does not deter him from ultimately abandoning natural law and "natural rights" in favor of "the historical school" and the prescriptive "rights of Englishmen." See Strauss, "On Natural Law," in *Studies in Platonic Political Philosophy*, 146.

84. For a critique of Strauss's reading of Burke on this point, see Joseph Baldacchino, "The Value-Centered Historicism of Edmund Burke," *Modern Age* 27, no. 2 (1983): 139–145; Robert P. Kraynak, "Strauss, Voegelin, and Burke: A Tale of Three Conservatives," *Modern Age* 53, no. 4 (Fall 2011): 28–31.

85. Strauss associates Hobbes with Burke in *Natural Right and History*, 188. Once again, Strauss interprets Burke as a radical who prepares the ground for Hegel (*Natural Right and History*, 319). This line of thinking is consistent with Strauss's dismissal of conservatism as both modern and radical in origin. In his "Preface to the English Translation," Strauss further emphasizes the utterly modern origins of conservatism by pointing to the "typical mistake of the conservative" as "concealing the fact" that conservatism came into being through the rather unconservative process of "discontinuities, revolutions, and sacrileges" (27). In short, conservatism springs forth not as tradition but as a radical force in modernity. Strauss wrote this in the context of his critique of Hermann Cohen's attack on Spinoza.

86. Strauss, *Natural Right and History*, 317–318. The American Burkean philosopher Russell Kirk, who initially saw Strauss and his students "as the most vigorous and promising group" of political thinkers determined to reassert the natural law tradition in America, once even partially sympathized with the Straussian view that Burke's refusal to resist what he called "Providence" may have "opened the way, theoretically, for the triumph of much of what he detested." Nevertheless, Kirk also offered the cautionary view, particularly against

Harvey Mansfield's reading of Burke, that this Whiggish conservative was displaying an admirable prudence in recognizing that "theory divorced from social reality" cannot counteract massive historical change. See Russell Kirk, "Bolingbroke, Burke, and the Statesman," *Kenyon Review* 28 (June 1966): 429, 431. Although Kirk never wrote in detail about Strauss and his students, he eventually took a tough stance against their hermeneutic. In time, Kirk repudiated altogether the Straussian view that Burke advocated passivity in the face of revolution, since he called for relentless opposition to the Jacobin tyranny in France. See Russell Kirk, *Redeeming the Time*, edited with an introduction by Jeffrey O. Nelson (Wilmington, DE: ISI Books, 1996), 257–258. Harry Jaffa accuses Kirk of overemphasizing the conservatism of Burke without taking into account his liberal inclinations (which led him to support the American Revolution). Yet Jaffa does not explain how this reading of Burke fits with that of Strauss, who also portrays Burke as primarily a conservative. See Harry V. Jaffa, "Straussian Geography: A Memoir and Commentary," in Jaffa et al., *Crisis of the Strauss Divided*, 4.

87. Edmund Burke, *Reflections on the Revolution in France* (Harmondsworth: Penguin, 1982), 188.

88. Ibid., 248.

89. Edmund Burke, *On the American Revolution: Selected Speeches and Letters*, edited by Elliott R. Barkan (New York: Harper Torchbooks, 1966), 193. This passage is from a letter to John Farr and John Harris, Esquires, sheriffs of Bristol, on the affairs of America (April 1777). Spinoza makes a remarkably similar argument against superstitions that "turn the spirit of the multitude" in order to justify "servitude" in the name of religion. See Spinoza, *Theologico-Political Treatise*, preface, section 3, paragraph 3 (xviii).

90. Winston Churchill, "Moses: The Leader of a People," in *Thoughts and Adventures* (New York: W. W. Norton, 1990), 213–215. Churchill published this essay in 1932.

91. Harry V. Jaffa, "Can There Be Another Winston Churchill?" in *Statesmanship: Essays in Honor of Sir Winston S. Churchill*, edited by Harry V. Jaffa (Durham, NC: Carolina Academic Press, 1981), 29–30.

92. Strauss, *Spinoza's Critique of Religion*, 194.

93. Strauss, "Why We Remain Jews," 327.

94. Pangle, who follows Strauss, dismisses this Anglo-American attempt to identify "true religion" with moral teachings as an impious project that weakens the force of religion altogether. See Pangle, *Spirit of Modern Republicanism*, 83–84. Yet Pangle ignores the fact that the "true religion" to which Hobbes and Locke refer, that of charity, still requires the influence of Christianity to promulgate it. Churchill certainly never doubted this fact. See chapter four on Churchill's views on the indispensability of Christianity.

95. Levene, "Athens and Jerusalem," 137.

96. Strauss, "Plato," 208; Strauss, *The City and Man*, 2.

97. Strauss, *Thoughts on Machiavelli*, 231. Hobbes's term "the kingdom of darkness" is the subject of part 4 of his *Leviathan*. Elsewhere Strauss associates the rise of liberal democracy with this opposition to the "kingdom of darkness." See "Preface to the English Translation," 3. It follows logically, then, based on these two passages from Strauss, that in his view Machiavellianism was the catalyst for liberal democracy.

98. Strauss, *Political Philosophy of Hobbes*, 118–126.

99. Bloom, *Giants and Dwarfs*, 246; Peter Minowitz, "Machiavellianism Come of Age? Leo Strauss on Modernity and Economics," *Political Science Reviewer* 22 (1993): 178.

100. I am not the first reader of Strauss to critique his interpretation of Spinoza. See Polka, *Hermeneutics and Ontology*, 251–264. See also Errol E. Harris, *The Substance of Spi-*

noza (Atlantic Highlands, NJ: Humanities Press, 1995), 125–148; Nancy K. Levene, "Ethics and Interpretation, or How to Study Spinoza's *Tractatus Theologico-Politicus* without Strauss," *Journal of Jewish Thought and Philosophy* 10 (2000): 57–110; Grant Havers, "Romanticism and Universalism: The Case of Leo Strauss," *Dialogue and Universalism* 12, nos. 6–7 (2002): 155–167.

101. Strauss, "Preface to the English Translation," 16.

102. Smith, *Reading Leo Strauss*, 105.

103. Strauss, "Preface to the English Translation," 15, 18.

104. Strauss, *Thoughts on Machiavelli*, 50–51, 197.

105. Janssens, *Between Athens and Jerusalem*, 35.

106. Martin D. Yaffe, "Interpretive Essay," in *Spinoza's Theologico-Political Treatise*, 329.

107. Ernest L. Fortin, "Augustine, Spinoza, and the Hermeneutical Problem," in *Classical Christianity*, 116.

108. Pangle, *Spirit of Modern Republicanism*, 153.

109. Michael P. Zuckert, *Launching Liberalism: On Lockean Political Philosophy* (Lawrence: University Press of Kansas, 2002), 142, 155–156; Rahe, *New Modes and Orders*, 233–236.

110. Edwin Curley, "'I Durst Not Write So Boldly,' or How to Read Hobbes' Theological-Political Treatise," in *Hobbes e Spinoza: Scienza e politica. Atti del convegno internazionale, Urbino 14–17 ottobre, 1988*, edited by Daniela Bostrenghi (Naples: Bibliopolis, 1992), 571.

111. I discuss the demanding nature of charity in the political realm in my *Lincoln and the Politics of Christian Love*. It is interesting that Strauss, at least when he is not discussing Spinoza, does not interpret Christian morality (including the virtues of mercy and humility) as minimal in influence, since he occasionally worries that the tradition of classical political philosophy was "transformed but not broken" by this ethic. Fortunately for the classical tradition, statesmen like Churchill were not too beholden to this ethic in the war against Nazi Germany. See Strauss, "What Can We Learn from Political Theory?" 527.

112. See Minowitz, "Machiavellianism?"

113. Yaffe, "Interpretive Essay," 271, 273.

114. Despite Strauss's much discussed appreciation of Nietzsche, it is surprising that his "recovery" of the ancient Greeks was undeterred by Nietzsche's late in life rejection of the Greeks as "too alien, and also too fluid, to have an imperative effect, a 'classical effect'" on the moderns. See Nietzsche, "What I Owe to the Ancients," no. 2, in *Twilight of the Idols*, translated by Richard Polt (Indianapolis and Cambridge: Hackett, 1997), 86–87.

115. Strauss, *Thoughts on Machiavelli*, 13–14; Strauss, *What Is Political Philosophy?* 47.

116. Clifford Orwin, "Machiavelli's Unchristian Charity," *American Political Science Review* 72 (1978): 1223. See also Strauss, *Thoughts on Machiavelli*, 50–51, 197.

117. Strauss, *What Is Political Philosophy?* 45–46.

118. In chapter 18 of *The Prince*, Machiavelli notes that a ruler at times must be "uncharitable, inhumane, and irreligious" if he is to hold onto power. Charity, then, is associated with weakness. Yet Machiavelli does not adequately explain how the power of Christian charity, in the hands of the lower classes, dethroned the "manly" ruling class of Rome. For an insightful discussion of these issues, see Vickie B. Sullivan, *Machiavelli's Three Romes: Religion, Human Liberty, and Politics Reformed* (DeKalb: Northern Illinois University Press, 1996), 101–121.

119. See Ranieri, *Disturbing Revelation*, 103–130, 158–180.

120. Strauss, *What Is Political Philosophy?* 171; see also Strauss, *Political Philosophy of Hobbes*, 116.

121. Thomas Jefferson, *The Life and Selected Writings of Thomas Jefferson*, edited by Adrienne Koch and William Peden (New York: Modern Library, 1998), 515, 519, 522, 634.

122. For a thought-provoking discussion of Jefferson's views on charity, see Matthew S. Holland, *Bonds of Affection: Civic Charity and the Making of America—Winthrop, Jefferson, and Lincoln* (Washington, DC: Georgetown University Press, 2007), 93-157.

123. Montesquieu, *The Spirit of Laws*, book 24, chapters 1 and 6. These quotes are from *The Spirit of Laws: A Compendium of the First English Edition*, edited with an introduction by David Wallace Carrithers (Berkeley and Los Angeles: University of California Press, 1977), 321, 326.

124. Novak, *On Two Wings*, 101-106.

125. Jonathan Israel, *Radical Enlightenment: Philosophy and the Making of Modernity, 1650-1750* (Oxford: Oxford University Press, 2001), 268; Steven Nadler, *Spinoza's Heresy: Immortality and the Jewish Mind* (Oxford: Oxford University Press, 2001); Antonio Negri, *Subversive Spinoza: (Un)contemporary Variations*, edited by Timothy S. Murphy (Manchester: Manchester University Press, 2004), 52n4; J. Samuel Preus, *Spinoza and the Irrelevance of Biblical Authority* (Cambridge: Cambridge University Press, 2001); Yirmiyahu Yovel, *Spinoza and Other Heretics: The Marrano of Reason* (Princeton: Princeton University Press, 1989).

126. The Thomistic philosopher Frederick D. Wilhelmsen accused Strauss and his students of being anti-Christian Averroists. See his *Christianity and Political Philosophy* (Athens: University of Georgia Press, 1978), 211.

127. See Batnitzky, *Strauss and Emmanuel Levinas*, 142-144; Kenneth Hart Green, *Jew and Philosopher: The Return to Maimonides in the Jewish Thought of Leo Strauss* (Albany: SUNY Press, 1993), 10-11.

128. For a useful discussion of this stage in Strauss's life, see Michael Zank, "Introduction," in Strauss, *Early Writings*, 3-11.

129. Strauss, "Preface to the English Translation," 6. Once again, this remark is an attack on German liberalism, not the Anglo-American version that Strauss cherishes. As Strauss contends throughout this preface, the age-old negative association of Jewishness with the most destabilizing forces of modernity (the Enlightenment, liberalism, democracy) in the traditional German mind-set created a "precarious" situation for German Jews even before the rise of Hitler (2-3). For an insightful discussion of this historic context, see Christopher Vasillopulos, *The Triumph of Hate: The Political Theology of the Hitler Movement* (Lanham, MD: University Press of America, 2012), 247-257.

130. Altman, *German Stranger*, 517.

131. Himmelfarb, "On Leo Strauss," 64.

132. McAllister, *Revolt against Modernity*, 84-191.

133. Ranieri, *Disturbing Revelation*, 28.

134. Hadley Arkes, "Athens and Jerusalem: The Legacy of Leo Strauss," in *Leo Strauss and Judaism: Jerusalem and Athens Critically Revisited* (Lanham, MD: Rowman and Littlefield, 1996), 21.

135. See Novak, "Introduction," in *Leo Strauss and Judaism*, ix. Strauss himself notes that the conflation of Judaism with a "religion of reason" is atheism, since it reduces God to a mere "idea," and revelation to the status of a work contrived by the "human imagination." See "Preface to the English Translation," 8.

136. Hermann Cohen, *Religion of Reason: Out of the Sources of Judaism*, translated with an introduction by Simon Kaplan (Atlanta: Scholars Press, 1995), 3.

137. Strauss, "Introductory Essay," in ibid., xxxi-xxxv.

138. Emil L. Fackenheim, *To Mend the World: Foundations of Future Jewish Thought*

(New York: Schocken Books, 1982), 39. Fackenheim dedicated this book to the memory of Leo Strauss.

139. Strauss, "Introductory Essay," xxxviii.

140. Steven B. Smith contends that Cohen's faith in Jewish messianism (as leftist politics) is, in Strauss's implicit view, as "Machiavellian" as Spinoza's philosophy. See Steven B. Smith, "How to Commemorate the 350th Anniversary of Spinoza's Expulsion, or Leo Strauss's Reply to Hermann Cohen," *Hebraic Political Studies* 3, no. 2 (Spring 2008): 166.

141. In his 1924 essay, "Cohen's Analysis of Spinoza's Bible Science," the young Strauss faults Cohen for ignoring the political context of Dutch Calvinism, which posed great dangers to Spinoza. See Strauss, *Early Writings*, 145–147; Green, *Jew and Philosopher*, 55; Eugene R. Sheppard, *Leo Strauss and the Politics of Exile: The Making of a Political Philosopher* (Waltham, MA: Brandeis University Press, 2006); 50; Ranieri, *Disturbing Revelation*, 25–26; Smith, "How to Commemorate," 166. Even Bloom ambivalently praises Spinoza for using "secret writing" in order to create a regime (liberal democracy) that would no longer require philosophers to practice this ancient art. "His use of it [secret writing] was in the service of overcoming it." See Bloom, *Giants and Dwarfs*, 244. Bloom does not explain, however, why this tactic of Spinoza's was a bad thing, since it made possible the one regime that extended full political rights to Jews.

142. For parallels between Strauss and Adorno on modern reason, see Brittain, "Resourceful Odysseus," 147–163. See also Xenos, *Cloaked in Virtue*, 68.

143. Perhaps for this reason Strauss has been called the "conservative Doppelgänger" of Adorno. See Lars Fischer, "After the 'Strauss Wars,'" *East European Jewish Affairs* 40, no. 1 (April 2010): 66. See also Havers, "Kierkegaard, Adorno."

144. Max Horkheimer and Theodor W. Adorno, *Dialectic of Enlightenment*, translated by John Cumming (New York: Continuum, 2002), 95–96. This work was originally published in German in 1944.

145. Ibid., 90.

146. Bloom (*Closing*, 146–147) blames Adorno and the Frankfurt School for introducing nihilistic German philosophy into the American mainstream, and thus undermining democratic values.

147. According to Aschheim, Strauss and Adorno exhibited a typical "Weimar" antipathy to liberalism that was common among Jewish intellectuals from the Left and the Right of that period (*Beyond the Border*, 111–112).

148. See Theodor W. Adorno, *Kierkegaard: Construction of the Aesthetic*, translated, edited, and with a foreword by Robert Hullot-Kentor (Minneapolis: University of Minnesota Press), 110–112; Theodor W. Adorno, *The Jargon of Authenticity*, translated by Knut Tarnowski and Frederic Will (London: Routledge and Kegan Paul, 1973), 31–32.

149. Strauss, "Preface to the English Translation," 6; Adorno and Horkheimer, *Dialectic of Enlightenment*, 200.

150. Smith, "How to Commemorate," 171–172.

151. Strauss, "Preface to the English Translation," 30–31.

152. Strauss, "Re-education of Axis Countries," 533.

153. Strauss, "Progress or Return?" 310.

154. Ibid., 265. Elsewhere Strauss appreciates Nietzsche's view that the separation of biblical morality from belief in the biblical God (who manifests mercy and compassion) will lead to the triumph of the ruthless and amoral "overman." See "Preface to the English Translation," 12–13. For a useful discussion of related issues, see also Corine Pelluchon, "Strauss

and Christianity," *Interpretation* 33, no. 2 (Spring 2006): 200–201. For a discussion of the Straussian reluctance to ground ethics in biblical revelation, due to their attachment to "natural rights," see Grant Havers, "Natural Rightism and the Biogenetic Revolution," in *Values and Technology: Religion in Public Life*, vol. 37, edited by Gabriel R. Ricci (New Brunswick, NJ: Transaction, 2011), 93–105.

155. See Havers, *Lincoln and the Politics of Christian Love*, chapters 5–6. Social conservatism is far less important to supporters of American democracy than it may often appear to be. Hadley Arkes was genuinely surprised by the negative reaction to his attempt—in an essay he contributed to *First Things* in 1996—to question the moral legitimacy of the American regime because of its tolerance of mass abortion. See Arkes, *Natural Rights and the Right to Choose*, 150–151. His surprise may have been based on his misunderstanding that neoconservatives (including Straussians like Mansfield, as discussed at the start of this chapter) are just as concerned with preserving traditionalist stances on issues like abortion as they are with winning broad support for American democratic ideals across the political spectrum.

4: Churchill, the Anglo-American Greek?

1. Strauss, "What Can We Learn from Political Theory?" 527. In *On Tyranny*, Strauss similarly asks whether classical social science is obsolete, because of "the triumph of the biblical orientation" (177–178). Given the shining example of Churchill, as Strauss portrays him, the answer is clearly no.

2. Strauss, "German Nihilism," 363. The "teacher" to whom Strauss refers here is Oswald Spengler. See note 11 to this lecture for full citation information.

3. Strauss, "Correspondence concerning Modernity," 111 (original italics). This letter is dated August 20, 1946. Just before his remark on Churchill, Strauss notes how "incomprehensible" and "foreign" Aristotle's concept of magnanimity (greatness of soul) was to him until he recognized Churchill as the incarnation of this quality. Jaffa has noted that the significance of this letter lies in the fact that Strauss credits Churchill for helping him understand Aristotle. See Harry V. Jaffa, "Aristotle and the Higher Good," *New York Times*, July 1, 2011. See also Harry V. Jaffa, "Strauss at One Hundred," in Deutsch and Murley, *Leo Strauss, the Straussians*, 44.

4. Leo Strauss, "Churchill's Greatness," *Weekly Standard* 5, no. 16, January 10, 2000. Strauss delivered this eulogy to his class at the University of Chicago on January 25, 1965. Once again, "magnanimity" is a term associated with Aristotle's philosophy. I discuss below the meaning of this term and how well it applies to Churchill.

5. Jaffa, *How to Think*, 173.

6. Jaffa, "Strauss at One Hundred," 44.

7. See Gottfried, *Leo Strauss*, 24, 59–60.

8. John Ramsden, *Man of the Century: Winston Churchill and His Legend since 1945* (New York: Columbia University Press, 2002), 579.

9. Russell Kirk, *The Politics of Prudence* (Wilmington, DE: ISI Books, 1993), 40. However, Kirk, in *The Conservative Mind: From Burke to Eliot*, 7th revised edition (Washington, DC: Regnery Gateway, 2001), followed T. S. Eliot in contending that Balfour was the intellectual superior of Churchill (475). See also Lord, *Modern Prince*, 109–110.

10. Berns, *Making Patriots*, ix.

11. Smith, *Reading Leo Strauss*, 105.

12. Joseph Cropsey, *Polity and Economy: With Further Thoughts on the Principles of Adam Smith* (South Bend, IN: St. Augustine's Press, 2001), 137–138.

13. Fukuyama, *End of History*, 318.

14. James Mann, *Rise of the Vulcans: The History of Bush's War Cabinet* (New York: Viking, 2004), 27.

15. Anne Norton, *Leo Strauss and the Politics of American Empire* (New Haven: Yale University Press, 2004), 127–130. See my review of her book in *European Legacy* 10, no. 7 (2005): 758–759. I have omitted discussion of the Straussian portrait of Lincoln here, whose defects have been discussed in my *Lincoln and the Politics of Christian Love*, because Strauss himself makes little mention of the president (apart from a reference to Lord Charnwood's biography of Lincoln in *Natural Right and History*, 70n). In chapter two, I provide some comments on Jaffa's and Arkes's Hellenized portraits of Lincoln.

16. Harry V. Jaffa, "Humanizing Certitudes and Impoverishing Doubts: A Critique of *The Closing of the American Mind* by Allan Bloom," *Interpretation* 16, no. 1 (Fall 1988): 135; Jaffa, "Dear Professor Drury," 324–325; Harry V. Jaffa, "Leo Strauss's Churchillian Speech and the Question of the Decline of the West," *Teaching Political Science* 12, no. 2 (Winter 1985): 65–67.

17. "If I Were an American," in Winston S. Churchill, *The Great Republic: A History of America* (New York: Modern Library, 1999), 390. This piece is excerpted from *Life*, April 14, 1947. It is relevant here to note that Churchill's mother was American, and he was famously proud of his Anglo-American ancestry.

18. Quoted in Irwin Stelzer, "Neoconservatives and Their Critics: An Introduction," in *The Neocon Reader*, edited with an introduction by Irwin Stelzer (New York: Grove Press, 2004), 10.

19. Michael Gove, "The Very British Roots of Neoconservatism and Its Lessons for British Conservatives," in Stelzer, *The Neocon Reader*, 276–277.

20. Andrew Roberts, *Eminent Churchillians* (London: Phoenix, 2004), 216–241.

21. Howard is quoted in Robert Rhodes James, "The Enigma," in *Churchill as Peacemaker*, edited by James W. Muller (Cambridge: Cambridge University Press, 1997), 7. See also Manfred Weidhorn, *A Harmony of Interests: Explorations in the Mind of Sir Winston Churchill* (London: Associated University Presses, 1992), 110.

22. Jaffa, *How to Think*, 17–18. Churchill praises southern gentlemen like General Lee in his speculative essay "If Lee Had Not Won the Battle of Gettysburg," in Churchill, *The Great Republic*, 248. Steven Smith denies that the Straussian admiration for Churchill amounts to "hero worship" or the "great man theory of history" (*Reading Leo Strauss*, 197). Rather, Churchill's knowledge of statesmanship should be studied and celebrated. Even so, I discuss this admiration as an example of the "great man theory of history" below.

23. Strauss and his students attribute this idea to Churchill, but I cannot find it anywhere in Churchill's writings. See Zuckert and Zuckert, *The Truth*, 62.

24. Strauss, *On Tyranny*, 209.

25. Churchill, *Thoughts and Adventures*, 182; see Weidhorn, *Harmony of Interests*, 163–166.

26. See Strauss, *Natural Right and History*, 27, 318 (especially on the nobility of "last-ditch resistance," which the historicist Edmund Burke allegedly could not grasp).

27. See Bloom, *Giants and Dwarfs*, 265–266.

28. Daniel J. Mahoney, *The Conservative Foundations of the Liberal Order: Defending Democracy against Its Modern Enemies and Immoderate Friends* (Wilmington, DE: ISI Books,

2011), 54. See also Gottfried (*Leo Strauss*, 5), who describes Mahoney as someone "affected" by Straussian ideas but not "unreservedly" Straussian.

29. Altman, in his *German Stranger*, is one of the very few leftist critics to mention Strauss's admiration for Churchill expressed in "German Nihilism." Without any evidence, however, Altman simply dismisses this praise as Strauss's secret celebration of Hitler. Since both leaders called on their nations to sacrifice for war, it follows (for Altman) that Strauss's exoteric praise for Churchill is esoteric praise for Hitler (316n and 317).

30. Winston S. Churchill, *The Birth of Britain*, vol. 1 of *A History of the English-Speaking Peoples* (New York: Bantam, 1963), 163–165; *The New World*, vol. 2 of *A History of the English-Speaking Peoples* (New York: Bantam, 1963), 214. See also Weidhorn, *Harmony of Interests*, for his dismissal of Greco-Roman honor, which lacks the humaneness of Christian piety (54).

31. Churchill considered the classics to have "arrived at fairly obvious reflections" upon the great philosophical questions, a conclusion that did not encourage further study on his part. See his autobiography, *My Early Life, 1874–1904*, with a new introduction by William Manchester (New York: Touchstone, 1996), 23. Lord Birkenhead recounts the story of a friend who lent Churchill a copy of Aristotle's *Nicomachean Ethics*, with the request that he should read what his friend considered to be the "greatest book" ever written. Although Churchill enjoyed reading it, he also remarked with a hint of faint praise that "it is extraordinary how much of it I had already thought out for myself." See Lord Birkenhead, *Contemporary Personalities* (London: Cassel, 1924), 115. Yet Jaffa insists that, despite Churchill's lack of interest in Aristotle, "the classical tradition informed more of his upbringing, at home and at school, than he realized." See Jaffa, "Aristotle and the Higher Good." Other Straussians portray Churchill as a statesman who possessed classical Greek virtues. See James W. Muller, "The Aftermath of the Great War," in Muller, *Churchill as Peacemaker*, 155; Kirk Emmert, *Winston S. Churchill on Empire* (Durham, NC: Carolina Academic Press and the Claremont Institute for the Study of Statesmanship and Political Philosophy, 1989), xv–xvi.

32. Winston S. Churchill, *Closing the Ring*, vol. 5 of *The Second World War* (Boston: Houghton Mifflin, 1951), 533. This statement is quoted in Jaffa, "Can There Be Another Winston Churchill?" 29.

33. Winston S. Churchill, "The Flame of Christian Ethics," in *Winston Churchill: His Complete Speeches*, vol. 7, *1943–1949*, edited by Robert Rhodes James (New York and London: Chelsea House Publishers, 1974), 7645.

34. Jaffa, "Strauss at One Hundred," 44.

35. Patrick J. Buchanan, *Churchill, Hitler, and the "Unnecessary War": How Britain Lost Its Empire and the West Lost the World* (New York: Crown Publishers, 2008), 399.

36. Quoted in Mahoney, *Conservative Foundations*, 82.

37. Strauss, *Early Writings*, 65.

38. Strauss, *Thoughts on Machiavelli*, 178–179.

39. Paul A. Rahe, "*The River War*: Nature's Provision, Man's Desire to Prevail, and the Prospects for Peace," in Muller, *Churchill as Peacemaker*, 99. Rahe is likely building on Strauss's view that an "ethics of intention," which he took from Weber's sociology, is unsuitable for the political world if it is not tempered by an "ethics of responsibility," which takes into account the consequences of actions. See Strauss, *Natural Right and History*, 70 (Strauss refers to Churchill's biography of his famous ancestor, the Duke of Marlborough, in 70n29).

40. Rahe, "*The River War*," 99. Rahe's description of Gordon is reminiscent of the tender-minded Christian evangelicals of the Victorian era who went out of their way to empathize with the empire's enemies while trusting that the same human beings desired English

democracy. Ironically, these evangelicals are perhaps forerunners of neoconservatives who also believe that English (and American) democratic ideals are desired by all human beings. See Correlli Barnett, *The Collapse of British Power* (London: Pan Books, 2002), 61–63.

41. Rahe, *"The River War,"* 118. Compare Mahoney on the civic virtue and manly courage of Churchill as "indispensable supports of human freedom" (*Conservative Foundations*, 83). Unlike Rahe, Mahoney represents Churchill's thought as a synthesis of classical, modern, and Christian ideas (73).

42. See Robert Kaplan, *Warrior Politics: Why Leadership Demands a Pagan Ethos* (New York: Vintage, 2001). Kaplan, a popular neoconservative journalist, describes Churchill as a true "pagan" warrior. See my review of his book in *European Legacy* 11, no. 1 (2006): 98–99.

43. Bloom, *Giants and Dwarfs*, 263–266.

44. Strauss, "German Nihilism," 371.

45. Ibid., 372. Strauss praises Churchill's policy of KMT (keep muddling through) in his lecture "What Can We Learn from Political Theory?" 517–518. Altman, in his *German Stranger*, believes that Strauss's praise for English virtues and even Churchill is still insincere, since Strauss is determined to conceal his hatred of English democracy (312–320).

46. Susan Shell, "'To Spare the Vanquished and Crush the Arrogant': Leo Strauss's Lecture on 'German Nihilism,'" in *The Cambridge Companion to Leo Strauss*, edited by Steven B. Smith (Cambridge: Cambridge University Press, 2009), 191.

47. Harry Jaffa writes: "Shakespeare was the great vehicle within the Anglo-American world for the transmission of an essentially Socratic understanding of the civilization of the West" (*Conditions of Freedom*, 7). For a brief critique of the Strauss-Jaffa interpretation of Shakespeare, see Grant Havers, "Lincoln, *Macbeth*, and the Illusions of Tyranny," *European Legacy* 15, no. 2 (April 2010): 143–144.

48. Strauss, "German Nihilism," 372.

49. George Parkin Grant, *English-Speaking Justice* (Toronto: House of Anansi, 1974), 52–53. Like Strauss, however, Grant credits the English with being immune to the radical philosophies that emanated from Germany, due to the famous English virtue of moderation.

50. Isaiah Berlin, *Mr. Churchill in 1940* (Cambridge, MA: Riverside Press, 1964), 12. Berlin, who wrote this essay in 1949, pointedly contrasts Churchill's historical sense with Roosevelt's naïve optimism about the world (especially Stalin).

51. Jaffa, "Churchillian Speech," 67. See also Fukuyama, *End of History*, 153–161. Weidhorn agrees that Churchill "scorned mere survival" (*Harmony of Interests*, 61). As Churchill observes in *The New World*, the instability during the reign of Charles I proved that tranquility is only one of many goods sought by humanity (151).

52. Strauss, *Political Philosophy of Hobbes*, 126; Strauss, *Natural Right and History*, 178; Minowitz, *Straussophobia*, 182.

53. Strauss, *What Is Political Philosophy?* 49.

54. Ibid., 172. See also Strauss, *Natural Right and History*, 194–195.

55. Strauss, *Natural Right and History*, 318. In the same work, Strauss associates historicism with the fatalistic view that the individual is trapped in the currents of historical change (27).

56. Winston Churchill, *The Gathering Storm*, vol. 1 of *The Second World War* (Boston and New York: Houghton Mifflin, 1948), 320–321. See also David Dilks, *The Great Dominion: Winston Churchill in Canada, 1900–1954*, foreword by Lady Soames (Toronto: Thomas Allen, 2005), 141. This statement serves as the epigraph to Harry V. Jaffa's study *Thomism and Aristotelianism: A Study of the Commentary by Thomas Aquinas on the "Nicomachean Ethics"* (Chicago: University of Chicago Press, 1952). This study is a lengthy critique of the

Thomistic view that Aristotle's philosophy of virtue and statesmanship is compatible with Christian morality.

57. Strauss, "Marsilius of Padua," in *Liberalism: Ancient and Modern*, 196.

58. Churchill, *Gathering Storm*, 265–266.

59. Dilks, *The Great Dominion*, 142. Churchill, at least in private moments, sometimes embraced the nineteenth-century view that the progress of rationalism would render religion obsolete. See Richard Toye, *Churchill's Empire: The World that Made Him and the World that He Made* (New York: Henry Holt, 2010), 28.

60. Norman Rose, *Churchill: An Unruly Life* (London: Tauris Parke Paperbacks, 2009), 38.

61. Churchill, *Gathering Storm*, 265–266; Strauss, "Churchill's Greatness." Churchill cites "magnanimity in victory" as a "moral of the work," in the epigraph to *The Second World War*.

62. Aristotle, *Posterior Analytics* 97b 15–25. Here I quote from *The Basic Works of Aristotle*, 179.

63. Winston S. Churchill, *The Great Democracies*, vol. 4 of *A History of the English-Speaking Peoples*, 203.

64. Aristotle, *Nicomachean Ethics*, book 4, chapter 3, 1124b 17–25, 27, and 1125a, 1. For Strauss's contrasting of humility with magnanimity, see "Progress or Return?" 277.

65. Churchill, "The Upkeep of the Aristocracy (17 December, 1909)," in *Never Give In! The Best of Winston Churchill's Speeches*, selected by his grandson Winston S. Churchill (New York: Hyperion, 2003), 38.

66. See Carson Holloway, "Christianity, Magnanimity, and Statesmanship," *Review of Politics* 61 (1999): 602. See also Larry Arnhart, "Statesmanship as Magnanimity: Classical, Christian, and Modern," *Polity* 16 (Winter 1983): 265–267. Holloway's article is in part a response to Arnhart's essay.

67. Martin Gilbert, *The Will of the People: Winston Churchill and Parliamentary Democracy* (Toronto: Vintage Canada, 2006), 114. Churchill expressed these sentiments during the civil war in Greece in 1944.

68. Churchill, "Mass Effects in Modern Life," in *Thoughts and Adventures*, 182–192. For de Gaulle, see Angelo Codevilla, "De Gaulle: Statesmanship in the Modern State," in Jaffa, *Statesmanship*, 213–233. Strauss was also an admirer of de Gaulle; for his praise of de Gaulle as an "outstanding European conservative," see *Liberalism: Ancient and Modern*, viii; Gottfried, *Leo Strauss*, 64.

69. Churchill, "Moses: The Leader of a People," in *Thoughts and Adventures*, 213–215.

70. Aristotle attributes this quality to the philosopher as well. See *Nicomachean Ethics* book 10, chapter 7, 1177b 1.

71. For Christianity's influence on Roman Britain, see Churchill, *The Birth of Britain*, 27. For his views on Christianity's influence on America, see Weidhorn, *Harmony of Interests*, 119.

72. Martin Gilbert, *Churchill's Political Philosophy* (Oxford: Oxford University Press, 1981), 78.

73. C. E. M. Joad, "Churchill the Philosopher," in *Churchill by His Contemporaries*, edited by Charles Eade (London: Hutchinson, 1953), 477.

74. Churchill, "Liberalism and Socialism," in Winston S. Churchill, *Liberalism and the Social Problem: A Collection of Early Speeches as a Member of Parliament* (Rockville, MD: Arc Manor, 2007), 39. Churchill gave this speech in 1906, eight years before the outbreak of World War I.

75. Churchill, *My Early Life*, 66.

76. Churchill, "Leon Trotsky, *Alias* Bronstein," in Winston S. Churchill, *Great Contemporaries* (Chicago: University of Chicago Press, 1973), 201.

77. Strauss, *On Tyranny*, 192.

78. Churchill, "Mass Effects in Modern Life," in *Thoughts and Adventures*, 182.

79. Churchill, "Liberalism and Socialism," in *Liberalism and the Social Problem*, 43.

80. Churchill, "Mass Effects in Modern Life," in *Thoughts and Adventures*, 184–185.

81. Ibid., 185.

82. Ibid., 191. See also Churchill, *My Early Life*, 65–66, 72.

83. Mahoney, *Conservative Foundations*, 61; Churchill, "Mass Effects in Modern Life," in *Thoughts and Adventures*, 185.

84. Strauss, *On Tyranny*, 178. Strauss here associates modern tyranny with the belief in the unlimited progress in the "conquest of nature" that is made possible by modern science.

85. Mahoney, *Conservative Foundations*, 61.

86. Ibid.

87. Jaffa, "Can There Be Another Winston Churchill?" 27.

88. Strauss, "Liberal Education and Responsibility," in *Liberalism: Ancient and Modern*, 24–25.

89. Strauss, "What Is Liberal Education?" in *Liberalism: Ancient and Modern*, 5. Oddly, this comment seems to conflict with Strauss's recognition of Plato's position that a democracy is "not designed for inducing the non-philosophers to attempt to become as good as they possibly can, for the end of democracy is not virtue but freedom, i.e., the freedom to live either nobly or basely according to one's liking" (Strauss, *The City and Man*, 132). Nevertheless, Strauss's students, like Kenneth L. Deutsch, follow their teacher in calling for "the founding of an aristocracy within democratic mass society" that can contribute "qualities of dedication, concentration, breadth, and depth to democratic practice." Only this elite can reinvigorate liberal democracies and help their citizens "yearn for the prudent defeat of tyranny, seek the recovery of human excellence, and demonstrate a public-spirited concern for the common good instead of the joyless quest for joy." See Kenneth L. Deutsch, "Leo Strauss's Friendly Criticism of American Liberal Democracy: Neoconservative or Aristocratic Liberal?" in Kenneth L. Deutsch and Ethan Fishman, eds., *The Dilemmas of American Conservatism* (Lexington: University Press of Kentucky, 2010), 175–202.

90. Kirk, "Bolingbroke, Burke," 429. See also Rosen, *Hermeneutics as Politics*, 137. See chapter three, note 86, above. Rosen overstates the "conservative" nature of Strauss's idea of aristocracy when he considers it incompatible with modern democracy.

91. Strauss, "Liberal Education and Responsibility," in *Liberalism: Ancient and Modern*, 15, 21. See also *What Is Political Philosophy?* 36–38.

92. Strauss, "Liberal Education and Responsibility," in *Liberalism: Ancient and Modern*, 24.

93. Ibid.

94. See Gottfried, *After Liberalism*, 81–83.

95. Ibid., 81.

96. Strauss, *What Is Political Philosophy?* 43, also 37–38. Strauss also stresses this point in *Natural Right and History*, 193.

97. As Stephen Holmes quips: "Reading Plato in Greek will not stop Hitler in his tracks." See *Anatomy*, 83.

98. Churchill, *My Early Life*, 359.

99. Weidhorn, *Harmony of Interests*, 108.

100. Ibid., 49–54.

101. Toye, *Churchill's Empire*, 241. Defenders of Churchill usually argue that this belief had more to do with "culture, history, and values than pure ethnicity." See Jeremy Havardi, *The Greatest Briton: Essays on Winston Churchill's Life and Political Philosophy* (London: Shepheard-Walwyn, 2009), 352.

102. Churchill, *The New World*, 231, 282.

103. Even defenders of Churchill who sympathize with the Straussian hermeneutic sometimes acknowledge Churchill's views on Anglo-Saxon superiority. See Will Morrisey, "The Statesman as Great-Souled Man: Winston Churchill," in *Magnanimity and Statesmanship*, edited by Carson Holloway (Lanham, MD: Lexington Books, 2008), 210.

104. Churchill, "Abandoning India," in *Never Give In!* 98. Churchill gave this speech on March 18, 1931.

105. Burke, *Reflections*, 345. For this reason, Churchill agreed with Burke that the colonial Americans were fighting for their rights as Englishmen (*The Age of Revolution*, 151, 210). Straussians typically dismiss this argument as historicist. See Jaffa, *How to Think*, esp. 143.

106. See Churchill, "Consistency in Politics," in *Thoughts and Adventures*, 24. Although Jaffa notes Churchill's praise of Burke in this essay, he is silent on how this favorable portrait of Burke by Strauss's favorite statesman clashes with his teacher's reading of Burke as a philosopher of fatalism. See Jaffa, "Too Good to Be True?" 226; Kraynak, "Strauss, Voegelin, and Burke," 28–31.

107. See Hannah Arendt's illuminating discussion concerning Burke on this point, in *The Origins of Totalitarianism* (New York: Harcourt, 1951), 300.

108. Strauss, *Natural Right and History*, 316. In Burke's view, "metaphysical jurisprudence" refers to the ahistorical ideals of liberty and equality that came out of the French Revolution.

109. Weidhorn, *Harmony of Interests*, 164 (also 165–166). Although I usually concur with Weidhorn's analysis, I disagree with his harsh view that Churchill did not understand socioeconomic or historical forces (144). Churchill's preoccupation with class power is the best evidence against this judgment.

110. Churchill, *The Birth of Britain*, 231.

111. Ibid., 182, 271–273.

112. Churchill, *The Age of Revolution*, 222.

113. Churchill, "Unemployment," in *Liberalism and the Social Problem*, 97.

114. I am not the first reader to associate Churchill with Burnham. Christopher Hitchens contended that Burnham was deeply influenced by Churchill's famous "Iron Curtain" speech. See Christopher Hitchens, *Blood, Class, and Empire: The Enduring Anglo-American Relationship* (New York: Nation Books, 2004), 243–246.

115. James Burnham, *The Managerial Revolution* (Harmondsworth: Penguin, 1962). This work was originally published in 1942. See Churchill, "Mass Effects," in *Thoughts and Adventures*, 186, 189.

116. Burnham, *Managerial Revolution*, 231.

117. For the Straussian idea of "moral equivalence," see Gottfried, *Leo Strauss*, 60.

118. Gottfried, *After Liberalism*. Gottfried is heavily influenced by Burnham's analysis

here. Perhaps the closest Strauss gets to advancing a critique of the managerial state is his analysis of Weber's fact-value dichotomy as a dangerously instrumental approach to reason. See Strauss, *Natural Right and History*, 36–78. Yet this analysis does not lead Strauss to doubt the persistence of "liberal" democracy in the face of technocratic rulers who employ this mode of reason.

119. Burnham, *Managerial Revolution*, 232.

120. Jaffa, "Can There Be Another Winston Churchill?" 27.

121. Burnham also correctly predicted that America would become the "receiver" for the disintegrating British Empire (*Managerial Revolution*, 237). By the end of World War II, it was obvious that Churchill had to go along with Roosevelt's insistence that the empire be liquidated, despite his best efforts to reverse this subordination of Britain to the American sphere of influence. For a useful discussion of these historical shifts after the war, see Toye, *Churchill's Empire*, 230.

122. Strauss wrote an appreciative letter (dated March 10, 1964) to the John Day Company, which published Burnham's *Suicide of the West*, stating that Burnham's polemic was "excellent" and that he and Burnham had reached "practically the same conclusions" from different premises. See Daniel Kelly, *James Burnham and the Struggle for the World*, foreword by Richard Brookhiser (Wilmington, DE: ISI Books, 2002), 289n64.

123. See Grant Havers, "James Burnham's Elite Theory and the Postwar American Right," *Telos* 154 (Spring 2011): 33–36.

124. See George Dangerfield, *The Strange Death of Liberal England*, with a foreword by Peter Stansky (Stanford: Stanford University Press, 1997). This classic was first published in 1935.

125. Throughout his four-volume *History of the English-Speaking Peoples*, Churchill's admiration for Beard is evident. He makes use of Beard's analysis of the Reformation (see *The New World*, 6–7) as well as the American Constitution (see *The Age of Revolution*, 214) and Andrew Jackson's struggle with the Federal Bank (see *The Great Democracies*, 109).

126. Bloom, *Closing*, 29.

127. These men were the "salvation" of England. See Winston S. Churchill, *Marlborough: His Life and Times* (Toronto: Ryerson Press, 1933–1938), vol. 1, 82.

128. Kirk, *Conservative Mind*. See Louis Hartz, *The Liberal Tradition in America: An Interpretation of American Political Thought since the Revolution* (New York: Harcourt Brace, 1955). Straussians like Willmoore Kendall are hostile to Burke because his conservatism is too aristocratic for the more populist American tradition. See, for example, Kendall and George W. Carey, *The Basic Symbols of the American Political Tradition* (Washington, DC: Catholic University of America Press, 1995), 15–16.

129. Strauss, *Natural Right and History*, 298, 316. See also Baldacchino, "Value-Centered Historicism"; Kraynak, "Strauss, Voegelin, and Burke," 28–31.

130. Weidhorn, *Harmony of Interests*, 114–117, 133. Note Churchill's dismissal of the "superficial resemblances" drawn by his wartime ally Roosevelt, who supported independence for India, between the eighteenth-century American revolutionaries and the Indian movement for democracy in the twentieth century. See Winston S. Churchill, *The Hinge of Fate*, vol. 4 of *The Second World War* (Boston: Houghton Mifflin, 1950), 214. For identical reasons, Churchill fumed over Woodrow Wilson's desire to create "world democracy in his own image," while he presumed to speak for "plain people" (Europeans) who knew nothing about how to "make a just and durable peace" at the end of World War I. See Winston S. Churchill, *The World Crisis: The Aftermath* (London: Thornton Butterworth, 1929), 128.

131. Strauss, *Natural Right and History*, 143. Strauss did not always think in these abstract terms. As we have seen, his study of Hobbes, which represents his earlier receptivity to the role of class interests, portrays Hobbes as a defender of the bourgeoisie.

132. Kojève was perhaps the first reader of Strauss to doubt whether his "Platonic" view of philosophy would actually lead to an avoidance of political praxis, given the fact that philosophers like Plato and Spinoza occasionally took on the position of advising rulers. See Kojève, "Tyranny and Wisdom," in Strauss, *On Tyranny*, 158–164.

5: The Anglo-American Struggle with Strauss

1. It may be odd to associate Grant with an Anglo-American tradition, given his famous antipathy to America. My own view is that Grant was Anglo-American in the sense that his Loyalist ancestors were originally Americans as well. See Grant, *Technology and Empire*, where he comments that the Loyalists were no more interested in questioning modernity than the American revolutionaries were (68). Grant also has some American admirers who have tried to integrate his thought into the American conservative tradition. See the article on Grant by Jeremy Beer in *American Conservatism: An Encyclopedia*, edited by Bruce Frohnen, Jeremy Beer, and Jeffrey O. Nelson (Wilmington, DE: ISI Books, 2006), 361–362.

2. Harold A. Innis, "The Church in Canada," in Harold Innis, *Essays in Canadian Economic History*, edited by Mary Q. Innis (Toronto: University of Toronto Press, 1956), 383. For Innis's laments over the Canadian Protestant inattention to the Greeks, see pages 385, 390, and 392.

3. Grant, "Harold Adams Innis," in *The George Grant Reader*, edited by William Christian and Sheila Grant (Toronto: University of Toronto Press, 1998), 356.

4. Grant, "Letter of Resignation (1960)," in ibid., 189.

5. George Parkin Grant, *Philosophy in the Mass Age* (Toronto: University of Toronto Press, 1995), 122.

6. George Parkin Grant, *Lament for a Nation: The Defeat of Canadian Nationalism* (Ottawa: Carleton University Press, 1991), 95–96. This famous work was originally published in 1965. For Grant's early Hegelianism, see Robert C. Sibley, *Northern Spirits: John Watson, George Grant, and Charles Taylor—Appropriations of Hegelian Political Thought* (Montreal and Kingston: McGill-Queen's University Press, 2008), 109–167. Even late in life, when Grant had become more critical of "the silliness of some of [Strauss's] epigones," he still credited Strauss with having saved him "from the grip of Hegel." See Grant, *Selected Letters*, edited with an introduction by William Christian (Toronto: University of Toronto Press, 1996), 369.

7. Kirk, "Bolingbroke, Burke," 429. As already noted, Kirk later in life became a fierce critic of Strauss, his students, and the neoconservatives. See 190n.86.

8. H. D. Forbes, "George Grant and Leo Strauss," in *George Grant and the Subversion of Modernity: Art, Philosophy, Politics, Religion, and Education*, edited by Arthur Davis (Toronto: University of Toronto Press, 1996), 189–190.

9. See Charles Taylor, *Radical Tories* (Toronto: House of Anansi Press, 2006), 135–136. This book was originally published in 1982. See also Grant Havers, "Northern Right," *American Conservative* (March 2011): 33–36.

10. In an interview in the 1970s, Grant remarked: "How to express a proper love of one's own within a Christian life? That is very hard—a very difficult question." See *George*

Grant in Process: Essays and Conversations, edited by Larry Schmidt (Toronto: House of Anansi Press, 1978), 21.

11. Grant uneasily urged his fellow English Canadians to maintain their faith in the civilizing mission of the declining British Empire even after World War II, when America and the Soviet Union had already displaced the British in global influence. See George Parkin Grant, "The Empire: Yes or No?" in *Collected Works of George Grant*, vol. 1, *1933-1950*, edited by Arthur Davis and Peter Emberley (Toronto: University of Toronto Press, 2000), 97-126. This essay was published in 1945. Grant eventually abandoned his view that Canadians should keep their ties to the empire, in the face of overwhelming American influence over Canada.

12. Grant, "An Ethic of Community," in *George Grant Reader*, 70.

13. Carl Berger, *The Sense of Power: Studies in the Ideas of Canadian Imperialism, 1867-1914* (Toronto: University of Toronto Press, 1970), 223-226.

14. C. P. Champion, *The Strange Demise of British Canada: The Liberals and Canadian Nationalism, 1964-1968* (Montreal and Kingston: McGill-Queen's University Press, 2010), 18, 47, 49, 145.

15. Grant, *Lament for a Nation*, 21. For this reason, Grant castigated the Conservative prime minister John Diefenbaker for believing that French Canadians were the same as all other ethnic Canadians and did not deserve any favorable status, despite their historic role as one of Canada's founding peoples.

16. Dilks, *The Great Dominion*, 58.

17. Peter Brimelow, *The Patriot Game: National Dreams and Political Realities* (Toronto: Key Porter Books, 1986), 144.

18. Grant, *Technology and Empire*, 69-71. When Grant asked a man of the interwar generation (1918-1939) why Canada was allowed to "slip into the slough of despond" that drew the nation into the hegemony of the United States, he replied: "We had our guts shot away in France" (70).

19. Grant, *Philosophy in the Mass Age*, 77-89; see also Grant, *Technology and Empire*, 65-66. Grant's critique of twentieth-century Anglo-American Protestantism anticipated the historian James Kurth's analysis of the "Protestant Deformation." See James Kurth, "George W. Bush and the Protestant Deformation," *American Interest* 1, no. 2 (2005): 4-16.

20. Grant, *English-Speaking Justice*, 60-65. See also Grant, *Technology and Empire*, 18-25; Longley, *Chosen People*, 27.

21. Grant, *English-Speaking Justice*, 52. See Strauss, "German Nihilism," 372.

22. Grant, *Lament for a Nation*, 72.

23. Ibid., 62.

24. Grant, *English-Speaking Justice*, 55.

25. Strauss thought that secularization was a modern, even Machiavellian, ruse to use religion for political purposes. See Leo Strauss, "The Three Waves of Modernity," in Strauss, *Introduction to Political Philosophy*, 81-98 (83). See also "Reason and Revelation," in Meier, *Strauss and the Theologico-Political Problem*, 143. For Strauss and Voegelin on Protestantism, see Emberley and Cooper, *Faith and Political Philosophy*, 71. Other Straussians dismiss the secularization thesis; see Bloom, *Closing*, 211.

26. Grant, "The Minds of Men in the Atomic Age (1955)," in *George Grant Reader*, 57.

27. See Grant, *English-Speaking Justice*, 63-65. For an illuminating discussion of Grant's perspective on liberalism and Protestantism, see Clifford Orwin's review of this work in *University of Toronto Law Journal* 30 (1980): 110.

28. See Strauss, *Natural Right and History*, 61n, 199n.

29. Wayne Whillier, "George Grant and Leo Strauss: A Parting of the Way," in *"Two Theological Languages" by George Grant and Other Essays in Honour of His Work*, edited by Wayne Whillier (Toronto: Edwin Mellen, 1990), 73.

30. Arthur Davis, "Did George Grant Change His Politics?" in *Athens and Jerusalem: George Grant's Theology, Philosophy, and Politics*, edited by Ian Angus, Ron Dart, and Peg Peters (Toronto: University of Toronto Press, 2006), 75–76.

31. Gad Horowitz, "Commentary," in *By Loving Our Own: George Grant and the Legacy of "Lament for a Nation,"* edited by Peter C. Emberley (Ottawa: Carleton University Press, 1990), 78.

32. See Grant, "A Critique of the New Left (1966)," in *George Grant Reader*, 84–87; Grant, *Technology and Empire*, 63–65.

33. For Grant on Strauss's views on biblical religion, see *Technology and Empire*, 108. Late in life, Grant admitted in private correspondence that he was "fundamentally more in Voegelin's ambience rather than Strauss's," because of Voegelin's greater sympathy toward Christianity. See Grant, *Selected Letters*, 380. See also John von Heyking and Barry Cooper, "'A Cow Is just a Cow': George Grant and Eric Voegelin on the United States," in Angus, Dart, and Peters, *Athens and Jerusalem*, 166. These authors take pains to distinguish Grant's polemics against Protestantism from Voegelin's allegedly more appreciative view of this faith tradition (see 181–183), even though Voegelin himself (unlike Strauss) often harshly judged the Protestant heritage of his adopted land, America. See Ranieri, *Disturbing Revelation*, 152–153.

34. It is unsurprising that Grant's positions on American foreign policy and social equality made him a darling of the Canadian Left, at least in the 1960s (before he opposed the legalization of abortion in the 1970s). Leftist admirers even labeled Grant a "Red Tory." For a useful discussion of the leftist admiration for Grant, see Ron Dart, "Stephen Leacock and George Grant: Tory Affinities," in Angus, Dart, and Peters, *Athens and Jerusalem*, 18–19.

35. Grant, "Tyranny and Wisdom," in *Technology and Empire*, 93–94.

36. Grant, *Lament for a Nation*, 64–66. Strauss clearly gives this impression in his preface to *Liberalism: Ancient and Modern*, ix.

37. Grant, *Technology and Empire*, 107–109. For Strauss's implicitly historicist acceptance of Kojève's devaluation of Christianity, see Planinc, "Paradox and Polyphony," 32–33.

38. Grant, *Technology and Empire*, 108.

39. Grant writes at the end of *Lament for a Nation*: "My lament is not based on philosophy but on tradition." He adds that it is not evident that the loss of the older Canadian traditions "will lead to some greater political good" (96).

40. See Strauss, "Preface," *Liberalism: Ancient and Modern*, x.

41. Ibid. (My italics).

42. Forbes, "George Grant and Leo Strauss," 186–187. For a critique of the scholarly consensus that Grant rightly saw Strauss as anti-liberal and anti-modern, see Grant Havers, "George Grant and Leo Strauss: Modernist and Postmodernist Conservatisms," *Topia* 8 (Fall 2002): 92–93.

43. Davis, "Did George Grant Change His Politics?" 65.

44. Strauss, *Natural Right and History*, 5.

45. Strauss, "German Nihilism," 358–359.

46. George Parkin Grant, *Time as History*, edited with an introduction by William Christian (Toronto: University of Toronto Press, 1995), 11–12. Grant gave these lectures,

which are known as the Massey Lectures (in honour of his uncle, former Governor-General Vincent Massey) on CBC radio in 1969.

47. Ibid., 6, 14.

48. Ibid., 50.

49. Bloom, *Closing*, 147; for Grant's views on the New Left, see "A Critique of the New Left (1966)," in *George Grant Reader*, 84–90.

50. Grant, *Technology and Empire*, 33, 39.

51. Ibid., 30–31. See the editor's comments in *George Grant Reader*, 394.

52. See Robert Blumstock, "Anglo-Saxon Lament," *Canadian Review of Sociology and Anthropology* 3 (1966): 100.

53. See Strauss, *What Is Political Philosophy?* 43; also his comments on Marx in *Natural Right and History*, 143.

54. According to Grant, Strauss believed that Christianity contributed to an "over-extension of the soul." See William Christian, "Introduction," *George Grant Reader*, 19. Although Grant never explained what this meant, it is likely that Strauss meant Christian charity was too demanding for the political life. See Ranieri, *Disturbing Revelation*, 161–180. Strauss once referred to the "deepening of the soul" that biblical monotheism encourages, but he did not elaborate on what he meant by this. See Strauss, "Heideggerian Existentialism," 41. Elsewhere Strauss acknowledges (without necessarily accepting) Nietzsche's view that the "most profound change which the human soul has hitherto undergone, the most important enlargement and deepening which it has hitherto experienced," is due to the Bible (and not simply Christianity). See "The Preface to the English Translation," 12.

55. George Parkin Grant, "Two Theological Languages," in Grant, *"Two Theological Languages" by George Grant*, 11–12. I discuss Grant's failure to challenge, on philosophical grounds, the validity of Strauss's dualistic separation of Athens and Jerusalem in Grant Havers, "Leo Strauss's Influence on George Grant," in Angus, Dart, and Peters, *Athens and Jerusalem*, 124–135.

56. Clark A. Merrill, "Leo Strauss's Indictment of Christian Philosophy," *Review of Politics* 62, no. 1 (2000): 87–90.

57. Strauss, *Natural Right and History*, 144, 164. See also Jaffa, "Leo Strauss, the Bible, and Political Philosophy," 208–209. Whether Strauss and Jaffa are correct in attributing this exclusivist view to Thomism, which emphasizes that all human beings can comprehend the truth by reason or revelation, is another question. For a Thomistic critique of the Straussian interpretation of Aquinas, see Christopher S. Morrissey, "Thomas Aquinas on Providence, Prudence, and Natural Law," in *Politics in Theology*, vol. 38 of *Religion and Public Life*, edited by Gabriel R. Ricci (New Brunswick, NJ: Transaction, 2012), 133–145.

58. See Fortin's review of Wilhelmsen's book, *Christianity and Political Philosophy*, in *Classical Christianity*, 357.

59. Janet Ajzenstat, *The Canadian Founding: John Locke and Parliament* (Montreal and Kingston: McGill-Queens, 2007), 102. For her inaccurate portrait of Grant as a theocrat, see Ajzenstat, "The Conservatism of the Canadian Founders," in *After Liberalism: Essays in Search of Freedom, Virtue, and Order*, edited by William D. Gairdner (Toronto: Stoddart, 1998), 21. To my knowledge, Grant never supported a theocratic version of statecraft in the modern era and would have considered such an option to be woefully obsolete and oppressive.

60. Kaufmann, *Rise and Fall*, 279.

61. Grant, "An Ethic of Community," in *George Grant Reader*, 69.

62. Grant, *English-Speaking Justice*, 76–77.

63. For an insightful discussion of how the Canadian policy of multiculturalism clash-

es with Grant's vision of an historically Protestant nation, see Anthony J. Parel, "Multicultur-alism and Nationhood," in *George Grant and the Future of Canada*, 139–150.

64. Michael Ignatieff, "Human Rights: The Midlife Crisis," *New York Review of Books*, May 20, 1999, 58. In the 2011 federal election, Ignatieff, as leader of the Liberal Party of Canada, led the party to its worst defeat in its history.

65. Grant, *English-Speaking Justice*, 75–76.

66. I discuss this Straussian blind spot on the religious origins of morality, along with the views of Fukuyama and Kass, in Havers, "Natural Rightism and the Biogenetic Debate," 93–105.

67. In the discussion that follows, I focus a great deal on the writings of Harry Jaffa. It may be objected here that Jaffa's positions on the mission of America are too extreme to rep-resent all Straussians. After all, Jaffa has clashed with prominent Straussians like Bloom. See Jaffa, "Humanizing Certitudes." Yet Jaffa and Bloom, among other Straussians, fundamen-tally agree that the mission of America in the world is to spread her democratic ideals and fight tyrannies that resist this imperative. Bloom sounds just like Jaffa when he writes that the credos of liberty and equality "are rational and everywhere applicable," and that World War II was an "educational project" to impose these ideals on nations that objected to them (*Closing*, 153).

68. Jaffa, *How to Think*, 118–120.

69. Jaffa occasionally compares the year 1776 with the year 1940, when he remarks that Tom Paine's ideas "did for the turning points of the American Revolution what Churchill's speeches did to rally Britain, in the dark days after Dunkirk" (*How to Think*, 72–73).

70. Ceaser, *Nature and History*, 22.

71. There are even signs of a slight revival of interest in Kendall's thought today. See Grant Havers, "Willmoore Kendall for Our Times," *Modern Age* 53, nos. 1–2 (Winter–Spring 2011), 121–124; Daniel McCarthy, "Willmoore Kendall, Man of the People," in Deutsch and Fishman, *Dilemmas*, 175–202; Mark Nugent, "Willmoore Kendall and the Deliberate Sense of the Community," *Political Science Reviewer* 36 (2007): 228–265.

72. Gary Wills, *Confessions of a Conservative* (New York: Penguin, 1979), 24, 34.

73. Kendall, "The Part-Time Sage of Ithaca," in *Willmoore Kendall Contra Mundum*, 72.

74. Kendall and Carey, *Basic Symbols*, 15–17.

75. Steven Lenzner, "Leo Strauss and the Conservatives," *Policy Review* (April–May 2003): 80.

76. Strauss, letter to Kendall dated May 14, 1961, in Kendall, "Willmoore Kendall–Leo Strauss Correspondence," Murley and Alvis, *Willmoore Kendall*, 237.

77. George Anastaplo, "Leo Strauss at the University of Chicago," in Deutsch and Murley, *Leo Strauss, the Straussians*, 24n7.

78. William F. Buckley Jr., "The Relevance of Social Science," in Buckley, *American Conservative Thought*, 398. Buckley knew Kendall more personally, having been his student at Yale in the late 1940s. He later invited his former teacher to be a contributor to *National Review*, a role that Kendall fulfilled, uneasily, until he left the magazine in the early 1960s. Shortly after that, he dramatically ended his friendship with Buckley. For a discussion of the circumstances that led to the end of their friendship, which in part involved Kendall's misgivings over the direction in which Buckley was leading the conservative movement, see Jeffrey Hart, *The Making of the American Conservative Mind: "National Review" and Its Times* (Wilmington, DE: ISI Books, 2005), 161–162.

79. See chapter three, note 86, and note 99 below.

80. See Kelly, *James Burnham*, 289n64; Havers, "James Burnham's Elite Theory," 33–36.

81. George H. Nash, *The Conservative Intellectual Movement in America since 1945* (New York: Basic Books, 1976), 226.

82. Willmoore Kendall, *The Conservative Affirmation in America* (Chicago: Gateway Editions, 1985), 260. Kendall wrote this near the end of his review of Strauss's *What Is Political Philosophy?* Nellie Kendall, his widow, dedicated his translation of Rousseau's *The Government of Poland* (Indianapolis: Hackett, 1985) to Strauss under whom "he put himself to school again to learn what the ancients and the moderns have to teach us." In the preface to the 1985 printing, Harvey Mansfield Jr. praises Kendall's introductory essay to this translation as "still the best analysis" of Rousseau's work (viii).

83. Kendall, "Thoughts on Machiavelli," in *Willmoore Kendall Contra Mundum*, 454. Kendall wrote this in his review of Strauss's study of Machiavelli.

84. Under the influence of Strauss, Kendall revised his earlier reading of Locke, in his 1965 essay "John Locke Revisited," in *Willmoore Kendall Contra Mundum*, 418–448. His early work on Locke, which was his doctoral dissertation, was published as *John Locke and the Doctrine of Majority-Rule* (Urbana: University of Illinois Press, 1965). In his introductory essay to his translation of Rousseau's *The Government of Poland*, Kendall, a lifelong admirer of Rousseau, admits he now accepts Strauss's portrait of Rousseau as a Machiavellian opponent of the ancients (xxxiv–xxxv). In the preface to *Conservative Affirmation*, Kendall also refers to Strauss as "his greatest teacher" (xxix). John E. Alvis, a former student of Kendall, provides an insightful discussion of Strauss's influence on his former teacher in "The Evolution of Willmoore Kendall's Political Thought," in Murley and Alvis, *Willmoore Kendall*, 54–66.

85. Kendall, *Conservative Affirmation*, 203. Kendall wrote these comments in a favorable review of Walter Berns's study of the First Amendment. Berns studied with Strauss. Kendall was particularly impressed with his friend Jaffa, whom he ranked alongside Strauss, Voegelin, and Richard Weaver as the greatest conservative thinkers of their generation. See *Willmoore Kendall Contra Mundum*, 395.

86. Strauss, letter to Kendall dated May 14, 1961, in Kendall, "Willmoore Kendall–Leo Strauss Correspondence," 237. Strauss noted he was "mortified" that Kendall, a far better known theorist than he, was having trouble finding a job (after Kendall left Yale).

87. Hart, *American Conservative Mind*, 162. See also Lenzner, "Leo Strauss and the Conservatives," 76. John East praised Kendall as "the most original, innovative, and challenging interpreter of any period" in American history. See John East, "The Political Thought of Willmoore Kendall," *Political Science Reviewer* 3 (1973): 201.

88. See Sam Tanenhaus, "Will the Tea Get Cold?" *New York Review of Books*, March 8, 2012.

89. See Willmoore Kendall, "Natural Law and 'Natural Right,'" *Modern Age* 6, no. 1 (1961–1962), 95. Kendall's article is a long review of John Courtney Murray's *We Hold These Truths: Catholic Reflections on the American Proposition*, introduction by Peter Augustine Lawler (Lanham, MD: Rowman and Littlefield, 2005).

90. Alvis notes that Kendall could have benefited from Strauss's teaching that "majoritarian premises" are not only "less than self-evident" but even "quite evidently false." See Alvis, "Evolution," 55.

91. Kendall, "The True Sage of Woodstock," in *Willmoore Kendall Contra Mundum*, 81. This essay is also an appreciative review of Murray's work.

92. Kendall, "How to Read Richard Weaver: Philosopher of 'We (the Virtuous) Peo-

ple,'" in *Willmoore Kendall Contra Mundum*, 401.

93. George Carey, "How to Read Willmoore Kendall," *Intercollegiate Review* (Winter–Spring 1972): 64; Lenzner, "Leo Strauss and the Conservatives," 77.

94. Kendall, "True Sage of Woodstock," 74–89; Carey, "How to Read Willmoore Kendall," 64–65.

95. Kendall, "True Sage of Woodstock," 83; Murray, *We Hold These Truths*, 23–24, 49–51. Both men agreed that Americans would still need "instruction" in the lessons of virtue (see Murray, *We Hold These Truths*, 120).

96. Willmoore Kendall, *Oxford Years: Letters of Willmoore Kendall to His Father*, edited by Yvona Kendall Mason, foreword and epilogue by George W. Carey (Bryn Mawr, PA: Intercollegiate Studies Institute, 1993), 59. This is from a letter to his father dated October 11, 1932. See also Sam Francis, *Beautiful Losers: Essays on the Failure of American Conservatism* (Columbia, MO: University of Missouri Press, 1993), 87.

97. Kendall, *Willmoore Kendall Contra Mundum*, 35.

98. Gerald J. Russello, "Russell Kirk and Territorial Democracy," *Publius: The Journal of Federalism* 34, no. 4 (Fall 2004): 121–122.

99. Kendall, *Conservative Affirmation*, xxv. In private correspondence, Kendall admitted that his *Conservative Affirmation* was a "declaration of war" against Kirk (Nash, *Conservative Intellectual Movement*, 245). Although both men of the Right emphasized the Christian origins of America, Kendall tended to follow the Straussian line against Kirk that he placed too much focus on the aristocratic origins of American politics. Kendall even accused Kirk of adhering too closely to Burkean views on Providence and the near impossibility of effecting change, an argument that is reminiscent of Strauss's main objection against Burke. See Kendall, "The Benevolent Sage of Mecosta," in *Willmoore Kendall Contra Mundum*, 35–39. Martin Diamond, another Straussian scholar, went so far as to accuse Kirk of misunderstanding the American Founding altogether, since he purportedly sided with the leftist views of Charles Beard and Richard Hofstadter that the Founders were opposed to (majority-rule) democracy. Both Diamond and Kendall agreed that majoritarian democracy is the chief principle of the Founding. See Martin Diamond, *As Far as Republican Principles Will Admit: Essays by Martin Diamond*, edited by William A. Schambra (Washington, DC: AEI Press, 1992), 72–73. Ironically enough, Kirk's later repudiation of the Straussian project of overemphasizing Lockeanism (in its most secular form) as the true foundation of American republicanism may well have resonated with Kendall. See Russell Kirk, *The Conservative Constitution* (Washington, DC: Regnery Gateway, 1990), 65. Jaffa later accused Kendall of devoting "the last years of his life to an extraordinary effort to read John Locke out of the American political tradition" (Jaffa, *How to Think*, 37).

100. Jaffa, "Willmoore Kendall: Philosopher of Consensus?" in *American Conservatism*, 194, 198. Catherine and Michael Zuckert, following Jaffa, also see Kendall as an opponent of the "Straussian approach to American politics" (*The Truth*, 240). Yet in *Basic Symbols*, which questions the American preoccupation with equality, Kendall refers to Strauss as "another great political philosopher" who, besides Eric Voegelin, would support his hermeneutic of the American Founding (23).

101. Drury, *Strauss and the American Right*, 129–135.

102. His former student William F. Buckley thought that Kendall's faith in the people reflected a "baffling optimism." See George H. Nash, "The Place of Willmoore Kendall in American Conservatism," in Murley and Alvis, *Willmoore Kendall*, 11. For a useful discussion of Kendall's attempt to project conservative beliefs onto post–World War II American

voters with mixed success, see Raymond Tatalovich and Thomas S. Engeman, *The Presidency and Political Science: Two Hundred Years of Constitutional Debate* (Baltimore: Johns Hopkins University Press, 2003), 12–24. See also Havers, "Leo Strauss, Willmoore Kendall, and the Meaning of Conservatism," 15–25.

103. Kendall supported the passage of this legislation as a great "conservative victory" on the grounds that it demonstrated how the American system can exhaust a radical political movement through debate and compromise. See "What Killed the Civil Rights Movement?" in *Willmoore Kendall Contra Mundum*, 457–468.

104. Kendall, *Conservative Affirmation*, 17.

105. Kendall to Strauss, December 2, 1956, in Kendall, "Willmoore Kendall–Leo Strauss Correspondence," 195.

106. Kendall and Carey, *Basic Symbols*, 34, 42.

107. M. E. Bradford, "How to Read the Declaration: Reconsidering the Kendall Thesis," *Intercollegiate Review* (Fall 1992): 45. For Bradford's disagreements with Jaffa, see his "The Heresy of Equality: A Reply to Harry Jaffa," in M. E. Bradford, *A Better Guide than Reason: Studies in the American Revolution*, introduction by Jeffrey Hart (La Salle, IL: Sherwood Sugden, 1979), 29–57.

108. Francis G. Wilson, "The Political Science of Willmoore Kendall," *Modern Age* 16 (Winter 1972): 42.

109. John A. Murley, "On the 'Calhounism' of Willmoore Kendall," in Murley and Alvis, *Willmoore Kendall*, 126.

110. Ibid., 103–104. Murley astutely notes that Jaffa and Kendall agree that the Declaration allows Americans to form any type of government they want, even one that is not democratic. Nevertheless, Jaffa has a more globalist view of America's mission than Kendall ever did.

111. Kendall, *Conservative Affirmation*, 249–252; Jaffa, *How to Think*, 38.

112. See note 100 of this chapter; Gottfried, *Leo Strauss*, 73. Shain's *Myth of American Individualism*, in rejecting the Straussian view of the Founding as a secular event, builds on Kendall and Carey's *Basic Symbols*. See Shain, *Myth of American Individualism*, 242, 249.

113. Jaffa, *New Birth*, 353. See also Harry V. Jaffa, *Original Intent and the Framers of the Constitution: A Disputed Question* (Washington, DC: Regnery Gateway, 1994), 315.

114. Bloom, *Closing*, 54.

115. Robert Kagan, *Dangerous Nation: America's Place in the World, from Its Earliest Days to the Dawn of the Twentieth Century* (New York: Vintage, 2007), 13.

116. Ceaser, *Nature and History*, 19.

117. Kendall, *Conservative Affirmation*, 100–120; Kendall, "The 'Open Society' and Its Fallacies," in *Willmoore Kendall Contra Mundum*, 634–649; see Jaffa, "On the Nature of Civil and Religious Liberty," in Buckley, *American Conservative Thought*, 221–238.

118. Drury, *Strauss and the American Right*, 129–136; Altman, *German Stranger*, 315, 317, 320.

119. Strauss, "German Nihilism," 358–359.

120. Strauss, *Natural Right and History*, 5.

121. Kendall, "The 'Open Society' and Its Fallacies," in *Willmoore Kendall Contra Mundum*, 637.

122. Strauss, "Preface to the English Translation," 1–3; Kendall, *Conservative Affirmation*, 114.

123. Strauss, "Preface to the English Translation," 3.

124. Ibid., 6.

125. Strauss, "Liberal Education and Responsibility," in *Liberalism: Ancient and Modern*, 15, 24. See also his "What Is Liberal Education?" in the same volume (3–8).

126. Kendall, "The People vs. Socrates Revisited," in *Willmoore Kendall Contra Mundum*, 157–167.

127. Strauss, *Socrates and Aristophanes*, 314.

128. Kendall, "The People vs. Socrates Revisited," in *Willmoore Kendall Contra Mundum*, 162–163.

129. Ibid., 160–161.

130. James Patrick, *The Magdalen Metaphysicals: Idealism and Orthodoxy at Oxford, 1901–1945* (Macon, GA: Mercer University Press, 1985), 154–155. In a letter to Strauss dated August 29, 1960, Kendall admits that the influence of his former tutor Collingwood "continues to weigh very heavily upon me." See Kendall, "Willmoore Kendall–Leo Strauss Correspondence," 228. In his response to Kendall on September 28, 1960, Strauss acknowledges his "very high regard for Collingwood," and even praises him as "the only 20th century Anglo Saxon known to me who was a genuine philosopher." Strauss implicitly associates Collingwood's thought with historicism, however, when he comments that Collingwood's philosophy, in its most radicalized form, "leads to Heidegger." See Kendall, "Willmoore Kendall–Leo Strauss Correspondence," 230. Some Straussians also suspect Kendall of historicism due to his admiration of Rousseau and Voegelin. See Leo Paul S. de Alvarez, "The Missing Passage of the 'Vanderbilt Lectures,'" in Murley and Alvis, *Willmoore Kendall*, 153.

131. Kendall, "American Conservatism and the 'Prayer' Decisions," in *Willmoore Kendall Contra Mundum*, 334.

132. Strauss, "Preface to the English Translation," 6.

133. Kendall, *Conservative Affirmation*, xxviii. This did not go far enough for the Catholic Right. A few contributors to the Catholic magazine *Triumph*, edited by Kendall's former student Brent Bozell, attacked Kendall's defense of church-state separation as insufficiently Christian. See Nash, *Conservative Intellectual Movement*, 313.

134. See Kendall, "How to Read Richard Weaver," 394–395 (esp. note 23). One wonders if Kendall was implicitly blaming Jaffa for the Goldwater debacle, since Jaffa wrote the famous speech in which Goldwater, at the Republican convention in 1964, uttered the stormy declaration: "Extremism in the defense of liberty is no vice."

135. Ibid.

136. Bloom, *Closing*, 39.

137. Zuckert, "Natural Rights and Protestant Politics," 25–30; Jaffa, *Crisis*, 229; Jaffa, *New Birth*, 164, 353. Zuckert has faced some criticism from a few Straussians for downplaying the influence of Christianity on the American Founding. See Peter Augustine Lawler, "Religion, Philosophy, and the American Founding," and Thomas G. West, "The Transformation of Protestant Theology as a Condition of the American Revolution." Both of these essays can be found in *Protestantism and the American Founding*, edited by Thomas S. Engeman and Michael P. Zuckert (Notre Dame, IN: University of Notre Dame Press, 2004). That said, both Jaffa and Zuckert agree that Kendall and Carey's *Basic Symbols* overemphasizes the importance of the Mayflower Compact as a founding event.

138. See Robert B. Kraynak, "Moral Order in the Western Tradition: Harry Jaffa's Synthesis of Athens, Jerusalem, and Peoria," *Review of Politics* 71 (2009): 181–206. See also Jaffa's reply to Kraynak in "Too Good to Be True?" Alvis correctly notes that Kendall generally took no interest in the differences between Strauss and Voegelin, whom he both admired,

on the relation between reason and revelation. See Alvis, "Evolution," 56–57. Perhaps one of the few examples in which Kendall showed any interest in their differences is in a letter to Voegelin dated October 14, 1959, where he explains the lack of interest that Strauss's students display toward Voegelin by referring to the fact that they are "almost exclusively" all "unbelievers" and that Strauss offers "a kind of training that tends to emphasize their unbelief." See Kendall, "The Eric Voegelin–Willmoore Kendall Correspondence," edited by Steven D. Ealy and Gordon Lloyd, *Political Science Reviewer* 33 (2004): 395.

139. Kendall, "What Killed the Civil Rights Movement?" in *Willmoore Kendall Contra Mundum*, 468.

140. Jaffa, *How to Think*, 18–25, 197.

141. Kendall, *Conservative Affirmation*, 252.

142. Jaffa, *How to Think*, 35.

143. Jaffa, *Crisis*, 243–244, 261.

144. Jaffa, *How to Think*, 56 (his italics).

145. Kendall and Carey, *Basic Symbols*, 151–154.

146. Ibid., 57. See also Harold Bloom, *The American Religion: The Emergence of the Post-Christian Nation* (New York: Touchstone Books, 1992). Hart notes that most postwar conservatives did not think deeply about the meaning of religion in politics and assumed too quickly that it would always take on a traditionalist face (*American Conservative Mind*, 110–111).

147. Jaffa, *New Birth*, 352. I critique Jaffa's reinvention of Lincoln's legacy in greater detail in Havers, *Lincoln and the Politics of Christian Love*, 139–142.

148. Jaffa, *How to Think*, 42.

149. Jaffa, "A Conversation with Harry Jaffa at Rosary College," in *American Conservatism*, 56.

150. Jaffa, *Crisis*, 231.

151. Jaffa, "Humanizing Certitudes," 134, 138. Yet there is no evidence that Bloom was less enthusiastic than Jaffa about American exceptionalism: see note 67 in this chapter. Jaffa also attacks Irving Kristol and Martin Diamond, who sympathized with Straussian teachings, for insufficient support of equality as the Founding credo (*How to Think*, 49–140).

152. See Kraynak, "Moral Order in the Western Tradition," 191–192, 200–206; Drury, *Strauss and the American Right*, 99–100.

153. See Strauss, "Progress or Return?" (257) for his doubts about America's "divine" status. On secularization, see Strauss, "Three Waves," 83. For Strauss on charity, see Ranieri, *Disturbing Revelation*, 103–130, 158–185.

154. Kendall takes these two, perhaps contradictory, positions in the same essay. See "True Sage of Woodstock," 79, 81.

155. See Justin Raimondo, *Reclaiming the American Right: The Lost Legacy of the Conservative Movement* (Wilmington, DE: ISI Books, 2008), 221–261. A few neoconservatives, like the late Irving Kristol and Jeane Kirkpatrick, opposed these crusades. See Dorrien, *Neoconservative Mind*, 123–125, 324–327. As Dorrien shows, however, even before the second Iraq War these were minority positions within the neoconservative movement.

156. Kendall, *Conservative Affirmation*, 3–4, 84; Kendall, "The Benevolent Sage of Mecosta," in *Willmoore Kendall Contra Mundum*, 35.

157. Kendall, *Conservative Affirmation*, 12.

158. Ibid., 91.

159. See Havers, "Willmoore Kendall." See also Kevin Phillips, *American Theocracy: The Peril and Politics of Radical Religion, Oil, and Borrowed Money in the Twenty-First Century* (New York: Viking, 2006).

160. I borrow this term from Paul E. Gottfried. See his *Encounters: My Life with Nixon, Marcuse, and Other Friends and Teachers* (Wilmington, DE: ISI Books, 2009), 40. For a similar argument from a Straussian perspective, see Berns, *Making Patriots*.

6: Leo Strauss and the Uniqueness of the West

1. Strauss, *The City and Man*, 1.

2. Ernest L. Fortin, "Rational Theologians and Irrational Philosophers: A Straussian Perspective," in *Classical Christianity*, 287–288, 295. James Schall has similarly argued that Strauss "succeeded in forcing us [Thomists] to reconsider the validity of revelation with its relation to thought and politics as such." See *Christianity and Politics*, 247.

3. Strauss, "Progress or Return?" 279–280. In the same essay, Strauss attributes the "secret vitality" of the West to this tension between the two traditions (295). This distinction that Strauss draws is perhaps the closest he comes to admitting that he is a modern, since he occasionally admits that the conflict between Athens and Jerusalem is "at the bottom of a kind of thought which is philosophic indeed but no longer Greek: modern philosophy." See Strauss, "Niccolo Machiavelli," in Strauss, *Studies in Platonic Political Philosophy*, 211. Strauss, however, does not develop the content of his modernism here. See chapter two for a discussion of his implicit modernist tendencies.

4. Strauss, "What Is Liberal Education?" in *Liberalism: Ancient and Modern*, 7.

5. Strauss cryptically refers to this "secular conflict" in his essay "Progress or Return?" 295.

6. Ibid., 273. See also Strauss, *Thoughts on Machiavelli*, 133, 157, 207.

7. Pierre Manent, a prominent French admirer of Strauss, asks a similar question about the difficulty of relating a particular faith like Judaism (Jerusalem) to the philosophy of universalism (Athens) in our time. Only a faith like Christianity can mediate this tension, whereas Strauss's "invocation of the intrinsic legitimacy of the chosen people" on one hand and "the philosophic idea of a borderless mankind" on the other cannot do so. See Pierre Manent, "Between Athens and Jerusalem," *First Things* (February 2012): 39. For the remainder of this chapter, I argue that what Strauss wrote about the morality of the Old Testament, however, can be compared to the morality of the Gospels, since both Scriptures are, in his view, incompatible with Greek political philosophy.

8. Strauss, "Progress or Return?" 274–275. In particular, Strauss notes that Plato's *Laws* teach the same lessons about morality as Moses did.

9. Strauss, "What Can We Learn from Political Theory?" 527. Bloom follows Strauss in arguing that the ethic of charity makes "impossible demands" on human nature (*Closing*, 165). What Bloom ignores here is that most defenders of the early social contract tradition (including the American version) still insisted on this ethical standard for citizens.

10. Strauss, "Progress or Return?" 279, 281.

11. Ibid., 277.

12. Ibid., 274.

13. Strauss, "Jerusalem and Athens," 389.

14. Ibid., 396. Clifford Orwin, who follows the Straussian hermeneutic, correctly notes that no Greek god of justice, in contrast to the God of Israel, "is reliably just or even attentive" toward humanity (*Humanity of Thucydides*, 95–96). Yet Orwin does not delve into the implications of this insight for his admiration of the "humane" Thucydides.

15. Strauss, "Jerusalem and Athens," 396. See also "Progress or Return?" 293.

16. Strauss, "Jerusalem and Athens," 403.

17. Thomas L. Pangle, "Introduction," in Strauss, *Studies in Platonic Political Philosophy*, 20. In this context, Pangle emphasizes that the conflict between Plato and the poets parallels the conflict between Athens and Jerusalem. The differences between Greek poetry and biblical revelation, which Pangle does not discuss, are "secondary" to this wider conflict, according to Pangle's Strauss. For a similar argument that Pangle offers in the context of Kierkegaard's thought, see Pangle, *Political Philosophy*, 172–181. For an incisive critique of Pangle's conclusions, see Polka, *Hermeneutics and Ontology*, 259–262.

18. Pangle, "Introduction," 11. Jaffa has criticized Pangle's understanding of Strauss in this context. See Harry V. Jaffa, "The Legacy of Leo Strauss," in Jaffa et al., *Crisis of the Strauss Divided*, 71–73. Jaffa objects to Pangle's portrayal of Strauss as an "Epicurean" (that is, a nihilist) who opposes both Athens and Jerusalem because of their strict teachings on morality. In his reply to Jaffa, Pangle contends that his philosophical opponent too closely identifies the life of the philosopher, who is committed to Socratic questioning, and that of the prophet, who is wedded to unquestioning obedience. See Thomas L. Pangle, "The Platonism of Leo Strauss: A Reply to Harry Jaffa," in Jaffa et al., *Crisis of the Strauss Divided*, 85–86. Although I agree with Pangle on this score, I argue in what follows that Pangle is equally wrong to identify the Bible with the moral lessons of ancient Greek poetry.

19. See Strauss, "Progress or Return?" 299, on the "blasphemous" usage of religion for political purposes. For similar passages, see also "On the Interpretation of Genesis," 362; "Jerusalem and Athens," 384. Strauss notes in "Jerusalem and Athens" that "the concept of poetry—as distinguished from that of song—is foreign to the Bible" (381).

20. Strauss, "Progress or Return?" 281. Strauss also writes: "It is for this reason that Greek poetry is inseparable from Greek philosophy" ("On the Interpretation of Genesis," 374). In the biblical era, however, revelation presents an unprecedented challenge to philosophy. Strauss, in his 1948 lecture "Reason and Revelation," notes that the Bible promises "knowledge" of God, which constitutes the only serious challenge to philosophy's exclusive claim to offer knowledge (149). Neither classical poetry nor politics, Strauss notes, ever challenged Greek philosophy in this way.

21. Strauss, *On Plato's "Symposium,"* 6.

22. Wilhelmsen, *Christianity and Political Philosophy*, 209–225; Schall, *Christianity and Politics*, 252.

23. Grant was critical of Protestant theologians like Reinhold Niebuhr and Anders Nygren for similarly adhering to a dualistic opposition between Greek philosophy and the Bible. See Grant, "Two Theological Languages," 11. See also Grant Havers, "Leo Strauss's Influence on George Grant," in Angus, Dart, and Peters, *Athens and Jerusalem*, 124–135 (esp. 127).

24. Drury, *Political Ideas*, 37–60; Altman, *German Stranger*, esp. xv. See also Lampert, *Leo Strauss and Nietzsche*.

25. Remi Brague, "Athens, Jerusalem, Mecca: Leo Strauss's 'Muslim' Understanding of Greek Philosophy," *Poetics* 19 (1998): 235–259.

26. For Jaffa's early views on this distinction, see his *Thomism and Aristotelianism*. For

his later views, see his "Strauss at One Hundred," 45–46. For a useful analysis of the twists and turns that characterize Jaffa's thought in this context, see Kraynak, "Moral Order in the Western Tradition."

27. See Moyn, "From Experience to Law," 174–194. For Strauss's early interest in Protestant theologians like Karl Barth and their contribution to debates over the Enlightenment's challenge to orthodox theology in the Weimar era, see Leo Strauss, "Preface to *Hobbes Politische Wissenschaft*," in *Jewish Philosophy*, 453. Altman, who usually argues that this distinction between Athens and Jerusalem is a sign of Strauss's "Nazism," admits that Tertullian first made this distinction. But then he concludes that Tertullian is a "proto-Straussian" (*German Stranger*, 522).

28. See Owen Barfield, *Saving the Appearances: A Study in Idolatry* (New York: Harcourt, Brace, and World, 1988), 182.

29. See José Porfirio Miranda, *Marx and the Bible: A Critique of the Philosophy of Oppression*, translated by John Eagleson (Maryknoll, NY: Orbis Books, 1974).

30. For the similarities between Strauss and Voegelin, see Ranieri, *Disturbing Revelation*. See also Strauss's letter to Voegelin dated February 25, 1951, in Emberley and Cooper, *Faith and Political Philosophy*, 78.

31. Eric Voegelin, *Plato* (Baton Rouge: Louisiana State University Press, 1966), 141, 105. Ranieri, in his comparative study of Strauss and Voegelin, also notes that Voegelin was far more openly critical of the biblical tradition than Strauss was (*Disturbing Revelation*, 161).

32. Strauss, "Progress or Return?" 282; Barfield, *Saving the Appearances*, 182.

33. Strauss, "Progress or Return?" 286–287.

34. Strauss, "On the Interpretation of Genesis," 369; Strauss, "Progress or Return?" 281–282. See also Strauss, "Freud on Moses and Monotheism," where he writes: "The Bible is the document of the greatest effort ever made to deprive all heavenly bodies of all possibility of divine worship" (293).

35. Strauss, "Jerusalem and Athens," 396. Strauss is discussing the poetry of Hesiod as well as Aristotle's *Metaphysics* in this context. See also note 14 of this chapter.

36. Jürgen Habermas, "Israel and Athens, or to Whom Does Anamnesic Reason Belong?" in *The Frankfurt School on Religion: Key Writings by the Major Thinkers*, edited by Eduardo Mendieta (New York: Routledge, 2005), 295.

37. Ibid., 299–300.

38. On secularization, see Strauss, "Three Waves," 83; on Kojève, see Strauss, *On Tyranny*, 191.

39. Jürgen Habermas, "On the Relation between the Secular Liberal State and Religion," in *The Frankfurt School on Religion*, 344. See also Jürgen Habermas, *The New Conservatism: Cultural Criticism and the Historians' Debate*, edited and translated by Shierry Weber Nicholsen (Cambridge, MA: MIT Press, 1989), 137; also his essay "'The Political': The Rational Meaning of a Questionable Inheritance of Political Theology," in *The Power of Religion in the Public Sphere*, edited and introduced by Eduardo Mendieta and Jonathan VanAntwerpen (New York: Columbia University Press, 2011), 16. Habermas gave a seminar on Schmitt and Strauss at the State University of New York in 2009.

40. Habermas, "Israel and Athens," 299.

41. Ibid., 300.

42. Charles Taylor, "Multiculturalism and 'The Politics of Recognition,'" in *Ethical Issues: Perspectives for Canadians*, 3rd edition, edited by Eldon Soifer (Peterborough: Broadview Press, 2009), 609.

43. See Habermas's and Taylor's comments in *The Power of Religion*, 37, 61, 66–67.

44. My reading here is exactly opposite to that of Drury, who believes that Strauss saw religion as the only foundation of morality for citizens in a democracy. See Drury, *Strauss and the American Right*, 66. Zuckert correctly notes that Strauss opposed the Averroistic usage of biblical religion as a mere "civil theology" (*Postmodern Platos*, 197).

45. See Shell, "To Spare the Vanquished," 186; Daniel Tanguay, *Leo Strauss: An Intellectual Biography* (New Haven: Yale University Press, 2007), 101, 205–207. See also Smith, "Athens and Washington," 123. Strauss notes that Heidegger may have played some role in creating a "Christianity without God" (*What Is Political Philosophy?* 252).

46. Strauss, "Three Waves," 83. Strauss may have learned this skeptical attitude from Lessing, the subject of his early writings. In his 1937 essay "Introduction to *Mendelssohn's Morning Hours* and *To the Friends of Lessing*," Strauss quotes Lessing's argument against "rational Christianity" based on Lessing's view that "one doesn't really know either where reason comes in or where Christianity comes in." See Leo Strauss, *Leo Strauss on Moses Mendelssohn*, translated and edited with an interpretive essay by Martin D. Yaffe (Chicago: University of Chicago Press, 2012), 75. Strauss's doctoral dissertation, which was supervised by Ernst Cassirer, was on F. H. Jacobi, a key participant in the late-eighteenth-century controversy over Lessing's "Spinozism" and Mendelssohn's attempts to defend Lessing from this accusation after his death in 1781.

47. Spinoza, *Spinoza's Critique of Religion*, 232. For the record, I agree with Xenos that Strauss's early study of Spinoza is central to understanding the rest of his oeuvre (*Cloaked in Virtue*, 65–68).

48. Strauss, "Preface to the English Translation," 18. Strauss admits elsewhere that he has "leaned very heavily" on Spinoza ("Progress or Return?" 307).

49. Strauss, *Spinoza's Critique of Religion*, 245.

50. Spinoza, *Theologico-Political Treatise*, chapter 14, section 1, paragraphs 38–47 (165). These dogmas include belief in God's mercy, uniqueness, omnipresence, and love.

51. See Yaffe, "Interpretive Essay," 329. See also Strauss, *Persecution and the Art of Writing*, 162, 193. Spinoza insists on this point when he acknowledges, following Hobbes, that the "state of nature" cannot teach or command morality. See *Theologico-Political Treatise*, chapter 16, from section 2, paragraph 5, to section 4, paragraph 2 (179–181).

52. Strauss, "Jerusalem and Athens," 396.

53. Ibid., 381.

54. Ibid., 398–99, 403. For a useful discussion of Strauss's critique of Cohen in this essay, see Susan Orr, *Jerusalem and Athens: Reason and Revelation in the Work of Leo Strauss* (Lanham, MD: Rowman and Littlefield, 1995), 127–128. Strauss is discussing Cohen's essay "The Social Ideal in Plato and the Prophets," in *Reason and Hope: Selections from the Jewish Writings of Hermann Cohen*, translated by Eva Jospe (New York: W. W. Norton, 1971), 66–77.

55. Strauss, "Cohen's Analysis of Spinoza's Bible Science (1924)," in Strauss, *Early Writings*, 144. Ironically, Strauss and his students are similarly accused of wanting "Christian consequences in the social order without Christianity in their public orthodoxy." See Wilhelmsen, *Christianity and Political Philosophy*, 213.

56. See J. Judd Owen, *Religion and the Demise of Liberal Rationalism: The Foundational Crisis of the Separation of Church and State* (Chicago: University of Chicago Press, 2001). Like Strauss, Owen contrasts the early social contractarians' usage of religion with the utter hostility to religion that secular liberals manifest today.

57. Habermas, "Israel and Athens," 300; Habermas, "Secular State and Religion," 348; Paul Edward Gottfried, *Multiculturalism and the Politics of Guilt: Toward a Secular Theocracy* (Columbia, MO: University of Missouri Press, 2002). Strauss also associates guilt with the biblical virtues, not the pagan ones. See "Progress or Return?" 279.

58. See Miguel Vatter's excellent analysis of Habermas's defective political theology in "Habermas between Athens and Jerusalem: Public Reason and Atheistic Theology," *Interpretation* 38, no. 3 (2011): 253–256.

59. Strauss, "Progress or Return?" 279.

60. Strauss, *Thoughts on Machiavelli*, 298.

61. See Strauss, "Re-education of Axis Countries," 533–536. In this lecture, which he gave at the New School for Social Research in 1943, Strauss insisted that a postwar German government of reconstruction be run by Germans, not by the Allied conquerors. See also Minowitz, *Straussophobia*, who persuasively argues that Strauss would not have supported the imposition of "regime change" on a nation (118, 158).

62. See Strauss, "Preface," in *Liberalism: Ancient and Modern*, vi–vii; also Gottfried, *Leo Strauss*, 63–64.

63. See Strauss, "Relativism," 17. On a rare occasion, Strauss acknowledges the power of historical relativity when he admits that the "answer to the universal question of the best political order as such" is usually shaped by the regime to which a citizen belongs. For example, "a man who defends democracy" will portray it as the best regime, just as a citizen in a monarchy will defend it in identical terms. See Strauss, *What Is Political Philosophy?* 85. However, he does not apply this insight to his own preference for a democratic regime.

64. Natan Sharansky, *Defending Identity: Its Indispensable Role in Protecting Democracy*, with Shira Wolosky Weiss (New York: Public Affairs, 2008), 84.

65. See Harold A. Innis, *Empire and Communications*, with a general introduction by Alexander John Watson (Toronto: Dundurn Press, 2007), 196. For the postwar Right's turn away from "history," see Gottfried, *Search for Historical Meaning*.

66. Fukuyama, *End of History*, 198, 261.

67. Ibid., 216–217.

68. Francis Fukuyama, *Trust: The Social Virtues and the Creation of Prosperity* (New York: Free Press, 1995), 92–93, 287. See also Theodore de Bary, *The Trouble with Confucianism* (Cambridge: Harvard University Press, 1985); Brayton Polka, "What Is Democracy? Reflections on Sen's Idea of Justice," *European Legacy* 15, no. 6 (2010): 773–775. Polka questions Amartya Sen's view that ancient Hinduism was democratic and counters that only the biblical tradition can accurately make such a claim of influencing and fostering true democracy.

69. Leon J. Podles, *The Church Impotent: The Feminization of Christianity* (Dallas: Spence Publishing, 1999), 63. Podles cites Strauss's "On the Interpretation of Genesis" to buttress his argument.

70. See Ricardo Duchesne, *The Uniqueness of Western Civilization* (Leiden: Brill, 2011). Duchesne, like Strauss, also emphasizes the unique contributions that both Greek philosophy and the Bible have made to the identity of the West.

Bibliography

Adams, John. *The Works of John Adams, Second President of the United States: With a Life of the Author, Notes and Illustrations, by his Grandson Charles Francis Adams*. Boston: Little, Brown and Co., 1856.

Adorno, Theodor W. *The Authoritarian Personality*. 2 vols. New York: Harper and Row, 1950.

———. *The Jargon of Authenticity*. Translated by Knut Tarnowski and Frederic Will. London: Routledge and Kegan Paul, 1973.

———. *Kierkegaard: Construction of the Aesthetic*. Translated, edited, and with a foreword by Robert Hullot-Kentor. Minneapolis: University of Minnesota Press, 1989.

Ajzenstat, Janet. *The Canadian Founding: John Locke and Parliament*. Montreal and Kingston: McGill-Queen's University Press, 2007.

———. "The Conservatism of the Canadian Founders." In *After Liberalism: Essays in Search of Freedom, Virtue, and Order*. Edited by William D. Gairdner. Toronto: Stoddart, 1998. 17–32.

Altman, William H. F. "The Alpine Limits of Jewish Thought: Leo Strauss, National Socialism, and *Judentum ohne Gott*." *Journal of Jewish Thought and Philosophy* 17, no. 1 (Spring 2009): 1–46.

———. *The German Stranger: Leo Strauss and National Socialism*. Foreword by Michael Zank. Lanham, MD: Lexington Books, 2011.

Alvarez, Leo Paul S. de. "The Missing Passage of the 'Vanderbilt Lectures.'" In Murley and Alvis, *Willmoore Kendall*, 141–155.

Alvis, John E. "The Evolution of Willmoore Kendall's Political Thought." In Murley and Alvis, *Willmoore Kendall*, 47–97.

Anastaplo, George. "Leo Strauss at the University of Chicago." In Deutsch and Murley, *Leo Strauss, the Straussians*, 3–30.

Angus, Ian, Ron Dart, and Peg Peters, eds. *Athens and Jerusalem: George Grant's Theology, Philosophy, and Politics*. Toronto: University of Toronto Press, 2006.

Arendt, Hannah. *Between Past and Future: Six Exercises in Political Thought*. New York: Meridian Books, 1963.

———. *On Revolution*. London and New York: Penguin, 1990.

———. *The Origins of Totalitarianism*. New York: Harcourt, 1951.

Aristotle. *The Basic Works of Aristotle*. Edited by Richard McKeon. New York: Modern Library, 2001.

Arkes, Hadley. "Athens and Jerusalem: The Legacy of Leo Strauss." In *Leo Strauss and Judaism: Jerusalem and Athens Critically Revisited*. Lanham, MD: Rowman and Littlefield, 1996. 1–23.

———. *Natural Rights and the Right to Choose*. Cambridge: Cambridge University Press, 2002.

Arnhart, Larry. "Statesmanship as Magnanimity: Classical, Christian, and Modern." *Polity* 16 (Winter 1983): 263–283.

Aschheim, Steven E. *Beyond the Border: The German-Jewish Legacy Abroad*. Princeton: Princeton University Press, 2007.

Baldacchino, Joseph. "The Value-Centered Historicism of Edmund Burke." *Modern Age* 27, no. 2 (1983): 139–145.

Barfield, Owen. *Saving the Appearances: A Study in Idolatry*. New York: Harcourt, Brace, and World, 1988.

Barnett, Correlli. *The Collapse of British Power*. London: Pan Books, 2002.

Bary, Wm. Theodore de. *The Trouble with Confucianism*. Cambridge: Harvard University Press, 1985.

Batnitzky, Leora. *Leo Strauss and Emmanuel Levinas: Philosophy and the Politics of Revelation*. Cambridge: Cambridge University Press, 2006.

Behnegar, Nasser. *Leo Strauss, Max Weber, and the Scientific Study of Politics*. Chicago: University of Chicago Press, 2003.

Berger, Carl. *The Sense of Power: Studies in the Ideas of Canadian Imperialism, 1867–1914*. Toronto: University of Toronto Press, 1970.

Berlin, Isaiah. *Mr. Churchill in 1940*. Cambridge, MA: Riverside Press, 1964.

Berns, Walter. *Making Patriots*. Chicago: University of Chicago Press, 2001.

———. *Taking the Constitution Seriously*. New York: Simon and Schuster, 1987.

Birkenhead, Lord, Earl of. *Contemporary Personalities*. London: Cassel, 1924.

Bloom, Allan. *The Closing of the American Mind: How Higher Education Has Failed Democracy and Impoverished the Souls of Today's Students*. Foreword by Saul Bellow. New York: Simon and Schuster, 1987.

———. *Giants and Dwarfs: Essays, 1960–1990*. New York: Simon and Schuster, 1990.

———. "Introduction." In Jean-Jacques Rousseau, *Émile, or On Education*. Introduction, translation, and notes by Allan Bloom. New York: Basic Books, 1979.

Bloom, Harold. *The American Religion: The Emergence of the Post-Christian Nation*. New York: Touchstone Books, 1992.

Blumstock, Robert. "Anglo-Saxon Lament." *Canadian Review of Sociology and Anthropology* 3 (1966): 98–105.

Bradford, M. E. "The Heresy of Equality: A Reply to Harry Jaffa." In M. E. Bradford, *A Better Guide than Reason: Studies in the American Revolution*. Introduction by Jeffrey Hart. La Salle, IL: Sherwood Sugden, 1979. 29–57.

———. "How to Read the Declaration: Reconsidering the Kendall Thesis." *Intercollegiate Review* (Fall 1992): 45–50.

Brague, Remi. "Athens, Jerusalem, Mecca: Leo Strauss's 'Muslim' Understanding of Greek Philosophy." *Poetics* 19 (1998): 235–259.

Brimelow, Peter. *The Patriot Game: National Dreams and Political Realities*. Toronto: Key Porter Books, 1986.

Brittain, Christopher. "Leo Strauss and Resourceful Odysseus: Rhetorical Violence and the Holy Middle." *Canadian Review of American Studies* 38, no. 1 (2008): 147–163.

Brown, David S. *Richard Hofstadter: An Intellectual Biography*. Chicago: University of Chicago Press, 2006.

Buchanan, Patrick J. *Churchill, Hitler, and the "Unnecessary War": How Britain Lost Its Empire, and the West Lost the World*. New York: Crown Publishers, 2008.

Buckley, William F., Jr. "The Relevance of Social Science." In Buckley, *American Conservative Thought*, 397–400.

Buckley, William F., Jr., ed. *American Conservative Thought in the Twentieth Century*. Indianapolis and New York: Bobbs-Merrill, 1970.

Burke, Edmund. *On the American Revolution: Selected Speeches and Letters*. Edited by Elliott R. Barkan. New York: Harper Torchbooks, 1966.

———. *Reflections on the Revolution in France*. Harmondsworth: Penguin, 1982.

Burnham, James. *The Managerial Revolution*. Harmondsworth: Penguin, 1962.

Calvin, John. *Genesis*. Translated and edited by John King, MA. London: The Banner of Truth Trust, 1975.

———. *Institutes of the Christian Religion*. Translated by Henry Beveridge. Grand Rapids, MI: Eerdmans, 1989.

Carey, George W. "How to Read Willmoore Kendall." *Intercollegiate Review* (Winter–Spring 1972): 63–65.

Ceaser, James W. "Multiculturalism and American Liberal Democracy." In *Multiculturalism and American Democracy*. Edited by Arthur Melzer, Jerry Weinberger, and M. Richard Zinman. Lawrence: University Press of Kansas, 1998. 139–156.

———. *Nature and History in American Political Development: A Debate*. Cambridge: Harvard University Press, 2006.

Champion, C. P. *The Strange Demise of British Canada: The Liberals and Canadian Nationalism, 1964–1968*. Montreal and Kingston: McGill-Queen's University Press, 2010.

Chomsky, Noam. *Necessary Illusions: Thought Control in Democratic Societies*. Toronto: Anansi, 2003.

———. "Reinhold Niebuhr." *Grand Street* 6, no. 2 (Winter 1987): 197–212.

Churchill, Winston S. *The Age of Revolution*. Vol. 3 of *A History of the English-Speaking Peoples*. New York: Bantam, 1963.

———. *The Birth of Britain*. Vol. 1 of *A History of the English-Speaking Peoples*. New York: Bantam, 1963.

———. *Closing the Ring*. Vol. 5 of *The Second World War*. Boston: Houghton Mifflin, 1951.

———. "The Flame of Christian Ethics." In *Winston S. Churchill: His Complete Speeches*. Vol. 7, *1943–1949*. Edited by Robert Rhodes James. New York and London: Chelsea House Publishers, 1974. 7643–7644.

———. *The Gathering Storm*. Vol. 1 of *The Second World War*. Boston and New York: Houghton Mifflin, 1948.

———. *Great Contemporaries*. Chicago: University of Chicago Press, 1973.

———. *The Great Democracies*. Vol. 4 of *A History of the English-Speaking Peoples*. New York: Bantam, 1963.

———. *The Great Republic: A History of America*. New York: Modern Library, 1999.

———. *The Hinge of Fate*. Vol. 4 of *The Second World War*. Boston: Houghton Mifflin, 1950.

———. *Into Battle: Speeches by the Right Hon. Winston S. Churchill*. Compiled by Randolph S. Churchill. London: Cassel, 1943.

———. *Liberalism and the Social Problem: A Collection of Early Speeches as a Member of Parliament*. Rockville, MD: Arc Manor, 2007.

———. *Marlborough: His Life and Times*. 4 vols. Toronto: Ryerson Press, 1933–1938.

———. *My Early Life, 1874–1904*. With an introduction by William Manchester. New York: Touchstone, 1996.

———. *Never Give In! The Best of Winston Churchill's Speeches*. Selected by his grandson Winston S. Churchill. New York: Hyperion, 2003.

———. *The New World*. Vol. 2 of *A History of the English-Speaking Peoples*. New York: Bantam, 1963.

———. *Thoughts and Adventures*. New York: W. W. Norton, 1990.

———. *The World Crisis: The Aftermath*. London: Thornton Butterworth, 1929.

Codevilla, Angelo. "De Gaulle: Statesmanship in the Modern State." In *Statesmanship: Essays in Honor of Sir Winston S. Churchill*. Edited by Harry V. Jaffa. Durham, NC: Carolina Academic Press, 1981. 213–233.

Cohen, Hermann. *Religion of Reason: Out of the Sources of Judaism*. Translated with an introduction by Simon Kaplan. Atlanta: Scholars Press, 1995.

———. "The Social Ideal in Plato and the Prophets." In *Reason and Hope: Selections from the Jewish Writings of Hermann Cohen*. Translated by Eva Jospe. New York: W. W. Norton, 1971. 66–77.

Collingwood, R. G. *The Idea of History*. New York: Oxford University Press, 1956.

Cooper, Barry. "The Revival of Political Philosophy." In *By Loving Our Own: George Grant and the Legacy of "Lament for a Nation."* Edited by Peter C. Emberley. Ottawa: Carleton University Press, 1990. 97–119.

Corbett, Ross J. "Locke's Biblical Critique." *Review of Politics* 74 (2012): 27–51.

Coulanges, Numa Denis Fustel de. *The Ancient City: A Study of the Religions, Laws, and Institutions of Greece and Rome*. Garden City, NY: Doubleday Anchor Books, 1956.

Cropsey, Joseph. *Polity and Economy: With Further Thoughts on the Principles of Adam Smith*. South Bend, IN: St. Augustine's Press, 2001.

Curley, Edwin. "'I Durst Not Write So Boldly,' or How to Read Hobbes' Theologico-Political Treatise." In *Hobbes e Spinoza: Scienza e politica. Atti del convegno internazionale Urbino 14–17 ottobre, 1988*. Edited by Daniela Bostrenghi. Naples: Bibliopolis, 1992. 497–593.

Dangerfield, George. *The Strange Death of Liberal England*. Foreword by Peter Stansky. Stanford: Stanford University Press, 1997.

Dart, Ron. "Stephen Leacock and George Grant: Tory Affinities." In Angus, Dart, and Peters, *Athens and Jerusalem*, 5–28.

Davis, Arthur. "Did George Grant Change His Politics?" In Angus, Dart, and Peters, *Athens and Jerusalem*, 62–79.

Deutsch, Kenneth L. "Leo Strauss's Friendly Criticism of American Liberal Democracy: Neoconservative or Aristocratic Liberal?" In Deutsch and Fishman, *Dilemmas*, 175–202.

Deutsch, Kenneth L., and Ethan Fishman, eds. *The Dilemmas of American Conservatism*. Lexington: University Press of Kentucky, 2010.

Deutsch, Kenneth L., and John A. Murley, eds. *Leo Strauss, the Straussians, and the American Regime*. Lanham, MD: Rowman and Littlefield, 1999.

Deutsch, Kenneth L., and Walter Nicgorski, eds. *Leo Strauss: Political Philosopher and Jewish Thinker*. Lanham, MD: Rowman and Littlefield, 1994.

Diamond, Martin. *As Far as Republican Principles Will Admit: Essays by Martin Diamond*. Edited by William A. Schambra. Washington, DC: AEI Press, 1992.

Diggins, John P. *Up from Communism: Conservative Odysseys in American Intellectual History*. New York: Harper and Row, 1975.

———. *Why Niebuhr Now?* Chicago: University of Chicago Press, 2011.

Dilks, David. *The Great Dominion: Winston Churchill in Canada, 1900–1954*. Foreword by Lady Soames. Toronto: Thomas Allen, 2005.

Dorrien, Gary. *The Neoconservative Mind: Politics, Culture, and the War of Ideology*. Philadelphia: Temple University Press, 1993.

Drolet, Jean-François. *American Neoconservatism: The Politics and Culture of a Reactionary Idealism*. London: Hurst, 2011.

Drucker, Peter F. "A Key to American Politics: Calhoun's Pluralism." In *Liberalism versus*

Conservatism: The Continuing Debate in American Government. Edited by Willmoore Kendall and George W. Carey. New York: D. Van Nostrand, 1966. 436–446.

Drury, Shadia B. *Alexandre Kojève: The Roots of Postmodern Politics.* New York: St. Martin's Press, 1994.

———. *Leo Strauss and the American Right.* New York: St. Martin's Press, 1997.

———. *The Political Ideas of Leo Strauss.* Updated edition, with a new introduction by the author. 1988. New York: Palgrave Macmillan, 2005.

Duchesne, Ricardo. *The Uniqueness of Western Civilization.* Leiden: Brill, 2011.

East, John. "The Political Thought of Willmoore Kendall." *Political Science Reviewer* 3 (1973): 201–239.

Emberley, Peter, and Barry Cooper, translators and editors. *Faith and Political Philosophy: The Correspondence between Leo Strauss and Eric Voegelin, 1934–1964.* University Park: Pennsylvania State University Press, 1993.

Emmert, Kirk. *Winston S. Churchill on Empire.* Durham, NC: Carolina Academic Press and the Claremont Institute for the Study of Statesmanship and Political Philosophy, 1989.

Fackenheim, Emil L. *To Mend the World: Foundations of Future Jewish Thought.* New York: Schocken Books, 1982.

The Federalist. New York: Modern Library, 1937.

Fessard, Gaston. "Two Interpreters of Hegel's Phenomenology." *Interpretation* 19, no. 2 (Winter 1991–1992): 195–199.

Feuer, Lewis. *Spinoza and the Rise of Liberalism.* Boston: Beacon Press, 1958.

———. "Spinoza's Political Philosophy: The Lessons and Problems of a Conservative Democrat." In *The Philosophy of Baruch Spinoza.* Edited by Richard Kennington. Washington, DC: Catholic University of America Press, 1980. 133–153.

Fischer, Lars. "After the 'Strauss Wars.'" *East European Jewish Affairs* 40, no. 1 (April 2010): 61–79.

Forbes, H. D. "George Grant and Leo Strauss." In *George Grant and the Subversion of Modernity: Art, Philosophy, Politics, Religion, and Education.* Edited by Arthur Davis. Toronto: University of Toronto Press, 1996. 169–198.

Fortin, Ernest L. *Classical Christianity and the Political Order: Reflections on the Theologico-Political Problem.* Edited by J. Brian Benestad. Lanham, MD: Rowman and Littlefield, 1996.

Francis, Sam. *Beautiful Losers: Essays on the Failure of American Conservatism.* Columbia, MO: University of Missouri Press, 1993.

Friedrich-Walling, Karl. "Was Alexander Hamilton a Machiavellian Statesman?" In *Machiavelli's Liberal Republican Legacy.* Edited by Paul A. Rahe. Cambridge: Cambridge University Press, 2006. 254–278.

Frohnen, Bruce, Jeremy Beer, and Jeffrey O. Nelson, eds. *American Conservatism: An Encyclopedia.* Wilmington, DE: ISI Books, 2006.

Fromm, Erich. *The Fear of Freedom.* London: Routledge, 1991.

Fukuyama, Francis. *America at the Crossroads: Democracy, Power, and the Neoconservative Legacy.* New Haven: Yale University Press, 2006.

———. *The End of History and the Last Man.* New York: Simon and Schuster, 1992; Free Press, 2006.

———. *Trust: The Social Virtues and the Creation of Prosperity.* New York: Free Press, 1995.

Gates, Henry Louis, Jr. "Whose Canon Is it Anyway?" *New York Times*, February 26, 1989.

Genovese, Elizabeth Fox-, and Eugene D. Genovese. *The Mind of the Master Class: History and Faith in the Southern Slaveholders' Worldview.* Cambridge: Cambridge University Press, 2005.

Gilbert, Martin. *Churchill's Political Philosophy.* Oxford: Oxford University Press, 1981.

——. *The Will of the People: Winston Churchill and Parliamentary Democracy.* Toronto: Vintage Canada, 2006.

Gillespie, Michael Allen. *The Theological Origins of Modernity.* Chicago: University of Chicago Press, 2008.

Gottfried, Paul Edward. *After Liberalism: Mass Democracy in the Managerial State.* Princeton: Princeton University Press, 1999.

——. *Carl Schmitt: Politics and Theory.* New York: Greenwood Press, 1990.

——. "Concepts of Government." *Modern Age* 37, no. 3 (Spring 1995): 264–269.

——. *Conservatism in America: Making Sense of the American Right.* London: Palgrave, 2007.

——. "Cryptic Fascist?" *American Conservative* (February 2011): 47–49.

——. *Encounters: My Life with Nixon, Marcuse, and Other Friends and Teachers.* Wilmington, DE: ISI Books, 2009.

——. *Leo Strauss and the Conservative Movement in America: A Critical Appraisal.* Cambridge: Cambridge University Press, 2012.

——. *Multiculturalism and the Politics of Guilt: Toward a Secular Theocracy.* Columbia, MO: University of Missouri Press, 2002.

——. *The Search for Historical Meaning: Hegel and the Postwar American Right.* DeKalb: Northern Illinois University Press, 1986.

——. "Strauss and the Straussians." *Humanitas* 18, nos. 1–2 (2005): 26–30.

Gove, Michael. "The Very British Roots of Neoconservatism and Its Lessons for British Conservatives." In *The Neocon Reader.* Edited and with an introduction by Irwin Stelzer. New York: Grove Press, 2004. 271–288.

Grant, George Parkin. "The Empire: Yes or No?" In *Collected Works of George Grant.* Vol. 1, *1933–1950.* Edited by Arthur Davis and Peter Emberley. Toronto: University of Toronto Press, 2000. 97–126.

——. *English-Speaking Justice.* Toronto: House of Anansi, 1974.

——. *The George Grant Reader.* Edited by William Christian and Sheila Grant. Toronto: University of Toronto Press, 1998.

——. *Lament for a Nation: The Defeat of Canadian Nationalism.* 1965. Reprint. Ottawa: Carleton University Press, 1991.

——. *Philosophy in the Mass Age.* 1959. Reprint. Toronto: University of Toronto Press, 1995.

——. *Selected Letters.* Edited with an introduction by William Christian. Toronto: University of Toronto Press, 1996.

——. *Technology and Empire: Perspectives on North America.* Toronto: House of Anansi, 1969.

——. *Time as History.* Edited with an introduction by William Christian. 1969. Reprint. Toronto: University of Toronto Press, 1995.

——. "Two Theological Languages." In *"Two Theological Languages" by George Grant and Other Essays in Honour of His Work.* Edited by Wayne Whillier. Toronto: The Edwin Mellen Press, 1990. 6–19.

Green, Kenneth Hart. *Jew and Philosopher: The Return to Maimonides in the Jewish Thought of Leo Strauss.* Albany: SUNY Press, 1993.

Habermas, Jürgen. "Israel and Athens, or to Whom Does Anamnesic Reason Belong?" In *The Frankfurt School on Religion: Key Writings by the Major Thinkers*. Edited by Eduardo Mendieta. New York: Routledge, 2005. 293–301.

———. *The New Conservatism: Cultural Criticism and the Historians' Debate*. Edited and translated by Shierry Weber Nicholsen. Cambridge, MA: MIT Press, 1989.

———. "On the Relation between the Secular Liberal State and Religion." In *The Frankfurt School on Religion: Key Writings by the Major Thinkers*. Edited by Eduardo Mendieta. New York: Routledge, 2005. 339–348.

———. "'The Political': The Rational Meaning of a Questionable Inheritance of Political Theology." In *The Power of Religion in the Public Sphere*. Edited and introduced by Eduardo Mendieta and Jonathan VanAntwerpen. New York: Columbia University Press, 2011. 15–33.

Hamilton, Alexander. "The War in Europe." In *The Papers of Alexander Hamilton*. Vol. 20, *January 1796–March 1797*. Edited by Harold C. Syrett. New York: Columbia University Press, 1974. 339–340.

Harris, Errol E. *The Substance of Spinoza*. Atlantic Highlands, NJ: Humanities Press, 1995.

Hart, Jeffrey. *The Making of the American Conservative Mind: "National Review" and Its Times*. Wilmington, DE: ISI Books, 2005.

Hartz, Louis. *The Liberal Tradition in America: An Interpretation of American Political Thought since the Revolution*. New York: Harcourt Brace, 1955.

Havardi, Jeremy. *The Greatest Briton: Essays on Winston Churchill's Life and Political Philosophy*. London: Shepheard-Walwyn, 2009.

Havers, Grant. "Between Athens and Jerusalem: Western Otherness in the Works of Leo Strauss and Hannah Arendt." *European Legacy* 9, no. 1 (2004): 19–29.

———. "Carl Schmitt, Leo Strauss, and the Necessity of Political Theology." In *Politics in Theology: Religion and Public Life*, vol. 38. Edited by Gabriel R. Ricci. New Brunswick, NJ: Transaction, 2012. 15–31.

———. "Conservatism True and False in America: Evaluating Leo Strauss from the Right." http://libertylawsite.org/2012/04/15/conservatism-true-and-false-in-america-evaluating-leo-strauss-from-the-right/

———. "The Final Volley in the Strauss Wars?" *European Legacy* 18, no. 1 (2013): 78–82.

———. "George Grant and Leo Strauss: Modernist and Postmodernist Conservatisms." *Topia* 8 (Fall 2002): 91–106.

———. "James Burnham's Elite Theory and the Postwar American Right." *Telos* 154 (Spring 2011): 29–50.

———. "Kierkegaard, Adorno, and the Socratic Individual." *European Legacy* (forthcoming).

———. "Leo Strauss, Willmoore Kendall, and the Meaning of Conservatism." *Humanitas* 18, nos. 1–2 (2005): 5–25.

———. "Leo Strauss's Influence on George Grant." In Angus, Dart, and Peters, *Athens and Jerusalem*, 124–135.

———. "Lincoln, *Macbeth*, and the Illusions of Tyranny." *European Legacy* 15, no. 2 (April 2010): 137–147.

———. *Lincoln and the Politics of Christian Love*. Columbia, MO: University of Missouri Press, 2009.

———. "The Meaning of 'Neo-Paganism': Rethinking the Relation between Nature and Freedom." In *Humanity at the Turning Point: Rethinking Nature, Culture, and Freedom*. Edited by Sonja Servomaa. Helsinki: Renvall Institute, 2006. 159–169.

———. "Natural Rightism and the Biogenetic Debate." In *Values and Technology: Religion and Public Life*, vol. 37. Edited by Gabriel R. Ricci. New Brunswick, NJ: Transaction, 2011. 93–105.

———. "Northern Right." *American Conservative* (March 2011): 33–36.

———. *Philosophy and Psychoanalysis: A Critical Study of Spinoza and Freud.* Unpublished Ph.D. dissertation, Program in Social and Political Thought, York University, Toronto, 1992.

———. Review of Allan Lichtman, *White Protestant Nation. European Legacy* 15, no. 3 (2010): 375–376.

———. Review of Anne Norton, *Leo Strauss and the Politics of American Empire. European Legacy* 10, no. 7 (2005): 758–759.

———. Review of Harvey C. Mansfield, *Manliness. European Legacy* 12, no. 6 (2007): 764–765.

———. Review of Peter Minowitz, *Straussophobia: Defending Leo Strauss and Straussians against Shadia Drury and Other Accusers. European Legacy* 16, no. 4 (2011): 553–554.

———. Review of Robert D. Kaplan, *Warrior Politics: Why Leadership Demands a Pagan Ethos. European Legacy* 11, no. 1 (2006): 98–99.

———. Review of Ronald J. Pestritto, *Woodrow Wilson and the Roots of Modern Liberalism. European Legacy* 13, no. 1 (2008): 112–113.

———. "Romanticism and Universalism: The Case of Leo Strauss." *Dialogue and Universalism* 12, nos. 6–7 (2002): 155–167.

———. "Was Spinoza a Liberal?" *Political Science Reviewer* 36 (2007): 143–174.

———. "Willmoore Kendall for Our Times." *Modern Age* 53, nos. 1–2 (Winter–Spring 2011): 121–124.

Hegel, G. W. F. *Lectures on the History of Philosophy.* Vol. 3, *Medieval and Modern Philosophy.* Translated by E. S. Haldane and Frances H. Simson. Lincoln and London: University of Nebraska Press, 1995.

———. *The Philosophy of History.* Translated by J. Sibree. Amherst, NY: Prometheus Books, 1991.

Henrie, Mark C. "Thomas Pangle and the Problems of a Straussian Founding." *Modern Age* 36, no. 2 (1993): 128–138.

Himmelfarb, Milton. "On Leo Strauss." *Commentary* 58, no. 2 (August 1974): 60–66.

Hitchens, Christopher. *Blood, Class, and Empire: The Enduring Anglo-American Relationship.* New York: Nation Books, 2004.

Hobbes, Thomas. *Leviathan.* Edited by Michael Oakeshott. New York: Macmillan, 1962.

Holland, Matthew S. *Bonds of Affection: Civic Charity and the Making of America—Winthrop, Jefferson, and Lincoln.* Washington, DC: Georgetown University Press, 2007.

Holloway, Carson. "Christianity, Magnanimity, and Statesmanship." *Review of Politics* 61 (1999): 581–604.

Holmes, James R. *Theodore Roosevelt and World Order: Police Power in International Relations.* Washington, DC: Potomac Books, 2006.

Holmes, Stephen. *The Anatomy of Antiliberalism.* Cambridge: Harvard University Press, 1993.

Horkheimer, Max, and Theodor W. Adorno. *Dialectic of Enlightenment.* Translated by John Cumming. New York: Continuum, 2002.

Horowitz, Gad. "Commentary." In *By Loving Our Own: George Grant and the Legacy of "Lament for a Nation."* Edited by Peter C. Emberley. Ottawa: Carleton University Press, 1990. 75–82.

Hunter, Graeme. *Radical Protestantism in Spinoza's Thought*. Burlington, VT: Ashgate, 2005.

Ignatieff, Michael. "Human Rights: The Midlife Crisis." *New York Review of Books*, May 20, 1999.

Innis, Harold A. "The Church in Canada." In Harold Innis, *Essays in Canadian Economic History*. Edited by Mary Q. Innis. Toronto: University of Toronto Press, 1956. 383–393.

———. *Empire and Communications*. With a general introduction by Alexander John Watson. Toronto: Dundurn Press, 2007.

Israel, Jonathan. *Radical Enlightenment: Philosophy and the Making of Modernity, 1650–1750*. Oxford: Oxford University Press, 2001.

Jaffa, Harry V. *American Conservatism and the American Founding*. Claremont, CA: Claremont Institute, 1984.

———. *The American Founding as the Best Regime: The Bonding of Civil and Religious Liberty*. Claremont, CA: Claremont Institute, 1990.

———. "Aristotle and the Higher Good." *New York Times*, July 1, 2011.

———. "Can There Be Another Winston Churchill?" In *Statesmanship: Essays in Honor of Sir Winston S. Churchill*. Edited by Harry V. Jaffa. Durham, NC: Carolina Academic Press, 1981. 25–39.

———. *The Conditions of Freedom: Essays in Political Philosophy*. Claremont, CA: Claremont Institute, 2000.

———. *Crisis of the House Divided: An Interpretation of the Issues in the Lincoln-Douglas Debates*. Chicago: University of Chicago Press, 1982.

———. "Dear Professor Drury." *Political Theory* 15, no. 3 (August 1987): 316–325.

———. "Dear Sirs." In Jaffa et al., *Crisis of the Strauss Divided*, 163–165.

———. *How to Think about the American Revolution: A Bicentennial Celebration*. Durham, NC: Carolina Academic Press, 1978.

———. "Humanizing Certitudes and Impoverishing Doubts: A Critique of *The Closing of the American Mind* by Allan Bloom." *Interpretation* 16, no. 1 (Fall 1988): 111–138.

———. "The Legacy of Leo Strauss." In Jaffa et al., *Crisis of the Strauss Divided*, 57–79.

———. "Leo Strauss, the Bible, and Political Philosophy." In Deutsch and Nicgorski, *Leo Strauss*, 195–210.

———. "Leo Strauss's Churchillian Speech and the Question of the Decline of the West." *Teaching Political Science* 12, no. 2 (Winter 1985): 61–67.

———. *A New Birth of Freedom: Abraham Lincoln and the Coming of the Civil War*. Lanham, MD: Rowman and Littlefield, 2000.

———. "On the Nature of Civil and Religious Liberty." In *American Conservative Thought in the Twentieth Century*. Edited by William F. Buckley Jr. New York: Bobbs-Merrill, 1970. 221–238.

———. *Original Intent and the Framers of the Constitution: A Disputed Question*. Washington, DC: Regnery Gateway, 1994.

———. "Strauss at One Hundred." In Deutsch and Murley, *Leo Strauss, the Straussians*, 41–48.

———. "Straussian Geography: A Memoir and Commentary." In Jaffa et al., *Crisis of the Strauss Divided*, 1–34.

———. *Thomism and Aristotelianism: A Study of the Commentary by Thomas Aquinas on the "Nicomachean Ethics."* Chicago: University of Chicago Press, 1952.

———. "Too Good to Be True? A Reply to Robert Kraynak's 'Moral Order in the Western Tradition: Harry Jaffa's Grand Synthesis of Athens, Jerusalem, and Peoria.'" In Jaffa et al., *Crisis of the Strauss Divided*, 223–239.

Jaffa, Harry V., et al. *Crisis of the Strauss Divided: Essays on Leo Strauss and Straussianism, East and West*. Lanham, MD: Rowman and Littlefield, 2012.

James, Robert Rhodes. "The Enigma." In Muller, *Churchill as Peacemaker*, 6–23.

Janssens, David. *Between Athens and Jerusalem: Philosophy, Prophecy, and Politics in Leo Strauss's Early Thought*. Albany: SUNY Press, 2008.

Jefferson, Thomas. *The Life and Selected Writings of Thomas Jefferson*. Edited by Adrienne Koch and William Peden. New York: Modern Library, 1998.

Jividen, Jason R. *Claiming Lincoln: Progressivism, Equality, and the Battle for Lincoln's Legacy in Presidential Rhetoric*. DeKalb: Northern Illinois University Press, 2011.

Joad, C. E. M. "Churchill the Philosopher." In *Churchill by His Contemporaries*. Edited by Charles Eade. London: Hutchinson, 1953. 477–487.

Kagan, Robert. *Dangerous Nation: America's Place in the World, from Its Earliest Days to the Dawn of the Twentieth Century*. New York: Vintage, 2007.

Kaplan, Robert. *Warrior Politics: Why Leadership Demands a Pagan Ethos*. New York: Vintage, 2001.

Kaufmann, Eric P. *The Rise and Fall of Anglo-America*. Cambridge: Harvard University Press, 2004.

Kelly, Daniel. *James Burnham and the Struggle for the World*. Foreword by Richard Brookhiser. Wilmington, DE: ISI Books, 2002.

Kendall, Willmoore. *The Conservative Affirmation in America*. Chicago: Gateway Editions, 1985.

———. "The Eric Voegelin–Willmoore Kendall Correspondence." Edited by Steven D. Ealy and Gordon Lloyd. *Political Science Reviewer* 33 (2004): 357–412.

———. "Introduction: How to Read Rousseau's *Government of Poland*." In Jean-Jacques Rousseau, *The Government of Poland*. Translated with an introduction and notes by Willmoore Kendall. Indianapolis: Hackett, 1985. ix–xxxix.

———. *John Locke and the Doctrine of Majority-Rule*. Urbana: University of Illinois Press, 1965.

———. "Natural Law and 'Natural Right.'" *Modern Age* 6, no. 1 (1961–1962): 93–96.

———. *Oxford Years: Letters of Willmoore Kendall to His Father*. Edited by Yvona Kendall Mason, with foreword and epilogue by George W. Carey. Bryn Mawr, PA: Intercollegiate Studies Institute, 1993.

———. "Thoughts on Machiavelli." In *Willmoore Kendall Contra Mundum*, 449–456.

———. "The True Sage of Woodstock." In *Willmoore Kendall Contra Mundum*, 74–89.

———. *Willmoore Kendall Contra Mundum*. Edited by Nellie D. Kendall. New York: University Press, 1994.

———. "Willmoore Kendall–Leo Strauss Correspondence." In Murley and Alvis, *Willmoore Kendall*, 191–261.

Kendall, Willmoore, and George W. Carey. *The Basic Symbols of the American Political Tradition*. Washington, DC: Catholic University of America Press, 1995.

Kirk, Russell. "Bolingbroke, Burke, and the Statesman." *Kenyon Review* 28 (June 1966): 426–431.

———. *The Conservative Constitution*. Washington, DC: Regnery Gateway, 1990.

———. *The Conservative Mind: From Burke to Eliot*. 7th revised edition. Washington, DC: Regnery Gateway, 2001.

———. *The Politics of Prudence*. Wilmington, DE: ISI Books, 1993.

———. *Redeeming the Time.* Edited with an introduction by Jeffrey O. Nelson. Wilmington, DE: ISI Books, 1996.

Kojève, Alexandre. "Hegel, Marx, and Christianity." *Interpretation* 1 (1970): 21–42.

———. "Tyranny and Wisdom." In Leo Strauss, *On Tyranny. Revised and Expanded Edition. Including the Strauss-Kojève Correspondence.* Edited by Victor Gourevitch and Michael S. Roth. Chicago: University of Chicago Press, 2000. 135–176.

Kraynak, Robert B. "Moral Order in the Western Tradition: Harry Jaffa's Synthesis of Athens, Jerusalem, and Peoria." *Review of Politics* 71 (2009): 181–206.

———. "Strauss, Voegelin, and Burke: A Tale of Three Conservatives." *Modern Age* 53, no. 4 (Fall 2011): 24–35.

Kristol, Irving. *Neoconservatism: The Autobiography of an Idea.* Chicago: Elephant Paperbacks, 1995.

Kristol, William. "The West Fights Back." *Weekly Standard* 18, no. 12 (December 3, 2012).

Kurth, James. "George W. Bush and the Protestant Deformation." *American Interest* 1, no. 2 (2005): 4–16.

Lampert, Laurence. *Leo Strauss and Nietzsche.* Chicago: University of Chicago Press, 1996.

Lawler, Peter Augustine. *Homeless and at Home in America.* South Bend, IN: St. Augustine's Press, 2007.

———. "Introduction to the ISI edition." In Orestes A. Brownson, *The American Republic: Its Constitution, Tendencies, and Destiny.* Wilmington, DE: ISI Books, 2003. xiii–cviii.

———. "Religion, Philosophy, and the American Founding." In *Protestantism and the American Founding.* Edited by Thomas S. Engeman and Michael P. Zuckert. Notre Dame: University of Notre Dame Press, 2004. 165–185.

———. "Strauss, Straussians, and Faith-Based Students of Strauss." *Political Science Reviewer* 36 (2007): 3–12.

———. "What Is Straussianism (according to Strauss)?" *Society* (2011): 50–57.

Lenzner, Steven. "Leo Strauss and the Conservatives." *Policy Review* (April–May 2003): 75–82.

Levene, Nancy K. "Athens and Jerusalem: Myths and Mirrors in Strauss's Vision of the West." *Hebraic Political Studies* 3, no. 2 (Spring 2008): 113–155.

———. "Ethics and Interpretation, or How to Study Spinoza's *Tractatus Theologico-Politicus* without Strauss." *Journal of Jewish Thought and Philosophy* 10 (2000): 57–110.

Lévy, Bernard-Henri. *The Testament of God.* Translated by George Holoch. New York: Harper and Row, 1979.

Lichtman, Allan J. *White Protestant Nation: The Rise of the American Conservative Movement.* New York: Atlantic Monthly Press, 2008.

Lippmann, Walter. *Liberty and the News.* Preface by Robert W. McChesney. Mineola, NY: Dover, 2010.

Locke, John. *A Letter concerning Toleration.* Edited and introduced by James H. Tully. Indianapolis: Hackett, 1983.

———. *The Reasonableness of Christianity, with a Discourse of Miracles and Part of a Third Letter concerning Toleration.* Edited by I. T. Ramsey. Stanford: Stanford University Press, 1958.

Longley, Clifford. *Chosen People: The Big Idea that Shapes England and America.* London: Hodder and Stoughton, 2002.

Lord, Carnes. *The Modern Prince: What Leaders Need to Know Now.* New Haven: Yale University Press, 2003.

Machiavelli, Niccolò. "The Prince" and "The Discourses." Translated by Max Lerner. New York: Modern Library, 1950.

Macpherson, C. B. The Political Theory of Possessive Individualism: Hobbes to Locke. Oxford: Oxford University Press, 1962.

Mahoney, Daniel J. The Conservative Foundations of the Liberal Order: Defending Democracy against Its Modern Enemies and Immoderate Friends. Wilmington, DE: ISI Books, 2011.

———. "Moral Principle and Realistic Judgment." In Churchill's "Iron Curtain" Speech Fifty Years Later. Edited by James W. Muller. Columbia, MO: University of Missouri Press, 1999. 69–81.

Maistre, Joseph de. The Works of Joseph de Maistre. Edited and translated by Jack Lively. New York: Macmillan, 1965.

Manent, Pierre. "Between Athens and Jerusalem." First Things (February 2012): 35–39.

———. La Raison des nations: Réflexions sur la démocratie en Europe. Paris: Éditions Gallimard, 2006.

Mann, James. Rise of the Vulcans: The History of Bush's War Cabinet. New York: Viking, 2004.

Mansfield, Harvey C., Jr. Manliness. New Haven: Yale University Press, 2006.

———. "Preface to the 1985 Reprinting." In Jean-Jacques Rousseau, The Government of Poland. Translated with an introduction and notes by Willmoore Kendall. Indianapolis: Hackett, 1985. Vii–viii.

———. "Providence and Democracy." Claremont Review of Books 11, nos. 1–2 (Winter 2010–Spring 2011): 74–78.

———. "Roundtable Discussion: The Influence of German Philosophy." In Hannah Arendt and Leo Strauss: German Emigrés and American Political Thought after World War II. Edited by Peter Graf Kielmansegg, Horst Mewes, and Elisabeth Glaser-Schmidt. Cambridge: Cambridge University Press, 1995. 163–171.

———. Taming the Prince: The Ambivalence of Modern Executive Power. New York: Free Press, 1989.

Mansfield, Harvey C., Jr., and Delba Winthrop. "Editors' Introduction." In Alexis de Tocqueville, Democracy in America. Translated, edited, and with an introduction by Harvey C. Mansfield Jr. and Delba Winthrop. Chicago: University of Chicago Press, 2000. Xvii–lxxxvi.

Marcuse, Herbert. A Study on Authority. Translated by Joris de Bres. London: Verso Press, 2008.

McAllister, Ted V. Revolt against Modernity: Leo Strauss, Eric Voegelin, and the Search for a Postliberal Order. Lawrence: University of Kansas Press, 1995.

McCarthy, Daniel. "Willmoore Kendall, Man of the People." In Deutsch and Fishman, Dilemmas, 175–202.

McIntyre, Kenneth B. "'What's Gone and What's Past Help…': Oakeshott and Strauss on Historical Explanation." Journal of the Philosophy of History 4, no. 1 (2010): 65–101.

McNamara, Robert S., and James G. Blight. Wilson's Ghost: Reducing the Risk of Conflict, Killing, and Catastrophe in the Twenty-First Century. New York: PublicAffairs, 2001.

Meier, Heinrich. Leo Strauss and the Theologico-Political Problem. Translated by Marcus Brainard. Cambridge: Cambridge University Press, 2006.

Merrill, Clark A. "Leo Strauss's Indictment of Christian Philosophy." Review of Politics 62, no. 1 (2000): 77–106.

Miller, Eugene F. "Leo Strauss: The Recovery of Political Philosophy." In Contemporary Political Philosophers. Edited by Anthony de Crespigny and Kenneth Minogue. London: Methuen, 1976. 67–99.

Minowitz, Peter. "Machiavellianism Come of Age? Leo Strauss on Modernity and Econom-
ics." *Political Science Reviewer* 22 (1993): 157–197.
———. *Straussophobia: Defending Leo Strauss and Straussians against Shadia Drury and Other
Accusers.* Lanham, MD: Lexington Books, 2009.
Miranda, José Porfirio. *Marx and the Bible: A Critique of the Philosophy of Oppression.* Trans-
lated by John Eagleson. Maryknoll, NY: Orbis Books, 1974.
Molnar, Thomas. *The Pagan Temptation.* Grand Rapids: Eerdmans, 1987.
Montesquieu, Baron de. *The Spirit of Laws: A Compendium of the First English Edition.* Edited
with an introduction by David Wallace Carrithers. Berkeley and Los Angeles: Univer-
sity of California Press, 1977.
Moots, Glenn. *Politics Reformed: The Anglo-American Legacy of Covenant Theology.* Colum-
bia, MO: University of Missouri Press, 2010.
Morrisey, Will. "The Statesman as Great-Souled Man: Winston Churchill." In *Magnanim-
ity and Statesmanship.* Edited by Carson Holloway. Lanham, MD: Lexington Books,
2008. 197–220.
Morrissey, Christopher S. "Thomas Aquinas on Providence, Prudence, and Natural Law." In
Politics in Theology. Vol. 38 of *Religion and Public Life.* Edited by Gabriel R. Ricci. New
Brunswick, NJ: Transaction, 2012. 133–145.
Moyn, Samuel. "From Experience to Law: Leo Strauss and the Weimar Crisis of the Philoso-
phy of Religion." *History of European Ideas* 33, no. 2 (June 2007): 174–194.
Muller, James W. "The Aftermath of the Great War." In Muller, *Churchill as Peacemaker,*
153–185.
Muller, James W., ed. *Churchill as Peacemaker.* Cambridge: Cambridge University Press, 1997.
Murley, John A. "On the 'Calhounism' of Willmoore Kendall." In Murley and Alvis, *Will-
moore Kendall,* 99–139.
Murley, John A., and John E. Alvis, eds. *Willmoore Kendall: Maverick of American Conser-
vatives.* With a foreword by William F. Buckley Jr. Lanham, MD: Lexington Books,
2002.
Murray, John Courtney. *We Hold These Truths: Catholic Reflections on the American Proposi-
tion.* Introduction by Peter Augustine Lawler. Lanham, MD: Rowman and Littlefield,
2005.
Nadler, Steven. *A Book Forged in Hell: Spinoza's Scandalous Treatise and the Birth of the Secular
Age.* Princeton: Princeton University Press, 2011.
———. *Spinoza's Heresy: Immortality and the Jewish Mind.* Oxford: Oxford University Press,
2001.
Nash, George H. *The Conservative Intellectual Movement in America since 1945.* New York:
Basic Books, 1976.
———. "The Place of Willmoore Kendall in American Conservatism." In Murley and Alvis,
Willmoore Kendall, 3–15.
Negri, Antonio. *Subversive Spinoza: (Un)contemporary Variations.* Edited by Timothy S. Mur-
phy. Manchester: Manchester University Press, 2004.
Nelson, Eric. *The Greek Tradition in Republican Thought.* Cambridge: Cambridge University
Press, 2004.
———. *The Hebrew Republic: Jewish Sources and the Transformation of European Political
Thought.* Cambridge: Harvard University Press, 2010.
Nichols, Mary P. *Citizens and Statesmen: A Study of Aristotle's "Politics."* Savage, MD: Row-
man and Littlefield, 1992.

Niebuhr, Reinhold. *The Irony of American History*. New York: Charles Scribners' Sons, 1962.
———. *Moral Man and Immoral Society: A Study in Ethics and Politics*. New York: Charles Scribner's Sons, 1932.
Nietzsche, Friedrich. *Twilight of the Idols*. Translated by Richard Polt. Indianapolis and Cambridge: Hackett, 1997.
Nisbet, Robert. *History of the Idea of Progress*. New York: Basic Books, 1980.
Norton, Anne. *Leo Strauss and the Politics of American Empire*. New Haven: Yale University Press, 2004.
Novak, David. "Introduction." In *Leo Strauss and Judaism: Jerusalem and Athens Critically Revisited*. Lanham, MD: Rowman and Littlefield, 1996. vii–xvi.
Novak, Michael. *On Two Wings: Humble Faith and Common Sense at the American Founding*. San Francisco: Encounter Books, 2002.
———. *The Spirit of Democratic Capitalism*. New York: Madison Books, 1991.
Nugent, Mark. "Willmoore Kendall and the Deliberate Sense of the Community." *Political Science Reviewer* 36 (2007): 228–265.
Nussbaum, Martha. *The Fragility of Goodness: Luck and Ethics in Greek Tragedy and Philosophy*. Cambridge: Cambridge University Press, 2001.
O'Meara, Michael. *New Culture, New Right: Anti-liberalism in Postmodern Europe*. Bloomington, IN: 1stBooks, 2004.
O'Neill, John. *Plato's Cave: Desire, Power, and the Specular Functions of the Media*. Norwood, NJ: Ablex Publishing, 1991.
O'Neill, Johnathan. "Straussian Constitutional History and the Straussian Political Project." *Rethinking History* 13, no. 4 (December 2009): 459–478.
Orr, Susan. *Jerusalem and Athens: Reason and Revelation in the Work of Leo Strauss*. Lanham, MD: Rowman and Littlefield, 1995.
Orwin, Clifford. *The Humanity of Thucydides*. Princeton: Princeton University Press, 1994.
———. "Machiavelli's Unchristian Charity." *American Political Science Review* 72 (1978): 1217–1228.
———. Review of *English-Speaking Justice* by George Parkin Grant. *University of Toronto Law Journal* 30 (1980): 106–115.
———. "'Straussians' in the News: The World Trembles." *National Post*, June 17, 2003, A12.
Owen, J. Judd. *Religion and the Demise of Liberal Rationalism: The Foundational Crisis of the Separation of Church and State*. Chicago: University of Chicago Press, 2001.
Pangle, Thomas L. *The Ennobling of Democracy: The Challenge of the Postmodern Age*. Baltimore: Johns Hopkins University Press, 1992.
———. "Introduction." In Strauss, *Studies in Platonic Political Philosophy*, 1–26.
———. *Leo Strauss: An Introduction to His Thought and Intellectual Legacy*. Baltimore: Johns Hopkins University Press, 2006.
———. "The Platonism of Leo Strauss: A Reply to Harry Jaffa." In Jaffa et al., *Crisis of the Strauss Divided*, 81–88.
———. *Political Philosophy and the God of Abraham*. Baltimore: Johns Hopkins University Press, 2003.
———. *The Spirit of Modern Republicanism: The Moral Vision of the American Founders and the Philosophy of Locke*. Chicago: University of Chicago Press, 1988.
Parel, Anthony J. "Multiculturalism and Nationhood." In *George Grant and the Future of Canada*. Edited by Yusuf K. Umar, with a foreword by Barry Cooper. Calgary: University of Calgary Press, 1992. 139–150.

Patrick, James. *The Magdalen Metaphysicals: Idealism and Orthodoxy at Oxford, 1901–1945*. Macon, GA: Mercer University Press, 1985.

Pelluchon, Corine. "Strauss and Christianity." *Interpretation* 33, no. 2 (Spring 2006): 185–203.

Pestritto, Ronald J. *Woodrow Wilson and the Roots of Modern Liberalism*. Lanham, MD: Rowman and Littlefield, 2005.

Phillips, Kevin. *American Theocracy: The Peril and Politics of Radical Religion, Oil, and Borrowed Money in the Twenty-First Century*. New York: Viking, 2006.

Planinc, Zdravko. "Paradox and Polyphony in Grant's Critique of Modernity." In *George Grant and the Future of Canada*. Edited by Yusuf K. Umar, with a foreword by Barry Cooper. Calgary: University of Calgary Press, 1992. 17–45.

Plato. *Plato's "Statesman."* Part 3 of *The Being of the Beautiful*. Translated and with a commentary by Seth Benardete. Chicago: University of Chicago Press, 1986.

Pocock, J. G. A. *Politics, Language, and Time: Essays on Political Thought and History*. London: Methuen, 1972.

———. "Prophet and Inquisitor, or, A Church Built upon Bayonets Cannot Stand: A Comment on Mansfield's 'Strauss's Machiavelli.'" *Political Theory* 3, no. 4 (November 1975): 385–401.

Podles, Leon J. *The Church Impotent: The Feminization of Christianity*. Dallas: Spence Publishing, 1999.

Polka, Brayton. *The Dialectic of Biblical Critique: Interpretation and Existence*. New York: St. Martin's Press, 1986.

———. *Hermeneutics and Ontology*. Vol. 1 of *Between Philosophy and Religion: Spinoza, the Bible, and Modernity*. Lanham, MD: Lexington Books, 2007.

———. *Politics and Ethics*. Vol. 2 of *Between Philosophy and Religion: Spinoza, the Bible, and Modernity*. Lanham, MD: Lexington Books, 2007.

———. "What Is Democracy? Reflections on Sen's Idea of Justice." *European Legacy* 15, no. 6 (2010): 769–777.

Preus, J. Samuel. *Spinoza and the Irrelevance of Biblical Authority*. Cambridge: Cambridge University Press, 2001.

Rahe, Paul A. *The Ancien Régime in Classical Greece*. Vol. 1 of *Republics Ancient and Modern*. Chapel Hill and London: University of North Carolina Press, 1994.

———. *Inventions of Prudence: Constituting the American Regime*. Vol. 3 of *Republics Ancient and Modern*. Chapel Hill and London: University of North Carolina Press, 1994.

———. *New Modes and Orders in Early Modern Political Thought*. Vol. 2 of *Republics Ancient and Modern*. Chapel Hill and London: University of North Carolina Press, 1994.

———. "*The River War*: Nature's Provision, Man's Desire to Prevail, and the Prospect for Peace." In Muller, *Churchill as Peacemaker*, 82–119.

———. "Thucydides' Critique of Realpolitik." *Security Studies* 5, no. 2 (Winter 1995–1996): 105–141.

Raimondo, Justin. *Reclaiming the American Right: The Lost Legacy of the Conservative Movement*. Wilmington, DE: ISI Books, 2008.

Ramsden, John. *Man of the Century: Winston Churchill and His Legend since 1945*. New York: Columbia University Press, 2002.

Ranieri, John J. *Disturbing Revelation: Leo Strauss, Eric Voegelin, and the Bible*. Columbia, MO: University of Missouri Press, 2009.

Roberts, Andrew. *Eminent Churchillians*. London: Phoenix, 2004.

Roberts, Jennifer Tolbert. *Athens on Trial: The Antidemocratic Tradition in Western Thought.* Princeton: Princeton University Press, 1994.

Rogers, Melvin L. "Rorty's Straussianism, or, Irony against Democracy." *Contemporary Pragmatism* 1, no. 2 (December 2004): 95–121.

Rose, Norman. *Churchill: An Unruly Life.* London: Tauris Parke Paperbacks, 2009.

Rosen, Stanley. *The Ancients and the Moderns: Rethinking Modernity.* New Haven: Yale University Press, 1989.

———. *Hermeneutics as Politics.* Oxford: Oxford University Press, 1987.

———. "Politics or Transcendence? Responding to Historicism." In Emberley and Cooper, *Faith and Political Philosophy,* 261–266.

Rossiter, Clinton. *Seedtime of the Republic: The Origin of the American Tradition of Political Liberty.* New York: Harcourt, Brace, and World, 1953.

Russello, Gerald J. "Russell Kirk and Territorial Democracy." *Publius: The Journal of Federalism* 34, no. 4 (Fall 2004): 109–124.

Ryn, Claes G. *America the Virtuous: The Crisis of Democracy and the Quest for Empire.* New Brunswick, NJ: Transaction, 2003.

———. "Leo Strauss and History: The Philosopher as Conspirator." *Humanitas* 18, nos. 1–2 (2005): 31–58.

Schall, James V., SJ. *Christianity and Politics.* Boston: St. Paul Editions, 1981.

———. "A Latitude for Statesmanship? Strauss on St. Thomas." In Deutsch and Nicgorski, *Leo Strauss,* 212–215.

Schmidt, Larry, ed. *George Grant in Process: Essays and Conversations.* Toronto: House of Anansi, 1978.

Shain, Barry Alan. *The Myth of American Individualism: The Protestant Origins of American Political Thought.* Princeton: Princeton University Press, 1994.

Sharansky, Natan, with Shira Wolosky Weiss. *Defending Identity: Its Indispensable Role in Protecting Democracy.* New York: Public Affairs, 2008.

Shell, Susan. "'To Spare the Vanquished and Crush the Arrogant': Leo Strauss's Lecture on 'German Nihilism.'" In *The Cambridge Companion to Leo Strauss.* Edited by Steven B. Smith. Cambridge: Cambridge University Press, 2009. 171–192.

Sheppard, Eugene R. *Leo Strauss and the Politics of Exile: The Making of a Political Philosopher.* Waltham, MA: Brandeis University Press, 2006.

Sibley, Robert C. *Northern Spirits: John Watson, George Grant, and Charles Taylor—Appropriations of Hegelian Political Thought.* Montreal and Kingston: McGill-Queen's University Press, 2008.

Smith, Adam. *The Theory of Moral Sentiments.* Edited by D. D. Raphael and A. L. Macfie. Indianapolis: Liberty Classics, 1982.

Smith, Gregory Bruce. "Athens and Washington: Leo Strauss and the American Regime." In Deutsch and Murley, *Leo Strauss, the Straussians,* 103–127.

Smith, Steven B. "How to Commemorate the 350th Anniversary of Spinoza's Expulsion, or Leo Strauss's Reply to Hermann Cohen." *Hebraic Political Studies* 3, no. 2 (Spring 2008): 155–176.

———. *Reading Leo Strauss: Politics, Philosophy, Judaism.* Chicago: University of Chicago Press, 2006.

Sokolowski, Robert. *The God of Faith and Reason: Foundations of Christian Theology.* Washington, DC: Catholic University of America Press, 1982.

Spinoza, Benedict de. *The Letters.* Translated by Samuel Shirley. Indianapolis: Hackett, 1995.

———. *Spinoza's Theologico-Political Treatise.* Translated by Martin D. Yaffe. Newburyport, MA: Focus Philosophical Library, 2004.

Stelzer, Irwin. "Neoconservatives and Their Critics: An Introduction." In *The Neocon Reader.* Edited and with an introduction by Irwin Stelzer. New York: Grove Press, 2004. 3–28.

Strauss, Leo. "Churchill's Greatness." 1965. Reprint. *Weekly Standard* 5, no. 16, January 10, 2000.

———. *The City and Man.* Chicago: University of Chicago Press, 1964.

———. "Correspondence concerning Modernity: Karl Löwith and Leo Strauss." *Independent Journal of Philosophy* 4 (1983): 105–119.

———. *The Early Writings, 1921–1932.* Translated and edited by Michael Zank. Albany: State University of New York Press, 2002.

———. "An Epilogue." In Strauss, *Introduction to Political Philosophy*, 125–155.

———. "Freud on Moses and Monotheism." In Strauss, *Jewish Philosophy*, 285–309.

———. "German Nihilism." *Interpretation* 26, no. 3 (Spring 1999): 353–378.

———. "How to Begin to Study Medieval Philosophy." In Strauss, *Rebirth of Classical Political Rationalism*, 207–226.

———. "An Introduction to Heideggerian Existentialism." In Strauss, *Rebirth of Classical Political Rationalism*, 27–46.

———. *An Introduction to Political Philosophy: Ten Essays by Leo Strauss.* Edited with an introduction by Hilail Gildin. Detroit: Wayne State University Press, 1989.

———. "Introductory Essay." In Hermann Cohen, *Religion of Reason: Out of the Sources of Judaism.* Translated with an introduction by Simon Kaplan. Atlanta: Scholars Press, 1995. xxiii–xxxviii.

———. "Jerusalem and Athens: Some Preliminary Reflections." In Strauss, *Jewish Philosophy*, 377–405.

———. *Jewish Philosophy and the Crisis of Modernity: Essays and Lectures in Modern Jewish Thought by Leo Strauss.* Edited with an introduction by Kenneth Hart Green. Albany: SUNY Press, 1997.

———. *Leo Strauss on Moses Mendelssohn.* Translated and edited with an interpretive essay by Martin D. Yaffe. Chicago: University of Chicago Press, 2012.

———. "Letter to Karl Löwith (May 19, 1933)." *Constellations* 16, no. 1 (2009): 82–83.

———. *Liberalism: Ancient and Modern.* Foreword by Allan Bloom. Chicago: University of Chicago Press, 1989.

———. *Natural Right and History.* Chicago: University of Chicago Press, 1953.

———. "Niccolo Machiavelli." In Strauss, *Studies in Platonic Political Philosophy*, 210–228.

———. "Notes on Carl Schmitt, *The Concept of the Political.*" In Carl Schmitt, *The Concept of the Political.* Translated and with an introduction by George Schwab. Chicago: University of Chicago Press, 1996. 83–107.

———. "On Classical Political Philosophy." In Strauss, *Introduction to Political Philosophy*, 59–79.

———. "On Collingwood's Philosophy of History." *Review of Metaphysics* 5, no. 4 (June 1952): 559–586.

———. "On Natural Law." In Strauss, *Studies in Platonic Political Philosophy*, 137–146.

———. *On Plato's "Symposium."* Edited and with a foreword by Seth Benardete. Chicago: University of Chicago Press, 2003.

———. "On the Interpretation of Genesis." In Strauss, *Jewish Philosophy*, 359–376.

———. *On Tyranny: Including the Strauss-Kojève Correspondence.* Revised and expanded edition. Edited by Victor Gourevitch and Michael S. Roth. Chicago: University of Chicago Press, 2000.

———. *Persecution and the Art of Writing.* Chicago: University of Chicago Press, 1952.

———. *Philosophy and Law: Contributions to the Understanding of Maimonides and His Predecessors.* Translated with an introduction by Eve Adler. Albany: State University of New York Press, 1995.

———. "Plato." In Strauss, *Introduction to Political Philosophy,* 167–245.

———. *The Political Philosophy of Hobbes: Its Basis and Its Genesis.* Translated by Elsa M. Sinclair. 1936. Reprint. Chicago: University of Chicago Press, 1963.

———. "Preface to *Hobbes Politische Wissenschaft.*" In Strauss, *Jewish Philosophy,* 453–456.

———. "Preface to the English Translation." In Leo Strauss, *Spinoza's Critique of Religion.* Translated by E. M. Sinclair. New York: Schocken Books, 1982. 1–31.

———. "The Problem of Socrates: Five Lectures." In Strauss, *Rebirth of Classical Political Rationalism,* 103–183.

———. "Progress or Return? The Contemporary Crisis in Western Civilization." In Strauss, *Introduction to Political Philosophy,* 249–310.

———. "Reason and Revelation." In Heinrich Meier, *Leo Strauss and the Theologico-Political Problem.* Translated by Marcus Brainard. Cambridge: Cambridge University Press, 2006. 141–180.

———. *The Rebirth of Classical Political Rationalism: An Introduction to the Thought of Leo Strauss.* Essays and lectures selected and introduced by Thomas L. Pangle. Chicago: University of Chicago Press, 1989.

———. "The Re-education of Axis Countries concerning the Jews." *Review of Politics* 69, no. 4 (Fall 2007): 530–538.

———. "Relativism." In Strauss, *Rebirth of Classical Political Rationalism,* 13–26.

———. Review of C. B. Macpherson, *The Political Theory of Possessive Individualism: Hobbes to Locke.*" In Strauss, *Studies in Platonic Political Philosophy,* 229–231.

———. *Socrates and Aristophanes.* Chicago: University of Chicago Press, 1966.

———. *Spinoza's Critique of Religion.* Translated by E. M. Sinclair. New York: Schocken Books, 1982.

———. *Studies in Platonic Political Philosophy.* With an introduction by Thomas L. Pangle. Chicago: University of Chicago Press, 1983.

———. *Thoughts on Machiavelli.* Chicago: University of Chicago Press, 1958.

———. "The Three Waves of Modernity." In Strauss, *Introduction to Political Philosophy,* 81–98.

———. "An Unspoken Prologue to a Public Lecture at St. John's College in Honor of Jacob Klein." In Strauss, *Jewish Philosophy,* 449–452.

———. "What Can We Learn from Political Theory?" *Review of Politics* 69, no. 4 (Fall 2007): 515–529.

———. "What Is Political Philosophy?" In Strauss, *Introduction to Political Philosophy,* 3–57.

———. *What Is Political Philosophy? and Other Studies.* Chicago: University of Chicago Press, 1988.

———. "Why We Remain Jews: Can Jewish Faith and History still Speak to Us?" In Strauss, *Jewish Philosophy,* 311–356.

Strong, Tracy B. "Foreword: Dimensions of the New Debate around Carl Schmitt." In Carl Schmitt, *The Concept of the Political.* Translated and with an introduction by George Schwab. Chicago: University of Chicago Press, 1996. ix–xxvii.

Sullivan, Vickie B. *Machiavelli's Three Romes: Religion, Human Liberty, and Politics Reformed.* DeKalb: Northern Illinois University Press, 1996.

Sunic, Tomislav. *Against Democracy and Equality: The European New Right.* Preface by Paul Gottfried. Newport Beach, CA: Noontide Press, 2004.

Tanenhaus, Sam. "Will the Tea Get Cold?" *New York Review of Books,* March 8, 2012.

Tanguay, Daniel. *Leo Strauss: An Intellectual Biography.* New Haven: Yale University Press, 2007.

Tarcov, Nathan, and Thomas L. Pangle. "Epilogue: Leo Strauss and the History of Political Philosophy." In *History of Political Philosophy.* 3rd edition. Edited by Leo Strauss and Joseph Cropsey. Chicago: University of Chicago Press, 1987. 907–934.

Tatalovich, Raymond, and Thomas S. Engeman. *The Presidency and Political Science: Two Hundred Years of Constitutional Debate.* Baltimore: Johns Hopkins University Press, 2003.

Taylor, Charles. "Multiculturalism and the 'Politics of Recognition.'" In *Ethical Issues: Perspectives for Canadians.* 3rd edition. Edited by Eldon Soifer. Peterborough, ON: Broadview Press, 2009. 599–616.

Taylor, Charles. *Radical Tories: The Conservative Tradition in Canada.* Toronto: House of Anansi, 2006.

Thompson, C. Bradley, with Yaron Brook. *Neoconservatism: An Obituary for an Idea.* Boulder: Paradigm Publishers, 2010.

Tierney, Brian. *The Idea of Natural Rights: Studies on Natural Rights, Natural Law, and Church Law, 1150–1625.* Grand Rapids: William B. Eerdmans, 1997.

Tocqueville, Alexis de. *Democracy in America.* Translated, edited, and with an introduction by Harvey C. Mansfield Jr. and Delba Winthrop. Chicago: University of Chicago Press, 2000.

Toye, Richard. *Churchill's Empire: The World that Made Him and the World that He Made.* New York: Henry Holt, 2010.

Vasillopulos, Christopher. *The Triumph of Hate: The Political Theology of the Hitler Movement.* Lanham, MD: University Press of America, 2012.

Vatter, Miguel. "Habermas between Athens and Jerusalem: Public Reason and Atheistic Theology." *Interpretation* 38, no. 3 (2011): 243–259.

Voegelin, Eric. *Plato.* Baton Rouge: Louisiana State University Press, 1966.

Von Heyking, John, and Richard Avramenko. "Introduction: The Persistence of Friendship in Political Life." In *Friendship and Politics: Essays in Political Thought.* Edited by John von Heyking and Richard Avramenko. Notre Dame: Notre Dame University Press, 2008. 1–17.

Von Heyking, John, and Barry Cooper. "'A Cow Is Just a Cow': George Grant and Eric Voegelin on the United States." In Angus, Dart, and Peters, *Athens and Jerusalem,* 166–189.

Weidhorn, Manfred. *A Harmony of Interests: Explorations in the Mind of Sir Winston Churchill.* London: Associated University Presses, 1992.

West, Thomas G. "The Transformation of Protestant Theology as a Condition of the American Revolution." In *Protestantism and the American Founding.* Edited by Thomas S. Engeman and Michael P. Zuckert. Notre Dame: University of Notre Dame Press, 2004. 187–223.

Whillier, Wayne. "George Grant and Leo Strauss: A Parting of the Way." In *"Two Theological Languages" by George Grant and Other Essays in Honour of His Work.* Edited by Wayne Whillier. Toronto: Edwin Mellen, 1990. 63–81.

Wilhelmsen, Frederick D. *Christianity and Political Philosophy.* Athens: University of Georgia Press, 1978.

Wills, Gary. *Confessions of a Conservative*. New York: Penguin, 1979.

Wilson, Francis G. "The Political Science of Willmoore Kendall." *Modern Age* 16 (Winter 1972): 38–47.

Xenos, Nicholas. *Cloaked in Virtue: Unveiling Leo Strauss and the Rhetoric of American Foreign Policy*. New York: Routledge, 2008.

Yaffe, Martin D. "Interpretive Essay." In *Spinoza's Theologico-Political Treatise*. Translated by Martin D. Yaffe. Newburyport, MA: Focus Philosophical Library, 2004. 267–347.

Yovel, Yirmiyahu. *Spinoza and Other Heretics: The Marrano of Reason*. Princeton: Princeton University Press, 1989.

Zank, Michael. "Introduction." In Leo Strauss, *The Early Writings, 1921–1932*. Translated and edited by Michael Zank. Albany: State University of New York Press, 2002. 3–49.

Zuckert, Catherine H. *Postmodern Platos: Nietzsche, Heidegger, Gadamer, Strauss, Derrida*. Chicago: University of Chicago Press, 1996.

Zuckert, Catherine, and Michael Zuckert. *The Truth about Leo Strauss: Political Philosophy and American Democracy*. Chicago: University of Chicago Press, 2006.

Zuckert, Michael P. *Launching Liberalism: On Lockean Political Philosophy*. Lawrence: University Press of Kansas, 2002.

———. "Natural Rights and Protestant Politics." In *Protestantism and the American Founding*. Edited by Thomas S. Engeman and Michael P. Zuckert. Notre Dame: University of Notre Dame Press, 2004. 21–75.

Index

www.ingramcontent.com/pod-product-compliance
Lightning Source LLC
Chambersburg PA
CBHW032346280326
41935CB00008B/473